Challenging Orthodoxy In Special Education:
Dissenting Voices

Deborah J. Gallagher
University of Northern Iowa

With:

Lous Heshusius
York University

Richard P. Iano
Temple University (Emeritus)

Thomas M. Skrtic
University of Kansas

D1145802

Dedicated
To John
With love and admiration

Published by Love Publishing Company
P.O. Box 22353
Denver, Colorado 80222
www.lovepublishing.com

Library of Congress Catalog Card Number 2003111568

Copyright © 2004 by Love Publishing Company
Printed in the United States of America
ISBN 0-89108-301-4

Contents

6   The Tale of a Reluctant Empiricist   231
Richard P. Iano

7   Accidental Tourist and Deliberate Seeker: Two True Stories   251
Thomas M. Skrtic

Preface

For more than a decade a vigorous discussion has been taking place among educators in special education and disability studies, a discussion that, despite its importance, has had relatively few participants. This conversation is of crucial importance because it confronts the fundamental frameworks within which the debates over full inclusion, disability definitions, labeling, and the like, are actually deliberated. Why is this so crucial? Because, ultimately, the framework chosen to address these debates either enhances or diminishes our possibilities for resolving them.

This conversation about the fundamental frameworks for asking and answering questions has to do with an area of study known as *epistemology,* or the study of knowledge. Epistemology explores how knowledge claims are justified and what assumptions are made in various claims for knowing. As this pertains to special education, for instance, what does it mean to say that we know a child has a learning disability or a behavioral disorder? What does it mean to say that we know which teaching methods are most effective? Underlying all knowledge claims are certain assumptions about the nature of knowledge itself. Unless we can agree on what these assumptions are, it is nearly impossible to decide how best to resolve the most important questions we face as professionals.

The reason this discussion is less familiar to most educators is because it has taken place on the philosophical or conceptual level—the level of our beliefs and understandings. For this reason, it is more difficult to see the crucial connection between the "abstract" nature of these discussions and our everyday practical concerns. The irony is that our most pressing practical questions are unlikely to be resolved unless the dialogue is opened up to the larger community of special educators whose daily lives are deeply affected by the very questions this discussion raises.

Understanding and participating in this discussion does, however, require some background in the philosophy of science—information to which few of us have been exposed in our professional preparation programs. Without this background, joining the discussion is a formidable task.

The purpose of this book is, quite simply, to help address this situation. The first chapter introduces in straightforward, accessible language the fundamental information required to gain an intellectual foothold on the existing literature. This chapter starts at the very beginning by clarifying what the philosophy of science has to do with special education and also by presenting the historical context and core concepts necessary to engage the ideas at the core of this discussion.

Chapters 2 through 4 consist of seminal articles by Lous Heshusius, Richard Iano and Thomas Skrtic, the three authors featured in this book whose early and ongoing work has been at the center of this exchange. At this point the reader will be well positioned to read these pieces with depth and understanding. To further facilitate readers' access to these works, each is preceded by a commentary highlighting and clarifying the central issues raised by each author and relating them to the core philosophical concepts discussed in Chapter 1.

In the subsequent portions of the book, readers are introduced to the three authors from a more personal perspective. In chapters 5 through 7 each narrates his or her experiences as a special educator that raised questions and spurred a personal search for answers. Here readers can relate to each of the authors as people who contend with the professional day-to-day events and problems, many of which we might recognize as having been part of our own experiences. This serves to deepen our realization that the practical aspects of our work are inseparable from, and deeply affected by, the ideas and concepts that inform them.

In the ensuing chapters, the authors offer their reflections on the future possibilities of special education. Will the field function much as it does currently, or are informed, coherent changes possible? If so, what will special education look like, and what will it take to get there? Here, readers will have the opportunity to gain insights into how beliefs and understandings profoundly affect what is done and also what is possible to do.

The concluding chapter integrates and provides commentary on the work as a whole, providing an appropriate jumping-off place for the broader community of educators (special and general alike) to participate in a sustained, informed dialogue about the ideas and assumptions that shape our everyday work.

What prompted the writing of this book? I was not acquainted with the work of Heshusius, Iano, or Skrtic until I had nearly completed my doctoral work in special education. I was, of course, well aware of the heated debates about full inclusion, labeling, definitions of disabilities, and the like. The literature on these issues was certainly interesting enough but ultimately unsatisfying in terms of helping me to come to any personal resolution about these pressing problems. Indeed, it appeared that the field had divided itself into opposing camps whose point/counterpoint arguments defied resolution, leaving me to tread water in the wide gulf that separated them. I seemed to have two choices: Remain in a state of suspended animation or decide to join one side or the other. The first choice was out of the question, and I could not simply join one side or the other without a reason or framework for making such a choice.

Still searching for some sense of direction, I began my academic career in an odd and disconcerting state of confusion. Looking back, I count it as a stroke of tremendous good fortune that I just happened to stumble across the work of these authors. What definitively set them apart from my previous readings was the level at which they approached the questions at hand. Their conceptual and philosophical approach cut to the core of what special education is all about. Although it required several readings of their work, I realized that these authors had moved the debates to another level, one that dealt with the foundational assumptions underlying the point/counterpoint exchanges I had previously encountered. Once exposed to their clear-text application of these concepts, I also realized the potential of these ideas to clarify my own thinking because their work gave me a basis for making more deeply informed decisions about the problems facing special education.

In my growing enthusiasm I was anxious to ask my fellow special education colleagues across the United States if they had read these author's writings and, if so, what their thoughts were. Their responses were interesting, and somewhat troubling. Some had never heard of these scholars and others were not sure what to think about their work. Either I had overrated the importance of these authors' work or something else was going on.

I might have gone on wondering why I had responded so differently had I not seen the reaction of my graduate students in an issues seminar I taught twice yearly. Having regretted not coming across this literature during my graduate-school days, I felt a serious obligation to expose them to it. I really was not surprised to find that my students found it as powerful as I had. Their responses differed, to be sure but no one was indifferent or unaffected. It has become almost predictable that at the end of each semester, one student will ask in all earnestness and incredulity why he or she had never heard all of these ideas before. Once this student breaks the ice, the others nod in agreement. Bolder students have told me they feel cheated by not having had an opportunity to read this work earlier in their careers. After all, most of them had majored in special education as undergraduates, had been special educators, and many were near completion of their graduate degrees. How could they have progressed so far without an inkling of the most important ideas and exchanges in their field? I could identify with their incredulity, but I had few answers as to why they had not been made aware of this literature earlier. On the one hand, I suspected that most teacher educators lacked sufficient background in philosophy of science, making this debate more difficult to follow and understand. On the other hand, to the extent that the work of these authors was understood, it broke so dramatically from the core tenants and beliefs driving special education at the time that it might have been considered subversive. The experiences of these authors in the process of publishing their work, and those I encountered with publishing after them, provides some substantiation for this possibility.

In the ensuing years I committed myself to reading the literature on the philosophy of science, sociology, disability studies, and general education. These works, combined with my earlier reading, had a deep influence on my own writing as I continued to search for answers to the questions I struggled with after completing my graduate studies. When I began submitting my work to special education journals, I had what can only be called a "rude awakening." I was not so naïve as to think that my ideas would be popular, as they were in fact critical of traditional thought in the field. But I did expect that at least the ideas would be genuinely engaged. If I were incorrect in my appraisals of special education research and practices, the reviewers would explain why that might be the case. Thus, even if the work were rejected, I would get helpful critiques that would assist me in refining my ideas, or even change my mind altogether. That is not, however, what happened.

Instead, the reviewers expressed quite a bit of disdain for the ideas and issues I raised without ever really telling me why they were erroneous.

I will confess to being surprised by these reactions because they were so at odds with the ideals of academia. I always had believed that we, as academics, should epitomize the informed exchange and genuine engagement of ideas. This experience naturally led me to wonder what Heshusius, Iano, and Skrtic had undergone in their efforts to publish their work. I also wondered how they felt about their position as "outsiders" in the profession. This curiosity got the best of me one day as I was sitting alone in my office wondering where I was going with my work and, honestly, what to do about the situation. I did the only thing I could think of—I picked up the phone and began calling them. The responses I received were more than passingly interesting. Their stories portray a professional field that is highly politicized, closed to ideas, and reluctant at best to engage in free and open intellectual exchange. The concept for this book emerged from their stories.

Acknowledgments

I have many people to thank for their parts in making this book possible. First, of course, are Lous Heshusius, Richard Iano, and Tom Skrtic. This book serves as a testament to the profound influence their work has had on me, both professionally and personally. And, to my husband John Smith, whose steadfast encouragement has meant more than words can ever capture. I also owe a debt of gratitude to Sandra Alper, head of the Department of Special Education at the University of Northern Iowa. I am immeasurably grateful for her deep commitment to the ideals of scholarship, her generosity of spirit, and the collegial support she has provided. For his sage advice, I thank Stan Love of Love Publishing, along with Erica Lawrence for her skillful editing and impressive attention to detail.

Finally, to my mother and stepfather, Jean Stout and Louis Stout, my sister and brother-in-law, Helen and Danny Robertson, and my niece, Sarah Crowley, I am forever thankful for all you have given me and what you have meant in my life.

PART ONE

Exploring the Past

Chapters

Entering the Conversation: The Debate Behind the Debates in Special Education

Deborah Gallagher

P|assage of the Education for All Handicapped Children Act, Public Law 94–142, marked the beginning of a great many changes for the better. For the first time, the strength of federal legislation asserted the rights of people with disabilities to have access to equal educational opportunities, and in a larger sense it asserted their right to basic human dignity. Without doubt, this expansion of civil rights has gone a long way toward broadening public attitudes and concern toward people who previously had been largely forgotten and essentially marginalized. That notwithstanding, agreement about how to fulfill the intentions behind this legislation has been neither straightforward nor simple. Even before this legislation was passed, special educators were deeply divided on a number of issues that continue to form the basis of sometimes contentious contemporary debates (Deno, 1970; Dunn, 1968). The literature in professional journals and books chronicles the struggle by those in the profession to come to terms with problems that seem at this point almost to defy resolution.

This literature reveals four major problems about which much is stated, argued, and countered, but ultimately left unresolved.

1. *How we understand disability.* While many, if not most special education scholars, view this as a matter of scientific refinement of disability definitions and identification criteria, others maintain that the very concept of disability has been misconstrued from the beginning.

2. *Research or knowledge production.* As volumes are devoted to the quest to codify an empiricist version of scientific knowledge for special education, some have argued that this goal is neither attainable nor desirable and that the version of science on which it is based is hopelessly flawed.

3. *Teacher preparation.* For those who believe that special education practices should be informed by this kind of scientific research, good teacher preparation is a matter of training teachers to use research in practice. Conversely, those who question the utility of this version of scientific research maintain that such an approach to teacher preparation actually precludes sound teaching practices.

4. *Place, or where students should receive instruction.* The question of place is intimately related to the first three. Currently known as the full-inclusion debate, it constitutes the most publicly visible debate in special education. Because those opposed to full inclusion are generally disposed toward believing that disability is scientifically definable and identifiable (at least theoretically) and that specialized teaching practices can be derived through empiricist scientific research that teachers can and should be trained to use, they believe instruction often should take place in separate environments. In challenging all of these premises, others have countered that the question of full inclusion is fundamentally, and inevitably, a moral one.

As the debate rages on, relatively few special educators have participated in this conversation directly, in large measure because most have had little exposure to the background knowledge and vocabularies required to engage the essential concepts of those who offer alternative perspectives. Consequently, it can be difficult to understand why these few scholars have taken the position that special education took a wrong turn when it embraced empiricism as its guiding philosophy and why they urge us to reconsider the grounding assumptions that continue to dominate the field. Yet, their ideas are of tremendous importance if we are to gain an informed understanding about the most pressing problems confronting education in general, and special education in particular. If the field of special education is to advance beyond surface debate about its longstanding problems, this discussion requires broader participation.

The information covered in this chapter has been recorded in a number of excellent sources, beginning with the works of the three authors featured in this book. My purpose is to acquaint readers with the concepts and vocabularies needed for their participation, to bring this knowledge to the fore, to make it central rather than peripheral, and ultimately to facilitate participation of the larger community of educators, especially as this information relates specifically to the challenges facing special education. The ideas presented here are designed to frame and introduce those expressed in the upcoming chapters by Heshusius (1989), Iano (1986), and Skrtic (1991). Because this chapter is an introduction to their work, I will not attempt to cite each one as I go.

Before returning to the four problems, we have to examine the key assumptions of empiricism (the dominant framework in special education) and to interrogate their adequacy in the face of this challenge. This examination is vital because these assumptions form the basis or foundation of all subsequent knowledge claims. In essence, these assumptions, and the challenges to them, are at the very core of disagreement between the opposing sides in the debates. Put in plainer terms, if the foundational assumptions of the empiricist framework can withstand scrutiny, those who side with the traditional arrangements of special education can safely maintain their positions. If these assumptions turn out to be inadequate, as the dissenters have submitted they are, whatever knowledge these assumptions produce must accordingly be called into question.

The focus of this discussion centers on ideas that form the conceptual basis for practical choices and action. Because these ideas are so fundamental, discussion of them inevitably cuts to the core of deeply held values and ideals, which in turn makes for a provocative discussion. The intent of this discussion is not to criticize people who hold one position or the other but, rather, to engage in reasoned deliberation about the assumptions that undergird those positions.

How Do We Know What We Know?

To begin, I pose what may seem to be a rather simple question: How do we, as humans, distinguish between truth and fabrication? When we say something is true, or a fact, what is our criteria for that assertion? In an informal sense, to say that we know something is true describes a general belief based on our experience. In a formal sense, however, this question comprises an intriguing field of philosophy known as *epistemology*, the study of knowledge.

When asked how we know that something is true, the typical response is, "Something is true when it is based on the facts." This response may seem sufficient, but a second question can then be posed. What is a fact? Again, the usual reply would be, "A fact is a condition that exists whether we believe it or are aware of it." One might go on to add that facts are the conditions that comprise reality, and reality is objective or separate from our everyday opinions. Facts impose on us a certain discipline that prevents us from being misled by bias, self-indulgence, and, in some cases, intentional dishonesty on the part of others.

A central premise of the above account is that facts are objective because they are conditions that exist in that separate sphere understood as reality. This assumption is formally referred to as the *fact/value distinction*. It is a foundational assumption of empiricism and the reason why empiricist educational researchers place so much faith in the scientific method. From the empiricist perspective, using scientific procedures provides the means to separate facts from values or opinion because the procedures are themselves neutral (Smith, 1993).

Correspondence Theory of Truth

These "procedures of verification" are seen as being neutral because they rely on observation of evidence we can detect in the physical realm; hence the well-known adage, "Seeing is believing." Of course, this applies to other information in addition to the visual, data we can touch, hear, or perceive through our other senses. This physically detectable evidence is known as *sense data*, and the formal procedures of verification center on the accumulation of this kind of information. The premise or theory is that a statement is true if it corresponds to or depicts physical reality. Philosophers of science refer to this premise as the *correspondence theory of truth*.

The advent of the scientific method with which we are all so familiar was based on this understanding of what constitutes truth, and, in turn, the scientific method is the result of the version of science known as empiricism. The acceptance and domination of empiricism in the physical sciences, and later in educational research, has a fascinating history. Because it is beyond the scope and purpose of the present discussion, this history will not be recounted here. Suffice it to say, though, that the empiricist approach to knowledge acquisition, with the specificity of its procedures, seemed to hold great promise for generating reliable knowledge and reducing the uncertainty of educators' actions in the classroom. It is little wonder that it was accepted as the dominant philosophy in educational research. It promised a means for "getting at" objective reality, establishing prediction and control, and, in the end, grounding reliable, authoritative knowledge.

During the past several decades, serious faults have come to light in the assumptions that support this approach to generating knowledge. This is difficult to come to terms with because the acceptance of these assumptions has become so entrenched in educators' professional culture that questioning the assumptions seems unnecessary, even unthinkable. We accept these assumptions as a matter of course, and, as a result, they are continually reconfirmed as "the way things are." We accept them as the definitive foundations of our professional knowledge. As it turns out, these foundational assumptions are not only questionable but also have been effectively discredited.

I begin my examination by returning to the correspondence theory of truth. Correspondence theory holds that facts can be verified through systematic methods of observation or gathering of sense data. According to this theory of truth, facts can be distinguished from human values or opinions in this way. For it to work, observation itself must be free from any form of distortion. We have to be able to ensure that what we see is not influenced by our predispositions to "see" certain things and "not see" others. If an observation is to be objective, it cannot be subject to the beliefs one holds, nor can it be influenced by the constraints of the observer's experiences in the world. In short, it cannot be subject to his or her current knowledge, values, biases, or opinions. If the observation is subject to these influences, what is produced is not simply an objective statement or description of the facts but, rather, an *interpretation* of sense data or what was "seen."

Can human observers set aside their knowledge, values, biases, and opinions so they can make objective observations or know things as they really are? The short answer to this question is—no. To do so, we would have to step outside of ourselves, in a manner of speaking, leaving behind all experience, previous knowledge, beliefs, and so forth. We even would have to be able to transcend the limits of our language and culture. Putnam (1981), expresses this situation in a particularly useful manner, explaining that to transcend these influences would be the functional equivalent of gaining "a God's eye point of view." Nagel (1981) likened it to the ability to view the world from no particular place in it. This inability to get outside of oneself is what prompted the assertion that there is *no theory-free knowledge*.

Once the recognition sets in that we cannot make observations free of our own preexisting theories or unmediated by our own interpretations, we cannot sustain the notions that facts can be separated from values, that an objective reality exists outside of our beliefs and understanding of the world, and that we have the means to discover reality through methods of observation no matter how scientifically disciplined the applications of those methods may be.

Subject-Object Dualism

Another aspect of knowing things "as they really are" is the idea that we can make observations without affecting or altering whatever we are observing. The assumption underlying this is referred to as *subject/object dualism*. If, in the act of observing, we affect or alter in any way the object (or in educational research, the people or classrooms) we are observing, obviously whatever or whomever it was cannot be known as it really is or they really are. And, again, as many philosophers of science have pointed out, we cannot avoid having such an effect. Succinctly put, the knower and the known are inseparable in the sense that each influences the other.

To provide an example from survey research, a commonly employed approach in educational research, the individuals completing a given survey are inevitably constrained by the type of questions the researcher asks, the order in which the questions are asked, and the phraseology used in the survey instrument (Cicourel, 1964). Perhaps this is why those who have agreed to complete surveys often explain their answers in the margins of the survey form and why they become uneasy and think the prescribed responses fail to capture what they really think.

In much the same manner, classroom-based research and researchers affect the objects of study (the teacher and the students) because the classroom must be altered to carry out the course of the research (Danziger, 1990). When researchers are present, few would maintain that teachers and students are not aware of and responsive to the researchers' presence. Their seemingly "objective" research is permeated with their own personal beliefs.

Interestingly, physical scientists provided the world with the first inkling that the very fundamental assumptions we make about the nature of truth and reality are problematic at best. Heisenberg's Uncertainty Principle is frequently offered as an example of how human choices in the methods of observation influence what researchers see. (Heisenberg's principle is referred to in the works of the authors contributing to this book.) Werner Heisenberg, a theoretical physicist, found that, when measuring a subatomic particle, the more accurate the measurement of the particle's momentum, the more inaccurate was the measurement of its position. The implications of this realization are stunning because it essentially demonstrates that we can never know "things" as they really are, even in the physical realm, because the very act of observation changes or alters what we observe.

In Heisenberg's case, the choice was between measuring the momentum or the position of a subatomic particle. He found that whenever he attempted to measure the momentum of a subatomic particle, his method of measurement changed its position. Conversely, whenever he tried to pinpoint its position, its momentum was altered. He reached the inevitable conclusion that observations are inevitably influenced by the researcher's *choices* of what to measure and the tools he or she employs as a measurement device.

Albert Einstein's theory of the quantum nature of light presents us with another example of how our ability to observe is limited by our ability to perceive. When faced with the inherently paradoxical realization that light consists of both particles and waves, depending on how the researcher chooses to observe it, physicists concluded that the limitations of the human mind, our inability to get outside of ourselves, force us to construct ways of thinking about things that serve our purposes, but this does not mean that is the way things "really" are. What we take to be facts or reality are actually our own *constructions*. The notion that we discover reality is incorrect. Instead, it is unavoidable that we *make* things come out certain ways, and because this is the case, we should not confuse *making* or *constructing* reality with *finding* or *discovering* reality (Hazelrigg, 1989; MacIntyre, 1984).

What these theoretical physicists and philosophers of science also have pointed out is that our constructions of reality place limitations on future understanding and possibilities. Unless we are aware that we have engaged in the construction of our understanding, by confusing discovery with constructing, we have effectively placed even more serious limitations on ourselves. Put differently, if we believe that what we know consists of conditions that simply exist, it follows that we also have no influence or control over those conditions and, consequently, no possibility of changing them. But if we understand and acknowledge that what we know is the result of choices we make and our predispositions to "see" things in certain ways as a result of our values, experiences, and culture, among other influences, we then can consider alternative perspectives or different ways of understanding and changing conditions (Hazelrigg, 1989; Vico, 1968). As we shall see, the distinction between the metaphors of discovery versus the metaphors of construction are central to the debates in special education.

Discovery Versus Construction and the Problems Facing Special Education

Let's revisit the four problems posed at the beginning of the chapter. First is the question: What is the nature of disability? For empiricist special education scholars, this question has been construed as an issue of proper definition and identification criteria because those scholars understand disability as having an independent existence. In contrast, those who hold a constructivist perspective, as do the three scholars featured in this book, think very differently about disability. For them, disability is a matter of what meaning people bring to human differences in various social contexts.

The second problem concerns the issue of knowledge production. For empiricists, conducting research is a matter of using the scientific method to discover generalizable "effective technologies" that will allow for prediction and control of learning. From a constructivist perspective, knowledge consists of context-dependent mental constructions, and for this reason learning cannot be simply transferred by using specific techniques that acknowledge neither human interpretation nor the context in which it takes place.

The third problem pertains to the preparation of special education teachers. From the empiricist perspective, good teacher preparation is largely a matter of training teachers to use "effective technologies" derived from their research. Constructivists, in contrast, view teacher preparation as a time for prospective teachers to learn how to develop craft knowledge, how to understand their students and themselves as teachers, and how to think and solve problems contextually.

Finally, the question of place is posed. Is the place of instruction a matter that should be decided on the basis of scientific research as empiricists insist it is, or is inclusion a moral issue involving choices about how we view difference, understand the teaching/learning process, and the educational contexts we create?

Defining and Identifying Disability

That disability is largely understood as a condition that a person "has" is substantiated in the language of formal definitions and codified in the widespread practice of labeling special education students. Still, the nagging problem of how to "operationalize" these definitions has yet to be resolved. Although this is the case with all disability areas, it is especially intractable for the largest group of special education students, those identified as "having" learning disabilities. As a backdrop for discussion, the problem of defining learning disabilities is therefore extraordinarily instructive. What is at the root of all the difficulty in defining and identifying learning disabilities is the confusion between discovery and construction.

From the time the term *learning disability* was coined, the condition was characterized as stemming from or being caused by neurological pathology. A brief history of learning disability theory demonstrates that the logic underlying "discovery" of the condition is flimsy indeed. As documented in Carrier's (1986) work, researchers Werner and Strauss used the term "exogenous mental retardation" to describe children whose learning and behavioral patterns closely matched those of the brain-injured World War I soldiers that Goldstein studied. Werner and Strauss reasoned that if the children they were studying displayed the same behavioral patterns as the injured World War I soldiers who were known to have sustained brain injury, these children also must have some form of brain injury.

Cast in plain terms, this circular or tautological logic concluded that if brain injury causes certain behavioral patterns, the presence of these behaviors indicates brain injury. Early on, it was pointed out that Werner and Strauss had engaged in a terrific leap of inference by drawing this conclusion;

nevertheless, the weakness of this logic was largely ignored and went on to serve as the foundation for learning disability theory.

Learning disability theorists later conceded that because they could not actually observe physical tissue damage to the brains of individuals identified as learning disabled, the term "brain damage" should be changed to "minimal brain dysfunction" to reflect the inferential nature of this presumed cause for the observed learning difficulties. Still, the initial causal inference remained intact and continues to form the basis for how most professionals, as well as the general public, understand the nature of learning disabilities.

Quite telling, though, is that the current literature is replete with intense efforts to explain (see Kavale and Forness, 1985, 1995; Swanson, 1988), define (see Shaw, Cullen, McGuire, & Brinckerhoff, 1995), and locate the exact neurological cause (Hynd, Marshall, & Gonzalez, 1991) of learning disabilities. That none of these efforts has come to definitive fruition should prompt us to take serious pause because this situation begs the obvious questions: How is it that students are identified daily as having a learning disability when no one really knows what a learning disability is? And if we know what it is, why are we still looking? Nevertheless, many scholars and researchers argue that learning disabilities are "real," even if the precise nature of this condition cannot be pinned down. For example, in an effort to come to terms with the elusiveness of the category, Kavale and Forness (1995) state that "LD is a real phenomenon" and also that, "It is counterproductive to continue asking whether LD is real" (p. 333). Considering their following statement, however, one may wonder if continuing to ponder the nature of LD is indeed counterproductive.

> It should be understood that objections to the LD category stem from our own inability to understand LD. The ceaseless empirical, political, and philosophical debates in the LD field have undermined the LD concept, leaving it vulnerable to questions about its existence. Instead of discussing ways in which the LD *concept* might be *developed* in a logical and rational fashion, we have been reduced to bickering over whether the *object* of our discussion even *exists*. After some 25 years, this is not the level of debate that fosters confidence that we know what we are talking about [emphasis added]. (p. 333)

On the one hand, stating that learning disabilities are "real" implies that they have an objective existence apart from anyone's pretheoretical dispositions of what constitutes a disability; on the other hand, acknowledging that learning disabilities is a concept subject to development suggests that the condition cannot exist apart from one's beliefs about normal versus abnormal functioning. The intermingling of these two opposing understandings reveals the conceptual confusion that ensues when a construction of reality is mistaken for the discovery of reality.

A comparison of two scenarios further illustrates the distinction between discovery and construction. In the first scenario, the parents of an elementary-school child are welcomed into a school conference room. Members of the school eligibility committee are introduced, and the meeting is opened by various professionals (psychologist, social worker, and so on). Discussion ensues about Sammy's classroom academic, behavioral, and social performance. The school psychologist concludes the discussion by stating, "Sammy fits the profile of a student who has a learning disability."

The parents might react in any or all of the following ways: resigned (because they already had been told that this was suspected), relieved (because this explained why things were not going well for their little one in school), or stunned and saddened (even if they had been forewarned). The phrase "has a learning disability" implies that the origin of the problem has been discovered within the child. It says that the condition existed within the child and all we did was find it; hence, we have no responsibility for its existence. The learning disability exists independently of anyone's values or opinions.

The second scenario is the same, except that the psychologist offers a different statement: "Given the choices made at this school about teaching methods, curriculum, and classroom management, and about our expectations for how students should learn and behave, it makes sense to think of your child as having a learning disability, given the way he is currently performing." The parents' response to this would likely be very different. They might call into question all of the "choices" the school made. Choices, after all, are value statements—what is deemed as good, proper, and worthwhile, as opposed to what is not. They may become indignant or angry at the professionals' assumption that their child can be regarded as deficient because it "makes sense" to the professionals—unless, of course, the parents decide it makes sense to them, too.

The sheer unlikeliness of a professional uttering such a statement notwithstanding, it conveys that learning disability is a construction of meaning or a name given to the interpretation of a student's observed behavior within a given social context. This perspective acknowledges the deeply embedded values that are brought to bear on the situation. What is acknowledged is that the concept of a learning disability and its identification is not about finding something, regardless of all of the seemingly "objective" measures used in the assessment process. Instead, both are the products of a social process wherein values, understandings, and beliefs influence judgments about what kind of difference makes a difference or how people choose to think about difference in various social and cultural contexts.

When discovery is confused with construction, much in the way of understanding and alternative possibilities are closed to us. In the case with learning disabilities, as long as we are confined to the metaphors of discovery, the only possibility open to us is to continue in an endless search for that elusive, and unfortunate, deficiency within the individual. Also, educators are closed off from examining their practices, choices, and expectations that may be creating the conditions that result in "seeing" the disability in the first place. Further, they are precluded from seeing how those choices might require examination and how different ways of thinking about these things could open new possibilities.

If we believe that things simply are the way they are, there can be no responsibility for them, and likewise no possibility for changing them. If we understand that our knowledge about the world is a construction, our thinking becomes altered dramatically. Rather than thinking in terms of "this is reality," we begin to think in terms of "this is the way we have constructed reality." Subsequently, we begin to realize that what we construct we can deconstruct and reconstruct, and that we have the responsibility for doing so when "the way things are" has undesirable consequences (Smith, 1988; Schwandt, 1989).

At this point, we should note that, although learning disability provides one of the best examples of how disability is constructed, the same holds true for other disabilities as well. And although it is a rather straightforward undertaking to understand how this applies to the other mild disabilities such as behavior disorders and mild mental disability (which may well explain why distinguishing one from the other is so difficult to in many cases), it seems more difficult to apply to other areas, especially those involving physical differences such as severe mental disability, blindness, deafness, and so on. It is with these differences that more subtlety of thought is required to comprehend what is meant by the social construction of disability.

The most important feature of understanding this concept does not mean denying that we perceive difference. There is general consensus that everyone's brains, eyes, and ears do not function the same. The crucial consideration concerns what this means, or how we are to interpret the respective differences. For instance, individuals with Down syndrome are observed to have chromosomal differences that, in inappropriate stereotypic fashion, have come to be so closely associated with mental retardation that the presence of the former has meant occurrence of the latter (Kliewer, 1998), until the relatively recent past, when some children with Down syndrome were observed to have scored in the average range on IQ tests (Clunies-Ross, 1990). This represents something of a crisis of meaning for those who equate this chromosomal condition with mental disability.

The obvious question raised is: What does having Down syndrome now mean? The individuals who scored in the average range, it might be pointed out, had received excellent early intervention. This explanation acknowledges, perhaps unwittingly, that disability is not merely a matter of difference; it is a matter of how we interpret and interact with perceived difference. One now must ask to what extent what we "know" about Down syndrome and other disabilities contributes to their very creation.

An important point of clarification is in order here: Certainly one should not take this to mean that we create the chromosomal difference associated with Down syndrome. Rather, it means that, we decide through the act of interpretation what that difference means. This meaning is what guides our decisions about how an individual with this difference is to be interacted with, which in turn sets into motion the events that construct who he or she is and eventually becomes.

An earlier point deserves reiteration: To mistake "finding" (discovery) for "making" (construction) has deeply moral implications. In the words of Hazelrigg (1989), this confusion "authorizes that most pernicious modality of the justification of human deeds (bad or good), namely, justification as matter-of-factness achieved through/in the amnesia of a naturalization of the social" (p. 168). In the context of the present discussion, to claim that we discovered (an act of naturalization) learning disabilities or Down syndrome authorizes or empowers us to impose meaning (a social act) on human difference. And, by extension, it justifies our subsequent actions based on those meanings. By "forgetting" that we have naturalized the social, we exonerate ourselves from responsibility for imposition and self-justification. There is no moral responsibility for what one finds, but one is enormously responsible for what he or she makes.

In the following examination of the problem of codifying a special education knowledge base, we explore how this question also is affected by the foundational assumptions of fact/value distinction, subject/object dualism, and the metaphors of discovery.

The Knowledge Base of Special Education

If disabilities are understood as conditions we discover, it seems only logical that students who "have" the disabilities would require a separate set of teaching methods designed to address those specific conditions. It also would seem to follow that the methods of empiricist science—the same methods that led to the "discovery" of disability in the first place—would lead to the discovery of what "works" with these students. To do so requires that effective teaching methods be distinguished from ineffective ones that are in vogue or merely favored by teachers. The concept of separating fact from opinion (establishment of objective truth) is clearly evident here, as is the presumption that experimental science will yield a set of teaching methods that will allow us to predict and control learning outcomes.

The prospect of accumulating such a knowledge base, one that will eliminate the guesswork from teaching, no doubt holds a certain allure. People do not want to struggle with uncertainty or the consequences of making mistakes. When we set out to teach a student to read, we want to know ahead of time that the methods we use are actually going to result in the student learning to read. The problem, though, is that applying the scientific method to the study of teaching fails to accomplish this goal because it is misapplied to the study of human beings.

When educational researchers adopted the scientific method, as it was embraced across the social sciences as a whole, most believed that it would offer the same successes it had brought to the physical sciences. This seemed reasonable enough, given that the physical sciences, using experimental procedures, had accomplished amazing strides in the past century or so. Why not study people as other scientists study the natural world? The palpable enthusiasm for this project is recorded in the words of educational psychologist Edward Thorndike (1910), who, in the first issue of *The Journal of Educational Psychology,* stated:

> A complete science of psychology would tell every fact about everyone's intellect and character and behavior, would tell the cause of every change in human nature, would tell the result which every educational force—every act of every person that changed any other or the agent himself—would have. It would aid us to use human beings for the world's welfare with the same surety of the result that we now have when we use falling bodies or chemical elements. In proportion as we get such a science, we shall become masters of our own souls as we are now masters of heat and light. Progress toward such a science is being made. (p. 6)

Lawlike Generalizations

Knowing everything about "everyone's intellect and character and behavior," it was thought, would allow educators to develop lawlike generalizations that, in turn, would offer them the ability to predict, and therefore control, learning. They could know that applying a given teaching technique would result in a student's learning to read, just as we know that, under certain conditions (all other things being equal), heating water to 212 degrees Fahrenheit causes it to boil. The problem, which did not occur to researchers at the time and continues to be overlooked even today, is that people as objects of study do not lend themselves neatly to such an undertaking.

The term "lawlike generalization" means that once all the necessary conditions are specified, a given action(s) will lead to a precise outcome. The crucial aspect of a lawlike generalization is that it has to hold true all of the time under the specified conditions. Otherwise one could not exercise control over desired outcomes because he or she could not predict the results of certain actions. Lawlike generalizations are the crucial link between scientific knowledge and its practical application. They are the stuff of which scientific knowledge bases are made (Giddens, 1976).

In the physical sciences, because all of the conditions impinging on a particular outcome can often be delineated at the "macro-level" (above the level of the atom), the scientific method allows for the derivation of lawlike generalizations having practical application. This is so because, "at the macro level, we are dealing with large agglomerations of particles and atoms whose quantum effects in a sense cancel each other out" (Cziko, 1989, p.22). Substances in the physical world tend, overwhelmingly, to be predictable. The scientist can tell us what always will occur under certain conditions and also can supply what are referred to *as scope modifiers* (see MacIntyre, 1984), statements that identify the conditions under which an action will not lead to the predicted event.

The paramount problem with the quest to build a scientific knowledge base in the social sciences (special education being one of these) lies in the impossibility of deducing lawlike generalizations about people's behavior. This is the case because of a host of rather obvious reasons, the implications of which nonetheless seem largely ignored. In an eminently clear and readable article, Cziko (1989), discussed the following reasons for the unpredictability and indeterminism of human behavior.

First, no two people are exactly alike. Unlike, say, a molecule of oxygen, each of us differs with regard to those very things that make us human, such as cognition, background knowledge, experiences, interests, and so on. Because molecules of oxygen do not differ in ways that make them unpredictable, they can be brought, in a fairly straightforward fashion, under conditions that allow for prediction and control. Conversely, the qualities that humans possess "are at best extremely difficult to measure and impossible to control" (p. 18). Added to the profound complexity of the human mind, which is capable of functioning in a variety of states that are estimated to far exceed "the total number of elementary [subatomic] particles (electrons and protons) in the entire universe" (Sagan, 1977, as cited in Cziko, 1989, p. 18), the prospect of bringing individual differences under scientific control can be seen as only an exercise in futility.

Second, because people possess consciousness and the ability to change their mind at any given moment, human behavior is an inherently creative process, always novel because it is the product of meanings and intentions. The infinite variety of meanings that each person brings to his or her sum of unique experiences, none of which researchers can fully know or influence, leads to reactions that even the individual himself or herself could not have foreseen. How many teachers, for example, have realized to their dismay that the schedule of reinforcement that worked with Johnny yesterday actually prompts his misbehavior today because Johnny decided that frustrating the teacher was more rewarding than the "reinforcer."[1] An interesting thing about human beings is that we tend to dislike and resist being predictable to others even as we seek to make others predictable.

What all of this means to "scientific" educational research is that lawlike generalizations about people's behavior cannot be generated. MacIntyre's (1984, pgs. 88–108) telling discussion of this point leads him to conclude that if a putative lawlike generalization does not hold, and the reason(s) for the failure cannot be pinned down, all that can be salvaged from the research is a list of previous instances in which something seemed to influence a given future event. MacIntyre's distinction between a lawlike generalization and a list of instances sheds a whole new light on the assertion that a given teaching method or program has been scientifically proven to be effective. What the research is really saying is that the intervention worked, according to the criteria the researchers set, in the particular contexts and instances where they conducted their experiment(s). But the research cannot predict, in a scientific sense, that the intervention will work for the teacher who decides to use it.

When viewed from this standpoint, a very different picture emerges regarding the authoritative knowledge claims of scientific educational research. It is one thing to claim that scientific research allows us to predict the outcome of any given educational intervention and another thing altogether to acknowledge that all it can really offer is anticipation that it might work because it did in other broadly and not precisely definable contexts. Anticipation based on past experience—something we do in everyday life—can be useful but certainly does not inspire the same confidence as the ability to predict based on lawlike generalizations. To appreciate fully this distinction, we might ask who among us would drive over a bridge if the structural engineers who built it could offer only their anticipation that the bridge would hold.

When confronted with the inadequacies of scientific educational research, prominent defenders (e.g., Gage, 1989; 1991) contend that scientific educational research does not claim to locate lawlike generalizations. Instead, they believe that this research yields probabilistic generalizations like those generated by the physical sciences. The reasoning here is that although research cannot unfailingly predict the effects of any given educational intervention, it can predict the probability of desired outcomes. Therefore, it is better for teachers to employ a technique or program that has "worked" 90% of the time in research settings than to engage in guesswork.

This argument is problematic because the probabilistic generalizations of the natural sciences "are as law-like as any non-probabilistic generalizations" and "can be refuted by counter-examples [instances when the probabilistic generalization did not hold] in precisely the same way and to the same degree that other lawlike generalizations are" (MacIntyre, 1984, p. 91). In contrast, the probabilistic generalizations of educational research are neither lawlike (as discussed above) nor subject to refutation. When the probabilistic generalizations of educational research fail, the reason for the failure cannot be definitively established, again because of the fundamental differences between human beings and inanimate substances. Indeed, all the researcher—or the teacher for that matter—can know is that the intervention failed. The question of why it failed is anyone's guess, a situation that teachers placing their faith in scientific educational research are likely to find distressing to say the least.

The overarching conclusion drawn from this discussion is that using the scientific method (empiricism) in educational research does not make for very good science—if it can be rightly called a science at all. And, because this model is based on deeply flawed logic and erroneous assumptions, it never has, and never will, deliver on its promise to provide a scientific knowledge base despite arguments that we just have not given it enough time. As Giddens (1976) pointedly expresses this situation, if we persist in placing our hopes in this version of science, we "are not only waiting for a train that won't arrive, [but we are] waiting in the wrong station altogether" (p. 13). Despite protestations to the contrary, we cannot study human beings the same way we study the physical universe. The more we persist in this undertaking, the more inevitably problematic the situation becomes.

Reductionism

Because empiricism is grounded in the correspondence theory of truth and the gathering of sense data serves as a foundation for verification, the scientific method depends on *reductionism*. This is so for obvious reasons. For something to be observed and quantified, it first must be reduced to terms that eliminate, or attempt to eliminate, sources of human interpretation, both those of the researcher and those he or she researches. This is why all of the major concepts that we deal with in education—be they self-concept, motivation, intelligence, achievement, and so on—have been reduced to quantifiables. Whatever rich complexity these concepts have in our daily lives has been subordinated by the desire to naturalize the social to make it researchable in empiricist terms.

For example, the familiar term "on-task," which is meant to indicate a student's state of mind, is commonly defined by behavioral indices such as remaining seated with eyes on the teacher and the like. Because the student's frame of mind is entirely subject to interpretation and obviously not directly observable, visible indicators are made to stand for the actual topic of interest. Despite arguments that these behavioral indices often "seem" to go hand in hand with mental engagement, the student can exhibit all of the requisite "on-task" behavioral indicators during the teacher's review of long division even as the student's mind is wandering the slopes of the Himalayas. And even if it is not, what is going on in his or her mind is nowhere near captured in the observations of the student's physical behavior.

The important point to be made here is that learning and teaching are, by their very nature, interpretive acts. Both are about meanings and ideas people construct in a social environment. It makes little sense to strip away sources of human interpretation as a means to gain knowledge about that which is inherently interpretive. It is impossible to do so anyway. This, in itself, is problematic enough but does not nearly cover all that goes awry as a result of reductionism.

Decontexualization

Closely related to the need to reduce so that things can be made quantifiable in an uncomplicated way is the further need to treat these things as if they could be understood in the absence of context. We all know that the same action in a different context results in different interpretations of its meaning. Every teacher has had the experience of using a specific teaching approach that was a smashing success yesterday or last year only to realize that it was a disaster today. And, of course, it is well to remember that the observer is part of the context. On a day when the teacher is preoccupied by some recent troubling event, he or she might decide that the approach was a complete catastrophe when the students actually learned quite a bit. Yet, scientific educational research is forced to decontextualize; otherwise the research methods could not be applied. As Danziger (1990) noted, from the outset, "This enterprise depended on the crucial assumption that the variables studied would retain their identity irrespective of context" (p. 187). This assumption is crucial because if the variables studied were to take on alternate identities in other contexts, generalization and the prospect of prediction would be impossible.

Once the methods of teaching are separated from classroom context, teaching and learning are reduced to a set of observable variables and the act of teaching becomes the mechanical application of a set of techniques. The teacher, in turn, becomes a technician. Being a good teacher comes to mean that he or she is able to use correctly and consistently certain materials or procedures that educational researchers have developed and "validated." Teaching is depicted as a matter of following the steps, much as one would follow a set of technical procedures for building a bridge or a recipe for making quiche. When teaching is understood as the application of technique, the implications for teacher preparation and instructional arrangements in schools are troublesome, to say the least.

Teacher Preparation and the Question of Place

It makes sense to discuss the third and fourth problems—the preparation of special education teachers and organizational arrangements for instruction—together for two reasons. *First,* because they are predominantly informed by the assumptions of the empiricist paradigm (worldview), teacher preparation and school organization are based on the acquisition of skills leading to certain kinds of expertise and specific roles in the schools. For example, teachers are "trained" and granted credentials in specialty areas such as teaching students with behavioral disorders, meaning that they have specific expertise (skills and knowledge) to work with a specific kind of student. Schools also are organized to accommodate instructional arrangements that reflect technical specialization. So teacher preparation is influenced by the kinds of instructional roles that teachers will eventually fill and vice versa.

Second, at this point, all we have discussed leading up to this moment begins to merge as it finds its way into the everyday school practice. The complex and interrelated ways in which this occurs serves to intensify the hegemony of "real world" arguments offered by those who wish to maintain the status quo.

In special education, an often stated goal is to *train* teachers to use the most effective methods available (Kauffman, 1994). Prominent special education journals have devoted a great deal of attention to the questions of why teachers do not use research findings in special education practice and how they might be facilitated to do so (Carnine, 1997; Gersten & Brengelman, 1996; Gersten, Vaughn, Deshler, & Schiller, 1997; Wong, 1997; Pressley & El-Dinary, 1997). An interesting aspect of this discussion is the use of the term "teacher-training" as a synonym for teacher preparation. That these two terms are often used interchangeably illustrates how educators have come to see their work largely as a technical undertaking as even in its broadest sense the word "training" implies the transfer of specific skills and techniques. The ideal scenario is that researchers develop "effective" techniques, strategies, and programs that teachers then can be trained to utilize efficiently in the classroom. Teacher-preparation programs then are responsible for equipping teachers with these skills.

Knowledge Construction

Although this might seem reasonable enough at face value, the drive to increase certainty of practice, to create a technology of teaching that teachers will actually use, simply has not come to fruition. To understand why the expected did not, and will not, occur, it is useful to return to the concept of knowledge as a social construction. Because teaching and learning are the very essence of knowledge construction, the roles of teachers' and students' interests, intentions, purposes, cultures, values, and previous experiences in the world are integral to the educational process. These constitute the very essence of the classroom context that is stripped away in the empiricist development of a technological knowledge base designed to generalize to all classrooms. What these technologies actually represent is the constructed knowledge of the researchers who developed them. In effect, they are an attempt to bypass the act of knowledge construction, or sense-making, on the part of teachers and students, treating knowledge as prepackaged material that can be transferred and implanted.

Technique-Centered Teacher Training

One of the most notable effects of this knowledge as a transferable material commodity is that teachers and students stop insisting that things make sense, or that they even possess the capacity to make sense of new information. Instead, teaching becomes the less than fully engaged act of material coverage and exposure, and learning becomes the passive act of absorption and storage. Teachers and students alike abandon the act of making sense of ideas and meaningfully integrating concepts and skills into their everyday lives.

On several occasions I witnessed this effect with special education pre-service and inservice teachers in my role as a university practicum supervisor. During one particularly interesting visit to a special education resource room, the practicum student was teaching a well-known and thoroughly researched strategy for identifying unknown reading vocabulary. The three sixth-grade students in the group were carefully instructed on the steps of the strategy, using the direct instruction model, as they read passages from the classic book, *Roll of Thunder, Hear My Cry*. Each time they encountered an unfamiliar word, the teacher took them through the steps of the strategy, mastery of which constituted the overall objective of her lesson plan. As the lesson progressed, the students dutifully recited and performed the steps, but it was evident from their occasional comments and questions that they were becoming captivated by the richness of language and thematic depth of the novel. Over time, these comments and questions began to diminish as mastering the strategy steps continued throughout to be the focal point of the lesson.

After the lesson, the practicum student and I met for the usual discussion session, and I began, as I usually do, by asking her how she thought the lesson went. My purpose in doing this was to offer the student an opportunity to engage in genuine reflection without having to respond to any evaluative information from me. In the beginning, she told me that she was really pleased with the way the lesson had gone, that she thought she had met the lesson objective and appreciated the cooperation from the students. In short, she counted the lesson a success.

As I waited for her to go on, she added, "But there are a lot of things I would like to have done." When I asked her what those things were, she explained that she would liked to have discussed the book more and went on to discuss enthusiastically the kinds of questions and insights about the novel she would have shared with the students.

"Was there any reason why you didn't?" I asked. "Well..." she replied hesitantly, "I couldn't get that to fit the steps of the direct-instruction lesson plan form we were told to use in methods class." She finally added that she did not think the students would really use the strategy on their own because she could not imagine using it herself in her own personal reading.

What was clear to me from this encounter, and others like it, was that this preservice teacher was well on her way toward believing that technique should take precedence over meaning, and that her own sense of what it means to teach and learn was neither legitimate nor trustworthy. That technique-centered teacher training accomplishes just this was brought home to me one day in a graduate seminar when a veteran special education teacher shared with the class that she had spent her career looking for the next curricular program or set of materials that would get her students to achieve the objectives on their Individualized Education Plans. In her concluding remark she stated, "I just never believed that teaching my students came from inside of me."

Taken to its extreme, but nevertheless logical, conclusion, the technological teaching framework would ameliorate the teacher's role as anything other than a technician. In a world in which teachers deliver scripted lessons, teacher preparation would merely inculcate competencies for script delivery. One must then ask: What makes a teacher a teacher? After all, any reasonably intelligent person can follow a script.

In this regard, teachers' work becomes a collection of tasks, what Darling-Hammond (1985) refers to as semiskilled work, in which there is no room for the constructed, practical knowledge of teachers, or very much like what Polanyi (1966) refers to as *tacit knowledge*. In fact, recognition of and use of teachers' tacit knowledge actually interferes with the smooth and efficient application of technique, and one of the goals of standardizing teaching is to "teacher-proof" it (Darling-Hammond, 1985). If the technical view of teaching is incompatible with the use of practical knowledge, it is little wonder that empiricist special education researchers struggle with the gap between theory and practice. Their dilemma is that any margin granted to teachers' practical knowledge and contextual decision-making reduces the generalizability of their research while eliminating them actually produces the theory-practice gap.

Educational Context

Under the technical view of teaching, it would seem to make sense that schools should be organized accordingly. If different kinds of teachers possess distinct, specialized technical expertise, nondisabled students should be taught in the general education classroom with general education teachers and special education students should be taught in special education classrooms with special education teachers according to their special needs. This organizational scheme flows logically from the empiricist paradigm or framework. Underneath it all, though, lies the assumptions that disability is real and exists within the individual, knowledge is discovered, prediction and control of the educational environment is possible and desirable, and teaching is a matter of correct application of technique.

But if disabilities are the product of social consensus—about what kind of difference makes a difference, knowledge is constructed rather than discovered, prediction and control of the educational environment is neither possible nor desirable, and teaching is the context-bound act of making meaning—the rationale for separate environments for different types of students is not a response to the way things are as much as it is a consequence of the way we have made them.

This means that from the constructivist framework, once educators recognize that they have made or constructed the way things are, they also can realize the moral responsibility to reconstruct them when they prove to be inadequate. In the context of the full-inclusion debate, for example, if the general classroom is inadequate for some children, we should reconstruct these environments rather than exclude those students. This would involve reconstructing the way we conceptualize students' differences and also our understanding of the teaching/learning processes, knowledge production, teacher preparation, teaching methodology, curriculum, assessment, and school organization. As Sapon-Shevin (1996) has noted, each time we identify exceptional students and segregate them in separate classrooms, we are actually choosing to avoid opportunities to improve the regular classroom. As difficult as it may seem to make these changes, realizing that we can go beyond accepting things "as they really are" offers us an opportunity to move forward, making deliberate choices toward how we would have them be.

Conclusion

As we will come to see, the authors contributing to this book have pointed out that the untenable assumptions of the empiricist paradigm have literally produced the very problems that empiricist special education scholars have sought to resolve. Rather than reconsidering the foundational assumptions of their conceptual framework, many continue struggling with definitions of disability, laboring to codify a scientific knowledge base, and ardently seeking validation for the traditional continuum of services. The resolution they hope for will nevertheless remain elusive, for the way out is not the same path that brought them to where they now find themselves.

The next three chapters consist of seminal works by the three authors featured in this volume. These works provide the next step toward entering a conversation that began more than a decade ago. And because they elucidate the past, they are of crucial importance if we are to understand the present and shape the future of special education.

References

Carnine, D. (1997). Bridging the research-to-practice gap. *Exceptional Children, 63,* 513–521.

Carnine, D. (1987). A response to "False standards, a distorting and disintegrating effect on education, turning away from useful purposes, being inevitably unfulfilled, and remaining unrealistic and irrelevant." *Remedial and Special Education, 8*(1), 42–43.

Carrier, J. G. (1986). *Learning disability: Social class and the construction of inequality in American education.* Westport, CT: Greenwood Press.

Cicourel, A. V. (1964). *Method and measurement in sociology.* New York: Free Press.

Clunies-Ross, G. (1990). *The right to read: Publishing for people with disabilities.* Canberra: National Library of Australia.

Cziko, G. A. (1989). Unpredictability and indeterminism in human behavior: Arguments and implications for educational research. *Educational Researcher, 18*(3), 17–25.

Danziger, K. (1990). *Constructing the subject.* Cambridge, UK: Cambridge University Press.

Darling-Hammond, L. (1985). Valuing teachers: The making of a profession. *Teachers College Record, 87,* 210.

Deno, E. (1970). Special education as developmental capital. *Exceptional Children, 37,* 229–237.

Dunn, L. M. (1968). Special education for the mildly retarded—Is much of it justifiable? *Exceptional Children, 35,* 5–22.

Gage, N. L. (1989). The paradigm wars and their aftermath: A "historical" sketch of research on teaching since 1989. *Educational Researcher, 18,* 4–10.

Gage, N. L. (1991). The obviousness of social and educational research results. *Educational Researcher, 20,* 10–16.

Gersten, R., & Brengelman, S. U. (1996). The quest to translate research into classroom practice: The emerging knowledge base. *Remedial and Special Education, 17*(2), 67–74.

Gersten, R., Vaughn, S., Deshler, D., & Schiller, E. (1997). What we know about using research findings: Implications for improving special education practice. *Journal of Learning Disabilities, 30,* 466–476.

Giddens, A. (1976). *New rules of sociological method: A positive critique of interpretive sociologies.* New York: Basic Books.

Hazelrigg, L. (1989). *A wilderness of mirrors: On the labor of making found worlds.* Tallahassee: Florida State University Press.

Heshusius, L. (1989). The Newtonian mechanistic paradigm, special education, and contours of alternatives: An overview. *Journal of Learning Disabilities, 22,* 403–415.

Hynd, G. W., Marshall, R., & Gonzalez, J. (1991). Learning disabilities and presumed central nervous system dysfunction. *Learning Disability Quarterly, 14,* 283–296.

Iano, R. P. (1986). The study and development of teaching: With implications for the advancement of special education. *Remedial and Special Education, 7*(5), 50–61.

Kauffman, J. M. (1994). Places of change: Special education's power and identity in an era of educational reform. *Journal of Learning Disabilities, 27,* 610–618.

Kavale, K. A., & Forness, S. R. (1985). *The science of learning disabilities.* San Diego, CA: College Hill Press.

Kavale, K. A., & Forness, S. R. (1995). *The nature of learning disabilities: Critical elements of diagnosis and classification.* Mahweh, NJ: Lawrence Erlbaum.

Kliewer, C. (1998). *Schooling children with Down syndrome: Toward an understanding of possibility.* New York: Teachers College Press.

MacIntyre, A. (1984). *After virtue.* Notre Dame, IN: University of Notre Dame Press.

Nagel, T. (1981). *Mortal questions.* New York: Cambridge University Press.

Polanyi, M. (1966). *The tacit dimension.* Garden City, NY: Doubleday.

Poplin, M. S. (1988). Holistic/constructivist principles of the teaching/learning process: Implications for the field of learning disabilities. *Journal of Learning Disabilities, 21,* 401–416.

Pressley, M., & El-Dinary, P.B. (1997). What we know about translating comprehension-strategies instruction research into practice. *Journal of Learning Disabilities, 30,* 486–488, 512.

Putnam, H. (1981). *Reason, truth and history.* Cambridge, UK: Cambridge University Press.

Sagan, C. (1977). *The dragons of Eden: Speculations on the evolution of human intelligence.* New York: Random House.

Sapon-Shevin, M. (1996). Including all students and their gifts within regular classrooms. In W. Stainback & S. Stainback (Eds.), *Controversial issues confronting special education: Divergent perspectives* (2d ed., pp. 69–95). Needham Heights, MA: Allyn & Bacon.

Schwandt, T. (1989). Recapturing moral discourse in evaluation. *Educational Researcher, 18*(8), 11–16.

Shaw, S. F., Cullen, J. P., McGuire, J. M.. & Brinckerhoff, L. C. (1995). Operationalizing a definition of learning disabilities. *Journal of Learning Disabilities 28,* 586–597.

Skrtic, T. M. (1991). The special education paradox: Equity as the way to excellence. *Harvard Educational Review, 61*(2), 148–206.

Smith, J. K. (1988). The evaluator/researcher as person versus the person as evaluator/researcher. *Educational Researcher, 17*(2), 18–23.

Smith, J. K. (1993). *After the demise of empiricism: The problem of judging social and educational inquiry.* Norwood, NJ: Ablex Publishing.

Swanson, H. L. (1988). Toward a metatheory of learning disabilities. *Journal of Learning Disabilities, 21,* 196–209.

Thorndike, E. L. (1910). The contribution of psychology to education. *Journal of Educational Psychology, 1,* 5–12.

Vico, G. (1968). *The new science* [3d ed.—original text 1744]. Trans. by T. G. Bergin & M. H. Fisch. Ithaca, NY: Cornell University Press.

Wong, B. Y. L. (1997). Clearing hurdles in teacher adoption and sustained use of research-based instruction. *Journal of Learning Disabilities, 30,* 482–485.

Zukav, G. (1979). *The dancing Wu Li masters.* New York: William Morrow.

Note

1. Of course, in technical parlance, a positive reinforcer is defined as an event following a certain desired (target) behavior that increases the behavior. As Carnine (1987) points out, a reinforcer cannot be defined *apriori* (ahead of time). This means that if the "reinforcer" fails to increase the behavior, it cannot then be termed a reinforcer. One might wonder, then, how the efficacy of positive reinforcement (and other behavioral interventions) can be "scientifically" tested since defining a reinforcer is simply a matter of affirming the consequent.

Reading Heshusius:
An Introduction

Deborah Gallagher

I s the universe a giant clock whose functioning, once fully understood, is eminently ordered and predictable? Ever since the 17th century, Isaac Newton's description of the mechanistic universe has served as the guiding metaphor for intellectual and practical understanding of our world. In the 1989 article, "The Newtonian Mechanistic Paradigm, Special Education, and Contours of Alternatives: An Overview," first published in the *Journal of Learning Disabilities,* Lous Heshusius provides compelling examples on how the fact-versus-value distinction fundamental to the Newtonian/mechanistic paradigm has affected the entire range of intellectual and practical activities in special education. This effect encompasses everything from our conceptions of teachers, learners, and instructional and assessment approaches, to our research methodology, and even the criteria we use for selecting problems to be solved.

As Heshusius aptly points out, once a person has tacitly adopted the assumptions of the Newtonian/mechanistic paradigm, it is difficult to consider alternative ways of understanding. Indeed, because this paradigm has dominated thought for centuries, most who have accepted its assumptions are unaware that they have done so. Paradigms, in other words, serve as a metaphors that provide not only a way of seeing but also a way of not seeing. Conversely, "Understanding paradigms is 'a knowing that we know how we know.'" In the absence of such awareness, little, if any, substantive change can take place.

The seeming intractability of special education's current problems attests to the limitations of its dominant paradigm. Yet, its "self-synchronizing" nature continues to exert a hold over the field despite deeply informed critiques of this framework. Heshusius indicates that failure to distinguish between theories and paradigms has resulted in theoretical changes being confused with paradigm shifts. The difficulty with this, as she thoroughly illustrates, is that confusion between theory and paradigm leads to the erroneous belief that the field has slipped the bonds of its prevailing paradigm when, in actuality, it has not. Consequently, all of our "changes" compound rather than ameliorate the original problems.

Citing a number of scholarly exchanges, Heshusius also discusses how and why special education scholars who have provided deeply informed critiques of the prevailing paradigm have, nonetheless, been accused of "fuzzy thinking." These conceptual critiques seem to elicit this kind of reaction because the very act of questioning the mechanistic assumptions of value-free objectivity apparently provokes a fear that the only alternative is to "collapse into either chaos or nothingness." Ironically, the tenants of the mechanistic paradigm are what incite such a fear. "The point is that once the mechanistic assumptions are seen to hold up no longer, the accusation of fuzziness (or engaging in anti-science, or in a kind of watered-down science) when not adhering to them is instantly rendered irrelevant." The accusation of "fuzziness" is predicated, after all, on the presumption of its opposite—objective knowing.

Heshusius goes on to explore how a number of "theoretical reorientations" consistent with the emerging alternative holistic paradigm has provided us with a conceptual foothold, so to speak, for moving beyond mechanistic assumptions. Among these theoretical reorientations are alternative sociological theories of exceptionalities, resistance theory, and a theory of empowerment. It is here that she so eloquently elucidates the new awareness made possible when knowledge is understood to be the product of human constructions. This new awareness, in turn, can provide more coherent ways of understanding the teaching–learning process, approaches toward inquiry, and eventually how we understand ourselves and the nature of our work.

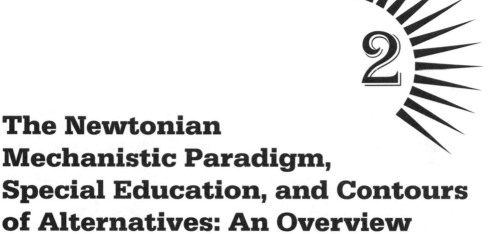

The Newtonian Mechanistic Paradigm, Special Education, and Contours of Alternatives: An Overview

Lous Heshusius

Increasingly, the concepts of paradigm and paradigm shifts are becoming major foci of discussion across the sciences and social sciences. As Adelman and Taylor note in their introduction to an article by Torgesen (1986), special education provides far too few broad overviews of paradigms and theories. Also different authors and different disciplines attach different meanings to the term "paradigm." In his major treatise on scientific revolutions, Kuhn (1970) brought the term "paradigm" into fashionable use. He employed the term, though, in at least 21 different ways to include metaphysical, sociological, and more directly concrete meanings (see Masterman, 1970; Note 1).

For the present purposes I use the term *paradigm* in a focused metaphorical sense rather than equating it—as is perhaps more typical within the social sciences—to model of inquiry (see, e.g., Popkewitz, 1984) or with

From "The Newtonian Mechanistic Paradigm, Special Education, and Contours of Alternatives: An Overview" by Lous Heshusius, 1989, *Journal of Learning Disabilities, 22,* 403–415. Reprinted with permission.

theory (as is the case in some fields of study, including learning disabilities—an observation I will return to later). In doing so, I draw largely from contemporary philosophy of science and from literature on new paradigm thinking.

The concept of paradigm-as-metaphor points to a distinctly more fundamental level at which questions can be asked than is the case at the level of theory, or of model of inquiry. Paradigm-as-metaphor directs attention to the most fundamental ways in which we think about the concept of reality in the first place and how it is allowed to be known, not just within scientific inquiry but in all of life. *Paradigm-as-metaphor refers to the values, beliefs, perceptions, and practices that collectively constitute the decisions we make about what counts as real and how we allow each other to know about it.*

Within scientific inquiry, paradigm-as-metaphor gives rise not only to theory and research methodology but also to criteria for problem selection and for evaluation (Capra, 1986; Lakoff & Johnson, 1980; LeShan & Margenau, 1982; Lincoln & Guba, 1985; Ogilvy, 1986; Prigogine & Stengers, 1984; Sadawa & Caley, 1985). Paradigm-as-metaphor represents what Lincoln and Guba (1985, p. 15) call "the ultimate benchmarks against which *everything else* is tested" (emphasis theirs). It does not directly delineate the phenomenon of interest as does theory but, rather, presents a "way of seeing" that is also a way of not seeing. (Indirectly, of course, the paradigmatic assumptions manifest themselves also in how theory conceives of its phenomenon in the first place.) Paradigm-as-metaphor represents the beliefs by which we ultimately think and act. "Paradigms represent a distillation of what we *think* about the world (but cannot prove)" (Lincoln & Guba, 1985, p. 15). When made self-conscious and articulated, paradigms make explicit how we think about the phenomena of interest in any area of our lives. Paradigms describe who *we* are in our epistemological makeup. Understanding paradigms is "a knowing that we know how we know" (Ogilvy, 1986, p. 14). It demands a self-consciousness of ourselves as knowers, an understanding that we, as knowers, are *part of* the paradigm we function within. The process of becoming self- conscious about our ultimate benchmarks is bound to happen when the paradigm we un-self-consciously live by reaches its limitations. Then the full extent of its characteristics emerges (Capra, 1982, 1986; Kuhn, 1970; Lincoln & Guba, 1985; Prigogine & Stengers, 1984).

Many substantial accounts trace the dominant paradigm of the last three centuries to the rise of the natural sciences in the 17th century: Newtonian, mechanistic assumptions have guided intellectual and practical life since that time. A dawning self-consciousness about the paradigmatic boundaries we have lived within can be found in publications by increasing numbers of scientists and philosophers of science (e.g., Berman, 1984; Bernstein, 1983; Capra, 1982; Hesse, 1980; Jantsch, 1980; LeShan & Margenau, 1982; Prigogine & Stengers, 1984; Wolf, 1981).

Mechanistic assumptions are captured by the metaphor of the machine, initially set forth by René Descartes in his *De Homine*, a theory of man and animals as machines. Many have explicitly described the subsequent enormous influence of the machine metaphor upon the study of human behavior (e.g., Capra, 1982; Koestler, 1967; LeShan & Margenau, 1982; Von Bertalanffy, 1967, 1968).

Although discussions of the Newtonian mechanistic paradigm-as-metaphor typically relate to scientific inquiry, many sources also are available describing its influence on other areas in life (e.g., Capra, 1982—economy, ecology; Dodson-Gray, 1982, and French, 1985—patriarchy; Fox, 1983—religion; LeShan & Margenau, 1982—art, ethics; Lewis, 1983—politics & economics). In the social sciences similar discussions are appearing in areas of study directly related to special education, such as psychology, research methodology, and curriculum inquiry (e.g., Doll, 1986a, 1986b; Gergen, 1985; Lincoln & Guba, 1985; Polkinghorne, 1983; Sadawa & Caley, 1985; Smith & Heshusius, 1986; Valle, 1981).

Now I will (a) address the assumptions about the nature of reality and the nature of knowledge claims that underlie Newtonian mechanistic thought, particularly in relation to special education theory and practice; (b) discuss the discontent with mechanistic thought and the calls for a paradigm change across the social sciences; (c) note the conceptual misunderstandings within the field of special education that stand in way of paradigmatic change—notably, the recent tendency to rename theories as paradigms and the accusation of "fuzziness" against those who advocate new paradigmatic thought; (d) address the importance for special education of what I have called theoretical "reorientations"; and (e) outline the assumptions about what counts as real, how we can know about it within the emerging nonmechanistic, holistic paradigm, and its importance for special education theory, practice, and research.

The Newtonian Mechanistic Paradigm and Special Education

Table 2.1 explicitly traces how the tenets of the Newtonian mechanistic paradigm have directly dictated our conceptions of the learner and the teacher, instructional and assessment practices, research methods, theory building, and the criteria we choose for problem selection and evaluation. Without exception, the sources listed in that table take a critical perspective, engaging in creative discontent, or in what Gould (1981, p. 32) refers to as "positive debunking." Debunking is not a negative exercise (as it would be within a mechanistic paradigm, in which science moves toward truth in an additive

TABLE 2.1
Key Assumptions of the Mechanistic Paradigm and Translations Into Special Education Theory and Practice

Mechanistic Paradigm	Applications in Special Education
The Nature of Reality	
• Is objective; fact can be separated from value, the observer from the observed, the knower from the known	• Attempts to objectify knowledge and knowing; only that which can be reliably measured gains the status of formal knowledge; categorization of exceptionalities by objective diagnoses; right–wrong answers, errorless learning
• Is understood through a mathematical system	• Quantification and ranking (statistically significant findings, frequency counts, test scores) as indices of children's recall abilities; diagnostic testing
• Is reductionistic; the dynamics of the whole can be understood from the properties of the parts	• Learning equates lengthy sequences of processes, behaviors, and learning strategies; focus on deficits within the student
• Consists of components; knowledge of pieces adds up to knowledge of the whole	• Isolated skill training, worksheets, bottom-up approaches to literacy; task analysis; learning equates to mastery of predetermined, known curriculum outcomes
• Can be known with certainty with the gathering of sufficient data	• Predictive instruments, search for causality in diagnosis; answers to problems lie in "more research" and "more data"
The Nature of Progress	
• Is deterministic; all events have direct causes and consequences • Is additive, incremental, sequential, and continuous, which leads to prediction and control	• Causal linkages between diagnoses and instruction; task analysis, mastery learning; precision teaching; programmed and sequentialized materials; controlled vocabulary; daily charting, curriculum-based assessment; "individualized" education (meaning the same for all students but at their own pace)
• Is the same regardless of personal meaning and context	• Behaviorism, stimulus control, reinforcement, input–output models; unidirectional control of curriculum by teacher
The Nature of the Organism	
• Is reactive	

Synchronized

fashion, by gathering more and more data) but, rather, a positive and necessary act, as science advances not by addition but by replacement through a process in which the old is transformed by new understandings (Gould, 1981; Kuhn, 1970; LeShan & Margenau, 1982; Prigogine & Stengers, 1984).

Accounts of the Newtonian mechanistic paradigm point to the belief in *simplicity* as the foundation of the paradigm. All complexity is to be broken down into components. Translated into practice, this leads to, for instance, task analysis and isolated skill training. The whole is understood by understanding the components as logically and sequentially arranged—assumptions that lead to mastery learning, programmed materials, and behavioral objectives. Thus, causality, prediction, certainty, and control come to be seen as inherently possible, leading to predictive instruments, diagnostic testing, and diagnostic/prescriptive teaching.

In Newton's universe, time and space flowed uniformly and continuously (reflected in measured curriculum and curriculum-based assessment), and all movement was controlled by outside forces (assumptions that are reflected in stimulus control and systematic reinforcement practices). Fact was separated from value, the observer from the observed, the knower from the known.

Sources: *Curriculum Beyond Stability: Schon, Prigogine, Piaget,* by W. E. Doll, paper presented at Bergamo Curriculum Conference, Bergamo, OH, 1986; "Prigogine: A New Sense of Order, A New Curriculum," by W. E. Doll, 1986, *Theory into Practice, 25*(1), 10–16. "A Paradigm for Humanizing Special Education," by C. T. Fisher and A. A. Rizzo, 1974, *Journal of Special Education, 8,* 321–329; "At the Heart of the Advocacy Dilemma: A Mechanistic World View," by L. Heshusius, 1982, *Exceptional Children, 49,* 6–13; "Why Would They and I Want To Do It? A Phenomenological-Theoretical View of Special Education," by L. Heshusius, 1984, *Learning Disability Quarterly, 17,* 363–368; "Paradigm Shifts and Special Education: A Response to Ulman and Rosenberg," by L. Heshusius, 1986, *Exceptional Children, 52,* 461–465; "Pedagogy, Special Education, and the Lives of Young Children: A Critical and Futuristic Perspective," by L. Heshusius, 1986, *Journal of Education, 168*(3), 25–38; "The Study and Development of Teaching: With Implications for the Advancement of Special Education," 1986, by R. Iano, *Remedial and Special Education, 8*(1), 52–61; "Rebuttal: Neither the Absolute Certainty of Prescriptive Law Nor a Surrender to Mysticism," by R. Iano, 1987, *Remedial and Special Education, 7*(5), 52–61; "Is Professionalism Succumbing to a Push-button Mentality?" by R. M. Mitchell, 1980, *Counterpoint, 1*(2), 14; "Research Practices in Learning Disabilities," by M. Poplin, 1984, *Learning Disability Quarterly, 7,* 2–5; "Summary Rationalizations, Apologies, and Farewell: What We Don't Know About the Learning Disabled," by M. Poplin, 1984, *Learning Disability Quarterly, 7,* 130–135; "Toward an Holistic View of Persons with Learning Disabilities," by M. Poplin, 1984, *Learning Disability Quarterly, 7,* 130–135; "Reductionism from the Medical Model to the Classroom: The Past, Present, and Future of Learning Disabilities," by M. Poplin, 1985, *Research Communications in Psychology, Psychiatry and Behavior, 10*(1&2), 37–70.

(a) With the rise of mechanistic thought, quantification, became *the* epistemologically privileged way by which to make valid knowledge claims. The
humanities, the arts, intuitive knowing, personal knowledge, inner knowing—these were no longer considered valid ways to know. Measuring and
ranking (that is, assigning numbers to things and to relations between things)
became knowing. One doesn't even have to reflect about how the obsession
with quantification and ranking is translated into special education practice:
It permeates all we do. During the 17th-century rise of the natural sciences,
Galileo, Descartes, and Newton saw God as "chief mathematician of the
Universe." "Geometry existed before the creation, is coeternal with the mind
of God, is God himself," wrote Kepler (cited in LeShan & Margenau, 1982,
p. 246).

Paraphrasing Bohm (1980, pp. 21–22), before the rise of science, to
"measure" something meant to understand the totality of inner proportions,
to understand its "innermost being." A measure was a form of insight, and a
person's actions following on ways indicated by such insight would bring
about orderly action and harmonious living, in terms of physical health,
social order, and mental harmony. Insight was gained not by conforming to
external standards but instead by creative insight and understanding of the
deeper meaning of the structures and proportions of that which one wished
to understand. Only since the rise of 17th-century science has measuring
something come to mean comparing it to an external standard only, and
measurement has become routinized, habitual, and relatively gross and
mechanical.

The failure of the Newtonian mechanistic paradigm to understand
human behavior is reflected in disarray in the social sciences. Sarason (1981,
p. 14) describes this "disarray" as follows:

> [Social scientists] will admit that something is (and went) wrong,
> that the promise of social science has not paid off; that the world of
> affairs does not conform to social science models and paradigms; . .
> . that perhaps the natural science conception of solutions is not
> applicable to social problems.

Failure of the Newtonian mechanistic paradigm is also reflected in the
strong contemporary calls for personal, intuitive, and inner knowing and in
the call for the humanities and the arts to take their place alongside science
in the formal study of human behavior (see, among many others, Frye, 1981;
Leshan & Margenau, 1982; Prigogine & Stengers, 1984; Randall, 1984;
Scully, 1980; Winkler, 1985) and within special education (see Blatt, 1984;
Heshusius, 1988). None of this is to say that quantification should be eliminated but, rather, that quantification no longer can be equated with formal,

epistemologically privileged knowing. A judgment of significance, which within mechanistic thought is a quantitative/statistical one, must become a human judgment.

Reflection on the assumptions of mechanistic thought will demonstrate their synchronizing nature. Together they display internal coherence and interdependence. Each assumption, as Lincoln and Guba (1985, p. 85) also point out, is a *raison d'etre* for the others. One can't exist without instantly drawing on all others.

Different names are used at different times to refer to the mechanistic paradigm. Besides the term *mechanistic* or *Newtonian* (used by Berman, 1984; Capra, 1982; Doll, 1986a, 1986b; Heshusius, 1982; LeShan & Margenau, 1982), the term *component* or *atomistic* is used (Capra, 1982), as are the terms *reductionistic* (Poplin, 1985), *natural science* (Fisher & Rizzo, 1974), and *rational/technical paradigm* (Iano, 1986). A close look at Table 2.1 shows that these different labels stress individual assumptions.

Given the synchronizing nature of all assumptions, the different labels merely reflect the dimension the author is emphasizing. All other assumptions, however, are instantly implied. Similarly, whichever practice results as a manifestation of a given mechanistic assumption, all others are implied. One cannot, for instance, plan instruction by stipulating quantitatively measurable behavioral objectives without engaging in other manifestations of the mechanistic paradigm such as objectification and fragmentation of knowledge, right and wrong answers, task analysis, and reduced complexity of learning to predetermined sequences of behaviors.

Within the field of special education, Mann and Phillips (1967) must have been among the first to point to the danger of fragmentation resulting from our imitation of the emphasis of the natural sciences on manipulation of precisely delineated variables. Fisher and Rizzo (1974), Heshusius (1982), and Poplin (1984b, 1985) explicitly analyze the mechanistic Newtonian paradigm as paradigm-as-metaphor and relate its general characteristics to special education practices.

With regard to assessment, Iano (1987) and Doll (1986b) specifically address the influence of the mechanistic paradigm. Doll analyzes the measured curriculum in terms of Newtonian assumptions: The atomistic units of instruction and the linear sequencing and behavioral language in which the curriculum is described constitute a "modern day reincarnation of the 17th century's view of stability and order" (Doll, 1986a, p. 21).

Curriculum-based assessment (CBA), as practiced and advocated in special education, constitutes such Newtonian reincarnation. According to Tucker (1985, p. 200), gauging the degree of achievement according to CBA "can only happen when the expected curricular outcomes are known and measurable and where there is a method for the ongoing measurement of student progress." Objectification of knowing and of knowledge, additive and linear progress, quantification, right and wrong answers, mastery learning, and lack of consideration for context, meaning, and personal purposes are reflected in Tucker's statement.

CBA is no more than a "course to be run," to use Doll's (1986b, p. 11) expression (see also Iano, 1987). In a profound sense, CBA, like all manifestations of mechanistic/reductionist thought, has the answer before asking the question. Rather than a process of inquiry that leads to insights about children's learning, measured curriculum approaches such as CBA are processes of justification that are both dictated by and justify mechanistic assumptions about teaching and learning.

Mechanistic thought as translated into the never-ending search for objectivity, causality, and certainty in diagnoses and categorization of exceptionalities is specifically discussed by Iano (1986), Heshusius (1982), and Poplin (1985). All of the references cited here address in one way or another the mechanistic need to fragment in order to know, as expressed in task analysis, isolated skill training, endless worksheets, behavioral objectives, and so forth. The deficit-driven nature of our field, resulting from reductionist conceptions of learning problems, is frequently critiqued as well. The boredom that flows from mechanistically informed instruction and from the characterization of the human organism as reactive is specifically addressed by Heshusius (1982, 1984b), Mitchell (1980), Poplin (1984b, 1985), and Smith (1983, 1986).

The machinelike quality of the human being is at times blatantly acknowledged. For instance, Johnson (1977) devotes only one of 12 chapters "to research directed at the individual," and here we read:

> [In a case study] information is not limited to test scores and observations. Talking to the student may be necessary. The researcher *may* need to see the student as a human being in order to better understand certain problems. (p. 320; emphasis added)

Clearly, in none of the other chapters does Johnson deem it necessary to consider the human being. The following excerpt from a text in special education early childhood is an example of the machine metaphor taking the form of behavioral objectivism:

> Given Susie with her coat on and the verbal command "take off your coat," Susie will grab one edge of the coat at the chest within 10 seconds 5 out of 5 times for 3 consecutive days. (Thurman & Widerstrom, 1985, p. 179)

Specific to the field of learning disabilities, Poplin (1985) provides perhaps the most systematic analysis of the translations of mechanistic thought into our dominant theoretical approaches. Comparing the medical model, the psychological process model, the behavioristic model, and the cognitive learning strategies model, Poplin concludes that their differences are at a surface level and are not nearly as important as their commonalities, which have been reflected upon rarely. Each model shares a mechanistic/reductionistic heritage in which the child has to be reduced to be understood. Each model

- assumes that the problem of not learning is within the student
- segments learning into pieces (be it pieces of auditory/visual processes, pieces of behavior, or pieces of cognition)
- is deficit-driven, linking directly to instruction the perceived problems in the pieces of processes, behaviors, or cognition
- conceives of teaching as unidirectional; that is, the teacher gives to the student the preset tasks in a preordained sequence
- assumes that there are correct and incorrect strategies, facts, behaviors, and so forth, that directly, linearly, and indisputably flow from the theoretical assumptions of the specific theory
- reduces life goals almost exclusively to school goals.

There is insufficient evidence of generalization and maintenance for each model, which Poplin sees as a result of their common mechanistic/reductionistic heritage.

A powerful solidification of mechanistic thought is seen in the mandates of Public Law 94–142. As Reid and Hresko (1981) observed, behaviorism (which is the quintessential expression of Newtonian mechanistic thought) was legalized in Public Law 94–142 through the stipulation that goals have to be stated in the language of quantitatively measurable behavioral objectives (see also Poplin, 1985, and Heshusius, 1986a).

The "Family of Malcontents"

Special educators who critiqued mechanistic assumptions have been clearly joined by what Gergen and Gergen (1982, p. 128) call "the family of malcontents." Increasing numbers of scholars across the social sciences have outlined this discontent with the mechanistic, natural science assumptions. Lather (1986, p. 261), for instance, speaks of the "rich ferment" in the field of social science research methodology and of the "dramatic shift" in our understanding of scientific inquiry away from mechanistic assumptions. Bernstein (1983) compares the Cartesian "Age of Reason" with the contemporary "Rage Against Reason" (that is, reason as narrowly defined by

Cartesian/Newtonian assumptions). Gould (1981, p. 24) refers to our obsession with quantifying and ranking human behavior as the "ranking fallacy," by which he means "our propensity for ordering complex variation as a gradual ascending scale." Gergen (1985) speaks of the profound threat that contemporary thought poses to the traditional Western conception of objective, individualistic, ahistoric knowledge. Iano (1986) notes the mushrooming of a literature of discontent.

These references represent only a few members within this "family of malcontents." Without doubt, the social sciences are in turmoil and the discontent is centrally focused on the inadequacies of the ultimate, paradigmatic benchmarks of mechanistic thought.

Conceptual Misunderstandings with Special Education

As a result of the discontent, some major theoretical reorientations are occurring in an attempt to correct for some of the inadequacies of existing approaches. At a still more fundamental level, the formulation of an alternative, holistic paradigm is emerging. Within the field of special education, however, at least two conceptual misunderstandings inhibit exploration of substantial theoretical and paradigmatic alternatives:

1. The renaming of theories as paradigms
2. The accusation of "fuzziness" associated with those who stray from the mechanistic path

Without doubt, additional issues encumber the formulation of new knowledge. These include the difficulties of establishing legal mandates, policies, and practices; one's own, often unconscious, investment in established ways of thinking; the mere courage necessary to go against established practices; and so forth. I will deal with only the two conceptual misunderstandings listed above, as they seem to be most prevalent in the literature at this point.

Renaming Theories as Paradigms: Creating Illusions of Fundamental Change

Within the field of learning disabilities, several authors have been renaming existing theories as paradigms. I believe it is unfortunate, in that this creates the impression that something essential has changed or that a new level of inquiry has been reached, when in fact only variations in theory (however important they may be) are discussed while leaving the fundamental mechanistic paradigmatic assumptions firmly in place. Ritzer (1975) has expressed similar concerns within the field of sociology.

To clarify the distinction between theory and paradigm-as-metaphor, we have to be aware both of the different levels of inquiry possible and of the different focus of these levels: (a) the level of theory, directly delineating specific phenomena, and (b) the level of paradigm-as-metaphor, delineating the assumptions we hold of reality and of knowing itself (regardless of the phenomena of interest). Even Kuhn (1962, 1970), whose many meanings of the word *paradigm* included theory as one definition, never equates the two. As Masterman (1970) notes with reference to Kuhn's work, a paradigm already exists and functions when the theory is not there. Within a paradigm one can change, modify, or expand a "part" (e.g., a theory, a model, a research method, or a criterion for evaluation) without ever changing the paradigmatic benchmarks as such—that is, *how* we think about how we think about the phenomenon of interest.

Torgesen (1986) provides an example of the confusion over paradigms and theories. He discusses three major theories within the field of learning disabilities (neuropsychological, information processing, and applied behavioral analysis theory) but renames them as paradigms. In a brief attempt to distinguish paradigm from theories, Torgesen (p. 400) states that theory is "more narrowly focused" than paradigms, that theories are "systems of propositions and hypothetical constructs that are developed to explain specific phenomena." That is precisely what neuropsychological, information processing, and applied behavioral analysis theories do, and always have done.

In the remainder of Torgesen's article, the paradigm/theory confusion appears in his use of the terms "paradigms," "paradigmatic pluralism," "theoretical confusion," and "theoretical coherence" to refer to these same three theories or the relations between them. His recommendations for the future do not go beyond extending the existing theories. Torgesen leads the reader to believe that we have as many paradigms in the field as we once had theories, which must mean that there is no difference between these two concepts that makes a difference.

Radencich (1984) provides a particularly strong illustration of the confusion that the concept of paradigm has wrought in the field. After stating that the learning disabilities (LD) field has to be grounded in "a paradigm or a theoretical framework" (p. 79), Radencich moves from equating "paradigm" with "a field of study" (p. 80) to asserting that we had "a process of modality paradigm" (p. 82), while on the same page contending that we are "finding ourselves in a preparadigmatic stage." Radencich then moves on to the assertion that "the modality model did constitute a paradigm of sorts" (p. 82), followed by the statement that the LD field is "undergoing a scientific revolution (p. 86) (which means that one paradigm is being replaced by a new one).

Radencich concludes that we are "still searching for a common paradigm" (p. 87). This confusion might be a natural part of the processes that occur when established knowledge and its foundations are questioned, and as such it may be helpful in upsetting the established order, which is necessary before fundamental change can occur. It is not helpful, however, in clarifying the concept and functions of paradigms and of levels of inquiry.

Kavale and Forness (1985, p. 13), too, use the concept of paradigm in analyzing the field of learning disabilities, but unlike Torgesen, who proposes three paradigms, Kavale and Forness propose only one: They change the Strauss and Werner theory into a "paradigm" (quotation marks are theirs) on the basis that theories in the LD field have not substantially deviated from it. The Strauss and Werner "paradigm" is later referred to as a "fundamental theoretical orientation." The latter, of course, is true: The Strauss and Werner theory was a prototype for all theories in learning disabilities. That is to say, theories in the LD field have been variations on the same set of theoretical propositions. Kavale and Forness show this in detail.

Serving as a prototype, however, does not change a theory into a paradigm. It is still what it is: a set of propositions about a specific set of phenomena, not a set of beliefs, values, and assumptions about what counts as real and how we are allowed to claim knowledge. Kavale and Forness (1985, p. 19) conclude that, although we do have a Strauss and Werner "paradigm," the LD field is (somehow, nevertheless) "really in a preparadigmatic period" because we don't have a firm foundation yet.

What is necessary next, Kavale and Forness (1985, p. 19) assert to move from a preparadigmatic to a paradigmatic period, is to question whether the natural sciences model provides the most appropriate model for understanding LD phenomena. As I argue, the natural science, mechanistic paradigm *has been* the paradigm under which we have functioned. It has provided us not with a set of propositions about specific phenomena such as learning disabilities, as do theories, but, instead, with a metaphor to live by.

Clearly, the Strauss and Werner theory is not at the same level of explanatory power as is the mechanistic, natural science paradigm. One does not speak of "the natural science theory" as one speaks of, for instance, a psychoneurological theory, because the former provides a metaphor, not a set of specific propositions to directly denote phenomena of interest. From this perspective, Strauss and Werner did not initiate a paradigmatic framework, as Kavale and Forness (1985) state; rather, they initiated a theoretical framework against the backdrop of the Newtonian paradigm. Thus, I argue that the field of special education/learning disabilities does not contain paradigms within itself, nor does it constitute a preparadigm stage; rather, it *is part of* a paradigm that has dominated the sciences and social sciences for several centuries.

"Fuzziness": A Case of Mistaken Identity

Under Newtonian mechanistic assumptions of objectivity, predictability, certainty, control, and so forth, accusations of fuzziness, mere intuition, and being anti-science are quickly leveled against those who engage in the formulation of nonmechanistic thought. Lloyd's (1987) response to Iano's (1986) paper (in which Iano argues for an alternative paradigm conceptualization for the study of teaching) and the response by Ulman and Rosenberg (1986) to my earlier work (Heshusius, 1982) reflect these reactions. There is a fear in these reactions that, if we let go of fundamental mechanistic assumptions, we will collapse into either chaos or nothingness (see, particularly, Ulman and Rosenberg, 1986). Or the formulation of alternative thought is seen as constituting art rather than science (see, particularly, Lloyd, 1987). Others misinterpret or minimize the extent and seriousness of the paradigmatic differences, as does Carnine (1987, pp. 42–43) in his response to Iano (1986), by declaring that we should drop the "unnecessary battle" and go on with our work because there are really "no substantial differences."

A different reaction still is that engaging in a nonmechanistic paradigm means engaging in a sort of watered-down science. According to Kavale and Forness (1987, p. 47), we can do it, and even should do it, but then "our level of aspiration for scientific inquiry must be lowered in order to be realistic." Lowering scientific aspirations, however, is a compromise of expectations, not a transformation of assumptions. It is saying, "Too bad we can't get there completely, but we may get there halfway." The belief in the possibility of certainty, objectivity, prediction and control, separation of fact and value, of observer and observed, and so forth, is steadily left in place.

Clearly, Kavale and Forness, too, continue to think that the methods we borrowed from the natural sciences are not only capable of explaining human behavior but also are ultimately the most privileged ones and continue to constitute real science. Likewise, their support of the curriculum as "a course to be run" in the form of curriculum-based assessment firmly leaves in place the mechanistic assumptions about learning as outlined earlier.

At the heart of these reactions, then, lies the continuous belief in mechanistic assumptions. The accusations of "fuzziness" and being "anti-science" are mirror images of these assumptions, which is to say that they give rise to each other and are parasitic upon each other. As Lakoff and Johnson (1980, p. 189) note, each defines itself in opposition to the other; therefore, each *is* the other but sees the other as enemy. Any disturbance of mechanistic beliefs will automatically trigger the fuzziness accusation.

Iano (1986, p. 59) states similarly, with regard to the charge that "anything goes" in an alternative paradigm (a charge closely related to that of fuzziness), that such a charge is but a mirror image of mechanistic dogma and implies that no "real" truth or knowledge is to be had at all if not through the established methods of traditional science: If you cannot know mechanistically, you cannot know. The point is that *once* the mechanistic assumptions are seen to hold up no longer, the accusation of fuzziness (or engaging in anti-science, or in a kind of watered-down science) when not adhering to them is instantly rendered irrelevant. That accusation cannot hold up when that which gave rise to it in the first place is seen to be no longer adequate (see also Bernstein, 1983, and Rorty, 1982).

In a holistic paradigm, mechanistic assumptions are replaced by assumptions that directly emerge from human knowing and from relationality. As will be noted in the discussion of the emergent holistic paradigm, the paradigm shift constitutes a profound shift from the machine metaphor to a human metaphor. We do not collapse into nothingness or fuzziness but, instead, transform our understanding into something qualitatively, and therefore fundamentally, different. We rid our thinking of *both* "objectivity" and "fuzziness," as both are a measure of exactly the same: One portrays the presence of the possibility of certainty and of control, the other its absence, but both are centrally preoccupied with the Cartesian/Newtonian belief in the possibility of certainty and control and its related set of paradigmatic assumptions. The contemporary paradigm shift is transforming the very concept of science itself, and along with it the concepts of "objectivity," "method," and "research."

The contemporary turbulence and ferment that within the constraints of a mechanistic paradigm are seen as fuzziness, chaos, and anti-science, from the vantage point of a conscious and close examination of the paradigmatic boundaries themselves contain the roots and the information needed to move into the articulation of alternative paradigm thinking. To do so, much of what is sacred has to be relinquished. The difficulties experienced in doing so both individually and as a community are indeed enormous, as many have elaborated upon (e.g., Bernstein, 1983; Gergen, 1985; Kuhn, 1970; LeShan & Margenau, 1982).

Theoretical Reorientations

Processes of Social Interchange

Out of the malcontent with mechanistic assumptions, theories are emerging that address the specific phenomena of learning (and of not learning) in ways that attempt to transform certain assumptions of mechanistic thought. Alternative sociological theories of exceptionalities, of course, have been with us for some time—for example, viewing exceptionalities as social constructions rather than as deficits within the person (see, e.g., Blatt, Biklen, & Bogdan, 1977; Bogdan & Taylor, 1982; Tomlinson, 1982, with regard to mental retardation; and Carrier, 1983, and Sleeter, 1986, with regard to learning disabilities). Here, we want to refer briefly to the more recent theoretical trends that define *knowledge and knowing as a result of processes of social interchanges* for their importance to the field of special education. Knowledge and knowing no longer are seen as a matter of mental representation, as mapping the "truth-out-there" onto one's own mind, as mechanistic thought would have it, but instead are seen as direct outcomes of processes of social interactions. As Gergen (1985, p. 270) states, "Knowledge is not something people possess somewhere in their heads, but rather something people do together."

Although one may argue—correctly I believe—that yet another too-simplistic monism is created by lodging everything within social interchange and nothing in a person's head, conceptualizations that focus on social interchanges as a medium through which knowledge and knowing come about are nevertheless important. These conceptualizations pose a fundamental problem for the presumably objective, acontextual, individually acquired, and ahistoric knowledge base that mechanistic thought presents. Within these developments, cognitive anthropology and anthropological psychology have been particularly informative. Erickson's (1984) overview of research shows, for example, that mental abilities (including linguistic and mathematical) once thought relatively, or even absolutely, context-independent (as presumed by classical learning theory and Piagetian developmental theory), are much more labile. Human reasoning actually seems to consist of understandings that are constituted in the context of personal use and purpose.

By changing settings, tools, meanings, and symbols, and by changing the social forms of relations among people, education has profoundly changed the nature of the situation, the learning task, and the demands on the child's ability. This view would explain, for instance, Sarason's (cited in McKean, 1985, p. 25) surprise when he arrived one morning at the institution for individuals with mental retardation to hear that several of the residents he had tested and found wanting in intelligence had escaped from the institution. Residents who had not been able to successfully trace their way out of a simple maze had plotted their way out of a 24-hour supervised institution. From this point of view, as Erickson (1984) states:

> It is not surprising that a child can display arithmetic competence while dealing with change at the grocery store and yet seem to lack that performance when doing what seems to be the "same" arithmetic problem on a worksheet or at the blackboard . . . [Even] the

picture of a coin is not a coin, and relations with the teacher and fellow students are not the same as relations with a store clerk. . . . The nature of the task in the store and in the classroom is very different and so is the nature of the abilities required to accomplish it. (p. 529)

Differences in performance, states Erickson (1984), such as the arithmetic problem referred to above (and Sarason's subjects' differential performance on maze tests versus in a real life, purposeful situation) do not merely lie on the dimension of abstract–concrete, as we have assumed, but, rather, on the dimension of problem definition by self or other. When the person has ownership in the very formation of the problem, he or she goes through a series of decision-making points, each one involving abilities as well as processes of social interchange that do not come into play when, for instance, doing problems on worksheets or tracing mazes. It is not just that learning tasks are "out of context," as Erickson (1984, p. 533) notes, but instead that they are *in a context* in which the power relations and processes of social interchanges are such that the child has no influence on problem formulation and the tasks offer no context of personal use and purpose.

Resistance Theory

Resistance theory is also grounded in the web of social interchanges and processes and particularly challenges the passive-reactive nature of the human being as characterized by mechanistic thought. Resistance theory was articulated to account for active noncooperation and resistance by students of less privileged classes who are defined by schools as having less worth than others, as well as high school students who see schools as alienating and boring institutions. The students' defiance provides a more acceptable self-image to themselves than does agreement with the school's definition of them (Erickson, 1984; Giroux, 1983; Willis, 1977).

Resistance theory may well serve to explain some of the behaviors of special education students, who also are being defined by schools as less worthy, or at least as less "normal" or not "regular," and who often are bored under mechanistically conceived instruction. For instance, McDermott (1974, 1977) shows, in a detailed microanalysis of videotapes, how students in a lowest reading group worked actively at not reading. The students constructed a situation in which the teacher cooperated, apparently without being aware of it, and in which they received far less reading instruction than did the better readers.

Similarly, Miller (1985), in an ethnographic study involving 175 hours of observation, described how children with learning problems integrated into general education classrooms worked hard at not working. They were overwhelmed by the amount of work to be done and actively found many ways of otherwise occupying themselves that went largely unnoticed by the teachers, who nevertheless complained that these children were never ready with their work. Although conventional LD theories likely would assess these students as inattentive, having a short attention span, being hyperactive, or the like, resistance theory provides a framework for understanding these children's behavior as active resistance to a situation they find threatening, boring, or otherwise intolerable.

Another example of resistance theory can be seen in a interview with an adult with LD (Heshusius, 1984a) reflecting on his school years. He actively and also very consciously had resisted anything that could have put him on the spot as a poor reader. This active and conscious resistance shaped his behavior in school in dramatic ways, as he was determined not to "lose face." The system, however, reinterpreted his resistance behavior as further evidence of his deficits and labeled him emotionally disturbed in addition to learning disabled. In their 3-year participant observation study, Meek, Armstrong, Austerfield, Graham, and Plackett (1983) provide a sensitive account of how a group of poor readers at the secondary level used resistance as a personal/political act.

Resistance theory shows special education students as active, purposeful beings who have reasons for behaving as they do within their specific context and within specific processes of social interchanges. It raises questions such as: To what extent, and for what reasons and under what conditions do special education students engage in active resistance and work, as Erickson (1984) phrases it, on further "achieving" their own failure? And to what extent do we reinterpret active resistance behavior as further evidence of their deficits and low ability?

Toward a Theory of Empowerment

A third and related theoretical orientation, which places behavior and knowing within processes of social interchanges and views the student as an active, self-organized being, could be called an empowering orientation. This orientation sees empowerment of the student as the main purpose of teaching. Education is viewed as an agent of change in the service of those who have been judged inadequate. It represents a struggle for personal meaning and for possibilities, but always within the framework of the histories and experiences of those whom the system has judged inadequate.

Within special education an empowerment approach moves away from remediation (which is adjustment to the system) and directs teaching toward activities that allow students the fullest expression of who they are and where they are going. Holzman and LaCerva (1986) describe how they use the empowering approach with high school students with LD. Initially, their work was informed by, among others, Paulo Freire, who developed literacy programs for illiterate peasants in the Third World, based upon an empowering theory of learning. Increasingly their work has become influenced more explicitly by Vygotsky's theories.

Vygotsky postulates development of higher psychological processes that are sociocultural and historical in nature. Such grounding defies any approach emerging from simple stimulus-response models or medical models that postulate innate ability or deficiencies as a point of departure. Vygotsky views learning as a dialectical social-historical activity, not a private, mentalistic, or inside-the-head activity. He stresses the need to create an environment of social interchanges in which educational methods are adapted to who the students are in their historical/social setting:

> What do we need to build learning? We usually think of learning materials in a very limited way—as books, pens, paper, minds, intelligence, the teacher, etc.—but that only scratches the surface of what is available. What about the histories of the students—their individual as well as collective histories, and of you, the teacher; their emotions, their wants, needs, desire, skills, hobbies, joys, loves, pain, their conflicts—and yours? In the building of the social environment for learning and development to take place, we must use what we have. This means that nothing is off limits; everything should be considered potentially useful in the process. (Holzman & LaCerva, 1986, p. 5)

These indeed may be "unorthodox building materials" (Holzman & LaCerva, 1986, p. 5), but they are the most serious set of building blocks for learning that one can think of, and they take utterly seriously the commonplace saying that we need to motivate students. Motivating here does not mean designing nice activities for students to do. It means understanding students in *who they are* and letting instruction emerge in a dialectical manner in the process of coming to understand them and in assisting them to become empowered as persons. The means, as Freirian theory also holds, that educators have to work with the personal, historical, and political experiences students bring to school and make these experiences the object of debate and confirmation. It means legitimizing the experiences so as to give those who live and move within them a sense of affirmation and to provide the conditions for students to fully be who they are through learning.

Holzman and LaCerva (1986) describe, among other examples, how they taught social studies to a class for students with LD in an inner-city multiracial high school in New York. These were students who could not and would not write or read and who wanted to "burn all textbooks." The teachers reorganized, from an empowering perspective, the students' understanding of what learning could be. The teachers involved the students directly in generating discussions of major issues in their personal lives by starting a unit on poverty and racism in America. The class engaged in exchanges about painful events, and these issues then were related to how three different social studies texts presented "history" to them. One text was a college text of the 1960s, a period of great social movements; one was a new, conservative college text; and the third was a text chosen for them as learning disabled students with simple vocabulary and few concepts, centering only on the history of great (white) men.

The students came to see how accounts of history are constructed under constraints of the time period and external purposes and interests. They then decided they needed a text that would come out of their own experience and started to rewrite the text collectively from a more personal/political perspective.

> They caught on quite quickly. In fact, they began to question *me* about how I knew what I was talking about. They began to work actively, giving expression to their life histories, including their anger, but not as victims. They were now engaging in the cooperative, socially meaningful activity of producing a useful history book. (Holzman & LaCerca, 1986, p. 13)

As Erickson (1984, p. 84) stresses, a full appreciation of the role of context, personal purpose and use, and of processes of social interchanges would fundamentally reshape our conceptualizations of, and approaches to, both assessment and instruction. I believe it would particularly affect special education, as our dominant theories and models for assessment and instruction have been, more than any other field within education, based explicitly on the assumption that learning problems are lodged within the individual (problems, variously assessed as deficits, defects, delayed development, disabilities, disorders, deficiencies, auditory or visual memory deficits, faulty learning, deficits in cognitive strategies, and so forth).

The Emergent Alternative Holistic Paradigm

Elsewhere (Heshusius, 1982), when discussing the mechanistic paradigm in relation to special education, I noted that special education has not been wrong so much as it has attempted to do what we now know is impossible: to force the innately unpredictable into the predictable, the unmeasurable into the measurable, and wholeness into fragmentation. It has attempted to transform teachers and students into reactive individuals.

Paradigms do not offer "right" and "wrong" answers, nor do they offer perfect solutions. Rather, they provide sets of fundamental assumptions that are adequate (or no longer adequate) to generate the pertinent questions of the time and possibilities for their answers.

We have been told that now that legal mandates are in place and we have recorded progress in terms of numbers served and test scores obtained, we need to start asking questions of quality. The difficulty is that mechanistic thought can only conceive of first translating qualitative questions back into quantitative formulations so they are measurable and otherwise adhere to mechanistic assumptions. Although the latter have been adequate in terms of the assessment and instruction of academic skills in restricted settings and with regard to controlled tasks and in terms of quantitatively measuring the outcomes of such learning, they have not been adequate in understanding the *nature* of the processes and the nature of social interchanges through which learning does or does not occur. They have not resulted in significantly increasing students' meaningful functioning in their day-to-day interactions (see Iano, 1986; Poplin, 1984c; Reid & Hresko, 1981). They have nothing to say about the place and importance of dialectics, or about novelty. They do not address the question of how students actually construct the meaning of their school situation, and therefore they can't tell us anything about what really motivates students. They do not inform us about the impact of the relationship between teacher and student *as persons* on the student's learning. They have nothing to say about the ethical and moral dimensions of all we do.

It is generally acknowledged that the emergence of a holistic paradigm started with the revolutionary discoveries in quantum physics that signaled the demise of Newtonian mechanistic assumptions. Fundamental changes in the understanding of the very structure of reality and of knowing at the sub-atomic level show that the observer and the observed are *not* separate, as mechanistic assumptions would have it. The observer shapes, and in a profound way creates, the observed. In addition, particles—the ultimate pieces of the Newtonian mechanistic universe—turn out not to be particles but actually relations in the form of ever-changing electromagnetic field interactions. Systems, from molecules to complex human organizations, now are understood not through stimulus–response and deterministic frameworks but instead through active self-organizing, self- regulating principles that form unexpected properties that cannot be predicted from their antecedents.

Rhodes (1987) directly and explicitly relates the empowerment view of the child as a generator of her or his own reality (rather than as a receptor) to the discoveries of quantum physics by acknowledging that the separation between knower and known, between self and world, is erroneous. Valle (1981) provides a similar discussion within psychology.

The contemporary paradigm shift, then, is centrally concerned with the shift from a machine metaphor to a human metaphor. Prigogine and Stengers (1984, p. 23) speak of art forms as the new metaphor to characterize the pivotal importance of the inner and intuitive ways of knowing in today's science (Prigogine is a Nobel laureate chemist). Lincoln and Guba (1985, pp. 61-62) refer to the shift in metaphor from "machine to human being," or from "reality as a machine toward reality as a conscious organism." Philosopher of science Bernstein (1983) speaks about a shift from a "rationality of method" to a "human rationality." Valle (1981) speaks of a "person–world view."

Within the field of special education, Iano (1986) speaks of the shift from a "natural science model" to a "human science model." This fundamental shift characterizes emergent thinking in virtually every major discipline. The axioms of the emergent paradigm represent "the analytic residue remaining after the particulars of physics, chemistry, brain theory, mathematics and so on have been 'boiled off'" (Lincoln & Guba, 1985, p. 65).

The Emergent Paradigm and Special Education

Relative to human behavior, the holistic paradigm holds the human being (in our case, the student, the teacher, and the researcher) as both active and reflexive. "Active" *not* as defined by traditional science (that is, actively displayed in reaction to a task, question, or stimulus provided by someone else) but, rather, as is "immanently active," to use Von Bertalanffy's (1968) terminology—active as existing within, as self-generated, meaning-giving, as actively constructing and transforming reality. Behavior is seen to occur because active choices are constantly made based upon perceptions of the purpose and meaning rather than because of the explanatory power gained from external "objective" knowledge and the collection of more data.

As LeShan and Margenau (1982, p. 147) state: "The assumption—which has now collapsed—that if you have enough data, you can know what is going to happen, was a comfortable one." Central to contemporary understanding is that *purpose* is the driving force, replacing conventional cause-and-effect relations. Now seen as the keystones of our understanding of the nature of reality, including human behavior, are openness of systems, self-organizing and self-regulating principles, and progress through transformation guided by what we experience as the purpose of our actions (or the purpose of systems). Science now is understood to be epistemic (as the observer and the observed are not separate) rather than objective and independent of the human observer or measurer. That is, our own consciousness about the way we know has to be included explicitly in the description of the phenomena. (For elaborations on the above, see, among others, Battista 1982;

Berman, 1984; Bohm, 1980; Capra, 1982, 1986; Cousins, 1985; LeShan & Margenau, 1982; Prigogine and Stengers, 1984; Wolf, 1981).

Holistic assumptions reverse the reductionistic/mechanistic position. It is not the case that the dynamics of the whole can be understood from the properties of the parts but, rather, that the properties of the parts can be understood only from the dynamics of the whole. The whole is both different from and more than the sum of its parts. Knowledge of "parts" does not lead to knowledge of the whole. There are no fixed and reliable linkages among the "parts." For our purposes, it means that learners are always learning and that the learner is actively involved and also actively initiates this process by constantly judging the personal relevance of what is to be learned relative to what she or he already knows. And when we think that the learner is not learning, the learner is learning nevertheless, although not necessarily what we would like him or her to be learning.

Our theories of learning disabilities will depend on our constructs of learning abilities. Just as we do not have one theory of how the blood circulates or how the heart works for those who are healthy and suddenly a different theory of how the blood circulates or how the heart works for those who are not, we should not have one theory of learning that is holistic for those who learn normally and quite another theory that proposes mechanistic assumptions of learning for those who do not manage to learn well in our schools. Yet, that is what seems to be happening at present. When whole-language theories, for instance, are increasingly seen as more adequate explanatory systems by which to understand how a human being learns to talk, read, and write, educators turn to programmed materials, worksheets, mastery learning, direct instruction, errorless learning, measured curriculum, and so forth, for students who do not learn as well as we want them to.

Holistic education is not a matter of a new set of prescriptive strategies and techniques. Because holism understands human behavior and growth as immanently active—meaning constructive, self-organizing, and self-regulating—there cannot be a sequentially organized prescriptive approach to "how to be holistic." Once it is understood how holistic assumptions are fundamentally different from mechanistic ones, one starts *thinking* differently about the nature of learning, teaching, and assessing, and about curriculum. Authors collectively point to the following translations of the holistic paradigm into educational principles.

Learning is understanding *relations* rather than pieces of knowledge. It is the personal/social/cultural construction of meaning by the child, based on who the child is and on what she or he knows (not based on how *we* understand what children need to learn). Learners always bring to the situation their own personal, social, cultural, and political histories, purposes, and interpretations, whether we are or are not aware of it or acknowledge it.

Learning occurs at various but equally valid levels, including kinesthetic, intuitive, and nondiscursive.

Progress is transformative rather than additive and incremental. Progress occurs when concepts are seen in new ways. As the human organism is self-regulating and immanently active, what is learned is not necessarily directly and solely "caused" by how or what we teach. What is learned and how it is learned cannot be controlled by superimposing measurement theory, and cannot be captured by simple input–output feedback loop models. New knowledge is not added to previous knowledge but instead transforms the old, just as past knowledge influences and shapes the nature of new knowledge.

There is no one best way to teach or to assess. Attentiveness to how *the child* thinks and reasons in a nonpunitive environment is essential. Teaching is a fundamental pedagogical engagement before it is an instructional one, containing immediate social, cultural, moral, and political dimensions. Teachers capitalize on children's natural curiosity and natural interests. The teacher becomes a "reflective practitioner" (see Schön, 1983) instead of an "executor of prescription" (Heshusius, 1982).

Assessment focuses on what students do over time in purposeful (to the student) engagements, in natural, interactive settings. We no longer can separate the question of what this learner needs to learn from the question of how this learner constructs meaning in this situation. "Errors" are not wrong pieces of knowledge but, rather, ways of making sense that provide insights into how the child thinks and reasons. Assessment also includes assessing the actual teacher/student match (see also Messick, 1984, p. 5), the actual teacher/student instructional interactions, the value of the curriculum in the first place, and the child's motivational readiness (see also Adelman & Taylor, 1986). Clearly, then, the very criteria by which we evaluate learners change—from testing, and from counting and ranking correct responses to controlled tasks, to documenting and assessing real-life processes and accomplishments.

Possibilities and choices are essential in a curriculum for human learning. A holistic curriculum, for all learners, stresses the interdependence among concepts and areas of study (reading–writing–oral language; language–math; history–geography–social movements–the arts; etc.). It stresses the interdependence among individuals and the larger world around them, leading not just to getting to know the community but also to attending to crucial real-life issues of our times—for example, global awareness of ecology.

More specifically, well known scholars in literacy acquisition who base their research and theory-building on holistic principles have started to bring their work to the field of special education (see Church & Newman, 1986, and Smith, 1983, in reading, and Graves, 1985, in writing). Further, holistic language activities for children labeled learning disabled are offered by Rhodes and Dudley–Marling (1988), Leigh (1980), McNutt (1984), and Weaver (1988), and for hearing-impaired children by Ewoldt (1982). Holistic criteria for planning and evaluation are discussed by Dudley–Marling (1986) and by Hasselbriis (1982).

Once holistic educational principles are grasped, one cannot go back. One cannot return to worksheets, isolated skill training, stipulating short-term quantitatively measurable behavioral objectives, IQ testing, and so forth (see Note 2).

Research Within an Alternative Paradigmatic Framework

Within alternative thought, the concepts of "research" and "method" naturally undergo a transformation according to the differing assumptions about what counts as real and how we can know. Various forms of inquiry that have emerged within alternative paradigmatic thought include phenomenological research, qualitative/interpretive research, ethnography, naturalistic research, open ideological research, research as praxis, and research for empowerment. Their commonality lies in the rejection of mechanistic assumptions, and they overlap to a considerable extent in their specific inquiry strategies and assumptions. Their differences are of emphasis and purpose (for overviews of issues and approaches see, e.g., Jacob, 1987; Lather, 1986; Morgan, 1983; Polkinghorne, 1983). These forms of inquiry collectively hold to the view of the person as an immanently active, meaning-constructing being, to the importance of context, and to the pivotal role of "lived experience." This fundamentally changes the role of the subject in traditional inquiry to that of research–participant. Understanding of the real, natural life context is seen as crucial to gain insights, and inquiry occurs in real-life settings and in relation to real-life events.

The role of the researcher in these forms of inquiry changes from a measurer, controller of variables, and executor of research design to that of a careful and aware listener, observer, absorber, participator, organizer of data, and able narrator. The privileged symbol system for data gathering, data organization, reporting of findings, and a judgment of significance shifts from a mathematical symbol system to the language of our everyday discourse. "Method" is no longer an unambiguous set of fixed rules but instead is defined as organized inquiry and careful accounting of data-gathering and analysis strategies, which always are in the service of, rather than in control of, the research question, the context, and the flow of events. Quantification through application of conventional method is no longer seen to be episte-mologically privileged to render knowledge claims.

To quote Lincoln and Guba (1985, p. 156): "The necessity for human judgment is not only *not* an embarrassment, but is elevated to the level of precondition" [emphasis theirs]. In the present post-positivistic era, we are moving "Beyond Method" (Morgan, 1983). We are moving from a "ration-ality of method " to a "human rationality" (Bernstein, 1983). Needless to say, such dramatic reconstruction of key dimensions of the processes of inquiry has brought about many debates between proponents of the various para-digms, a discussion of which, does not lie within the scope of this chapter.

The impact of new paradigm inquiry on the field of special education research is not yet great, but it does exist. Some examples include the work by Bogdan and Taylor (1982), Edgerton (1967), and Heshusius (1981) in the area of mental retardation, Ewoldt (1985) in the area of hearing impairment, Miller (1985) and Sanders (1986) in the area of learning disabilities. In his inquiry into successful mainstreaming programs, Biklen (1985) and Mehan, Hertweck, and Meihls (1986), and Smith (1982) in the study of assessment decisions in school.

Conclusion

A nonmechanistic paradigm is emerging from our increased consciousness of having painted a now several centuries old picture of reality, and of know-ing and finding it wanting. Although holism is certainly not "just around the corner"—not in our practice and not in mainstream academia—its influence is slowly but steadily becoming visible in North America and internationally (e.g., Prigogine & Stengers, 1984; Van Steenbergen, 1986). As LeShan and Margenau (1982) and Polkinghorne (1983) note, for the first time in 400 years, we are asking fundamental questions again. Much remains to be fur-ther explored and articulated. But it took the mechanistic paradigm more than three centuries to work out its assumptions and implications in order to fulfill and then outlive its promises. It may well take longer for a holistic par-adigm to do so, because it acknowledges understanding complexity, rather than reduction of simplicity, as its major task. Grasping complexity, guided by human rationality, will be far more difficult than inquiry informed by a machine metaphor of reality. But the effort will be more worthy of human beings, will result in more relevance, and is bound to be farther-reaching.

I express my gratitude to Mary Poplin, Claremont Graduate School, John Smith and Loree Rackstraw, University of Northern Iowa, and Michael Wheeler, Dufferin-Peel School Board, Toronto, whose knowledge and sus-tained discussions have for many years fostered the development of my own understandings. I also thank Carolyn Ewoldt, York University, for her insightful comments on an earlier draft of this chapter.

References

Adelman, H. S., & Taylor, L. (1986). *An introduction to learning disabilities.* Glenview, IL: Scott, Foresman.

Battista, J. R. (1982). The holistic paradigm and general systems theory. In W. Gray, J. Fidler, & J. Battista (Eds.), *General systems theory and the psychological sciences* (Vol. 1 pp. 209–210). Seaside, CA: Intersystem Publications.

Berman, M. (1984). *The reenchantment of the world.* New York: Bantam Books.

Bernstein, R. (1983). *Beyond objectivity and relativity: Science, hermeneutics, and praxis.* Philadelphia: University of Pennsylvania Press.

Biklen, D. (1985). *Achieving the complete school, strategies for effective mainstreaming.* New York: Teachers College, Columbia University.

Blatt, B. (1984). On distorting reality to comprehend distortion. *Journal of Learning Disabilities, 17,* 627–628.

Blatt, B., Biklen, D., & Bogdan, R. B. (Eds.). (1977). *An alternative textbook in special education.* Denver: Love.

Bogdan, R.. B., & Taylor, S.A. (1982). *Inside out: The social meaning of mental retardation.* Toronto: University of Toronto Press.

Bohm, D. (1980). *Wholeness and the implicate order.* Boston: Routledge & Kegan Paul.

Capra, F. (1982). *The turning point: Science, society and the rising culture.* New York: Simon & Schuster.

Capra, F. (1986). The concept of paradigm and paradigm shift. *Revision, Journal of Consciousness and Change, 9*(1), 11–17.

Carnine, D. (1987). A response to "false standards, a distorting and disintegrating effect on education, turning away from useful purposes, being inevitably unfulfilled, and remaining unrealistic and irrelevant." *Remedial and Special Education, 8*(1), 42–43.

Carrier, J. G. (1983). Explaining educability: An investigation of political support for the Children with Learning Disabilities Act of 1969. *British Journal of Sociology of Education, 4*(2), 125–140.

Church, S. & Newman, J. M. (1986) Danny. A case history of an instructionally induced reading problem. In J. M. Newman (Ed.), *Whole language, theory and practice* (pp. 169–179). Portsmouth, NH: Heinemann.

Cousins, N. (1985). *Nobel Prize conversations by Sir John Eccles, Roger Sperry, Ilya Prigogine, Brian Josephson.* Dallas: Saybrook Publishing.

Dodson-Gray, E. (1982). *Patriarchy as a conceptual trap.* Wellesley, MA: Roundtable Press.

Doll, W. E. (1986a). *Curriculum beyond stability: Schon, Prigogine, Piaget.* Paper presented at Bergamo Curriculum Conference, Bergamo, OH.

Doll, W. E. (1986b). Prigogine: A new sense of order, a new curriculum. *Theory into Practice, 25*(1), 10–16.

Dudley–Marling, C. (1986). Assessing the written language development of learning disabled children: An holistic perspective. *Canadian Journal of Special Education, 2*(1), 33–43.

Edgerton, R. (1967). *The cloak of competence: Stigma in the lives of the mentally retarded.* Berkeley: University of California Press.

Erickson, F. (1984). School literacy, reasoning, and civility: An anthropologist's perspective. *Review of Educational Research, 54*(4), 525–546.

Ewoldt, C. (1982). *The Kendell demonstration elementary school language arts curriculum guide.* Washington, DC: Gallaudet University, KDES Outreach.

Fisher, C. T., & Rizzo. A. A. (1974). A paradigm for humanizing special education. *Journal of Special Education, 8,* 321–329.

Forness, S. R., & Kavale, K. A. (1987). Holistic inquiry and the scientific challenge in special education: A reply to Iano. *Remedial and Special Education, 8*(1), 47–51.

Fox, H. (1983). *Original blessing: A primer in creation spirituality.* Santa Fe, NM: Bear & Co.

French, M. (1985). *Beyond power: On women, men, and morals.* New York: Ballantine.

Frye, N. (1981). Where metaphors and equations meet: A convergence of the arts and sciences. *The Chronicle of Higher Education, 21*(7), 65.

Gergen, K. (1985). The social construction movement in modern psychology. *American Psychologist, 40*(3), 266–275.

Gergen, K. & Gergen, M. (1982). Explaining human conduct: Form and function. In P. Secord (Ed.), *Explaining human behavior: Consciousness, human action, and social structure* (pp. 127–154). Beverly Hills, CA: Sage.

Giroux, H. A. (1983). Theories of reproduction and resistance in the new sociology of education: A critical analysis. *Harvard Educational Review, 53*(3), 257–293.

Gould, S. J. (1981). *The mismeasure of man.* New York: Norton.

Graves, D. H. (1985). All children can write. *Learning Disabilities Focus, 1*(1), 36–43.

Hasselbriis, P. (1982). I. E. P's and a whole language model of language arts. *Topics in Learning & Learning Disabilities, 1*(4), 17–21.

Heshusius, L. (1981). *Meaning in life as experienced by persons labeled retarded in a group home: A participant observation study.* Springfield, IL: Charles C Thomas.

Heshusius, L. (1982). At the heart of the advocacy dilemma: A mechanistic world view. *Exceptional Children, 49,* 6–13.

Heshusius, L. (1984a). The survival story of a nonreader: An interview. *Journal of Learning Disabilities, 7,* 472– 476.

Heshusius, L. (1984b). Why would they and I want to do it? A phenomenological–theoretical view of special education. *Learning Disability Quarterly, 7,* 363–368.

Heshusius, L. (1986a). Paradigm shifts and special education: A response to Ulman and Rosenberg. *Exceptional Children, 52,* 461–465.

Heshusius, L. (1986b). Pedagogy, special education, and the lives of young children: A critical and futuristic perspective. *Journal of Education, 168*(3), 25–38.

Heshusius, L. (1988). The arts, science, and the study of exceptionality. *Exceptional Children, 55*(1), 60–66.

Hesse, M. (1980). *Revolutions and reconstructions in the philosophy of science.* Bloomington: Indiana University Press.

Holzman, L. & LaCerva, C. (1986). *Development, learning and learning disabilities.* Paper presented at Eighth International Conference on Learning Disabilities, Kansas City, MO.

Iano, R. (1986). The study and development of teaching: With implications for the advancement of special education. *Remedial and Special Education, 8*(1), 52–61.

Iano, R. (1987). Rebuttal: Neither the absolute certainty of prescriptive law nor a surrender to mysticism. *Remedial and Special Education, 7*(5), 52–61.

Jacob, E. (1987). Qualitative research traditions: A review. *Review of Educational Research, 57*(1), 1–50.

Jantsch, E. (1980). *The self-organizing universe: Scientific and human implications of the emerging paradigm of education.* Oxford, England: Pergamon Press.

Johnson, M. C. (1977). *A review of research methods in education.* Chicago: Rand McNally.

Kavale, K. A., & Forness, S. R. (1985). Learning disability and the history of science: Paradigm or paradox? *Remedial and Special Education, 6*(4), 12–23.

Koestler, A. (1967). *The ghost in the machine.* London: Hutchinson.

Kuhn, T. S. (1962). *The structure of scientific revolutions.* Chicago: University of Chicago Press.

Kuhn, T. S. (1970). *The structure of scientific revolutions.* Chicago: University of Chicago Press.

Lakoff, G., & Johnson, M. (1980). *Metaphors we live by.* Chicago: University of Chicago Press.

Lather, P. (1986). Research as praxis. *Harvard Educational Review, 56*(3), 257–277.

Leigh, J. E. (1980). Whole language approaches: Premises and possibilities. *Learning Disability Quarterly, 3,* 62–69.

LeShan, L., & Margenau, H. (1982). *Einstein's space and van Gogh's sky: Physical reality and beyond.* New York: Macmillan.

Lewis, F. (1983, November 13). Quantum mechanics of politics and life. *Des Moines Sunday Register,* pp. 1, 3.

Lincoln, Y., & Guba, E. (1985). *Naturalistic inquiry.* Beverly Hills, CA: Sage.

Lloyd, J. W. (1987). The art and science of research on teaching. *Remedial and Special Education, 8*(1), 44–46.

Mann, L., & Phillips, W. A. (1967). Fractional practices in special education: A critique. *Exceptional Children, 33,* 311–317.

Masterman, M. (1970). The nature of a paradigm. In I. Lakatos & A. Mosgrave (Eds.), *Criticism and the growth of knowledge* (pp. 59–89). Cambridge, UK: Cambridge University Press.

McDermott, R. P. (1974). Achieving school failure: An anthropological approach to illiteracy and social stratification. In G. D. Spindler (Ed.), *Education and cultural process: Toward and anthropology of education* (pp. 82–118). New York: Holt, Rinehart & Winston.

McDermott, R. P. (1977). The ethnography of speaking and reading. In R. Shuy (Ed.), *Linguistics* (pp. 153–185). Newark, DE: International Reading Association.

McKean, K. (1985). Intelligence: New ways to measure the wisdom of man. *Discover, 6*(10), 25–41.

McNutt, G. (1984). A holistic approach to language arts instruction in the resource room. *Learning Disability Quarterly, 7,* 315–320.

Meek, M., Armstrong, S., Austerfield, V., Graham, J., & Plackett, E. (1983). *Achieving literacy: Longitudinal studies of adolescents learning to read.* Boston: Routledge, & Kegan Paul.

Mehan, H., Hertweck, A., & Meihls, L. (1986). *Handicapping the handicapped: Decision making in students' educational careers.* Stanford, CA: Stanford University press.

Messick, S. (1984). Assessment in context: Appraising student performance in relation to instructional quality. *Educational Researcher, 13*(1), 3–8.

Miller, C. M. M. (1985). *The viability of students with special learning needs remaining in regular classrooms: Perceptions of students, teachers, parents, and administrators, and observations of teachers' responses to student diversity.* Unpublished thesis, York University, Toronto.

Mitchell, R. M. (1980). Is professionalism succumbing to a push-button mentality? *Counterpoint, 1*(2), 14.

Morgan, G. M. (1983). *Beyond method: Strategies for social research.* Beverly Hills, CA: Sage.

Ogilvy, J. (1986). The current shift of paradigms. *Revision, A Journal of Consciousness and Change, 9*(1), 11–17.

Polkinghorne, D. (1983). *Methodology for the human sciences.* Albany: State University of New York Press.

Popkewitz, T. S. (1984). *Paradigm and ideology in educational research. The social functions of the intellectual.* New York: Falmer Press.

Poplin, M. (1984a). Research practices in learning disabilities. *Learning Disability Quarterly, 7,* 2–5.

Poplin, M. (1984b). Summary rationalizations, apologies, and farewell: What we don't know about the learning disabled. *Learning Disability Quarterly, 7,* 130–135.

Poplin, M. (1984c). Toward an holistic view of persons with learning disabilities. *Learning Disability Quarterly, 7,* 290–294.

Poplin, M. (1985). Reductionism from the medical model to the classroom: The past, present, and future of learning disabilities. *Research Communications in Psychology, Psychiatry and Behavior, 10*(1&2), 37–70.

Prigogine, I., & Stengers, I. (1984). *Order out of chaos: Man's new dialogue with nature.* New York: Bantam Books.

Radencich, M. C. (1984). The status of learning disabilities: The emergence of a paradigm or a paradigm shift? *Learning Disabilities, 3*(7), 79–89.

Randall, F. (1984). Why scholars become story-tellers. *New York Times Book Review,* pp. 1, 31.

Reid, D. K., & Hresko, W. P. (1981) *A cognitive approach to learning disabilities.* Toronto: McGraw-Hill.

Rhodes, L. K., & Dudley–Marking, C. C. (1988). *Teaching reading and writing to learning disabled and remedial learners: A holistic perspective.* Portsmouth, NH: Heinemann.

Rhodes, W. C. (1987). Ecology and the new physics. *Behavioral Disorders, 13*(1), 58–61.

Ritzer, G. (1975). Sociology: A multiparadigm science. *American Sociologist, 10,* 156–167.

Rorty, R. (1982). Method, social sciences, and social hope. In R. Rorty (Ed.), *Consequences of pragmatism* (pp. 191–229). Minneapolis: University of Minnesota Press.

Sadawa, D., & Caley, M. T. (1985). Dissipative structures: New metaphors for becoming in education. *Educational Researcher, 14*(3), 13–25.

Sanders, N. (1986). *Friendship perceptions of learning disabled students: a participant observation study.* Unpublished thesis, York University, Toronto.

Sarason, S. B. (1981). *Psychology misdirected.* New York: Macmillan/Free Press.

Schön, D. (1983). *The reflective practitioner.* New York: Basic Books.

Scully, M. G. (1980). Social scientists, unable to explain some issues, turning to humanists. *Chronicle of Higher Education, 20*(5), 1, 4.

Sleeter, C. E. (1986). Learning disabilities: The social construction of a special education category. *Exceptional Children, 53,* 46–54.

Smith, F. (1983). How children learn. In D. Carnine, D. Elkind, A. D. Hendrickson, D. Meichenbaum, R. L. Sieben, & F. Smith (Eds.), *Interdisciplinary voices in learning disabilities* (pp. 187–214). Austin, TX: Pro-Ed.

Smith, F. (1986). *Insult to intelligence.* New York: Arbor House.

Smith, J., & Heshusius, L. (1986). Closing down the conversation: The end of the quantitative-qualitative debate among educational researchers. *Educational Researcher, 15*(1), 4–12.

Smith, M. L. (1982). *How educators decide who is learning disabled: Challenge to psychology and public policy in the schools.* Springfield, IL: Charles C Thomas.

Thurman, S. K., & Widerstrom, A. H. (1985). *Young children with special needs: A developmental and ecological approach.* Newton, MA: Allyn & Bacon.

Tomlinson, S. (1982). *A sociology of special education.* London: Routledge & Kegan Paul.

Torgesen, J. K. (1986). Learning disabilities theory: Its current state and future prospects. *Journal of Learning Disabilities, 19,* 399–407.

Tucker, J. A. (1985). Curriculum-based assessment: An introduction. *Exceptional Children, 52*(3), 199–204.

Ulman, J. D., & Rosenberg, M. S. (1986). Science and superstition in special education. *Exceptional Children, 52*(5), 459–460.

Valle, R. S. (1981). Relativistic quantum psychology. In R. S. Valle & R. von Eckarteberg (Eds.), *The metaphors of consciousness* (pp. 417–434). New York: Plenum.

Van Steenbergen, B. (1986, October). Holisme schreeuwt om kritische sympathie. *Elseviers Magazine,* pp. 81–92.

Von Bertalanffy, L. (1967). *Robots, men, and minds.* New York: George Braziller.

Von Bertalanffy, L. (1968). *General system theory.* New York: George Braziller.

Weaver, C. (1988). *Reading process and practice: From socio–psycholinguistics to whole language.* Portsmouth, NH: Heinemann.

Willis, P. E. (1977) *Learning to labor: How working class kids get working class jobs.* Westmead, England: Saxon House.

Winkler, K. F. (1985). Questioning the science in social science. Scholars signal a "turn to Interpretation." *Chronicle of Higher Education, 30*(17), 1–3.

Wolf, F. A. (1981). *Taking the quantum leap.* New York: Harper and Row.

Note

1. The metaphysical notion included paradigm as myth, a general epistemological viewpoint, something that defines a broad sweep of reality, or an organizing principle governing perception itself. The sociological notion included paradigm as a recognized scientific achievement, or a set of political institutions. The more direct concrete notion included paradigm as an actual classic work, an exemplar, or a grammatical paradigm (see Masterman, 1970). In the second edition of his work, Kuhn (1970, postscript) acknowledges the confusion in his discussion

of paradigms and, in his attempts to clarify the concept, emphasizes the notion of paradigm as a concrete exemplar, which would come closest to the concept of theory and might have encouraged various scholars to misinterpret theories as paradigms, as Ritzer (1975) also has observed. Kuhn, however, does not equate paradigms with theories. He stresses that his viewpoints on fundamentals stayed unchanged. The postscript of his 1970 discussion does not include the metaphysical and sociological notions. A paradigm, also in the Kuhnian sense, as Masterman (1970) notes, already exists (and functions) when the theory is not there.

2. During my several years of teaching students in classes for students labeled learning disabled and in my present work with graduate students at York University (all practicing teachers and school administrators), the "way to holistic practice" is facilitated by keeping this set of educational principles literally pinned over our desks. They guide decision making and action in any concrete situation. Given the always present and immense pressures of function mechanistically that are built into the system, I have found (as have our students) that one needs a visible, immediately available clear reference to guide one's conceptualizations of actions throughout the day if one wishes to engage seriously in a paradigm shift.

Of course, in the present climate, compromise will be necessary almost always, as the system largely demands mechanistic procedures. Nevertheless, and without losing one's job, much can be done within one's own classroom, within one's own school, and much can be changed, however, slowly, through networking and raising consciousness with colleagues, parents, and administrators. From our experience, one thing can be stated with certainty: There is no problem in convincing children that the holistic principles are more adequate.

Reading Iano:
An Introduction

Deborah Gallagher

T he following article by Richard Iano, first published in *Remedial and Special Education* in 1986, was one of the first of its kind in the special education literature to address directly the powerful and pervasive limitations imposed through the use of the scientific method to study teaching and learning. Drawing on the work of eminent philosophers of science, Iano provided rather definitive, and sobering, examples of how the natural science–technical model has distorted education in general, and special education in particular.

As you will recall from Chapter 1, the purpose of using the scientific method is to produce lawlike generalizations by attempting to pin down the variables that affect the object of interest. In educational research, empiricist researchers believe that the development of lawlike generalizations will allow educators to predict, and hence control, the outcome of their actions. According to this reasoning, the ability to predict and control removes the uncertainties of teaching, and in the process makes teaching a matter of efficient application of techniques. From this reasoning, it also follows that well trained teachers are those who effectively apply the "knowledge base" composed of these techniques.

As Iano indicates, educational researchers found this approach to studying teaching attractive because it seemed to be a promising way to professionalize education. Throughout the article, he explains in clear and insightful detail why, after almost a century of "scientific" endeavor, the natural science–technical model never has (and never can) deliver on its promises. More important, though, are the pernicious consequences of this model on contemporary schooling. Chief among these are the inevitable separation between theory and practice, and the creation of a class (or caste) system among educators that results when university researchers produce decontextualized techniques that teachers then are expected somehow to wedge into the specific circumstances of their own classrooms. Iano provides a coherent response for all of the teachers out there who have wondered apprehensively why researchers and teacher educators do not simply tell them "how to do it."

Iano also addresses the deeply distorting effect of scientific, value-free objectivity on education. At the core of this enterprise lies the assumption that facts can be distinguished from values. As virtually all educators will acknowledge, education is a human undertaking that necessarily involves cultural values, individual interests, intentions, and the like. Because these human components cannot (and arguably should not) be subject to scientific manipulation, the natural science–technical model imposes its underlying ideology of neutrality, which denies the moral nature of teaching and learning. As Iano so cogently points out, the legacy of scientific neutrality strikes at the very heart of what education is all about. The inescapable result is a sense of detachment that reduces teaching to a set of procedures and treats people more like things.

The natural science–technical model, Iano suggests, has had an even more pronounced effect on the education of students with special needs. Because traditional special education is deeply rooted in the medical model, enduring practices in the field, such as the diagnostic–prescriptive teaching model, the study and development of the disability classification system, and even the procedures for individualized education programs, are subject to the same technical means/ends rationality and the ideology of scientific neutrality. Put another way, special education embraced more tightly what was presumed to be good for education as a whole. The upshot of all of this is that special education students and their teachers are even more subject to the distorting effects of this model.

To his great credit, Iano does not leave his readers without offering a thoughtfully rendered alternative to the natural science–technical model. What he offers in its place is a different "tradition of inquiry and practice," one that provides for the community of educators the possibility of genuinely progressive change. To achieve progressive change, Iano urges that positivist/empiricist ideology be abandoned. In its place, he envisions working teachers as active participants, "in identifying the problems and topics to be studied, the methods of investigation, and the conceptual schemes embracing studies." As he points out, this alternative requires a serious reconceptualization of teachers' preparation, expectations, and working conditions. Then, and only then, will educators be in a position to construct a tradition of practice that is truly progressive in its development and has as its hallmark the integrity of historical continuity.

When the original article was submitted for review, the journal's editor agreed to publish it under the condition that prominent special education researchers be provided an opportunity to respond to it in a subsequent issue of the journal. Interested readers are encouraged to read these responses, as well as Iano's published rebuttal. Whether one reads only the following chapter, or all of those involved in this exchange, a most striking aspect of this work is how pertinent it is to current conditions and contemporary discourse on special education reform. Along with the earlier work of Heshusius and Skrtic, this work stands as an important historical link to the present and future of special education.

The Study and Development of Teaching: With Implications for the Advancement of Special Education

Richard P. Iano

S|ince the beginning of the 20th century, education has been studied and developed primarily according to a "natural science–technical" model. The aim inspired by natural science assumptions has been to use methods of empirical research and theory construction to discover lawlike relationships. The aim inspired by technical assumptions has been to achieve control over the means and outcomes of education. The predominance of the natural science–technical model can be seen clearly in educational research and theory on teaching and learning.

This model of inquiry and development seems to have predominated especially in special education, perhaps because special educators are

From "The Study and Development of Teaching: With Implications for the Advancement of Special Education" by Richard P. Iano, 1986, *Remedial and Special Education, Vol. 7,* 50–61. Reprinted with permission.

inclined to view the remediation of learning difficulties as primarily a technical task. Special educators have generally looked to researchers and theoreticians for developing knowledge and understanding of the nature of learning difficulties and for developing effective remedial teaching methods. Also, the diagnostic–prescriptive teaching model so popular in special education is basically technical in its thrust, and most special educators believe the model is based in theory and research. More recent developments in the philosophies of science and social practice, however, have opened the way for reformulations of how education might be studied and developed.

One development that can help to stimulate reformulations in education is the emergence of a literature that is critical of positivist philosophy of science. At first, such critiques were primarily directed at positivist interpretations of the natural sciences (Brown, 1977; Kuhn, 1970; Lakatos & Musgrave, 1970; Suppe, 1972), but there soon followed a similar critical literature with respect to the social-behavior sciences (Bauman, 1978; Dallmayer & McCarthy, 1977; Gergen, 1982; Polkinghorne, 1983; Schrag, 1980). Second, within the field of special education itself, criticisms of the well-entrenched natural science-technical model have begun to appear with increasing frequency (Apple, Sibkoviak, & Lufler, 1979; Chamberlin, 1981; Eisner, 1979; Feinberg, 1983; Giroux, 1981). Third, alternatives to positivist views of inquiry and knowledge can suggest new ways of viewing education and its development.

Here, I examine the limitations of the natural science–technical model and its distorting effects on education, particularly with respect to the study of teaching. I also briefly consider some of the effects of the model on special education. Finally, I suggest a few alternative approaches to the study and development of education.

Some Effects of the Natural Science–Technical Model

In promoting false standards of knowledge, progress, and control, the natural science–technical model has had a distorting and disintegrating effect on education. Funds, energy, and institutional policies have been directed away from useful purposes toward the aim of technical control. The expectation that teaching, student learning, and the preparation of teachers can all be brought under technical control is unrealistic, and the aim of technical control is largely irrelevant for education.

As the expectation inevitably remains unfulfilled, educators are faulted for being incompetent. Eventually, pressures mount for systems of accountability and other kinds of external controls to be imposed on educators.

Furthermore, these pressures tend to move teachers and teacher educators toward those narrower areas that more nearly lend themselves to technical control, thereby neglecting more fundamental educational aims that less easily lend themselves to being defined and manipulated within the natural science–technical model.

Part of the attraction of the natural science–technical view of education is in the promise it makes to professionalize education. From the mid-19th century onward, the development and extension of public education has been one of the great national goals in the United States. A related goal has been to develop a public school system and a cadre of public school workers. Just as the prestigious social services of medicine and law have become professionalized, so have educators wished to professionalize their work. The wish to professionalize eventually led to placing the task of preparing public school teachers and administrators in colleges and universities.

Even more important, a positivist belief system supporting a natural science–technical model of study and development established itself as dominant in the work and thinking of most educators. This positivist belief system equates knowledge with the sciences, especially with the natural sciences, and sees the scientific method, theory construction, and the systematic development of empirical generalizations as major means of professional advancement.

The Separation of Theory and Practice

The aim of scientifically advancing and professionalizing education has resulted in an unfortunate separation of functions and a class system within education. The scientists and theoreticians—those who are to advance and professionalize education—are in colleges and universities, whereas the practitioners—those who teach and work directly with the students in public education—are in the public schools. In this way, a system of classes has developed in education, and it also has become institutionalized.

The lower class is composed of practitioners who teach and work in elementary and secondary schools. The upper class is composed of researchers and professors who are generally thought to be responsible for the scientific and professional development of the field. The responsibility for advancing educational practice is placed with the researchers and professors, even though they are remote from practice in the public schools. Thus, their research topics and aims, their studies, hypotheses, and data collections, often are entirely unrelated to what school teachers see as their central problems, interests, and concerns. It is easy to see why relating theory to practice has been a persistent problem in education: Studies and theories are developed in a context detached from ongoing school practice; then educators puzzle over how to get the "latest scientific knowledge and research findings" into schools and classrooms.

School teachers typically react in two ways to the researchers and theoreticians. Sometimes they are cynically contemptuous of researchers and theoreticians, who often seem to have little understanding of teachers' "real world" problems and tasks, and to have little of practical value to offer them. The other typical reaction of teachers is to stand in exaggerated awe of researchers and theoreticians and to look toward them for guidance in meeting the often overwhelming challenges and demands of their day-to-day work.

The separation of practice from theory in education has been institutionalized further in the working conditions of school teachers. The schools typically are organized so that teachers' work and time are rigidly controlled and strictly confined to the direct teaching of students. Moreover, teachers typically are treated as employees rather than as professionals who can shape and control their work (Lortie, 1975, pp. 162–186; Sizer, 1984). Unlike most fully professionalized workers, school teachers cannot ordinarily include within their official working time activities such as problem solving and systematic inquiry, or the sharing of questions and difficulties with colleagues. Teachers are not expected or encouraged to be contributors to the growth of professional knowledge. They are not expected to communicate and publish their problems, attempted solutions, or their findings.

In short, positivist ideology in concert with an institutionalized separation of theory and practice has worked against understanding the task of studying and developing education in other than a natural science–technical model. The consequences for education of following this model are next directed to the study of teaching.

Critique of the Dominant Tradition

The positivist ideology that underlies the natural science-technical model in education dominated the U.S. philosophy of science until the early part of the last century. Most research on teaching has been inspired by a particularly vulgarized version of positivism. In this version, prediction and control become primary and the ultimate aim and justification for scientific activity, rather than being only subsidiary and supportive to scientific theory, explanation, and understanding. Educational researchers have believed that the route to prediction and control is in the discovery of lawlike regularities and associations. These would be the basis for propositional generalizations and rules of teaching procedure, and such propositions would represent a body of distinctive professional knowledge. After some 80 years of research in education dating back to the early part of the last century, this natural science–technical model has largely failed to fulfill its promise to develop a distinctive, scientifically based body of professional knowledge. This suggests something seriously awry with the model. Indeed, a number of critiques challenge the use of this model in education (Egan, 1981; Ericson & Ellett, 1982; Fenstermacher, 1978; Tom, 1984).

A common response by advocates of the natural science–technical model is that human and social phenomena are much more complex than the physical phenomena of the unquestionably successful natural sciences. The recourse to complexity suggests that given more time and research, and following the same model of science, researchers eventually will succeed in unraveling the regularities or laws of human and social phenomena. But we have reached a point in educational theory and research at which it is no longer sufficient to appeal to the great complexity of its subject matter as a justification for unquestioningly adhering to the natural science-technical tradition. The claim of great complexity self-servingly underestimates the complexity of the physical systems that the natural sciences have dealt with successfully. Even more important, the appeal to complexity ignores the deeper conceptual problems in the basic aims and assumptions of the natural science–technical model.

Let us look more closely at how this research tradition has proceeded in attempting to discover lawlike regularities that could be used as the basis for predicting and controlling educational outcomes. Typically, these researchers observe, measure, and record teachers' and students' behavioral or verbal actions. These actions express teachers' and students' traits, dispositions, skills, knowledge, beliefs, intentions, and so on. The researchers generally want to find out which teachers' actions, as means, are "associated with," or are "related to," or "produce" which students' actions, as outcomes. To accomplish the aim, the researchers typically attempt to study teachers' means or actions and the students' outcomes they produce across numerous settings of teaching and learning, often comparing and contrasting different means and their outcomes.

In this natural science approach to research, the actions of teachers and students must be conceived as capable of being identified and studied across different settings. The actions also must be conceived as potentially capable of being formulated as lawlike regularities that apply across different settings of teaching and learning. To accommodate the natural science research strategy, therefore, the actions of teachers and students have been conceptualized as "variables" that recur in different times and places with different people.

Usually, researchers preselect the categories of variables to be studied and "operationally define" them in terms of their basic observational and measurement criteria of identification. Once the preselected variables are so labeled and defined, every action or event the researchers subsequently observe in the various settings of teaching and learning are recorded as instances of one of the variables. There are, however, grave difficulties with this tactic of treating actions as if they can be converted into fixed and abstracted variables. We next examine four of these difficulties.

Actions and Events Are Open

The first problem is that using abstracted categories of variables to represent the actions of teachers and students dissociates these actions from their concrete settings of origin so that they lose much of their original meaning. The treatment of these phenomena as capable of being operationally defined and fixed, and as abstracted variables, makes it seem that they can recur in different times and settings as the same phenomena with the same effects. But once we consider these phenomena in their original, ongoing, concrete settings, in the full contexts of teaching and learning, we can see just how dubious such treatment is. In contrast to actions being fixed and stable as they are made to appear when represented as variables in a model of natural science, we instead find in ongoing settings of teaching and learning that any given action is open to the influence and interactions of other actions and events in that setting.

Let us consider something as simple and ordinary as "teacher praise," a type of action that educators generally consider to be desirable and effective in motivating students. Even a type of action as simple and ordinary as this cannot be considered fixed and stable across different settings, times, and people. The meaning of the praise and its effects depend upon the maturity of the students, how the students feel about the teacher, what kinds of activities are being praised, what events immediately preceded the praise, how the teacher combines praise with other actions, and so on. Students may hold one teacher in high esteem so that they prize and seek praise from this teacher, whereas a teacher whom the students do not respect could find that he or she is unable to motivate and encourage students through the use of praise. Or a teacher might use praise so frequently and indiscriminately that it loses its effectiveness. Still another teacher might communicate praise in an unorthodox or subtle manner so it is not readily observable and recordable through standard techniques.

Nonetheless, a researcher following the model of natural science typically attempts to operationally define praise as a variable to be studied so it can be objectively observed, recorded, and measured as the same variable in different settings and at different times. The objectifying procedure can represent a great distortion of what actually occurs in the individual settings, either through recording under the same category of "praise" the actions of teachers that differ significantly in their meanings and effects, or by failing to record as "praise" some subtle and unorthodox actions that the operational procedure fails to identify. Similarly, any and all actions of teachers and students are continually open to the infinite varying influences and interactions of other actions and events in their specific setting.

Moreover, if we consider any typical setting of teaching and learning in its full context, actions and events do not seem to occur in a lawlike manner or in a manner that would allow prediction and control. Indeed, "naturalistic" studies of full and ongoing contexts of teaching and learning concur in finding that these settings are characterized by a great deal of openness and unpredictability (Eggleston, 1979; Jackson, 1968; Woods, 1980). These studies find that although teachers do plan and project in a general way when they are outside the ongoing settings of teaching, they nevertheless must be responsive to the immediacy of ongoing teaching and to the demand for on-the-spot decisions within the continuous flux of classroom life.

Ongoing teaching and learning typically are characterized by emerging and unanticipated events, such as changes in students' moods and interests, students' remarks and questions, difficulties or obstacles in learning tasks, sudden insights by students and teachers, and interferences from sources outside the classroom. Of course, these settings usually have predictable elements that, as already noted, permit teachers to plan and project in a general way. Even the more predictable elements, however, do not resemble lawlike regularities, and typical settings of teaching do not lend themselves to strict, technical prediction and control. Therefore, rather than using terms such as "law," "prediction," and "control," which beg the issue by their appeal to connotations of science and technicality, it might be better to use looser and more modest terms such as "routine," "order," habit," "plan," "project," and "anticipate." The latter terms are less inflated in their connotations, and they seem better suited to usual settings of teaching and learning, which are more like the settings of ordinary life than they are like the experimentally controlled settings of science.

It is little wonder, then, that a notorious separation has come to exist between the work of educational researchers and the work of practitioners. Educators constantly worry about how to get the findings of research into the schools and the work of practitioners. But when the data of research are detached from their practical settings by being abstracted as variables in the manner described above, it is not surprising that those data are not readily returnable or applicable to those settings.

Actions and Events Are Interpretive

A second, related problem arises with the way in which those who follow the model of natural science treat the objects of their research as abstracted variables. As a consequence of the idealized image of science that most of these researchers hold, they treat the subject matter of the social sciences similar to the way physical scientists treat their subject matter—as naturally occurring phenomena having objective existence independent of our language, constructs, and interpretations. Hermeneutical approaches, however, offer an alternative view of the subject matter of the social sciences. According to Bleicher (1980, p. 1), hermeneutics can be defined loosely as the theory or philosophy of the interpretation of meaning (see Note 1).

Hermeneutical approaches give adequate recognition to the reality that, in contrast to physical reality, the subject matter of the social sciences is entirely a human creation (Gadamer, 1975; Habermas, 1971; Polkinghorne, 1983; Radnitzky, 1973; Ricoeur, 1976). Drawing on these hermeneutical approaches, Taylor (1971/1977) showed that social reality and practices are interpretive in a way that the phenomena of the natural sciences are not.

Ericson and Ellett (1982) extended Taylor's observations and arguments to the subject matter of educational research. Taylor pointed out that the subject matter and the reality that the social scientist theoretically interprets is itself constituted by interpretation already. The subject matter is produced by those who are the subjects of the research, and its meaning is constituted by their interpretations. Thus, the social scientist, like the natural scientist, applies interpretive constructs and theory to subject matter. But, unlike the subject matter of the natural scientist, the object of the social scientist's interpretations is itself constituted by interpretation. This means that, for social scientists to know what they are studying, for them to know the meaning of the social practices that are the object of research, they first must know how the participants themselves interpret their practices and actions.

This does not mean that the subjects being studied necessarily have the "last word" on the meaning of their practices. It does mean, though, that before offering further elucidation, or deeper and better explanations, or even before offering straightforward veridical descriptions, social scientists must have a subject to elucidate, explain, and describe, and it means that their subject matter itself is constituted by the interpretations of the individuals being studied. Yet, this necessary prior step of understanding the basic subject matter or data is precluded when researchers follow the natural science–technical tradition.

How understanding of subject matter is precluded can be seen in the way the methods of natural science–technical research are applied in education. Educational phenomena, like any social phenomena, are practices constituted by interpretation. Teaching and learning occurrences are constituted by the intersubjective interpretations of teachers and students. To understand any teaching and learning occurrence, a researcher would, at a minimum, have to observe it in its unfolding and also have to communicate with the participating students and teacher to ascertain their interpretations and understandings of the occurrence.

Furthermore, the researcher would have to know something of the wider context that helped to produce the occurrence and helped to give it the meaning it has for the participants. We have seen already, however, that this is not how the natural science–technical researcher typically proceeds. Instead, the researcher preselects the variables to be studied, uses these abstracted variables as the categories for observing and collecting data from numerous settings of teaching and learning, and subsequently also uses these abstracted categories for presenting data. In this way, occurrences in different settings are made to fit into the same preselected and fixed interpretive categories of variables, even though these occurrences are likely to be constituted by varying interpretations, some of them perhaps differing widely from one another.

As Habermas (1983) warned, social practices are context-dependent for their interpretation and we cannot be sure in advance that others start from the same background assumptions and practices that we do. Yet, the researchers following the natural science–technical model preselect and apply their interpretive categories across teaching and learning settings as if they all start from the same background assumptions and practices, and as if they do know in advance what those background assumptions and practices are.

Suppose, for instance, that a researcher following the natural science–technical model decides to study a certain method to determine how the method relates to or affects student behavior or learning. In the usual procedure the researcher initially defines the major variables of the study operationally. In this instance, the major independent research variable would be the designated teaching method. The operational definition of the teaching method is likely to consist of fixed observational or measurement criteria to identify the method across different settings. As a next step, the researcher often identifies teachers who already are using the method, or trains teachers to use the method for the purposes of the study. The researcher also might include a contrast or control group of teachers in the study, who either do not use the method or who use some opposing method. In any case, the fixed operational criteria are used to identify teachers' activities and actions that supposedly represent the same teaching method across different settings of teaching and learning.

But participants in different settings might not see as the same a set of activities and actions that are designated as the "same" across settings according to fixed operational criteria. One teacher might consider the teaching activities and actions central to her major activities and purposes. Another teacher might consider those "same" activities and actions subsidiary to other activities and purposes that he sees as more fundamental. Or students will interpret actions by a teacher they admire and respect an entirely different way than the "same" actions by a teacher they perceive as ineffective or alienating. Again we see that the use of fixed categories or operational criteria and variables precludes accounting for the openness that characterizes variables in their concrete settings. We see in addition that these fixed categories cannot account for the participants' interpretations that constitute the practices and realities in those social settings.

The Inarticulate Component of Practice

The third problem with the natural science–technical model of research is in its commitment to the positivist ideal of knowledge as only that which can be fully articulated and specified. In applying this ideal to the practice of teaching, researchers have attempted to identify laws, generalizations, or technical rules of procedure that would produce specific educational outcomes. These laws, generalizations, and rules would be the basis for a codified, articulated body of scientific and professional knowledge. Many find this ideal highly attractive because of its promise to contribute to the development of a recognized profession. The articulated and scientifically established body of professional knowledge would justify the further study and development of education in university and research centers, and it would justify calling teaching a "profession" and placing the preparation of teachers in universities.

The regeneration of positivism in the early 20th century, especially in the philosophy of science, was inspired largely by the successes and achievements of the natural sciences. Since then, positivist accountings of science have been all but abandoned and various "post-positivist" alternatives have emerged. Also, the positivist ideal of knowledge has been criticized as being overly narrow and incapable of accounting for the full range and varieties of human knowing (Bernstein, 1983; Blanshard, 1973; Jaki, 1978; Mandelbaum, 1971; McCarthy, 1978). Particularly relevant to this discussion of educational and teaching practice—because of their emphasis on practical knowing—are the broader conceptions by Oakeshott (1962), Polanyi (1962), and Wittgenstein (cited in Lovibond, 1983, pp. 27–31). These three come remarkably close in their critiques and in the alternative view of knowing that they offer.

Oakeshott

According to Oakeshott, all human activities, including the activities of science, art, and practice, always involve two inseparable kinds of knowledge. Oakeshott has called one of these "technical knowledge." Technical knowledge can be formulated into rules and maxims; it can be deliberately learned, remembered, and put into practice; and it can be learned from books. The chief characteristic of technical knowledge is that it is susceptible to precise formulation. The second kind of knowledge, inseparable from the first and also involved in every human activity, is what Oakeshott has called "practical knowledge." In contrast to technical knowledge, practical knowledge is not reflective, it cannot be formulated into rules or prescriptions, and it exists only in use. Practical knowledge can never be explicitly imitated, taught, or acquired but, rather, is acquired only through practice and continuous contact with an authority, expert, or master.

Polanyi

Polanyi also has recognized both the articulate and the inarticulate aspects of knowledge. Every type of human knowledge, Polanyi has asserted—whether of the scientist, judge, artist, technician, or athlete—is shaped by skills, but the rules that are observed in the performance of these skills are not generally known by those who follow them. Articulated rules and maxims can guide, but they cannot replace practical knowledge; they are useful only to those who can integrate them into their already existing practical knowledge.

Wittgenstein

In a similar fashion, Wittgenstein has opposed positivist views of knowing. He has emphasized the fundamental importance of inarticulate elements in the acquisition of language and other social practices. Moreover, he, like the other two thinkers, has contended that a skill, art, or practice is not passed on by the deliberate teaching and learning of explicit rules but instead by use and practice, in the presence of a master who is unable to fully explicate what he or she knows and passes on to others.

Researchers who follow the natural science–technical model apply to the practice of teaching the positivist ideal of wholly explicit and theoretical knowledge. In doing so, they distort and misrepresent teaching. As we saw before, researchers typically study large numbers of teaching and learning settings, and they use preselected, fixed categories of variables in their attempts to identify the best or most efficient rules, procedures, and methods of teaching. Thus, researchers do not study methods of teaching in their full and ongoing contexts of teaching and learning. The consequence of this research strategy is that the specifiable components of teaching are abstracted from their unspecifiable components, although the two components are inseparable in actual teaching practice.

A strategy that in this way detaches actions and events from their settings and represents them as abstracted variables naturally poses the puzzle of how to get those "scientific" findings into the everyday practices of teachers in schools. The specifiable and formalized components of teaching are torn from their original contexts and lose their meaning. When placed in propositional form in manuals, texts, and guides, such rules and procedures of teaching strike practicing teachers as lacking in vitality, as trivial, or as irrelevant.

Educational Values

The fourth problem with the natural science–technical tradition of research is that of educational values. As a consequence of its adherence to positivist ideology, this tradition makes a sharp distinction between fact and value. Here, the notion of scientific objectivity is tied to that of value neutrality. Scientists are conceived of as objective in the sense of being entirely non-partisan and disinterested in the object of their studies and their outcomes. To achieve nonpartisan objectivity, scientists must confine themselves to facts, or to potential facts; they must confine themselves to empirical data and its related theory; and they must relentlessly keep values, norms, and interests from directing the aims and methods of their research. Scientists may study others' subjective values, norms, and interests, but only by turning them into objects of study and treating them as objective data, thereby retaining their own objective and value-free nonpartisanship. But the direct use of values, norms, and interests for the purposes of understanding, developing, or improving education is strictly relegated to unscientific opinion, subjective preference, and philosophical speculation—activities that are inherently arbitrary and devoid of rational justification according to positivist ideology.

When researchers committed to the natural science–technical tradition turn their attention to the ultimate aim of their research—the improvement of teaching and education—they retain their objective nonpartisanship position by interpreting their task in an entirely technical and efficient-means manner. That is, the researchers accept as "given" whatever value-based goals and objectives they happen to find in the schools, and they confine their efforts to investigating how these "given" goals and objectives might be achieved most efficiently. This separation of fact and technical means from human value and interest ensures that the researchers will fail to connect with central educational concerns.

Values, norms, and interests are not merely the subjective components of education that can be attached to just any set of objective means and techniques. Rather, values, norms, and interests are the very basis of the educational enterprise and educational activities are thoroughly informed by them. Our ultimate educational interest is in promoting a good society that sustains projects and institutions of fundamental worth, and in promoting the development of good people who understand, appreciate, and create products and practices of enduring value. To approach teaching and learning as if they were primarily technical and efficient-means tasks is thus to both miss the major point of what education is and to so narrow the focus of teaching and learning that education is undermined. Objective fact or efficient means cannot be studied or developed as separate and independent components of the educational enterprise, because they are always subordinate to the more fundamental value components.

Let us consider the teaching and learning of reading as an example. Our ultimate educational aims are that students integrate reading into their lives, that they appreciate and enjoy fine literature, that they read to enrich their lives and transform their experience, and that their reading contributes to worthy personal traits, interests, and aims. But those who base their research on the natural science–technical model attempt to identify the solely technical components of the teaching and learning of reading and to separate the technical from the "subjective" value components. Once identified, these technically efficient means and methods are supposedly capable of being applied by large numbers of teachers in different settings of teaching and learning. Yet, again, it is clear that these technical means and methods are torn from their original and full contexts so that not only are their interpretive components missing, as was noted earlier, but their value components are missing as well.

It is also clear that such neutralized and objectified technical means cannot have the same meaning and function in different contexts in which the values and interests of teachers and students alike will differ. Thus, aside from the broader problem of how such an approach could contribute to our understanding of education and its development, there is the question of how any such objectified techniques could be expected to achieve the same designated objective for different contexts.

Moreover, an adequate scheme of education must include a conception of students as persons, as ends in themselves, autonomous, capable of making value and moral choices, of succeeding and failing, and of being blamed and credited. In contrast, the natural science–technical model promotes a conception of students as "objects" to be technically manipulated in the interest of achieving given and externally imposed objectives. If researchers who use this model at any point seek to go beyond technical manipulation and control and to conceive of students as persons to be educated, they must abandon their objective detachment and enter the realm of values, interests, and norms. According to their positivist ideology, however, these are subjective, arbitrary, and outside the purview of rational justification or analysis.

In summary, based on a positivist ideology, educational research in the natural science–technical tradition has aimed at identifying lawlike regularities that could provide the basis for dependable generalizations. This tradition has been particularly interested in providing teachers with the technical means of prediction and control over educational outcomes in terms of improved student learning or behavior. In the service of these aims, researchers in this tradition typically have treated educational phenomena as abstracted categories of variables capable of being preselected, fixed, and applied across different settings, times, and people. This treatment has detached the subject matter and findings of research from their original settings in four important ways.

1. Preselected and fixed variables fail to faithfully represent traits as they are expressed and actions as they occur in ongoing settings of teaching and learning, where they are open, permeable, and therefore subject to interactive influence and modification in indefinite and unending ways.
2. Fixed and preselected variables fail to represent the practices and realities of teaching and learning settings because the variables are detached from the contextual backgrounds and from the interpretations that constitute the practices and realities of those settings.
3. In following the positivist ideal of knowledge as being fully formalized, articulated, and specified, the natural science–technical tradition distorts and misrepresents teaching by failing to account for its unspecifiable components that are inseparable from its specifiable ones.
4. The natural science–technical tradition attempts to "scientifically objectify" the study of education by a crude separation of facts from values, interests, and norms, thereby distorting what is inherently and fundamentally a value-based enterprise.

Some Effects in Special Education

This model of research has been followed in special education with the same effects and problems as described above for education and teaching in general. In addition, areas and practices within special education have been influenced, including diagnostic and prescriptive teaching, the development and use of diagnostic tests, individualized education programs (IEPs), and programs for students with severe disabilities. Especially interesting is how the natural science–technical tradition has influenced the study and development of the system for classifying exceptionalities in special education.

The Classification System

The classifications first became associated with special education in a formal way near the beginning of the 20th century, when certain new pressures in the public schools produced a demand for special education. These new pressures in the schools were, in turn, the consequence of interlocking social and educational changes that emerged during the last half of the 19th century: the rapid extension of public school education, the growth of urban centers and large schools serving greater numbers and varieties of pupils within a single school, and the organization and standardization of schooling, as exemplified

in specialized grade levels and grade-level teachers for each year of chronological age.

At about the same time there was a rapid growth in the use of standardized tests, and also of books, curricula, and various other kinds of learning and
teaching materials that were standardized by grade level. These changes combined to make much more insistent and explicit than ever before the demand
for common standards of achievement and social behavior from pupils.

There was a certain amount of flexibility and "give" in applying standards
of achievement and behavior to pupils, but it nevertheless was inevitable that
many pupils deviated noticeably from the standards for their age-grade level.
The minority of the pupils who deviated most extremely from their age-grade
peers were the most noticeable and troubling to teachers and to others in the
schools. These latter pupils were designated as belonging to the special education classification of "handicap" or "exceptionality."

The classification of most interest to our discussion here is not composed
of those who may be grouped as having "physical" disabilities, such as in
vision, hearing, and health conditions. Rather, our interest is in the conditions that may be grouped as "social-psychological" disabilities. In special
education three prominent classifications of handicap emerged, which fell
into the social–psychological grouping: mentally handicapped (especially at
the "mild" or "educable" level), emotionally disturbed or socially malad-
justed, and learning disabled. These distinctions reflected beliefs and
assumptions apparently held in common by most educators of the time.

Since the 1950s the social–psychological classifications have constantly
promoted confusion and controversy in special education, as seen in the special education literature on labeling, definition of handicap, diagnosis of
handicap, and the differential placement and treatment of pupils according to
handicap(s). Our inability in special education to significantly clarify the
issues and reduce the controversy surrounding the classification of handicaps
is, to a considerable extent, a result of the contradictions arising out of
assumptions in the natural science–technical model.

The need for special education and the need for the classification of disabilities both originate in the practical settings of teaching and learning, yet
the prevailing commitment to the natural science–technical model separates
efforts to study and develop the classifications from those practical settings.
Psychological theory and research have primarily determined the definitions
and conceptualizations of the classifications. There is nothing wrong, in
itself, with education drawing on psychology, but the action should be from
both directions—from the direction of educational practice as well as psychology—but with practice most often taking the initiating and predominat-
ing role. Instead, psychological theory, models, and research have exerted a
virtually one-sided influence.

During the 1960s and much of the 1970s, partly inspired by the growth of the new classification of learning disabilities in special education, considerable theory and research was devoted to the development of diagnostic models and tests, the development of remedial programs and materials, and the testing of the efficacy of these models, tests, programs, and materials. Many special educators were concerned with closing what they perceived to be a "diagnostic–remediation gap" in special education. That is, it was widely believed that the diagnostic and classification procedures that had been developed in special education generally failed to provide the practical and specific direction they should for remedial teaching purposes. But the study and development of problems and concepts related to diagnosis, classification, and remediation did not take their primary direction from practical settings of teaching and learning, with the consequence that today we know little about how these problems relate to the actual practices of teachers.

Labeling

Related to the general issue of classification is the considerable concern over the effects of labeling, not only on students who are labeled but also on teachers and their treatment of labeled students. Yet, other than the teacher-expectancy type of studies, which generally adopt a manipulative and external attitude toward teachers, there have been few direct studies of the interactions between labeling and teaching. Despite the considerable literature that has been devoted to the issue, we have little understanding of how diagnostic labeling and classification interacts with teaching, and a host of other basic questions remain unanswered:

Do special and general education teachers differ in their use of labels?

Do special education teachers who are sophisticated and experienced differ from those who are not?

After special education teachers have come to know the specific pupils they teach, do they use or refer to the diagnostic labels the pupils originally were given?

Do the teachers add further, more specific kinds of labels as they learn about their pupils?

Do labels enter into the planning, conceptualizations, and strategies of teachers?

Do the teachers modify and adapt the standard labels in certain ways according to teacher's experiences or beliefs?

If teachers do use labels in their teaching, is this use combined with other factors in the practical context of teaching and learning?

Do teachers ever really "diagnose," in the sense of carrying out intensive
studies of puzzling and problematic learning or behavioral problems?
If so, under what circumstances?

Is it actually possible for teachers to avoid labeling their students altogether, as some have claimed teachers ought to do? Or is labeling an
inevitable and necessary phenomenon even if only implicitly?

How do the primarily psychologically inspired diagnostic classifications,
definitions, models, and tests influence teachers, especially special
education teachers?

These questions, basic though they are, all remain unanswered. Progress
in answering these and related questions will continue to lag until we shift
from a natural science-technical orientation to one that gives primacy to the
practical setting and the problems and tasks that originate there. The latter
approach, if it is to be complete, should include practicing teachers as full
participants in the study and development of special education. The focus
would be on the problems and tasks that grow directly out of the work of
teaching, on how teachers proceed in meeting those problems and tasks, and
on how they interpret phenomena in settings of teaching and learning.

What could we look forward to with such research? Eventually, as a consequence of study and development centering on practice, a tradition of
inquiry would emerge, to include: a public consensus in special education on
its leading problems and tasks, on promising directions for further study, on
methods of study and development, and on promising solutions to common
problems. It also would include ongoing, public critique of current theories,
programs, solutions, and interpretations.

Alternatives to the Natural
Science-Technical Tradition

Returning to the discussion of general education: The natural science–technical program of research is limited, distorts teaching and education, and
after long and prodigious effort and the highest of expectations, has failed to
significantly advance educational practice. This should tell us that something
is awry in the program's basic assumptions and aims. One prominent
assumption that seems to be at least doubtful is that, by merely importing
ready-made "scientific methods" into educational practices, these practices
can be made "progressive" in the way the natural sciences and material technologies are considered to be "progressive."

The natural sciences did not become scientific merely because at one
point scientists decided to adopt scientific methods and be scientific (Harris,

1970; Kuhn, 1970; Polanyi, 1962). Moreover, it is obvious that there could be no formal, scientifically methodical way to discover or invent scientific methods before they existed. The natural sciences emerged through the efforts of mutually critical and communicating communities of scholars—those communities themselves only gradually emerging and becoming self-identifying—who defined the nature and boundaries of their disciplines, who located their problems, tasks, and questions, and who developed their methods.

The identification of a discipline—and its aims, problems, tasks, and methods of study—we may call the development of a "tradition of inquiry and practice." Any science, art, craft, or practice advances only as it develops a tradition of inquiry and practice in a mutually critical and communicating community. A tradition of inquiry and practice provides the community with a common set of aims, tasks, and standards of achievement, a public record of difficulties widely encountered, and a public record and analysis of methods that have been found to be especially effective, or that have failed. A tradition of inquiry also provides the basis for distinguishing progressive change from change that is transitory, haphazard, or even disruptive. Progressive change retains a continuity with past practices and conceptions at the same time that it transforms them, whereas change that lacks historical awareness and continuity tends to be mere novelty.

The beliefs and supporting institutional practices related to the natural science–technical model have been obstacles to establishing a tradition of practice and inquiry in teaching. Recall that the separation of the practitioner role from the research and theoretician roles has become institutionalized in education. This separation of roles has seemed to be rational as long as it has been supported by the positivist notion that the study and development of teaching could be made "scientific" by the mere application of an already known, ready-made, scientific method. Consequently, institutionalized working conditions and a prevailing positivist ideology have supported the imposition of external methods and strategies of research on education.

Teachers themselves are precluded from fully developing a tradition of inquiry and practice. Indeed, they are discouraged from becoming a genuine community of professionals who publicly communicate with and criticize one another with regard to their problems and tasks, trial and error efforts, and their successes and failures. Moreover, the researchers and theoreticians, who tend to be detached from the actual problems and tasks of teaching in the schools, are those whom teachers are constantly encouraged to look to for help in solving their problems and for development of the profession. A tradition of inquiry and practice cannot adequately develop when these conditions and attitudes prevail.

Regarding the inquiry component of teaching, a genuine tradition of inquiry can develop only if, at a minimum, working teachers are at least participants in identifying the problems and topics to be studied, the methods of investigation, and the conceptual schemes embracing the studies. Then, if some educators were to be designated as a specialist group of researchers, they would have to develop their studies as equal partners with teachers and also identify themselves primarily with the problems, tasks, and development of teaching. We should expect that working teachers themselves would often initiate studies of teaching. But, for teachers to become full participants in or initiators of research, clearly their prevailing conditions at work must be radically transformed. Time and opportunity to plan with other teachers, to develop proposals of inquiry, and to observe and study the teaching of others would have to be built into their daily routine. They must receive professional recognition for publicly reporting problems, methods, and findings, and for criticizing and analyzing the studies of others. And, of course, teachers must be inducted into teaching under standards and expectations very different from existing ones. Currently, from the time they are inducted into teaching until the end of their careers, teachers are encouraged to be recipients of the research findings and expert knowledge of others, rather then to be true students and developers of their profession.

If the working conditions of teaching and its standards and expectations were changed in the ways indicated above, both a tradition of inquiry and a tradition of practice would be supported and encouraged. If the professional work of teaching were to routinely include cooperative planning and working with colleagues, and if teachers were both encouraged and expected to share their tasks, problems, questions, methods, successes and failures, a tradition would systematically emerge. A genuine community of professional workers communicating with each other and criticizing each others' ideas, proposals, and interpretations would develop a set of standards for evaluating results and proposals. Then the short-term objectives and tasks for the professional community would gradually be identified.

Also, a fully developed professional community of this nature would provide the referent point for objectifying the beliefs, aims, and methods of individuals or particular groups of teachers. Unlike the current situation, with its constant arbitrary and externally imposed changes that have little to do with ongoing and established practices, a tradition of practice would provide a basis for discriminating between promising and unpromising proposals, for evaluating results, and for introducing changes that are truly reformative and progressive. In short, a tradition of practice would provide teaching with the necessary prerequisite to progressive development: historical continuity.

To return to the inquiring component of teaching, the limitations of the natural science–technical tradition show the need for an alternative approach to the study of teaching. Rather than studying preselected, fixed, and abstracted variables across numbers of teaching and learning settings, the settings must be studied singly, in depth, and in their full context. This does not mean eliminating large-scale, survey-type studies, for they have proven their value in providing information on prevailing practices, attitudes, and beliefs, on the sequences and hierarchies of students' development and learning, and on general and comparative trends in educational outcomes.

As we have seen, however, the natural science–technical tradition has not been able to fulfill its promise of significantly advancing our understanding of teaching, either through the discovery of lawlike regularities or through the identification of technically "best" educational means and teaching methods. It was argued above that the findings from this kind of research are irrelevant and indeterminate for teaching because the research detaches its subject matter from the settings of teaching and learning. Thus, what is called for is a more naturalistic or ethnographic type of research in which settings of teaching and learning are studied in their full and ongoing contexts. Research strategies related to this kind of alternative have constituted for some time a minor or counter-movement in education (Cicourel et.al., 1976; Jackson, 1968; Lightfoot, 1973; McPherson, 1972), and the use of such strategies initiated a trend (Eggleston, 1979; Elbaz, 1981, 1983; Goetz & LeCompte, 1984, Wilson, 1977). These kinds of studies can account for the emergent and unpredictable in events and actions, for participants' interpretations that constitute the practices and realities of teaching and learning settings, and they can account for the values, norms, and interests of participants in each setting.

Moreover, the study and development of teaching cannot be narrowly confined to existing practices, beliefs, and values. The educational enterprise involves us with almost every facet of human and social aspiration. When we propose to educate, we bring to the enterprise our conceptions of what makes good people, a good life, and a good society. The study and development of such a broad-based enterprise must join with the humanities and the behavioral sciences, and it also must draw on their methods, insights, and findings in a never-ending quest to understand the nature and possibilities of human and social life. If we persist in largely ignoring fundamental aims and values in our study and development of education, we can expect that educational practice will continue to be jostled this way and that by fashionable innovations and reforms that represent responses to the most superficial of social–cultural trends.

The arguments stated here are not intended to imply that there is nothing to be known about education and teaching and, therefore, that "anything goes" and one conviction is as good as another. That view is but a mirror image of the positivist dogma that only science and technology can establish a body of educational knowledge and truths. The exclusive reliance on science and technology easily leads to the conclusion that, because the requisite scientific knowledge has not been established, at least so far, there is no truth or knowledge at all to be had. In either of these mirror-image views, practice and its fruits are ideologically minimized.

There are things that may be learned about education and teaching, there are discriminations that may be developed, skills that may be refined, concepts that may be grasped, and so on. As it now stands, however, what is known about education and teaching is for the most part developed and passed on informally and unsystematically. The basic task is not to eliminate or replace informal and unsystematic knowledge—which is impossible to do anyway. The informal and unsystematic represents a necessary foundation and a permanent source to be drawn upon, but it badly needs to be supplemented by a more public and systematic tradition of inquiry and practice.

Finally, this examination contains implications for preparing and developing teachers. The natural science–technical tradition has promoted the view that teacher preparation and development is a matter of transmitting technical skills and "scientifically established" prescriptive rules of procedure. Instead, teachers need models of practice and programming that inspire and suggest a variety of educational possibilities. Teaching centers might be developed or identified as exemplary models and concrete expressions of various educational ideals. Teachers then could observe or work in these centers, and they could study films and narrative analyses of the activities of these centers—not for slavish imitation but, rather, for help in projecting and constructing personal teaching roles and educational values.

Conclusion

To conclude, the natural science–technical model in education has failed in its promise to progressively advance teaching, and it has had a stifling effect on the study and development of teaching. The criticisms that are made here, however, do not say whether teaching is, or can be, a science or scientifically based, whether it is more an art or a craft, or whether it is partly all of these. Rather, it is proposed that only if certain changes come about in the way teaching is viewed and in the prevailing working conditions of teachers in the schools, can a genuine tradition of inquiry and practice emerge that will advance the profession. Whether its methods of study and development will be those of a science, an art, a craft, or something else will depend on the character of the tradition that emerges.

References

Apple, M., Sibkoviak, M., & Lufler, H. S. (Eds.). (1979). *Educational evaluation, analysis, and responsibilities.* Berkeley, CA: McCutchen.

Bauman, Z. (1978). *Hermeneutics and social science.* New York: Columbia University Press.

Bernstein, R. J. (1983). *Beyond objectivism and relativism: Science, hermeneutics, and praxis.* Philadelphia: University of Pennsylvania Press.

Blanshard, B. (1973). *Reason and analysis.* LaSalle, IL: Open Court Publishing.

Bleicher, J. (1980). *Contemporary hermeneutics: Hermeneutics as method, philosophy, and critique.* Boston: Routledge & Kegan Paul.

Brown, H. I. (1977). *Perception, theory, and commitment.* Chicago: Precedent.

Chamberlin, J. G. (1981). *The educating act: A phenomenological view.* Washington, DC: University Press of America.

Cicourel, A. V., Jennings, K. H., Jennings, S. H. M., Letier, K. C. W., McKay, R., Mehan, H., & Roth, D. R. (1976). *Language use and school performance.* New York: Academic Press.

Dallmayer, F. R., & McCarthy, A. M. (Eds.). (1977). *Understanding and social inquiry.* Notre Dame, IN: University of Notre Dame Press.

Egan, K. (1981). Plato's theory of educational development: On the inappropriateness of applied psychology. *Curriculum Inquiry, 11*(2), 123–141.

Eggleston. J. (Ed.). (1979). *Teacher decision-making in the classroom.* Boston: Routledge & Kegan Paul.

Eisner, E. (1979). *The educational imagination: On the design and evaluation of school programs.* New York: Macmillan.

Elbaz, F. (1981). The teacher's "practical knowledge": Report of a case study. *Curriculum Inquiry, 11*(2), 42–71.

Elbaz, F. (1983). *Teacher thinking: A study of practical knowledge.* New York: Nichols.

Ericson, D. P., & Ellett, Jr., F. S. (1982). Interpretation, understanding, and educational research. *Teacher's College Record, 85*(1), 497–513.

Feinberg, W. (1983). *Understanding education: Toward a reconstruction of educational inquiry.* Cambridge, UK: Cambridge University Press.

Fenstermacher, G. D. (1978). A philosophical consideration of recent research on teacher effectiveness. In L. S. Shulman Ed., *Review of research in education* (Vol. 7, pp. 157–185). Itasca, IL: F. E. Peacock.

Gadamer, H. G. (1975). *Truth and method.* New York: Seabury Press.

Gergen, K. J. (1982). *Toward a transformation in social knowledge.* New York: Springer–Verlag.

Giroux, H. A. (1981). *Ideology, culture and the process of schooling.* Philadelphia: Temple University Press.

Goetz, J. P., & LeCompte, M. D. (1984). *Ethnography and qualitative design in educational research.* New York: Academic Press.

Habermas, J. (1971). *Knowledge and human interests.* Boston: Beacon Press.

Habermas, J. (1983). Interpretive social science vs. hermeneutics. In N. Haan et al. (Eds.), *Social science as moral inquiry* (pp. 251–269). New York: Columbia University Press.

Harris, E. E. (1970). *Hypothesis and perception. The roots of scientific method.* New York: Humanities Press.

Jackson, P. W. (1968). *Life in classrooms.* New York: Holt, Rinehart & Winston.

Jaki, J. S. (1978). *The road to science and the ways of God.* Chicago: University of Chicago Press.

Kuhn, T. S. (1970). *The structure of scientific revolutions* (2d ed.). Chicago: University of Chicago Press.

Lakatos, I., & Musgrave, A. (Eds.). (1970). *Criticism and the growth of knowledge.* Cambridge, UK: Cambridge University Press.

Lightfoot, S. L. (1973). Politics and reasoning: Through the eyes of teachers and children. *Harvard Educational Review, 43*(2), 197–244.

Lortie, D. C. (1975). *Schoolteacher: A sociological study.* Chicago: University of Chicago Press.

Lovibond, S. (1983). *Realism and imagination in ethics.* Minneapolis: University of Minnesota Press.

Mandelbaum, M. (1971). *History, man, and reason.* Baltimore: Johns Hopkins University Press.

McCarthy, T. (1978). *The critical theory of Jurgen Habermas.* Cambridge, MA: MIT Press.

McPherson, G. H. (1972). *Smalltown teacher.* Cambridge, MA: Harvard University Press.

Oakeshott, M. (1962). *Rationalism in politics.* London: Methuen.

Polanyi, M. (1962). *Personal knowledge.* Chicago: University of Chicago Press.

Polkinghorne, D. (1983). *Methodology for the social sciences: Systems of inquiry.* Albany: State University of New York Press.

Radnitzky, G. (1973). *Contemporary schools of metascience* (3d ed.). Chicago: Regency.

Ricoeur, P. (1976). *Interpretation theory: Discourse and the surplus of meaning.* Fort Worth: Texas Christian University Press.

Schrag, C. O. (1980). *Radical reflection and the origin of the human sciences.* West Lafeyette, IN: Purdue University Press.

Sizer, T. R. (1984). *High school reform and the reform of teacher education.* The 1984 DeGarmo Lecture of the Society of Professors of Education, Minneapolis.

Suppe, F. (Ed.). (1972). *The structure of scientific theories.* Urbana: University of Illinois Press.

Taylor, C. (1977). Interpretation and the sciences of man. In F. R. Dallmayer & T. A. McCarthy (Eds.), *Understanding and social inquiry* (pp. 101–131). Notre Dame, IN: University of Notre Dame Press. (Reprinted from *Review of Metaphysics,* 1971, 25, 3–24).

Tom, A. R. (1984). *Teaching as a moral craft.* New York: Longman.

Wilson, S. (1977). The use of ethnographic techniques in educational research. *Review of Educational Research, 44*(1), 245–265.

Woods, P. (Ed.). (1980). *Teacher strategies: Explorations in the sociology of the school.* London: Croom Helm.

Note

1. The origin of hermeneutics reaches back historically to the ancient art of interpreting meanings in sacred texts. In the 19th century, defenders of the humanities extended and developed hermeneutics into a distinctive discipline against claims that science and technology were the exclusive roads to knowledge, truth, and reality. More recently there has been a revival of interest in hermeneutics as part of the emergence of post-positivist philosophies of science and histories of science. This "new" hermeneutics also has played a major role in contemporary debates and reformulations of the human sciences.

Richard P. Iano received the Ed.D. from Syracuse University. A Professor of Special Education at Temple University, he is interested in philosophical implications for understanding and developing teaching and in developing interpretations of teaching as a practice.

Reading Skrtic:
An Introduction

Deborah Gallagher

To what extent students labeled as having disabilities should participate in the general education classroom has been the subject of debate for more than three decades. What is now referred to as the full-inclusion debate has its origins in the discussions of mainstreaming in the 1960s and 1970s and the sharply contentious exchanges arising from the regular education initiative (REI) in the 1980s. Skrtic's article, "The Special Education Paradox: Equity as a Way to Excellence," first published in *Harvard Educational Review* in 1991, builds its discussion around the REI to explain why the conceptual foundations of naive pragmatism and functionalism led to contradictions in the practices and organizational structures of schools, especially with regard to special education programs. Skrtic's conceptual and historical critique shows us that as long as educators maintain the assumptions of fact versus value distinctions, or value-free objectivity, any attempt to reform general and special education will reproduce, and even extend, the same problems we hope to ameliorate.

For example, Skrtic illustrates, in a multilayered account, how educators are caught in the crosscurrents between two organizational schemes: machine bureaucracy and professional bureaucracy. The machine bureaucracy, designed to simplify and standardize work, misconceptualizes teaching as a series of task-analyzed, technical activities. This, in effect, forces a theory/practice gap and obviates professional discretion and individualized instruction. Under these conditions, teachers are compelled to elevate the meeting of standards over the teaching of students.

Professional bureaucracy, despite its ostensive recognition of teachers' work as being complex, uncertain, and ambiguous—thus requiring professional discretion—also is designed to achieve a specialized division of labor. Because professional bureaucracy, too, is dominated by the functionalist framework, teachers' work is still standardized, with little room for discretion and individualization. This obviously hampers the democratic goals of education, and subsequent response to public demands for change are deflected by creating more separate programs. Thus, no substantive change can take place, even though, from the outside, the appearance is one of change.

Skrtic's work shares several themes in common with the work of Iano and Heshusius. The *first,* and most important shared theme relates to the distorting, contradictory effects that emerge from the flawed assumptions of value-free objectivity. *Second,* like Iano and Heshusius, Skrtic points out the self-synchronizing nature of the dominant paradigm. Achieving genuine organizational change, he asserts "requires a paradigm shift, which is difficult because the paradigm self-justifies itself by distorting new information so it is seen as consistent with the prevailing view."

Nevertheless, like his two counterparts, Skrtic sees change as possible because sooner or later a shift in values prompts a subsequent shift in paradigms. This shift in values occurs when "sufficient anomalies build up to undermine the prevailing paradigm." *Third,* all three authors point out the self-defeating consequences brought about by the desire to bring teaching under a form of predictable, mechanistic/technological control. *Fourth,* all three authors agree on the distorting effects of attempting to make education a value-free enterprise.

In place of the current bureaucracy around which schools are organized, Skrtic advances an alternative organizational approach that he refers to as "adhocracy." This approach acknowledges, and even embraces, the uncertain, ambiguous nature of teaching. In so doing, adhocracy is "premised on the principle of innovation rather than standardization." This being the case, schools organized around the principles of adhocracy allow educators to exercise genuine discretion and schools to operate as problem-solving organizations. The result is an organizational adaptability coherent with the democratic, egalitarian goals of public education in the United States.

The Special Education Paradox: Equity as the Way to Excellence

Thomas M. Skrtic

> The final result of political action often, no, even regularly, stands in completely inadequate and often even paradoxical relation to its original meaning.
>
> —Max Weber[1]

Although the Education for All Handicapped Children Act of 1975 (EHA) marked the end of a successful policy revolution in which the spirit of mainstreaming was formalized in law, the special education community knew that if the law was to amount to anything more than "a comprehensive set of empty promises" (Abeson & Zettel, 1977, p. 115), an implementation revolution would also have to be mounted and won (Abeson & Zettel, 1977; National Advisory Committee on the Education of the Handicapped, 1976; Weintraub, 1977). The strategy for winning the implementation revolution was to follow the letter of the law because special education professionals and advocates were convinced that the EHA "would work only if [they] and others made it work by using the procedures set forth in the law" (Weintraub, 1977, p. 114). At the time, of course, this appeared to be a prudent course of action. But the tragic irony is that the letter of the law has become the principal barrier to achieving the spirit of the law (see, for example, Gartner & Lipsky, 1987; Reynolds, Wang, & Walberg, 1987; Skrtic, Guba, & Knowlton, 1985; Stainback & Stainback, 1984; Walker, 1987).

Although no one in the special education community questioned the spirit of the EHA, or that some important implementation battles had been won, there was widespread concern that the implementation revolution had been lost (see, for example, Gartner & Lipsky, 1987; Reynolds, Wang, & Walberg, 1987; Stainback & Stainback, 1984; Will, 1986a). The sense of defeat was so pervasive that many of those who had been staunch supporters of the EHA called for a new revolution. This revolution—which came to be known as the regular education initiative (REI)—grew out of a number of proposals for achieving the spirit of the EHA for students with disabilities by extending its rights and resources to all students.

Despite opposition to the REI within the special education community, even its detractors agreed that there are serious problems with the EHA and that, in principle, the REI has some appealing features as well (for example, Kauffman, Gerber, & Semmel, 1988; Keogh, 1988). Those in opposition to the REI however, were rightfully concerned that a new revolution could mean the loss of hard-won rights and, in the worst case, a full-circle return to the unacceptable conditions that existed before the EHA (Kauffman, 1988, 1989b; Kauffman, Gerber, & Semmel, 1988).

The REI debate has paralleled the earlier mainstreaming debate in at least three ways. *First,* in both cases, the ethics and efficacy of special education practices are criticized and a new approach is proposed. In the 1960s, the practices associated with the segregated special classroom were criticized for being racially biased, instructionally ineffective, and socially and psychologically damaging; and mainstreaming (and eventually the EHA) emerged as the solution (Abeson & Zettel, 1977; Christophos & Renz, 1969; Deno, 1970; Dunn, 1968; Johnson, 1962). In the REI debate, the practices associated with mainstreaming and the EHA came under attack for virtually the same reasons (Heller, Holtzman, & Messick, 1982; Hobbs, 1980; Wang, Reynolds, & Walberg, 1987a), with the REI being advocated as the new solution.

Second, both debates originated during a period of apparent reform in public education, the character of which was seen as consistent with the proposed special education reform. In the 1960s, advocates of mainstreaming argued that nascent structural reforms and instructional innovations in public education (for example, team teaching, open classrooms, individualized instruction) were consistent with the mainstreaming concept (Dunn, 1968). In the 1980s, the REI proponents argued that the calls for school restructuring and the availability of new instructional technologies (for example, cooperative learning, teacher collaboration) were consistent with their reform proposals (Lipsky & Gartner, 1989a; Pugach & Lilly, 1984; Stainback, Stainback, & Forest, 1989; Wang 1989a,b; Wang, Reynolds, & Walberg, 1985, 1986).[2]

The *third* parallel explains the first two: Both debates are forms of naive pragmatism, a mode of analysis and problem resolution premised on an unreflective acceptance of the assumptions that lie behind social practices. As such, naive pragmatism is "socially reproductive, instrumentally and functionally reproducing accepted meanings and conventional organizations, institutions, and ways of doing things for good or ill" (Cherryholmes, 1988, p. 151). Thus, the problem with the mainstreaming and REI debates is that their criticism stops at the level of special education practices; neither one questions the assumptions in which these practices are grounded.

In the case of the mainstreaming debate, the result was that the new practices associated with the EHA and mainstreaming simply reproduced the special education problems of the 1960s in the 1980s (Skrtic, 1987a, 1988b). Moreover, although the REI debate implicates these assumptions and, thus, has been less naive than the mainstreaming debate, it does not explicitly recognize the connection between special education practices and assumptions, and therefore promises to reproduce the problems of the 1980s in the 1990s and beyond (Skrtic, 1988b, 1991a).

It is a given that resolving social problems requires one to be pragmatic. But being pragmatic in a just and productive way, in a way that does not merely reproduce and extend the original problems, requires a critical form of pragmatism, a mode of inquiry that accepts the fact that our assumptions themselves require evaluation and reappraisal (Cherryholmes, 1988). The advantage today is that revolutionary developments in the social disciplines are providing the conceptual and methodological insights for analyzing social practices from the perspective of their grounding assumptions.[3]

Although the REI and mainstreaming debates are forms of naive pragmatism, by appropriating these insights and applying them to special education practices, it is possible to address the field's past and present problems in terms of critical pragmatism—a mode of analysis in which the grounding assumptions of social practices are themselves treated as problematic (Cherryholmes, 1988; Skrtic, 1991a). Moreover, by conducting such an analysis of special education, and by extending it and its implication to public education per se, it is possible to address the broader question of educational reform in a way that reconciles the historical contradiction between the social goals of educational excellence and educational equity.

In subsequent sections I apply a form of critical pragmatism to three interrelated practices and their grounding assumptions[4] The practices are: (a) special education as a professional practice, (b) special education as an institutional practice of public education, and (c) public education as a social practice of our society. Because ultimately I am concerned with the legitimacy of public education, my approach is to subject it to an immanent critique—a form of criticism that asks whether public education's institutional practices are consistent with its democratic ideals. As such, I am interested in restoring the legitimacy of public education—that is, in transforming the real (actual practices) into the ideal by forcing the reader to consider whether it is living up to its own standards.[5]

To carry out the immanent critique of public education, I conduct critical readings of three discourses, each of which surrounds, shapes, and legitimizes one of the three practices noted above. The discourses are: (a) the REI debate in the field of special education, (b) the discourse on school organization and adaptability in the field of educational administration,[6] and (c) the discourse on school failure in the institution of public education. The purpose of reading the discourses critically is to deconstruct them—and thus the practices they legitimize—by exposing their silences, inconsistencies, contradictions, and incompleteness relative to their grounding assumptions.[7] The purpose of deconstructing the discourses and practices is to show that their grounding assumptions are inadequate and in need of reappraisal, that alternative assumptions are possible and desirable, and, most important, that choosing grounding assumptions is a political and moral act with implications for ethical practice and a just society.

The significance of the REI debate is that, when read critically, it provides the grounds to deconstruct special education as a professional practice, which, in conjunction with a critical reading of the discourse on school organization and adaptability, provides the grounds to deconstruct special education as an institutional practice of public education. The broader significance of deconstructing the institutional practice of special education is that, together with a critical reading of the discourse on educational excellence in general education,[8] it deconstructs the discourse on school failure in the institution of public education. Ultimately, without the legitimizing effect of the discourse on school failure, the immanent contradiction between its institutional practices and democratic ideals deconstructs 20th-century public education and prepares the way for reconstructing it according to its traditional democratic ideals and the changing historical conditions of the 21st century.

The remainder of this chapter is divided into seven major sections. The first is a genealogy of the 20th-century discourse on school failure, which provides an overview of my basic argument and identifies the assumptions that ground the professional and institutional practices and discourses of public education—the assumptions that I believe have to be reappraised.[9] In the second section I deconstruct special education as a professional practice by showing that a critical reading of the REI debate delegitimizes its grounding assumptions. The third section is a critical reading of the discourse on school organization and adaptability.

On the basis of this reading, I introduce an alternative way to conceptualize school organization and the problem of change, which I use in the fourth section to deconstruct special education as an institutional practice of public education. In the fifth section I combine my analysis of special education with a critical reading of the discourse on educational excellence in general education. My aim is to show how these critical readings converge to delegitimize the discourse on school failure and, ultimately, to deconstruct the institution of public education. After section five, my focus shifts to reconstructing public education. In the sixth section I propose an alternative organizational configuration for schooling that is both excellent and equitable. In the final section I consider the implications of this particular configuration for the emerging political and economic relevancies of the 21st century.

Functionalism and the
Problem of School Failure

Functionalism—the dominant mode of theorizing in the social disciplines (Bernstein, 1976; Rorty, 1979) and the professions (Glazer, 1974; Schön, 1983), including general education (Bowles & Gintis, 1976; Feinberg & Soltis, 1985; Giroux, 1981), educational administration (Griffiths, 1983, 1988), and special education (Heshusius, 1982; Iano, 1986; Skrtic, 1986)—presupposes that social reality is objective, inherently orderly, and rational, and thus that social and human problems are pathological (Foucault, 1954/1976, 1961/1973; Ritzer, 1980). As such, the functionalist worldview institutionalized the mutually reinforcing theories of organizational rationality and human pathology in society and in public education.

As a result, when industrialization and compulsory school attendance converged to produce large numbers of students who were difficult to teach in traditional classrooms, the problem of school failure was reframed as two interrelated problems: (a) inefficient organizations, and (b) defective students. This distorted the problem by largely removing it from the general education discourse and compartmentalizing it into two separate but mutually reinforcing discourses. The first was in the developing field of educational administration, which, in the interest of maximizing organizational efficiency, was compelled to rationalize its orientation according to the precepts of scientific management (Callahan, 1962). The second was in the new field of special education, which emerged as a means to remove and contain the most recalcitrant students in the interest of maintaining order in the rationalized school plant (Lazerson, 1983; Sarason & Doris, 1979).

The discourses of all three fields are shaped by explicit presuppositions grounded in their respective foundations of professional knowledge, as well as by implicit presuppositions grounded in the social norms of human pathology and organizational rationality. Because its professional knowledge is grounded in scientific management, educational administration presupposes explicitly that school organizations are rational (Clark, 1985; Griffiths, 1983) and implicitly that school failure is pathological (Skrtic, 1991a).[10] Conversely, special education's professional grounding in psychology and biology (medicine) means that it presupposes explicitly that school failure is pathological (Mercer, 1973; Skrtic, 1986) and implicitly that school organizations are rational (Skrtic, 1987a, 1988b). Given that its professional grounding is in psychology and scientific management (Cherryholmes, 1988; Oakes, 1985, 1986a,b; Spring, 1980), the general education discourse is grounded explicitly and implicitly in both presuppositions.

Taken together, these presuppositions yield four mutually reinforcing assumptions that shape the discourses and practices of all three fields and thus of public education itself. In the language of the special education discourse, these assumptions are (Bogdan & Knoll, 1988; Bogdan & Kuglemass, 1984; Mercer, 1973; Skrtic, 1986):[11]

1. Disabilities are pathological conditions that students have.
2. Differential diagnosis is objective and useful.
3. Special education is a rationally conceived and coordinated system of services that benefits diagnosed students.
4. Progress results from rational technological improvements in diagnostic and instructional practices.

Inquiry in all three fields is dominated by functionalist methodologies (Griffiths, 1983, 1988; Lincoln & Guba, 1985; Poplin, 1987; Skrtic, 1986), which favor data over theory and assume, more or less, that empirical data are objective and self-evident (Churchman, 1971; Mitroff & Pondy, 1974). Thus, each discourse is a form of naive pragmatism that produces and interprets empirical data on student outcomes and school effects intuitively, according to the four taken-for-granted assumptions about disability, diagnosis, special education, and progress. This reproduces the status quo in all three fields, which reaffirms the four assumptions and, ultimately, reinforces the functionalist presuppositions of organizational rationality and human pathology in public education and society.

Thus, the institutional practice of special education (and the very notion of student disability) is an artifact of the functionalist quest for rationality, order, and certainty in the field of education, a quest that is both intensified and legitimized by the institutional practice of educational administration.[12] As such, special education distorts the problem of school failure and, ultimately, prevents the field of education from entering into a productive confrontation with uncertainty. And because uncertainty is a necessary precondition for growth of knowledge and progress in communal activities such as the physical sciences (Kuhn, 1970), the social sciences (Barnes, 1982; Bernstein, 1983), and the professions (Schön, 1983; Skrtic, 1991a), the objectification and legitimization of school failure as student disability prevents public education from moving beyond its functionalist practices.

The problem in special education and educational administration has been that, although both fields have experienced enough uncertainty to call their traditional practices into question,[13] they have lacked a critical discourse for addressing their problems in a reflective manner (Bates, 1980, 1987; Foster, 1986; Skrtic, 1986, 1991a; Tomlinson, 1982). The problem in general education, however, is more fundamental. Not only has it lacked a critical discourse (Cherryholmes, 1988; Giroux, 1981, 1983; Sirotnik & Oakes, 1986), but it has been largely prevented from having to confront uncertainty altogether, precisely because of the objectification of school failure as student disability. Ultimately, the problem is that this distortion of school failure prevents public education from seeing that it is not living up to its democratic ideals.

Public education in a democracy must be both excellent and equitable. If the United States was to avoid tyranny and remain free, Thomas Jefferson argued, public education must produce excellent (intelligent, imaginative, reflective) citizens and assure that "[persons] of talent might rise whatever their social and economic origins" (Greer, 1972, p. 16). The problem with the Jeffersonian ideal, however, is that its democratic ends are contradicted by the bureaucratic means that were used to actualize universal public education in the 20th century. As such, the failure of public education to be either excellent or equitable can be understood in terms of the inherent contradiction between democracy and bureaucracy in the modern state (Weber, 1922/1978).

Special education, then, can be understood as the institutional practice that emerged to contain this contradiction in public education. And because social institutions are best understood from their dark side—from the perspective of the institutional practices that emerge to contain their failures (Foucault, 1983)—special education is a particularly insightful vantage point for deconstructing 20th-century public education. The paradox in all of this is that, when read critically, special education provides the structural and cultural insights that are necessary to begin reconstructing public education for the historical conditions of the 21st century and, ultimately, for reconciling it with its democratic ideals.

Special Education as a Professional Practice

Although the REI is generally thought of as a 1980s phenomenon, the first criticism of the EHA and mainstreaming, in the language of what was to become the REI, appeared in 1976 (Reynolds, 1976; Reynolds & Birch, 1977), barely a year after the EHA had been signed into law and nearly two full years before it was to become fully effective.[14] The next papers promoting the REI appeared in the early 1980s, and subsequently a body of supporting literature was produced by four teams of writers whose names have become synonymous with the pro-REI position.[15] This literature contains two lines of argument: one against the prevailing special education system, and one for certain general and special education reforms intended to correct the situation.

The arguments against the current system address an array of technical and ethical problems associated with the elaborate classification system required by the EHA, as well as instructional problems associated with the pull-out approach implied by mainstreaming. Although the reforms for addressing these problems are unique to particular teams of REI proponents, all four teams agree that the EHA and mainstreaming are fundamentally flawed, particularly for students classified as having mild to moderate disabilities—that is, students classified as having learning disabilities, emotional disturbance, and mental retardation, who made up more than two-thirds of the 4.5 million students served under the law in the late 1980's.[16]

Although the field's initial reaction to the REI was mixed, a full-blown controversy developed in 1988, when several leading figures in the three subfields of mild disability published a tour de force response criticizing the REI.[17] Thereafter, the controversy turned into a heated debate over the ethics and efficacy of the prevailing system of special education on the one hand, and the wisdom and feasibility of the REI reform proposals on the other.[18]

Criticism of the Special Education System

The debate over special education practices is important because it is implicitly a debate over the adequacy of special education's grounding assumptions, recast below in the form of questions.

Are Mild Disabilities Pathological?

Although the ensuing debate has been quite heated, there is virtually no disagreement that mild disabilities are based on a pathology.[19] Both the REI proponents (Gartner & Lipsky, 1987; Pugach & Lilly, 1984; Stainback & Stainback, 1984; Wang, Reynolds, & Walberg, 1986, 1987b) and opponents (for example, Braaten, Kauffman, Braaten, Polsgrove, & Nelson, 1988; Bryan, Bay, & Donahue, 1988; Council for Children with Behavioral Disorders, 1989; Kauffman, Gerber, & Semmel, 1988; Keogh, 1988) agreed that there are students for whom the "mildly handicapped" designation is an objective distinction based on pathology. Yet they also agreed that because of a number of definitional and measurement problems, as well as problems related to the will or capacity of teachers and schools to accommodate student diversity, many students identified as mildly handicapped are not truly disabled in the pathological sense. This was seen as particularly true for students identified as having learning disabilities.

Moreover, both sides in the early debate agreed that additional students in school remained unidentified and thus unserved. Although some of these students were considered to have mild pathological disabilities, others did not but nonetheless required assistance. Whereas the REI proponents recognized that many of these students, including those thought to have mild disabilities, presented difficult problems for classroom teachers, the proponents' point was simply that neither the general education system nor the special education system was sufficiently adaptable to accommodate the individual needs of those students (for example, Gartner & Lipsky, 1987; Pugach & Lilly, 1984; Wang, Reynolds, & Walberg, 1986), a point with which most REI opponents agreed (Bryan, Bay, & Donahue, 1988; Kauffman, 1988; Kauffman, Gerber, & Semmel, 1988; Keogh, 1988).[20]

Is Diagnosis Objective and Useful?

The REI proponents argued that differential diagnosis does not result in objective distinctions, either between the disabled and nondisabled designations or among the three mild disability classifications (Gartner & Lipsky, 1987; Stainback & Stainback, 1984; Wang, Reynolds, & Walberg, 1986, 1987a). As noted above, the REI opponents generally agreed that the disabled–nondisabled distinction is not objective. Moreover, they agreed that distinctions among the three mild disability classifications are not objective because, in addition to measurement and definitional problems, the process for making these decisions in schools is "embedded in a powerful economic, political, and philosophical network" (Keogh, 1988, p. 20; see also Council for Children with Behavioral Disorders, 1989; Gerber & Semmel, 1984; Hallahan & Kauffman, 1977; Kauffman, 1988, 1989a,b).

On the matter of the utility of differential diagnosis, the REI proponents argued that there are no instructionally relevant reasons for making the disabled–nondisabled distinction, or for distinguishing among the three mild-disability classifications. Their point is that all students have unique learning needs and, moreover, that students in the three mild-disability classifications, as well as those in the other special needs classifications, can be taught using similar instructional methods (for example, Lipsky & Gartner, 1989a; Reynolds, Wang, & Walberg, 1987; Stainback & Stainback, 1984, 1989; Wang, 1989a,b; Wang, Reynolds, & Walberg, 1986, 1987a). Here, too, most of the REI opponents agreed, admitting that "effective instructional and management procedures will be substantially the same for nonhandicapped and most mildly handicapped students" (Kauffman, Gerber, & Semmel, 1988, p. 8; see also Gerber, 1987; Hallahan & Kauffman, 1977).[21]

Is Special Education a Rational System?

The REI proponents argued that the only rational justification for the existence of the special education system is that it confers instructional benefit on students designated as "handicapped" (Lilly, 1986; Lipsky & Gartner, 1987; Reynolds, 1988; Reynolds, Wang, & Walberg, 1987; Stainback & Stainback, 1984; Wang, Reynolds, & Walberg, 1987a), a position with which the REI opponents agreed (Kauffman, Gerber, & Semmel, 1988; Keogh, 1988). On this basis, the REI proponents believed that, given the weak effects of special education instructional practices and the social and psychological costs of labeling, the prevailing system of special education was, at best, no more justifiable than simply permitting most students to remain unidentified in regular classrooms and, at worst, far less justifiable than regular-classroom placement in conjunction with appropriate in-class support services (Lipsky & Gartner, 1987, 1989a; Pugach & Lilly, 1984; Stainback & Stainback, 1984; Wang, Reynolds, & Walberg, 1987a). Thus, the REI proponents rejected the idea that special education is a rational system.

Though none of the REI opponents argued that special education had been shown to lead to direct instructional benefit (see, for example, Keogh, 1988; Hallahan, Keller, McKinney, Lloyd, & Bryan, 1988),[22] some of them argued that the "handicapped" designation is beneficial in a political sense. That is, they justified the prevailing system of special education on the political grounds that it targeted otherwise unavailable resources and personnel to designated students. Such targeting, they argued, was essential for these students to receive instructional assistance in the context of the resource allocation process in schools (Council for Children with Behavioral Disorders, 1989; Kauffman, 1988, 1989b; Kauffman, Gerber, & Semmel, 1988).

As noted, the REI opponents recognized that, to be justifiable, special education must confer instructional benefit on designated students, and that existing special education interventions did not confer such benefits. In effect, then, the REI opponents who justified special education on political grounds were saying that, although special education was not an instructionally rational system in its existing form, it is a politically rational system.

This is so, they maintained, because the nonadaptability and political inequality of the general education system made the pull-out logic of main-streaming and the targeting function of the EHA absolute necessities if designated students were to receive instructional assistance in school, even though that assistance did not appear to be effective.

As we will see, in response to the question posed next, on the nature of progress, the REI opponents (including those who justified special education on political grounds) argued that the special education system could be improved incrementally through additional research and development. Thus, their position on the nature of special education could not be separated from their position on the nature of progress in the field. In effect, when considering their positions on the third and fourth assumptions together, the REI opponents were saying that, although special education was not an instructionally rational system that time, it is a politically rational system that can be rendered instructionally rational in the future, given the assumption of the possibility of rational–technical progress. Thus, let us say, for present purposes, that the REI opponents were arguing that special education is an instructionally rational system, given the caveat that, to be rational in an instructional sense, rational–technical progress must be possible.[23]

Is Progress Rational and Technical?

This question asks whether progress can be made under the existing system through incremental technological improvements in its associated diagnostic and instructional practices. The REI proponents argued that the diagnostic and instructional practices of the prevailing system were fundamentally flawed and therefore could not and should not be salvaged. They believed that these practices and the entire system must be replaced through a fundamental restructuring of the special and general education systems (Lilly, 1986; Lipsky & Gartner, 1987, 1989a; Pugach & Lilly, 1984; Reynolds, Wang, & Walberg, 1987; Stainback & Stainback, 1984; Stainback, Stainback, & Forest, 1989)—which is an argument against the possibility of rational–technical change.

Although the REI opponents recognized that the prevailing special education system had serious problems, they believed that incremental progress is possible through additional research and development aimed at improving special education diagnostic and instructional practices while maintaining the system in place at that time (Braaten, Kauffman, Braaten, Polsgrove, & Nelson, 1988; Bryan, Bay, & Donahue, 1988; Council for Children with Behavioral Disorders, 1989; Hallahan, Keller, McKinney, Lloyd, & Bryan, 1988; Kauffman, 1988, 1989b; Kauffman, Gerber, & Semmel, 1988; Keogh, 1988; Lloyd, Crowley, Kohler, & Strain, 1988). This, of course, is an argument for the possibility of rational–technical change.

At this point in the critical reading, the REI proponents and opponents rejected the two grounding assumptions associated with the presupposition of human pathology, which were the explicit disciplinary grounding of special education's professional knowledge and practice ever since the field's inception. Moreover, the REI proponents rejected the two assumptions associated with the normative presupposition of organizational rationality. Thus, by rejecting the field's entire framework of grounding assumptions and presuppositions, the arguments of the REI proponents deconstructed special education as a professional practice. Nevertheless, by arguing that special education is a politically (if not an instructionally) rational system that can be improved in a rational–technical manner, the REI opponents retained the third and fourth assumptions and thus held out some hope for legitimacy of the field.

Although the REI proponents and opponents agreed that the field's grounding assumptions about the nature of disability and diagnosis were inadequate, their disagreement over the nature of special education and progress has resulted in total disagreement over an appropriate course of ameliorative action. On one hand, the REI proponents believed that, given the negative evidence on the ethics and efficacy of special education practices and the nonadaptability of the general education system, a completely new system should be formed by restructuring the two systems into a single adaptable one. On the other hand, the REI opponents believed that, the negative evidence on the adequacy of special education notwithstanding, the existing system and its associated practices should be retained for political purposes, given the nonadaptability of the general education system and the assertion that special education practices can be improved. Thus, the REI debate turns on the question of whether school organizations can and will be restructured into the adaptable system envisioned by the REI advocates.

The REI Proposals

Each of four REI proposals, to one degree or another, called for eliminating the EHA classification system and the pull-out approach of mainstreaming. Each also proposed restructuring the separate general and special education systems into a new system in which, depending on the proposal, most or all students requiring help in school would be provided with in-class assistance.[24] The REI proponents generally agreed that this restructured system should be "flexible, supple, and responsive" (Lipsky & Gartner, 1987, p. 72), a "totally adaptive system" (Reynolds & Wang, 1983, p. 199) in which professionals personalize instruction through "group problem solving ... shared responsibility, and ... negotiation" (Pugach & Lilly, 1984, p. 52). But they disagreed on which students should be integrated into the new system on a full-time basis.[25]

Who Should Be Integrated?

Each of the four teams of REI proponents believed that all students being served in compensatory and remedial education programs, as well as every other student needing help in school but not targeted for it, should remain in the regular classrooms of the restructured system on a full-time basis and receive whatever assistance they need in those classrooms. Where the teams differed was in which students classified as "handicapped" under the EHA should be served in this manner.

The Lilly and Pugach proposal was the least inclusive. In addition to the students noted above, it included only "the vast majority of students served as 'mildly handicapped'" (Lilly, 1986, p. 10) under the EHA, whereas students with moderate, severe, and profound disabilities would be taught by special educators in separate settings within regular school buildings.[26] The Reynolds and Wang proposal was somewhat more inclusive in that it maintained that "most students with special learning needs" (Wang, Reynolds, & Walberg, 1985, p. 13; Reynolds & Wang, 1983) should be in these regular classrooms on a full-time basis, while reserving the option of separate settings for some students, presumably those with severe and profound disabilities.[27]

The Gartner and Lipsky proposal included all students being served under each EHA classification, except those with the most severely and profoundly handicapping conditions. These students would receive their primary instruction in separate classrooms located in regular, age-appropriate school buildings (Gartner & Lipsky, 1987). Finally, in the most inclusive proposal, Stainback and Stainback (1984) argued for the integration of all students, including those with the most severely and profoundly disabling conditions, while recognizing the need to group students, "in some instances, into specific courses and classes according to their instructional needs" (p. 108).

What Should be Merged?

Although the strategy for creating the adaptable system necessary to implement the REI proposals is most often characterized as a merger of the general and special education systems, only the Stainback and Stainback and Gartner and Lipsky proposals actually called for a merger of the two systems at the classroom level.[28] The other two teams proposed a merger of instructional support personnel above the classroom level. Toward this end, Reynolds and Wang (1983) proposed eliminating the categorical special needs pull-out programs through a two-step merger.

The first merger was to be within special education, among the programs serving the three traditional classifications of mild disability. The second was to be between this merged or noncategorical special education program and the other "compensatory services that are provided for disadvantaged, bilingual, migrant, low-English-proficiency, or other children with special needs" (1983, p. 206). Supported by paraprofessionals, these generic specialists were to form a school-based support team that would work "mostly in the regular classrooms . . . to supply technical and administrative support to regular classroom teachers" (1983, p. 206).[29]

The Lilly and Pugach proposal would merge the special education resource and support programs that provided services "for the mildly handicapped, and primarily for the learning disabled" (Pugach & Lilly, 1984, p. 54) with the traditional general education support service of remedial education.[30] They recognized the need for support services but proposed a single, coordinated system of services based in general education and provided largely in regular classrooms, rather than the existing array of special pull-out programs (Lilly, 1986; Pugach & Lilly, 1984). Although the Reynolds and Wang and the Lilly and Pugach proposals modified the notion of instructional support services by replacing the categorical pull-out approach with a noncategorical or remedial model of in-class support services, both of them retained the traditional notion of a classroom, in the sense of one teacher with primary responsibility for a group of students.[31]

Although the Stainback and Stainback proposal called for merger at the classroom level, it actually would merge general and special education subject areas, not special education and general instructional programs or personnel. It called for disbanding special education programs and integrating the residual personnel into the general education system according to an instructional specialization. Each teacher in this system would have "a strong base in the teaching/learning process" (Stainback & Stainback, 1984, p. 107) and a particular specialization in a traditional general education subject (for example, science or reading) or a special education subject (for example, supported employment), and each would work individually in a separate classroom (Stainback & Stainback, 1987a; Stainback, Stainback, & Forest, 1989).

As with the first two proposals, this one called for support services above the classroom level. Here, however, the support personnel were organized as subject-area specialists rather than generic specialists, which modified the categorical pull-out approach by replacing it with in-class subject-area support services. As with the other two support services models, this one retained the traditional notion of a classroom in which one teacher would have primary responsibility for a group of students (see Stainback & Stainback, 1984, 1987a).

The Gartner and Lipsky proposal called for a merged or unitary system in which education would be "both one and special for all students" (Lipsky

& Gartner, 1987, P. 73). Such a system would mean the complete abandonment of a separate special education system for students with mild to moderate disabilities. The original Gartner and Lipsky proposal also emphasized the support services level (Gartner & Lipsky, 1987), but they later clarified and extended that proposal (Lipsky & Gartner, 1989a), emphasizing the classroom level by linking their proposal for a restructured system to the excellence movement in general education, which was, for them, the effective schools movement (Edmonds, 1979; Lezotte, 1989). As such, their basic assertion was that, through broad adoption of the principles and practices identified in the effective schools research, "the education of students labeled as handicapped can be made effective" (Lipsky & Gartner, 1989a, p. 281). They built their case for the effective schools approach by combining Edmonds's (1979) assertion that, if some schools are effective, all schools can be effective, with Gilhool's (1976) parallel assertion about effective integration of students with disabilities. They concluded that effective schools, and thus effective education for students labeled "handicapped," was a matter of will and commitment on the part of teachers and schools to adopt the principles and practices contained in the effective schools literature.[32]

Reactions to the REI Proposals

The REI opponents argued against the possibility of an adaptable system on historical and political grounds and concluded that special needs have not, are not, and simply cannot be met in regular classrooms. Kauffman (1988) and others (Council for Children with Behavioral Disorders, 1989) argued that, historically, the separate special education system emerged precisely because of the nonadaptability of regular classrooms and that, because nothing had happened to make contemporary classrooms any more adaptable (see Keogh, 1988), the REI most likely would lead to rediscovering the need for a separate system in the future.

In their political or macroeconomic criticism of the REI reform proposals, Kauffman, Gerber, & Semmel (1988; see also Gerber, 1988b; Gerber & Semmel, 1985) argued that "teachers, whether in regular or special class environments, cannot escape the necessary choice between higher means [that is, maximizing mean performance by concentrating resources on the most able learners) and narrower variances [that is, minimizing group variance by concentrating resources on the least able learners] as long as resources are scarce and students differ" (Gerber & Semmel, 1985, p. 19, cited in Kauffman, Gerber, & Semmel, 1988, p. 10). This is true, they argued, "whenever a teacher instructs a group of students . . . [except] when new resources are made available or more powerful instructional technologies are employed" (Kauffman, Gerber, & Semmel, 1988, p. 10).

Although these were compelling arguments, they ignored the reality that the REI proposals called for creating a system of adaptable classrooms by making new resources available and introducing more powerful instructional technologies, the exact conditions that can narrow group variances without negatively affecting class means, according to the macroeconomic argument itself. Thus, these were not arguments against the REI proposals; implicitly, they were compelling arguments against the traditional notion of a classroom. By arguing that both regular and special education classrooms are nonadaptable in a microeconomic sense, the REI opponents actually made a stronger case than the REI proponents against the existing system of special education. Moreover, by arguing that the regular classroom had not changed and that neither it nor the special classroom could change, the REI opponents contradicted their position on the possibility of rational–technical change, and thus their implicit support of the third and fourth assumptions.[33]

As we have seen, on the question of the adequacy of the existing system of special education, the REI proponents rejected all four of the field's grounding assumptions, and the opponents rejected the two about disability and diagnosis but retained the two about special education and progress. In their criticism of the REI proposals, however, the REI opponents reversed their position on the two assumptions about special education and progress, and thus implicitly agreed with the REI proponents that all four of the field's grounding assumptions were inadequate. At this point, then, the arguments for and against the field's current practices and those against the REI proposals rejected all four grounding assumptions and thus deconstructed special education as a professional practice. Although the deconstruction of special education appears to be complete, then, we will see in a subsequent discussion that the REI proponents reversed their position on the third and fourth assumptions as well.

As we know, in their criticism of the existing system, the REI proponents argued against the rationality of special education (and thus of the traditional organization of schools). When considering their reform proposals from an organizational perspective, however (see below), they actually reproduced and extended the traditional organization of schools and called for a rational–technical approach to change. Thus, both sides in the REI debate rejected the first two assumptions and thus the presupposition of human pathology that served as the field's explicit disciplinary grounding, but the two sides were contradictory and inconsistent about the third and fourth assumptions and thus about the presupposition of organizational rationality that served as the field's implicit normative grounding. Therefore, let us reserve judgment on whether the arguments in the REI debate deconstructed special education as a professional practice until we have considered the notion of organizational rationality in greater depth.

In the following section I address the legitimacy of the presupposition of organizational rationality by way of a critical reading of the discourse on school organization and adaptability in the field of educational administration. On the basis of this reading, I introduce two alternative ways to conceptualize school organization and the problem of change, which I combine in subsequent sections to carry out my deconstructions of the institutional practice of special education and the discourse on school failure, as well as my deconstruction and reconstruction of the institution of public education.

The Discourse on School Organization And Adaptability

Generally speaking, there are two sources of insight into school organization and adaptability: (a) the prescriptive discourse of educational administration, and (b) the theoretical discourse of the multidisciplinary field of organization analysis. The field of educational administration is grounded in the notion of scientific management, an extremely narrow view that presupposes that organizations are rational and that organizational change is a rational–technical process (Burrell & Morgan, 1979; Scott, 1981). Although scientific management is a purely functionalist approach for organizing and managing industrial firms, it was applied to schools and other social organizations during the social efficiency movement at the turn of the century (Callahan, 1962; Haber, 1964), and has remained the grounding formulation of educational administration ever since.[34]

The theoretical discourse of organization analysis is grounded in the social disciplines and thus, in principle, provides a much broader range of perspectives on organization and change. Ultimately, however, the theories produced in the field of organization analysis are shaped by the various modes of theorizing or paradigms that have been available to and, more important, historically favored by social scientists (Burrell & Morgan, 1979).[35] Because functionalism has been the favored mode of theorizing in the social sciences, the theoretical discourse on organization, like the prescriptive discourse of educational administration, has been dominated by the functionalist paradigm, and thus by the presupposition of organizational rationality (Burrell & Morgan, 1979). Ever since the 1950s the same revolutionary developments in the social disciplines that were noted previously have produced a number of new theories of organization grounded in other modes of social theorizing that had been underutilized in organizational research.[36]

One important substantive outcome of these developments has been a shift in emphasis on the question of the nature of organization and change itself. Whereas the functionalist notion of rational organizations (that is, prospective and goal-directed) and rational–technical change had been the exclusive outlook in organization analysis, many of the newer theories are premised on the idea that organizations are nonrational entities (that is, quasi-random, emergent systems of meaning or cultures) in which change is a nonrational–cultural process (Pfeffer, 1982; Scott, 1981). Methodologically, the trend in organization analysis, as in the social sciences generally, has been away from the traditional foundational notion of one best theory or paradigm for understanding organization. Thus, the contemporary discourse in organization analysis is characterized by theoretical diversity (Burrell & Morgan, 1979; Pfeffer, 1982; Scott, 1981) and, at the margins at least, by an antifoundational methodological orientation (Morgan, 1983).[37]

Drawing on these substantive and methodological developments, the following analysis considers school organization and adaptability from two general frames of reference that, together, include several theories of organization and change drawn from each of the modes of theorizing found in the social disciplines. The structural frame of reference combines configuration theory (Miller & Mintzberg, 1983; Mintzberg, 1979) and what will be referred to as "institutionalization theory" (Meyer & Rowan, 1977, 1978; Meyer & Scott, 1983). By combining these two theories, we can understand school organization as an inherently nonadaptable, two-structure arrangement. The cultural frame of reference contains what will be referred to as paradigmatic (Brown, 1978; Golding, 1980; Jonsson & Lundin, 1977; Rounds, 1979, 1981) and cognitive theories of organization (Weick, 1979, 1985), which, when combined, provide a way to understand school organizations as cultures or corrigible systems of meaning.

The two frames of reference are presented separately below and then integrated in the next major section, where the relationship between organization structure and culture is used to reconsider the four grounding assumptions of special education as an institutional practice of public education.[38] Although the reader no doubt will begin to see in the following analysis some of the organizational implications that I will emphasize in subsequent sections, at this point I will refrain from commenting on those implications. My aim here is merely to set the stage for the sections to follow.

The Structural Frame of Reference[39]

The central idea in configuration theory is that organizations structure themselves into somewhat naturally occurring configurations according to the type of work that they do, the means they have available to coordinate their work, and a variety of situational factors. Given these considerations, school organizations configure themselves as professional bureaucracies (Mintzberg, 1979), even though in the 20th century they were managed and governed as machine bureaucracies (Callahan, 1962; Meyer & Rowan, 1978; Weick, 1982). According to institutionalization theory, organizations such as schools deal with this contradiction by maintaining two structures: (a) a material structure that conforms to the technical demands of their work, and (b) a normative structure that conforms to the cultural demands of their institutionalized environments.

By combining the insights of configuration theory and institutionalization theory, school organizations can be understood in terms of two organizations, one inside the other. On the outside, their normative structure conforms to the machine bureaucracy configuration, the structure that people expect because of the social norm of organizational rationality. On the inside, however, the material structure of schools conforms to the professional bureaucracy configuration, the structure that configures itself around the technical requirements of their work.

Differences between the Machine and Professional Bureaucracies

The differences between the two organizations stem from the type of work they do and thus the way they can distribute it among workers (division of labor) and subsequently coordinate its completion. Organizations configure themselves as *machine bureaucracies* when their work is simple—when it is certain enough to be *rationalized* (or task-analyzed) into a series of separate subtasks, each of which can be prespecified and done by a different worker. Because it can be completely prespecified, simple work can be coordinated by standardizing the work processes through *formalization,* or the specification of precise rules for doing each subtask.

Organizations configure themselves as *professional bureaucracies* when their work is complex—when it is ambiguous and thus too uncertain to be rationalized and formalized. Because their work is too uncertain to be broken apart and distributed among a number of workers, division of labor in the professional bureaucracies is achieved through *specialization.* In the professional bureaucracy (which typically does client-centered work) clients are distributed among the workers, each of whom specializes in the skills that are needed to do the total job with his or her assigned client cohort. Given this form of division of labor, complex work is coordinated by standardizing the skills of the workers, which is accomplished through *professionalization,* or intensive education and socialization carried out in professional schools.

The logic behind rationalization and formalization in the machine bureaucracy is premised on minimizing discretion and separating theory from practice. The theory behind the work rests with the technocrats who rationalize and formalize it; they do the thinking, and the workers simply follow the rules. Conversely, specialization and professionalization are meant to increase discretion and to unite theory and practice in the professional. This is necessary because containing the uncertainty of complex work within the role of a particular professional specialization requires the professional to adapt the theory behind the work to the particular needs of his or her clients (Schein, 1972).

In principle, professionals know the theory behind their work and have the discretion to adapt it to the actual needs of their clients. In practice, however, the standardization of skills is circumscribed; it provides professionals with a finite repertoire of standard programs that are applicable to only a finite number of contingencies or presumed client needs. Given adequate discretionary space (see below), there is room for some adjustment. When clients have needs that fall on the margins or outside of the professional's repertoire of standard programs, however, they either must be forced artificially into the available programs or must be sent to a different professional specialist, one who presumably has the right standard programs (Perrow, 1970; Weick, 1976).

A fully open-ended process—one that seeks a truly creative solution to each unique need—requires a problem-solving orientation. But professionals are performers, not problem solvers. They perfect the programs they have; they do not invent new ones for unfamiliar contingencies. Instead of accommodating heterogeneity, professionals screen it out by squeezing their clients' needs into one of their standard programs or by squeezing them out of the professional-client relationship altogether (Segal, 1974; Simon, 1977).

An organization's division of labor and means of coordination shape the nature of interdependency or coupling among its workers (March & Olsen, 1976; Thompson, 1967; Weick, 1976). Because machine bureaucracies distribute and coordinate their work by rationalizing and formalizing it, their workers are highly dependent on one another and thus, like links in a chain, they are tightly coupled. Specialization and professionalization, however, create a loosely coupled form of interdependency in the professional bureaucracy, a situation in which workers are not highly dependent on one another. Because specialization requires close contact with the client and professionalization requires little overt coordination or communication among workers (everyone knows roughly what everyone else is doing by way of their common professionalization), each professional works closely with his or her clients and only loosely with other professionals (Weick, 1976, 1982).

Managing Professional Bureaucracies Like Machine Bureaucracies

Given the prescriptive discourse of educational administration and the social norm of organizational rationality, traditional school management (Weick, 1982), and governance (Meyer & Rowan, 1978; Mintzberg, 1979) practices force school organizations to adopt the rationalization and formalization principles of the machine bureaucracy, even though they are ill-suited to the technical demand of doing complex work. In principle, this drives the professional bureaucracy toward the machine bureaucracy configuration because, by misconceptualizing teaching as simple work that can be rationalized and formalized, it violates the theory/practice requirement and discretionary logic of professionalization. Thus, by separating theory and practice and reducing professional discretion, the degree to which teachers can personalize instruction. Complex work cannot be rationalized and formalized, except in misguided ways that force the professionals "to play the machine bureaucratic game—satisfying the standards instead of serving the clients" (Mintzberg, 1979, p. 377).

Fortunately, the imposition of rationalization and formalization does not work completely in school organizations because, from the institutionalization perspective, these structural contingencies are built into the outer machine bureaucracy structure of schools, which is decoupled from their inner professional bureaucracy structure where the work is done. That is, the outer machine bureaucracy structure of schools acts largely as a myth that, through an assortment of symbols and ceremonies, embodies the rationalization and formalization but has little to do with the way the work is actually done. This decoupled arrangement permits schools to do their work according to the localized judgments of professionals—the logic behind specialization and professionalization—while protecting their legitimacy by giving managers and the public the appearance of the rationalized and formalized machine bureaucracy that they expect.

But decoupling does not work completely either because, from the configuration perspective, no matter how contradictory they may be, misplaced rationalization and formalization require at least overt conformity to their precepts and thus circumscribe professional thought and action (Dalton, 1959; Mintzberg, 1979). Decoupling notwithstanding, managing and governing schools as if they were machine bureaucracies increases rationalization and formalization and thus decreases professional thought and discretion, which reduces even further the degree to which teachers can personalize instruction.

Similarities between the Machine and Professional Bureaucracies

Even though they are different in the respects noted above, the machine bureaucracy and the professional bureaucracy are similar in one important way: Both are inherently nonadaptable structures because they are premised on standardization. All bureaucracies are performance organizations—structures that are configured to perfect the programs they have been standardized to perform. Of course, the standardization of skills is intended to allow for enough professional thought and discretion to accommodate client variability. Even with adequate discretionary space, however, there is a limit on the degree to which professionals can adjust their standard programs. Moreover, they can adjust only the standard programs that are in their repertoires. In a professional bureaucracy, coordination through standardization of skills itself circumscribes the degree to which the organization can accommodate variability.

A fully open-ended process of accommodation requires a problem-solving organization, a configuration premised on inventing new programs for unique client needs. But the professional bureaucracy is a performance organization; it screens out heterogeneity by forcing its clients' needs into one of its existing specializations, or by forcing them out of the system altogether (Segal, 1974).

Because bureaucracies are performance organizations, they require a stable environment. They are potentially devastated under dynamic conditions, when their environments force them to do something other than what they were standardized to do. Nevertheless, machine bureaucracies can change by restandardizing their work processes, a more or less rational–technical process of rerationalizing their work and reformalizing worker behavior. When its environment becomes dynamic, however, the professional bureaucracy cannot respond by making rational–technical adjustments in its work because its coordination rests within each professional, not in its work processes.

At a minimum, change in a professional bureaucracy requires a change in what each professional does, because each professional does all aspects of the work individually and personally with his or her clients. Nevertheless, because schools are managed and governed as if they were machine bureaucracies, attempts to change them typically follow the rational–technical approach (Elmore & McLaughlin, 1988; House, 1979), which assumes that changes in, or additions to, the existing rationalization and formalization will result in changes in the way the work gets done. Of course, this fails to bring about the desired changes because the existing rationalization and formalization are located in the decoupled machine bureaucracy structure. Because such changes or additions require at least overt conformity, however, they act to extend the existing rationalization and formalization. This drives the organization farther toward the machine bureaucracy configuration, which reduces teacher thought and discretion even further, leaving students with even less personalized, and thus even less effective, services.

Even though schools are nonadaptable structures, their status as public organizations means that they must respond to public demands for change. From the institutionalization perspective, schools deal with this problem by using their outer machine bureaucracy structure to deflect the demands for change. That is, they relieve pressure for change by signaling the environment that a change has occurred, thereby creating the illusion that they have changed when they actually remain largely the same (Meyer, 1979; Rowan, 1980; Zucker, 1981). One way that school organizations signal change is by building symbols and ceremonies of change into their outer machine bureaucracy structure, which, of course, is decoupled from the actual work.

Another important signal of change is the ritual or decoupled subunit. Not only are the two structures of schools decoupled, but the various units (classrooms and programs) are decoupled from one another as well. As we know from the configuration perspective, this is possible because specialization and professionalization create precisely this sort of loosely coupled interdependency within the organization. As such, schools can respond to pressure for change by simply adding separate classrooms or programs—that is, by creating new specializations to deal with the change demand. This response acts to buffer the organization from the change demand because these subunits are decoupled from the rest of the organization, thereby making any substantive reorganization of activity unnecessary (Meyer & Rowan, 1977; Zucker, 1981).

The Cultural Frame of Reference

Organization theorists working from the cultural frame of reference think of organizations as bodies of thought, as schemas, cultures, or paradigms. Their theories are premised on the idea that humans construct their social realities through intersubjective communication (see Berger & Luckmann, 1967). As such, the cognitive and paradigmatic perspectives on organization and change are concerned with the way people construct, deconstruct, and reconstruct meaning and how this relates to the way action and interaction unfold over time in organizations. Cognitive theories emphasize the way people create and re-create their organizational realities; paradigmatic theories emphasize the way organizational realities create and re-create people. Together, these theories reflect the interactive duality of the cultural frame of reference—people creating culture and culture creating people (Pettigrew, 1979).

Organizations as Paradigms

Paradigmatic theorists conceptualize organizations as paradigms or shared systems of meaning. They are concerned with understanding the way existing socially constructed systems of meaning affect and constrain thought and action in organizations. From this perspective, an organizational paradigm is a system of beliefs about cause-effect relations and standards of practice and behavior. Regardless of whether these paradigms are true, they guide and justify action by consolidating disorder into an image of orderliness (Brown, 1978; Clark, 1972). From this perspective, organizational change requires a paradigm shift, which is difficult because the paradigm self-justifies itself by distorting new information so it is seen as consistent with the prevailing view. Nevertheless, when sufficient anomalies accumulate to undermine the prevailing paradigm, a new one emerges and action proceeds again under the guidance of the new organizing framework (Golding, 1980; Jonsson & Lundin, 1977).[40]

One way that anomalies are introduced into organizational paradigms is when values and preferences in society change. To the degree that the new social values are inconsistent with the prevailing paradigm, however, resistance emerges in the form of political clashes and an increase in ritualized activity, which act to reaffirm the paradigm that has been called into question (Rounds, 1979; see also Lipsky, 1975; Perrow, 1978; Zucker, 1977). Another way that anomalies are introduced is through the availability of technical information that indicates that the current paradigm is not working, which can bring about a paradigm shift in one of two ways (Rounds, 1981):

1. Through a confrontation between an individual (or a small constituency group), who rejects the most fundamental assumptions of the current paradigm on the basis of information that the system is not working, and the rest of the organization's members, who are acting in defiance of the negative information to preserve the prevailing paradigm.

2. When an initially conservative action is taken to correct a generally recognized flaw in what is otherwise assumed to be a viable system. Here, the corrective measure exposes other flaws that, when addressed, expose more flaws, and so on, until enough of the system is called into question to prepare the way for a radical reconceptualization of the entire organization.

Organizations as Schemas

From the cognitive perspective, an organization is a cognitive entity, a paradigm, or human schema, "an abridged, generalized, corrigible organization of experience that serves as an initial frame of reference for action and perception" (Weick, 1979, p. 50). That is, although an organizational paradigm orients the thought and action of its members, the members are active in creating and re-creating the paradigm. Through activity, selective attention, consensual validation, and luck, people in organizations unrandomize streams of random experience enough to form a paradigm that—correct or not—structures the field of action sufficiently so that meaningful activity can proceed (Weick, 1979, 1985). Members' sampling of the environment, and thus the paradigms they construct—are shaped by prior beliefs and values, which act as filters through which they examine their experiences.

Moreover, activity in organizations, which from the cognitive perspective is the pretext for sense-making, is shaped by material structures such as formalization, professionalization, and bureaucracy itself. These structural contingencies shape members' organizational realities because they influence the contacts, communication, and commands that they experience and thus affect the streams of experience, beliefs, values, and actions that constitute their organizational paradigms. Furthermore, the paradigm and its values and beliefs also "constrain contacts, communication, and commands. These constraints constitute and shape organizational processes that result in structures" (Weick, 1979, p. 48).

From this perspective, then, organization is a mutually shaping circularity of structure and culture. Depending on where one enters the circle, organization is a continuous process in which structural contingencies shape the work activities of organizational members, which, in turn, shape the members' value orientation and thus the nature of the organizational paradigms they construct to interpret the organization's structural contingencies.

From this perspective, school organizations are "underorganized systems" (Weick, 1985, p. 106), ambiguous settings that are shaped and reshaped by values and beliefs (see also Cohen, March, & Olsen, 1972). Change occurs in such contexts when organizational members believe, correctly or not, that a change in the environment was caused by their own actions. Although this may be an error, when environments are sufficiently malleable, acting on a mistaken belief can set in motion a sequence of activities that allows people to construct the reality that the belief is true. From the cognitive perspective, confident action based on a presumption of efficacy reinforces beliefs about efficacy contained in the paradigm. For good or ill, things are done in certain ways in ambiguous, underorganized systems because people believe their assumptions and presuppositions. And, because believing is seeing in these settings, things change when these beliefs change (Weick, 1985).

Thus, the very underorganized nature of schools that prevents change from a structural perspective is the precise condition that makes change possible from a cultural perspective. Under conditions of increased ambiguity and uncertainty, the presuppositions that underwrite the prevailing paradigm are called into question. Change occurs when someone or something introduces new presuppositions that explain the ambiguity and thereby reduce the uncertainty (Brown, 1978; Golding, 1980; Rounds, 1981; Weick, 1979). The recognition of an important, enduring ambiguity—an unresolvable anomaly in the prevailing paradigm—is an occasion when an organization may redefine itself. [From the cultural perspective, organizations such as schools are human constructions grounded in values. Schools change when apparently irresolvable ambiguities are resolved by confident, forceful, persistent people who manage to convince themselves and others to adopt a new set of presuppositions, which introduces innovation because the values embedded in these presuppositions create a new set of contingencies, expectations, and commitments (Weick, 1985).

Special Education as an Institutional Practice

The structural and cultural frames of reference on school organization and adaptability are combined in this section, and used to reconsider the four grounding assumptions relative to special education as an institutional practice of public education. The first three assumptions are addressed below. Following that, the fourth assumption is considered by way of an organizational analysis of the EHA and the REI proposals.

School Organization, Student Disability, and Special Education[41]

Participants in the REI debate came to reject the assumptions that mild disabilities are pathological and that diagnosis is objective and useful. They recognized instead that many students were identified as "handicapped" simply because of their needs that could not be accommodated in the regular classrooms of the general education system. This contradiction can be understood from an organizational perspective by redescribing student disability as an organizational pathology resulting from the inherent structural and cultural characteristics of traditional school organizations.

Structurally, schools are nonadaptable at the classroom level because professionalization ultimately results in "convergent thinking, in the deductive reasoning of the professional who sees the specific situation in terms of the general concept" (Mintzberg, 1979, p. 375). Given a finite repertoire of standard programs, students whose needs fall outside the standard programs must be forced into them or out of the classroom, a situation that is compounded by the rational–technical approach to school management, which, by introducing unwarranted rationalization and formalization, reduces professional thought and discretion and, thus, the degree to which teachers can personalize their standard programs.

The same phenomenon can be understood culturally by thinking of the standard programs as a paradigm of practice that persists because anomalies are distorted to preserve its validity. The principal distortion, of course, is the institutional practice of special education, which reaffirms the paradigm by removing students for whom it does not work. In effect, this prevents teachers from recognizing anomalies in their paradigms and thus, ultimately, removes a valuable source of innovation from the system.[42] Moreover, rationalization and formalization compound and further mystify the situation because they conflict with the values that ground the paradigm and thus increase ritualized activity, which further reduces thought and personalization.

Thus, whether we think of schools from the structural or the cultural frame of reference, the implication is that the first two grounding assumptions are inadequate and incomplete. In organizational terms, student disability is neither a human pathology nor an objective distinction; it is an organizational culture, the legitimacy of which is artificially reaffirmed by the objectification of school failure as a human pathology through the institutional practice of special education.

Participants in the REI debate reject the assumption that special education is an instructionally rational system and recognize that, at best, it is a politically rational system for targeting otherwise unavailable educational services to designated students, even though the targeting process stigmatizes the students and the services do not necessarily benefit them instructionally. This contradiction can be understood from an organizational perspective by reconceptualizing the institutional practice of special education as an organizational artifact that emerged to protect the legitimacy of a nonadaptable bureaucratic structure faced with the changing value demands of a dynamic democratic environment.

Even though specialization, professionalization, rationalization, and formalization make schools nonadaptable structures, these organizations maintain their legitimacy under dynamic social conditions by signaling to the public that changes have occurred through symbols, ceremonies, and decoupled subunits. As such, the segregated special classroom emerged in conjunction with compulsory school attendance to preserve the legitimacy of the prevailing organizational paradigm by symbolizing compliance with the public demand for universal public education.[43]

Structurally, special education is not a rational system; it is a nonrational system, an institutional practice that functions as a legitimizing device. Culturally, it distorts the anomaly of school failure and thus preserves the prevailing paradigm of school organization, which ultimately reaffirms the functionalist presuppositions of organizational rationality and human pathology in the profession of education and in society.[44]

School Organization and Progress

Both sides in the REI debate agree that most mild disabilities are not pathological and that diagnosis is neither objective nor useful. As such, the arguments put forth in the debate reject the presupposition of human pathology as a grounding for the institutional practice of special education. The two sides disagree, however, over an appropriate course of action because of conceptual confusion about the nature of special education and progress resulting from the presupposition of organizational rationality. As we have seen, this confusion among the REI opponents became evident in their defense of the existing system of special education and their criticism of the REI proposals. The same sort of confusion among the REI proponents can be illustrated at this point by considering their reform proposals from an organizational perspective, which I will turn to after analyzing the EHA. Before considering either reform measure, however, it will be helpful to introduce a third organizational configuration.

The Adhocracy

As we know, the professional bureaucracy is nonadaptable because it is premised on the principle of standardization (of skills), which configures it as a performance organization for perfecting standard programs. Conversely, the adhocracy configuration is premised on the principle of innovation rather than standardization and, as such, configures itself as a problem-solving organization for inventing new programs. It is the organizational form that configures itself around work that is so ambiguous and uncertain that neither the standard programs nor the skills for doing it are known (Mintzberg, 1979).[45]

Perhaps the best example of this configuration is the National Aeronautics and Space Administration (NASA) during its Apollo phase in the 1960s. Given its mission to put an American on the moon, it configured itself as an adhocracy because at that time there were no standard programs for this sort of manned space flight. At that point in its history, NASA had to rely on its workers to invent and reinvent these programs on an ad hoc basis—on the way to the moon, as it were. Although NASA employed professional workers, it could not use specialization and professionalization to distribute and coordinate its work because there were no special ties that had perfected the standard programs for doing the type of work that was required, and thus no professional fields whose existing repertoires of standard programs could contain its uncertainty. As such, during its Apollo phase, NASA's division of labor and means of coordination were premised on collaboration and mutual adjustment, respectively.

Under such an arrangement, division of labor is achieved by deploying professionals from various specializations on multidisciplinary project teams, a situation in which team members work collaboratively on the team's project and assume joint responsibility for its completion. Under mutual adjustment, coordination is achieved through informal communication among team members as they invent and reinvent novel solutions to problems on an ad hoc basis, a process that requires them to adapt, adjust, and revise their conventional theories and practices relative to those of their colleagues and the teams' progress on the tasks at hand (Chandler & Sayles, 1971; Mintzberg, 1979). Together, the structural contingencies of collaboration and mutual adjustment give rise to a discursive coupling arrangement that is premised on reflective thought, and thus on the unification of theory and practice in the team of workers (Burns & Stalker, 1966).

By contrast, during its Space Shuttle phase, NASA configured itself as a professional bureaucracy (Romzek & Dubnick, 1987), a performance organization that perfected a repertoire of standard launch and recovery programs that had been invented during its Apollo phase. This transformation from the adhocracy to the professional bureaucracy configuration begins when the organization assumes that it has solved all or most of its problems and thus that the programs it has invented can be standardized and used as solutions in the future. The difference between the two configurations is that, faced with a problem, the adhocracy "engages in creative effort to find a novel solution; the professional bureaucracy pigeonholes it into a known contingency to which it can apply a standard program. One engages in divergent thinking aimed at innovation; the other in convergent thinking aimed at perfection" (Mintzberg, 1979, p. 436).

Finally, under the organizational contingencies of collaboration, mutual adjustment, and discursive coupling, accountability in the adhocracy is achieved through a presumed community of interests—a sense among the workers of a shared interest in a common goal, in the well-being of the organization with respect to progress toward its mission—rather than through an ideological identification with a professional culture (professional bureaucracy) or a formalized relationship with an organization (machine bureaucracy) (Burns & Stalker, 1966; Chandler & Sayles, 1971; Romzek & Dubnick, 1987). Thus, rather than the professional-bureaucratic mode of accountability that emerges in two-structure configurations such as schools, the organizational contingencies of the adhocracy give rise to a *professional-political* mode of accountability, a situation in which work is controlled by experts who, although they act with discretion, are subject to sanctions that emerge within a political discourse among professionals and client constituencies (Burns & Stalker, 1966; Chandler & Sayles, 1971).[46]

Organizational Analyses of EHA and REI

The Education for All Handicapped Children Act

From an organizational perspective, the basic problem with the EHA is that it attempts to force an adhocratic value orientation on a professional bureaucracy by treating it as if it were a machine bureaucracy.[47] The EHA's ends are adhocratic because it seeks a problem-solving organization in which interdisciplinary teams of professionals and parents collaborate to invent personalized programs, or, in the language of the EHA, individualized education programs (IEPs). But this orientation contradicts the value orientation of the professional bureaucracy in every way, given that it is a performance organization in which individual professionals work alone to perfect standard programs. Culturally, this value conflict produces resistance in the form of political clashes, which undermine the ideal of collaboration, as well as an increase in ritualized activity, which, by further mystifying the prevailing paradigm of practice, intensifies the problem of professionalization and thus deflects the ideals of problem solving and personalization.[48]

Moreover, because the EHA's means are completely consistent with the value orientation of the machine bureaucracy structure—rationalization of instructional programs (see below) and formalization of procedures—the EHA extends and elaborates the existing rationalization and formalization in schools. Structurally, this both decouples the adhocratic ends of the EHA from the actual work and further reduces professional thought and discretion, a process that intensifies professionalization and thus reduces personalization. This results in even more students who fall outside the standard programs, many of whom must be identified as "handicapped" to protect the legitimacy of the prevailing paradigm.

Moreover, because there is a limit on the number of students who can be identified as "handicapped" under the EHA, as well as a political limit on the amount of school failure society will tolerate, the EHA, in conjunction with other rational–technical reforms associated with the excellence movement, helped to create the new "at-risk" category of student causalities, which became decoupled from both general education and special education.[49]

Because the EHA mandate required at least overt conformity, a number of symbols of compliance emerged, two of which are important for our purposes here. The symbol of compliance for programs serving students with severe and profound disabilities is the traditional decoupled subunit, the segregated special classroom. These programs were simply added to the existing school organization and, to one degree or another, decoupled from the basic operation. Because the nature of the needs of the students in these programs was beyond the standard programs of any single profession and thus required an interdisciplinary approach, their efficacy depended on school organizations providing the required team of professionals. Beyond this, these programs have had very little to do with the basic school operation.[50]

The resource room, a new type of decoupled subunit came to be the symbol of compliance for most students identified as "mildly handicapped." From an organizational perspective, the resource room is even more problematic than the special classroom because it violates the logic of the professional bureaucracy's means of coordination and division of labor.[51] Under the mainstreaming model, the responsibility for the student's instructional program is divided among one or more general classroom teachers and a special education resource teacher. This contradicts the division of labor in the requirement that the student's instructional program be rationalized and assigned to more than one professional. This was justified implicitly on the assumption that the professionals would work collaboratively to integrate the program. But the collaboration required to integrate the student's instructional program contradicted the logic of professionalization, and thus the loosely coupled form of interdependency among workers. Because professionalization locates virtually all of the necessary coordination within the teacher, there is no need for collaboration in schools, and thus it is difficult to accomplish.[52]

Given the adhocratic spirit of the EHA, it was intended to decrease the effects of student disability by increasing personalized instruction and general education integration. Given the bureaucratic value orientation of schools and of the procedural requirements of the law itself, however, the result has been an increase in the number of students classified as having a disability, a disintegration of instruction, and a decrease in personalization in general and special classrooms.[53]

The Regular Education Initiative Proposals[54]

The problem with the REI proposals is that each of them reproduces and extends the value contradictions of the EHA. This is so because, even though they reject the two assumptions associated with the notion of human pathology, ultimately they retain the assumptions that school organizations are rational and that changing them is a rational–technical process. In organizational terms, the result has been that, although the REI proposals call for an adhocratic value orientation, they have retained the professional bureaucracy inner configuration of schools and have extended their machine bureaucracy outer configuration. They retain the professional bureaucracy configuration because, by retaining the classroom teacher, each proposal retains a specialized division of labor and a professionalized means of coordination—a combination that yields loose coupling and thus deflects the ideal of collaboration.

In principle, as long as the work in schools is distributed through specialization and coordinated through professionalization, there is no need for teachers to collaborate. Collaboration emerges when work is distributed on the basis of a collaborative division of labor and coordinated through mutual adjustment, an arrangement that is premised on a team approach to problem solving and yielding a form of interdependency premised on reflective discourse. Although the Reynolds and Wang, Lilly and Pugach, and Stainback and Stainback proposals called for collaborative problem solving between a classroom teacher and a support services staff, by retaining the notion of a classroom and placing the support services staff above it, they actually extended the rationalization and formalization of the machine bureaucracy configuration and thus undermined the ideals of problem solving and personalized instructions That is, placing the support staff above the classroom teacher implies that the theory of teaching is at the support level while the mere practice of teaching takes place in the classroom, an administrative arrangement that maintains the misplaced convention of separating theory from practice.

Moreover, this politicizes and thus undermines the ideal of collaboration, because placing support personnel above the practice context makes them technocrats rather than support staff (Mintzberg, 1979). In an actual machine bureaucracy, technocrats are the people with the theory; they control and define the activities of the other workers. This is not collaboration in an organizational sense; it is bureaucratic control and supervision. In professional bureaucracies, where the notion of a technocracy within the organization violates the logic of professionalization (Mintzberg, 1979), technocrats are resisted, particularly change agents and other school-improvement personnel (Wolcott, 1977).

The same problems are inherent in the Gartner and Lipsky proposal, which retained the regular classroom and proposed to make it effective for all students by implementing the principles of effective schools research through school improvement projects. Here the assumption was that the theory of effective teaching—which is known by the school improvement and effective schools specialists apart from and prior to the classroom context—is contained in the principles identified in effective schools research, and that implementing these principles in the practice context is simply a matter of the teacher making a commitment to follow them. In principle, imposing such standards from above, their apparent efficacy in some other context notwithstanding, can only lead to an extension of existing rationalization and formalization, and thus to an increase in ritualized activity. Ultimately, this leads to an increase in professionalization and a corresponding decrease in personalization.[55]

Finally, the Stainback and Stainback proposal compounded both of these problems. Not only did it retain the notions of a classroom and the separation of theory and practice, thus politicizing and undermining the ideals of collaboration and problem solving, but also by creating a system of individual subject-area specializations, it disintegrated the student's instructional program across even more teachers than the mainstreaming approach. Ironically, the REI proposal that promoted total integration of students implied a virtually complete disintegration of instruction.

Although the arguments put forth in the REI debate reject the assumption of human pathology and thus represent progress relative to the mainstreaming debate, the outcome is the same. The adhocratic values of the REI proponents are distorted by the bureaucratic value orientation of school organization. Moreover, because they retain the presupposition of organizational rationality, their adhocratic ends are deflected by the bureaucratic value orientation of their own proposals.

Earlier in the analysis we saw that a critical reading of the REI debate rejected the presupposition of human pathology and thus left the legitimacy of special education as a professional practice hanging on the adequacy of the presupposition of organizational rationality. At this point, however, we have seen that a critical reading of the discourse on school organization and adaptability, in conjunction with an organizational analysis of the EHA and the REI proposals, rejects the presuppositions of human pathology and organizational rationality. Such a reading deconstructs special education, both as a professional practice and as an institutional practice of public education. In terms of the adequacy of its grounding assumptions, special education cannot be considered a rational and just response to the problem of school failure.

Public Education and the Discourse on School Failure

To this point in the analysis, we have been concerned with special education, first as a professional practice from the vantage point of the REI debate, then as an institutional practice from the perspective of school organization and adaptability. The focus of this section is the implications of the deconstruction of special education for the discourse on school failure and, ultimately, for the legitimacy of the institutional practice of public education. Considering these implications, however, will require broadening the analysis to include the voice of the general education community and what it has to say about school failure from the perspective of educational excellence. If we think of the mainstreaming and REI debates in special education as two debates within a broader discourse on educational equity, and the effective schools and school restructuring debates in general education as two debates within a broader discourse on educational excellence, we can begin to see how the equity and excellence discourses parallel, mirror, and, ultimately, converge upon one another.[56]

The first parallel is that the initial debate within each discourse was an extreme form of naive pragmatism that merely reproduced the problems it set out to solve. As in the case of mainstreaming and the EHA, the practices that emerged from the effective schools debate reproduced the original problems (Clark & Astuto, 1988; Cuban, 1983, 1989; Slavin, 1989; Stedman, 1987; Timar & Kirp, 1988; Wise, 1988). The second parallel is that the failure of the first debate within each discourse gave rise to the second debate, which, although less naive, was also a form of naive pragmatism that promised to reproduce current problems in the future.

As we will see below, although the restructuring debate is less naive than the effective schools debate, it does not explicitly recognize the connection between general education practices and the four assumptions. As such, like the REI debate in special education, it promises to reproduce the general education problems of the 1980s in the 1990s and beyond (see Cuban, 1983, 1989; Skrtic, 1991a; Wise, 1988).

Although the restructuring debate parallels the REI debate in this second respect, the effects of this pattern in the two debates are mirror images of one another. As we know, the REI debate implicates school organization in the problem of student disability. Thus, the first way that the two debates mirror each other is that, by pointing to the emergence and persistence of homogeneous grouping—curriculum tracking, in-class ability grouping, and compensatory pull-out programs—as an indication of deep structural flaws in traditional school organization (Cuban, 1989; Oakes, 1985, 1986a,b; Stedman, 1987; Wise, 1988), the restructuring debate implicates student disability in the problem of school organization. The second way that the REI and restructuring debates mirror each other is that, although both of them reject two of the four assumptions and question the other two, in the final analysis they retain the assumptions that they question. We saw this pattern for both the REI proponents and opponents relative to the assumptions about the rationality of school organization and change.

The mirror image of this contradiction in the restructuring debate is that, although it rejects the two assumptions about the rationality of school organization and change, it questions but retains the two assumptions about the nature of school failure and diagnosis. That is, although it criticizes the institutional practice of tracking, and even the overrepresentation of minority students in certain special education programs, it does not criticize special education as an institutional practice (see Goodlad, 1984; Oakes, 1986a,b; Sizer, 1984), and thus retains the assumptions that school failure is pathological and that diagnosis is objective and useful.[57]

The restructuring debate does not recognize special education as a form of tracking because its criticism of homogeneous grouping stops at the point of presumed pathology, which is the third and, for present purposes, most important way that the two debates mirror one another. Whereas the REI debate rejects the presupposition of human pathology but retains that of organizational rationality, the restructuring debate rejects organizational rationality but retains human pathology. The significance here, of course, is that the two debates—and thus the discourses on excellence and equity in public education—converge to reject both of the functionalist presuppositions that ground the 20th-century discourse of school failure, and thus they deconstruct it.

The broader significance of the deconstruction of the discourse on school failure is that it provides the grounds for an immanent critique of the institution of public education. That is, confronted with the fact that its practices are neither excellent nor equitable, public education must account for itself without recourse to the distorting and legitimizing effects of the functionalist discourse on school failure. Ultimately, to be able to continue making the claim that it embodies the Jeffersonian ideal of democratic education, public education must reconstruct itself to be both excellent and equitable.

Excellence, Equity, and Adhocracy

We can turn from deconstruction to reconstruction by considering the moments of truth contained in the convergence between excellence and equity in the REI and restructuring debates. As we know, the REI proponents call for virtually eliminating the regulatory requirements of the EHA. The corresponding argument among the proponents of restructuring is for eliminating scientific management as the approach to administration and change (for example, Boyer, 1983; Cuban, 1983, 1989; Goodlad, 1984; Oakes, 1985, 1986a,b; Sirotnik & Oakes, 1986; Sizer, 1984; Wise, 1988).

In organizational terms, the first convergence is that both sets of proponents are arguing for the elimination of rationalization, formalization, and tight coupling—the misplaced structural contingencies of the machine bureaucracy. The second convergence is between the REI proponents' arguments for merging the general and special education systems and the arguments of the restructuring proponents for merging the various general education tracks. Here, both sets of proposals call for the elimination of specialization, professionalization, and loose coupling—the structural contingencies of the professional bureaucracy configuration.

In practical terms, both sets of proponents seek an adaptable system in which increased teacher discretion will lead to more personalized instruction through collaborative problem solving among professionals and client constituencies (Boyer, 1983; Cuban, 1983, 1989; Goodlad, 1984; McNeil, 1986; Oakes, 1985; Sizer, 1984). Of course, because the restructuring proponents retain the assumption of pathology, there are differences between the two sets of proposals. But these are differences in degree, not in kind. In organizational terms, the participants in both debates argue for the introduction of collaboration, mutual adjustment, and discursive coupling—the structural contingencies of the adhocratic form. In principle, both sets of reform proposals require an adhocratic school organization and professional culture.

The REI opponents' position on equity has been that, given the nonadaptability of general education classrooms and school organizations, the targeting function of the EHA and the pull-out logic of mainstreaming must be maintained for political purposes, diagnostic and instructional inadequacies notwithstanding. The moment of truth in this position is the argument that, as long as resources are constant and students differ, no teacher, whether in a general or a special education classroom, can escape the necessary choice between excellence (higher class means) and equity (narrower class variances), unless more powerful instructional technologies are available. In organizational terms, this is true because the structural contingencies of rationalization and formalization circumscribe a finite set of resources relative to a prespecified set of activities and outcomes, while those of specialization and professionalization circumscribe a finite repertoire of standard programs relative to a finite set of presumed client needs. Thus, students whose needs fall on the margins or outside of these standard programs must either be squeezed into them or squeezed out of the classroom.

Given the inevitability of human diversity, a professional bureaucracy can do nothing but create students who do not fit the system. In a professional bureaucracy, all forms of tracking—curriculum tracking and in-class ability grouping in general education, as well as self-contained and resource classrooms in special, compensatory, remedial, and gifted education—are organizational pathologies created by specialization and professionalization and compounded by rationalization and formalization. Students are subjected to—and subjugated by—these practices because, given their structural and cultural contingencies, traditional school organizations cannot accommodate diversity and so must screen it out.

The problem with the REI opponents' argument, however, is that it assumes that nonadaptability is inherent in schooling, rather than in its traditional bureaucratic organization. Student diversity is not an inherent problem for school organizations; it is a problem only when these organizations are premised on standardization and thus configure themselves as performance organizations that perfect standard programs for known contingencies. As we have seen, the adhocratic form is premised on innovation. It configures itself as a problem-solving organization for inventing novel programs for unfamiliar contingencies. Regardless of its causes and its extent, student diversity is not a liability in a problem-solving organization; it is an asset, an enduring uncertainty, and thus the driving force behind innovation, growth of knowledge, and progress.

The problem with the REI and restructuring proposals in this regard is that, although their ends require the adhocratic configuration, their means reproduce the professional bureaucracy configuration. This is so because, by retaining the notion of a classroom, they retain a specialized division of labor, a professionalized means of coordination, and thus a loosely coupled form of interdependency. Both reform approaches eliminate rationalization and formalization—and thus the misplaced machine bureaucracy outer structure of schools—while retaining specialization and professionalization—and thus the professional bureaucracy inner structure.

From an organizational perspective, the argument for eliminating rationalization and formalization is an argument for uniting theory and practice in the professional. The problem with this move in the REI and restructuring proposals, however, is that, by retaining the professional bureaucracy configuration, they unite theory and practice in the individual professional rather than in a team of professionals.[58] From a structural perspective, innovation is "the building of new knowledge and skills, [which] requires the combination of different bodies of existing ones" (Mintzberg, 1979, p. 434). This requires a division of labor and a means of coordination that "break through the boundaries of conventional specialization," creating a situation in which "professionals must amalgamate their efforts [by joining] forces in multidisciplinary teams, each formed around a specific project of innovation" (Mintzberg, 1979, pp. 434–435). From a cultural perspective, repertoires or paradigms of practice are social constructions; innovation occurs when new paradigms emerge through confrontations over uncertainty within social groups (Brown, 1978; Rounds, 1981; Weick, 1979). From an organizational perspective, professional innovation is not a solitary act; when it does occur, it is a social phenomenon that takes place within a reflective discourse.

The problem of uniting theory and practice in the individual professional can be illustrated by considering the genealogy of special education as a professional and institutional practice.[59] The first special classroom teachers were general education teachers who thus had to invent new programs for students who, by definition, had needs that fell outside their repertoire of standard programs. Moreover, because special classrooms were decoupled from the machine bureaucracy structure and thus were relatively free from its rationalization and formalization, theory and practice were united in the special classroom teacher. Because these teachers were decoupled from other regular and special classroom teachers, however, and thus lacked the structural contingencies of collaboration, mutual adjustment, and discursive coupling, they were denied the structural conditions necessary for an adhocratic mode of professional practice to emerge.

The inadequacy of special education practices in the 20th century illustrates the problem with freeing teachers from the outer machine bureaucracy structure of school organizations while retaining the inner professional bureaucracy structure. Although such a move may permit teachers to invent new repertoires, it will not assure that the repertoires they invent will be any more effective, ethical, or, in the long run, much different from what they had been doing before being set free.[60]

From a structural perspective, the REI and restructuring proponents are right about eliminating the rationalization and formalization associated with scientific management and the EHA. At a minimum, achieving their adhocratic ends will require merging theory and practice. Nevertheless, if merging theory and practice is to have the adhocratic effects they desire, they will have to do more than merge general education tracks and the general and special education systems in the ways they have proposed. Achieving their adhocratic ends will require merging theory and practice in conjunction with eliminating specialization and professionalization. This will require eliminating the classroom, which, in structural terms, is an organizational artifact of the structural contingencies of the professional bureaucracy configuration and, in practical terms, the principal barrier to the introduction of collaboration, mutual adjustment, and discursive coupling, the structural contingencies of the adhocracy configuration.

Furthermore, from a cultural perspective, achieving their adhocratic ends will require that an adhocratic professional culture emerge and be sustained within public education. To emerge, such culture will require the structural contingencies of the adhocratic form. To be sustained, it will require an enduring source of uncertainty because, as we saw in the case of NASA, without problems to solve, adhocracies revert to bureaucracies.[61]

In political terms, the institution of public education cannot be democratic unless its practices are excellent and equitable. In organizational terms, its practices cannot be excellent and equitable unless school organizations are adhocratic. In structural and cultural terms, school organizations cannot be adhocratic—and thus cannot be excellent, equitable, or democratic—without the uncertainty of student diversity. In the adhocratic school organization, educational equity is the precondition for educational excellence.

History, Education, and Democracy

Although the evidence on educational excellence, equity, and adaptability is overwhelmingly negative, there are schools that are relatively effective, equitable, and adaptable, including some that have met or surpassed the intent of the EHA and the spirit of mainstreaming.[62] One way to explain this contradictory evidence theoretically is to think of schools as ambiguous, underorganized systems that are shaped by values. Of course, given the organizational history of public education, the value orientation of school organizations and their members tends to be bureaucratic. On occasion, however, someone, some group, or some event increases ambiguity enough to cast doubt on the prevailing paradigm and, under conditions of increased ambiguity, someone or some group, acting on a different set of values, manages to decrease the ambiguity by redefining the organization for itself and others. It is just this sort of organizational phenomenon that one finds in successful schools. Their success turns on human agency, on the values, expectations, and actions of the people who work in them.[63]

Schools can be effective, equitable, and adaptable, but when they are, they are operating more like adhocracies than bureaucracies. And they are operating this way because the people in them are thinking and acting more like problem solvers than performers. They are acting and thinking this way because someone or some group reduced uncertainty by reframing an ambiguous situation in terms of adhocratic values, a subtle process of deconstruction and reconstruction in which organizational members construct a new set of structural and cultural contingencies for themselves and their clients.

Although such an interpretation of today's successful schools provides further support for the adhocratic form, it does not account for the fact that the traditional industrial-era definitions of excellence and equity that have shaped the research on successful schools are losing their relevance with the emergence of post-industrialism. To assess the implications of post-industrialism for public education and the adhocratic form, it will be helpful to consider the arguments put forth in the social reconstruction debate, one of several debates within the progressive education movement earlier in this century (see Kliebard, 1988; Kloppenberg, 1986).

The proponents of social reconstruction were concerned that bureaucracy was distorting democracy. As Weber (1922/1978) explained, democracy and bureaucracy grow coincidentally because actualizing democratic government requires the bureaucratic administrative form. The problem is that, although democracy is supposed to be dynamic, the bureaucracy on which it depends resists change, a problem that, for Weber, was the central and irresolvable fact of the modern state.

In *The Public and Its Problems,* Dewey (1927/1988b) argued that, although industrialization had intensified the problem of bureaucracy, it also provided an opportunity to recover democracy. According to Dewey (1899, 1927/1988b), the problem of bureaucracy is intensified by industrialization because it places more of life—particularly work and education—under the bureaucratic form. This reduces the need for problem solving and discourse, which stunts the growth of reflective thought and, ultimately, undercuts the ability of the public to govern itself. The opportunity posed by industrialization was that it created an expanding network of social interdependencies that Dewey (1929–30/1988a) believed made possible and begged for a way of developing a new sense of social individualism to replace the possessive form of individualism of the 18th and 19th centuries.

For Dewey (1897, 1916, 1927/1988b) and other progressive reformers (see Kloppenberg, 1986), the only meaningful response to the problem and opportunity of the industrial era was to restore the public for democracy through a cultural transformation, which was to be actualized by instituting progressive education in the public schools. Dewey's (1897, 1899, 1916) notion of progressive education was particularly well suited to this end because, as a pedagogy grounded in the antifoundational epistemology of American pragmatism, it was premised on the belief that education in a democracy should both cultivate a sense of social responsibility by developing an awareness of interdependency, and engender a critical attitude toward received knowledge by promoting an appreciation of uncertainty.

The problem, of course, is that the value orientation of progressive education is pluralistic and adhocratic, which contradicts the individualistic and bureaucratic value orientation of public education. Thus, the circularity in the progressive argument for transforming society through education was and still is that:

> If the problems facing society can be traced to its individualism ... and reform must proceed by means of education, how can reformers get around the awkward fact that the educational system is imbued with precisely the values that they have isolated as the source of the problem? (Kloppenberg, 1986, p. 377)

No one grasped the circularity problem better than Weber (1922/1978). Whereas the problem of an unreflective public lay in the contradiction between democracy and bureaucracy in the modern state, he argued that the circularity of trying to solve it through education meant confronting an even greater problem in the logic of modernity itself: the contradiction among democracy, bureaucracy, education, and professionalization. Weber explained that the ever-increasing push to further bureaucratize government and the economy creates the need for more and more experts and thus continually increases the importance of specialized knowledge. But the logic of expertise contradicts democracy because it creates "the struggle of the 'specialist' type of man against the older type of 'cultivated' man" (1922/ 1978, p. 1090). And, because the progressive project is premised on restoring democracy by educating the cultivated citizen, it is stymied because public education itself becomes increasingly bureaucratized in the interest of training specialized experts.

Thus, democracy continues to decline, not only because the bureaucratic form resists change but also because the cultivated citizen continues to disappear. As more of life comes under the control of the professional bureaucracy's standard problem solutions, the need to solve problems and to engage in discourse diminishes even further. This tendency stunts the growth of reflective thought in society and in the professions, which not only undercuts the ability of the public to govern itself democratically but also the ability of the professions to see themselves critically.

The advantage today is that post-industrialism is premised on an even greater and more pervasive form of interdependency and social responsibility. Whereas the network of social interdependencies of industrialization stopped at the boundaries of industrial organizations themselves, post-industrialization extends the network into the very core of the post-industrial organizational form (Drucker, 1989; Naisbitt & Aburdene, 1985; Reich, 1983). The key difference is that industrial organization depended on the machine bureaucracy configuration and thus on the separation of theory and practice and an unreflective, mechanical form of interdependency among workers. Post-industrial organization, however, depends on the adhocratic form; on collaboration, mutual adjustment, and discursive coupling; and on a political form of accountability premised on a community of interests among workers, managers, and, ultimately, among the organizations members, consumers, and host community (Drucker, 1989; Mintzberg, 1979; Reich, 1983, 1990).

Reich (1990), characterized the adhocracies of the post-industrial economy as

> environments in which people can identify and solve problems for themselves," as contexts in which individual skills are integrated into a group.... Over time, as group members work through various problems ... they learn about each others' abilities. They learn how they can help one another perform better, what each can contribute to a particular project, and how they can best take advantage of one another's experience. (p. 201)

The system of education needed for the post-industrial economy is one that prepares young people "to take responsibility for their continuing education, and to collaborate with one another so that their combined skills and insights add up to something more than the sum of their individual contributions" (Reich, 1990, p. 202). As such, educational excellence in the post-industrial era is more than basic numeracy and literacy; it is a capacity for working collaboratively with others and for taking responsibility for learning (Drucker, 1989; Naisbitt & Aburdene, 1985; Reich, 1983).

Moreover, educational equity is a precondition for excellence in the post-industrial era, for collaboration means learning collaboratively with and from persons with varying interests, abilities, skills, and cultural perspectives, and taking responsibility for learning means taking responsibility for one's own learning and that of others. Ability grouping and tracking have no place in such a system because they "reduce young people's capacities to learn from and collaborate with one another" and work against developing a community of interests, a situation that is precluded unless "unity and cooperation are the norm" in schools (Reich, 1990, p. 208).

Given the relevancies of the post-industrial era, the successful school is one that prepares young people to work responsibly and interdependently under conditions of uncertainty. It does this by promoting in its students a sense of social responsibility, an awareness of interdependency, and an appreciation of uncertainty. It achieves these things by developing its students' capacity for experiential learning through collaborative problem solving and reflective discourse within a community of interests. The successful school in the post-industrial era is one that produces cultivated citizens by providing all of its students with the experience of a progressive education in an adhocratic setting. Given the emerging historical conditions of the 21st century, and the fact that democracy is collaborative problem solving through reflective discourse within a community of interests, the adhocratic school organization provides more than a way to reconcile the social goals of educational excellence and educational equity. It provides us with an opportunity to resume the critical project of American pragmatism in public education and, thus, with another chance to save democracy from bureaucracy.

References

Abeson, A., & Zettel, J. (1977). The end of the quiet revolution: The Education for All Handicapped Children Act of 1975. *Exceptional Children, 44*(2), 115–128.

Algozzine, B. (1976). The disturbing child: What you see is what you get? *Alberta Journal of Education Research, 22,* 330–333.

Algozzine, B. (1977). The emotionally disturbed child: Disturbed or disturbing? *Journal of Abnormal Child Psychology, 5*(2), 205–211.

Algozzine, B., & Korinek, L. (1985). Where is special education for students with high prevalence handicaps going? *Exceptional Children, 5*(5), 388–394.

Allington, R. L., & McGill-Franzen, A. (1989). Different programs: Indifferent instruction. In D. K. Lipsky & A. Gartner (Eds.), *Beyond separate education: Quality education for all* (pp. 75–97). Baltimore: Paul H. Brookes.

Antonio, R. J. (1981). Immanent critique as the core of critical theory: Its origins and developments in Hegel, Marx, and contemporary thought. *British Journal of Sociology, 32*(3), 330–345.

Antonio, R. J. (1989). The normative foundations of emancipatory theory: Evolutionary versus pragmatic perspectives. *American Journal of Sociology, 94*(4), 721–748.

Apter, S. J. (1982). *Troubled children, troubled systems.* New York: Pergamon Press.

Bacharach, S. B. (Ed.), (1990). *Education reform: Making sense of it all.* Boston: Allyn & Bacon.

Barnard, C. I. (1938). *Functions of the executive.* Cambridge, MA: Harvard University Press.

Barnes, B. (1982). *T. S. Kuhn and social science.* New York: Columbia University Press.

Bates, R. J. (1980). Educational administration, the sociology of science, and the management of knowledge. *Educational Administration Quarterly, 16*(2), 1–20.

Bates, R. J. (1987). Corporate culture, schooling, and educational administration. *Educational Administration Quarterly, 23*(4), 79–115.

Bennett, R. E., & Ragosta, M. (1984). *A research context for studying admissions tests and handicapped populations.* Princeton, NJ: Educational Testing Service.

Berger, P. L., & Luckmann, T. (1967). *The social construction of reality.* New York: Doubleday.

Berman, P., & McLaughlin, M. W. (1974–1978). *Federal programs supporting educational change* (Vols. 1–8). Santa Monica, CA: Rand.

Bernstein, R. J. (1976). *The restructuring of social and political theory.* Philadelphia: University of Pennsylvania Press.

Bernstein, R. J. (1983). *Beyond objectivism and relativism: Science, hermeneutics, and praxis.* Philadelphia: University of Pennsylvania Press.

Bidwell, C. E. (1965). The school as formal organization. In J. G. March (Ed.), *Handbook of organizations* (pp. 972–1022). Chicago: Rand McNally College Publishing.

Biklen, D. (1985). *Achieving the complete school: Strategies for effective mainstreaming.* New York: Columbia University Press.

Bishop, J. M. (1977). Organizational influences on the work orientations of elementary teachers. *Sociology of Work and Occupation, 4,* 171–208.

Bogdan, R. (1983). Does mainstreaming work? is a silly question. *Phi Delta Kappan, 64,* 425–434.

Bogdan, R., & Knoll, J. (1988). The sociology of disability. In E. L. Meyen & T. M. Skrtic (Eds.), *Exceptional children and youth: An introduction* (pp. 449–477). Denver: Love Publishing.

Bogdan, R., & Kugelmass, J. (1984). Case studies of mainstreaming: A symbolic interactionist approach to special schooling. In L. Barton & S. Tomlinson (Eds.), *Special education and social interests* (pp. 173–191). New York: Nichols.

Bowles, S., & Gintis, H. (1976). *Schooling in capitalist America.* New York: Basic Books.

Boyd, W. L., & Crowson, R. L. (1981). The changing conception and practice of public school administration. In D. C. Berliner (Ed.), *Review of research in education* (pp. 311–373). Itasca, IL: F. E. Peacock.

Boyer, E. L. (1983). *High school.* New York: Harper & Row.

Braaten, S. R., Kauffman, J. M., Braaten, B., Polsgrove, L., & Nelson, C. M. (1988). The regular education initiative: Patent medicine for behavioral disorders. *Exceptional Children, 55*(1), 21–27.

Bridges, E. M. (1982). Research on the school administrator: The state of the art, 1967–1980. *Educational Administration Quarterly, 18*(3), 12–33.

Brophy, J. E. (1983). Research in the self-fulfilling prophesy and teacher expectations. *Journal of Educational Psychology, 75*(5), 631–661.

Brown v. Board of Education (1954). 347 U.S. 483, 74 S.Ct. 686, 98 L.Ed. 873.

Brown, R. H. (1978). Bureaucracy as praxis: Toward a political phenomenology of formal organizations. *Administrative Science Quarterly, 23*(2), 365–382.

Bryan, T., Bay, M., & Donahue, M. (1988). Implications of the learning disabilities definition for the regular education initiative. *Journal of Learning Disabilities, 21*(1), 23–28.

Burns, T., & Stalker, G. M. (1966). *The management of innovation* (2d ed.). London: Tavistock.

Burrell, G., & Morgan, G. (1979). *Sociological paradigms and organizational analysis.* London: Heinemann.

Callahan, R. (1962). *Education and the cult of efficiency.* Chicago: University of Chicago Press.

Campbell, R. F., Fleming, T., Newell, L. J., & Bennion, J. W. (1987). *A history of thought and practice in educational administration.* New York: Teachers College Press.

Carlberg, C., & Kavale, K. (1980). The efficacy of special versus regular class placement for exceptional children: A meta-analysis. *Journal of Special Education, 14,* 295–309.

Chalfant, J., Pysh, M., & Moultrie, R. (1979). Teacher assistance teams: A model of within-building problem solving. *Learning Disabilities Quarterly, 2,* 85–86.

Chandler, J. T., & Plakos, J. (1969). *Spanish-speaking pupils classified as educable mentally retarded.* Sacramento: California State Department of Education.

Chandler, M. D., & Sayles, L. R. (1971). *Managing large systems.* New York: Harper & Row.

Cherryholmes, C. H. (1988). *Power and criticism: Poststructuralist investigations in education.* New York: Teachers College Press.

Christophos, F., & Renz, P. (1969). A critical examination of special education programs. *Journal of Special Education, 3*(4), 371–380.

Churchman, C. W. (1971). *The design of inquiry systems.* New York: Basic Books.

Clark, B. R. (1972). The organizational saga in higher education. *Administrative Science Quarterly, 17,* 178–184.

Clark, D. L. (1985). Emerging paradigms in organizational theory and research. In Y. S. Lincoln (Ed.), *Organizational theory and inquiry: The paradigm revolution* (pp. 43–78). Beverly Hills, CA: Sage.

Clark, D. L., & Astuto, T. A. (1988). *Education policy after Reagan—What next?* (Occasional Paper No. 6). Charlottesville: University of Virginia, Policy Studies Center of the University Council for Educational Administration.

Clark, D. L., Lotto, L. S., & Astuto, T. A. (1984). Effective schools and school improvement: A comparative analysis of two lines of inquiry. *Educational Administration Quarterly, 20*(3), 41–68.

Cohen, M. D., March, J. G., & Olsen, J. P. (1972). A garbage can model of organizational choice. *Administrative Science Quarterly, 17*(2), 1–25.

Conley, S. C. (1990). Reforming paper pushers and avoiding free agents: The teacher as a constrained decision maker. In S. B. Bacharach (Ed.), *Education reform: Making sense of it all.* Boston: Allyn & Bacon.

Council for Children with Behavioral Disorders. (1989). Position statement on the regular education initiative. *Behavioral Disorders, 14,* 201–208.

Cuban, L. (1979). Determinants of curriculum change and stability, 1870-1970. In J. Schaffarzick & G. Sykes (Eds.), *Value conflicts and curriculum issues.* Berkeley, CA: McCutchan.

Cuban, L. (1983). Effective schools: A friendly but cautionary note. *Phi Delta Kappan, 64*(10), 695–696.

Cuban, L. (1989). The "at-risk" label and the problem of urban school reform. *Phi Delta Kappan, 70*(10), 780–784, 799–801.

Cunningham, L. L., Hack, W. G., & Nystrand, R. O. (Eds.). (1977). *Educational administration: The developing decades.* Berkeley, CA: McCutchan.

Dallmayr, F. R., & McCarthy, T. A. (1977). *Understanding and social inquiry.* Notre Dame, IN: University of Notre Dame Press.

Dalton, M. (1959). *Men who manage.* New York: Wiley.

Davis, W. E. (1989). The regular initiative debate: Its promises and problems. *Exceptional Children, 55*(5), 440–446.

Davis, W. E., & McCaul, E. J. (1988). *New perspectives on education: A review of the issues and implications of the regular education initiative.* Orono, ME: Institute for Research and Policy Analysis on the Education of Students with Learning and Adjustment Problems.

Deno, E. (1970). Special education as developmental capital. *Exceptional Children, 37*(3), 229–237.

Derrida, J. (1982a). *Dissemination* (B. Johnson, Trans.). London: Athlone Press. (Original work published 1972)

Derrida, J. (1982b). *Margins of philosophy* (A. Bass, Trans.). Chicago: University of Chicago Press. (Original work published 1972)

Dewey, J. (1897). My pedagogic creed. *School Journal, 54*(3), 77–80.

Dewey, J. (1899). *The school and society.* Chicago: University of Chicago Press.

Dewey, J. (1916). *Democracy and education.* New York: Macmillan.

Dewey, J. (1988a). Individualism, old and new. In J. A. Boydston (Ed.), *John Dewey: The later works, 1925–1953:* Vol. 5. 1929–1930 (pp. 41–123). Carbondale: Southern Illinois University Press. (Original work published 1929–1930)

Dewey, J. (1988b). The public and its problems. In J. A. Boydston (Ed.), *John Dewey: The later works, 1925–1953:* Vol. 2. 1925–1927 (pp. 235–372). Carbondale: Southern Illinois University Press. (Original work published 1927)

Dreyfus, H. L., & Rabinow, P. (Eds.). (1983). *Michel Foucault: Beyond structuralism and hermeneutics.* Chicago: University of Chicago Press.

Drucker, P. F. (1989). *The new realities.* New York: Harper & Row.

Dunn, L. M. (1968). Special education for the mildly retarded—Is much of it justifiable? *Exceptional Children, 35*(1), 5–22.

Edgar, E. (1987). Secondary programs in special education: Are many of them justified? *Exceptional Children, 53,* 555–561.

Edmonds, R. (1979). Some schools work and more can. *Social Policy, 9*(5), 26–31.

Elmore, R. F. (1987). *Early experiences in restructuring schools: Voices from the field.* Results in Education series. Washington, DC: National Governors Association.

Elmore, R. F., & McLaughlin, M. W. (1982). Strategic choice in federal education policy: The compliance-assistance trade-off. In A. Lieberman & M. W. McLaughlin (Eds.), *Policy making in education: Eighty-first yearbook of the National Society for the Study of Education* (pp. 159–194). Chicago: University of Chicago Press.

Elmore, R. F., & McLaughlin, M. W. (1988). *Steady work: Policy, practice, and the reform of American education.* Santa Monica, CA: Rand.

Erickson, D. A. (1979). Research on educational administration: The state-of-the-art. *Educational Researcher, 8*(3), 9–14.

Feinberg, W., & Soltis, J. F. (1985). *School and society.* New York: Teachers College Press.

Foster, W. (1986). *Paradigms and promises: New approaches to educational administration.* Buffalo, NY: Prometheus Books.

Foucault, M. (1973). *Madness and civilization: A history of insanity in the age of reason* (R. Howard, Trans.). New York: Vintage/Random House. (Original work published 1961)

Foucault, M. (1975). *The birth of the clinic: An archeology of medical perception* (A. M. Sheridan Smith, Trans.). New York: Vintage/Random House. (Original work published 1963)

Foucault, M. (1976). *Mental illness and psychology.* Berkeley: University of California Press. (Original work published 1954)

Foucault, M. (1979). Discipline and punish: The birth of the prison (A. M. Sheridan Smith, Trans.). New York: Vintage/Random House. (Original work published 1975)

Foucault, M. (1980). *Power/knowledge: Selected interviews and other writings, 1972–1977* (C. Gordon, Ed.; C. Gordon, L. Marshall, J. Mepham, & K. Soper, Trans.). New York: Pantheon Books.

Foucault, M. (1983). The subject and power. In H. L. Dreyfus & P. Rabinow (Eds.), *Michel Foucault: Beyond structuralism and hermeneutics* (pp. 208–226). Chicago: University of Chicago Press.

Gadamer, H-G. (1975). *Truth and method* (G. Barden & J. Cumming, Eds. & Trans.). New York: Seabury Press.

Gartner, A. (1986). Disabling help: Special education at the crossroads. *Exceptional Children, 53*(1), 72–79.

Gartner, A., & Lipsky, D. K. (1987). Beyond special education: Toward a quality system for all students. *Harvard Educational Review, 57*(4), 367–390.

Gartner, A., & Lipsky, D. K. (1989). The yoke of special education: How to break it. Rochester, NY: National Center on Education and the Economy.

Geertz, C. (1983). *Local knowledge: Further essays in interpretive anthropology.* New York: Basic Books.

Gerardi, R. J., Grohe, B., Benedict, G. C., & Coolidge, P. G. (1984). I.E.P.—More paperwork and wasted time. *Contemporary Education, 56*(1), 39–42.

Gerber, M. M. (1987). Application of cognitive–behavioral training methods to teach basic skills to mildly handicapped elementary school students. In M. C. Wang, M. C. Reynolds, & H. J. Walberg (Eds.), *Handbook of special education: Research and practice: Vol. 1. Learner characteristics and adaptive education* (pp. 167–186). Oxford, UK: Pergamon Press.

Gerber, M. M. (1988a). Tolerance and technology of instruction: Implications for special education reform. *Exceptional Children, 54*(4), 309–314.

Gerber, M. M. (1988b, May 4). Weighing the regular education initiative: Recent calls for change lead to slippery slope. *Education Week,* pp. 36, 28.

Gerber, M. M., & Levine–Donnerstein, D. (1989). Educating all children: Ten years later. *Exceptional Children, 56*(1), 17–27.

Gerber, M. M., & Semmel, M. I. (1984). Teacher as imperfect test: Reconceptualizing the referral process. *Educational Psychologist, 19,* 137–148.

Gerber, M. M., & Semmel, M. I. (1985). The microeconomics of referral and reintegration: A paradigm for evaluation of special education. *Studies in Educational Evaluation, 11,* 13–29.

Getzels, J. W., & Guba, E. G. (1957). Social behavior and the administrative process. *School Review, 65,* 423–441.

Gilhool, T. K. (1976). Changing public policies: Roots and forces. In M. C. Reynolds (Ed.), *Mainstreaming: Origins and implications* (pp. 8–13). Reston, VA: Council for Exceptional Children.

Gilhool, T. K. (1989). The right to an effective education: From Brown to P. L. 94–142 and beyond. In D. K. Lipsky & A. Gartner (Eds.), *Beyond separate education: Quality education for all* (pp. 243–253). Baltimore: Paul H. Brookes.

Giroux, H. A. (1981). *Ideology, culture, and the process of schooling.* Philadelphia: Temple University Press.

Giroux, H. A. (1983). Theories of reproduction and resistance in the new sociology of education: A critical analysis. *Harvard Educational Review, 58*(3), 257–293.

Glazer, N. (1974). The schools of the minor professions. *Minerva, 12*(3), 346–364.

Golding, D. (1980). Establishing blissful clarity in organizational life: Managers. *Sociological Review, 28,* 763–782.

Goldman, J., & Gardner, H. (1989). Multiple paths to educational effectiveness. In D. K. Lipsky & A. Gartner (Eds.), *Beyond separate education: Quality education for all* (pp. 121–139). Baltimore: Paul H. Brookes.

Goodlad, J. I. (1975). *The dynamics of educational change.* New York: McGraw-Hill.

Goodlad, J. I. (1984). *A place called school: Prospects for the future.* New York: McGraw-Hill.

Greer, C. (1972). *The great school legend: A revisionist interpretation of American public education.* New York: Basic Books.

Griffiths, D. E. (1959). *Administrative theory.* New York: Appleton-Century-Crofts.

Griffiths, D. E. (1979). Intellectual turmoil in educational administration. *Educational Administration Quarterly, 15*(3), 43–65.

Griffiths, D. E. (1983). Evolution in research and theory: A study of prominent researchers. *Educational Administration Quarterly, 19*(3), 201–221.

Griffiths, D. E. (1988). Administrative theory. In N. J. Boyan (Ed.), *Handbook of research on educational administration* (pp. 27–51). New York: Longman.

Haber, S. (1964). *Efficiency and uptight: Scientific management in the progressive era, 1890–1920.* Chicago: University of Chicago Press.

Hallahan, D. P., & Kauffman, J. M. (1977). Categories, labels, behavioral characteristics: ED, LD, and EMR reconsidered. *Journal of Special Education, 11,* 139–149.

Hallahan, D. P., Kauffman, J. M., Lloyd, J. W., & McKinney, J. D. (1988). Introduction to the series: Questions about the regular education initiative. *Journal of Learning Disabilities, 21*(1), 3–5.

Hallahan, D. P., & Keller, C. E. (1986). *Study of studies for learning disabilities: A research review and synthesis.* Charleston: West Virginia Department of Education.

Hallahan, D. P., Keller, C. E., McKinney, J. D., Lloyd, J. W., & Bryan, T. (1988). Examining the research base of the regular education initiative: Efficacy studies and the adaptive learning environments model. *Journal of Learning Disabilities, 21*(1), 29–35; 55.

Halpin, A. W. (1970). Administrative theory: The fumbled torch. In A. M. Kroll (Ed.), *Issues in American education.* New York: Oxford University Press.

Halpin, A. W., & Hayes, A. E. (1977). The broken ikon, or Whatever happened to theory? In L. L. Cummingham, W. G. Hack, & R. O. Nystrand (Eds.), *Educational administration: The developing decades* (pp. 261–297). Berkeley, CA: McCutchan.

Hayes, D., & Pharis, W. (1967). *National conference of professors of educational administration.* Lincoln: University of Nebraska Press.

Hegel, G. W. F. (1977). *Phenomenology of spirit.* Oxford, UK: Clarendon Press. (Original work published 1807)

Heller, K., Holtzman, W., & Messick, S. (1982). *Placing children in special education: A strategy for equity.* Washington, DC: National Academy of Sciences Press.

Heller, W. H., & Schilit, J. (1987). The regular education initiative: A concerned response. *Focus on Exceptional Children, 20*(3), 1–6.

Heshusius, L. (1982). At the heart of the advocacy dilemma: A mechanistic world view. *Exceptional Children, 49*(1), 6–13.

Hobbs, N. (1975). *The futures of children: Categories, labels, and their consequences.* San Francisco: Jossey-Bass.

Hobbs, N. (1980). An ecologically oriented service-based system for the classification of handicapped children. In E. Salzinger, J. Antrobus, & J. Glick (Eds.), *The ecosystem of the "risk" child* (pp. 271–290). New York: Academic Press.

Horkheimer, M. (1974). *Eclipse of reason.* New York: Seabury. (Original work published 1947)

House, E. R. (1979). Technology versus craft: A ten-year perspective on innovation. *Journal of Curriculum Studies, 11*(1), 1–15.

Hoy, D. (1985). Jacques Derrida. In Q. Skinner (Ed.), *The return of grand theory in the human sciences* (pp. 83–100). Cambridge, UK: Cambridge University Press.

Iano, R. P. (1986). The study and development of teaching: With implications for the advancement of special education. *Remedial and Special Education, 7*(5), 50–61.

Johnson, G. O. (1962). Special education for the mentally handicapped—A paradox. *Exceptional Children, 29*(2), 62–69.

Jonsson, S. A., & Lundin, R. A. (1977). Myths and wishful thinking as management tools. In P. C. Nystrom & W. H. Starbuck (Eds.), *Prescriptive models of organizations* (pp. 157–170). New York: Elsevier North-Holland.

Kauffman, J. M. (1988). Revolution can also mean returning to the starting point: Will school psychology help special education complete the circuit? *School Psychology Review, 17,* 490–494.

Kauffman, J. M. (1989a). *The regular education initiative as Reagan–Bush education policy: A trickle-down theory of education of the hard-to-teach.* Austin, TX: Pro-Ed.

Kauffman, J. M. (1989b). The regular education initiative as Reagan–Bush education policy: A trickle-down theory of education of the hard-to-teach. *Journal of Special Education, 23*(3), 256–278.

Kauffman, J. M., Gerber, M. M., & Semmel, M. I. (1988). Arguable assumptions underlying the regular education initiative. *Journal of Learning Disabilities, 21*(1), 6–11.

Keogh, B. K. (1988). Improving services for problem learners: Rethinking and restructuring. *Journal of Learning Disabilities, 21*(1), 19–22.

Keogh, B. K., & Levitt, M. L. (1976). Special education in the mainstream: A confrontation of limitations? *Focus on Exceptional Children, 8,* 1–11.

Kiel, D. C., & Skrtic, T. M. (1988). *Modes of organizational accountability: An ideal type analysis.* Unpublished manuscript, University of Kansas, Lawrence.

Kirk, S. A., & Chalfant, J. D. (1983). *Academic and developmental learning disabilities.* Denver: Love.

Kliebard, H. M. (1988). The effort to reconstruct the modern American curriculum. In L. E. Beyer & M. W. Apple (Eds.), *The curriculum: Problems, politics, and possibilities* (pp. 19–31). Albany: State University of New York Press.

Kloppenberg, J. T. (1986). *Uncertain victory: Social democracy and progressivism in European and American thought, 1870–1920.* New York: Oxford University Press.

Kojeve, A. (1969). *Introduction to the reading of Hegel.* New York: Basic Books.

Kuhn, T. (1970). *The structure of scientific revolutions* (2d ed.). Chicago: University of Chicago Press.

Lazerson, M. (1983). The origins of special education. In J. G. Chambers & W. T. Hartman (Eds.), *Special education policies: Their history, implementation, and finance.* Philadelphia: Temple University Press.

Lehming, R., & Kane, M. (1981). *Improving schools: Using what we know.* Beverly Hills, CA: Sage.

Lezotte, L. W. (1989). School improvement based on the effective schools research. In D. K. Lipsky & A. Gartner (Eds.), *Beyond separate education: Quality education for all* (pp. 25–37). Baltimore: Paul H. Brookes.

Lieberman, A., & Miller, L. (1984). *Teachers, their world and their work: Implications for school improvement.* Alexandria, VA: Association for Supervision and Curriculum Development.

Lieberman, L. M. (1984). *Preventing special education ... for those who don't need it.* Newton, MA: GloWorm Publications.

Lieberman, L. M. (1985). Special education and regular education: A merger made in heaven? *Exceptional Children, 51*(6), 513–516.

Lieberman, L. M. (1988). *Preserving special education ... for those who need it.* Newton, MA: GloWorm Publications.

Lilly, M. S. (1986, March). The relationship between general and special education: A new face on an old issue. *Counterpoint, 6*(1), p. 10.

Lilly, M. S. (1987). Lack of focus on special education in literature on education reform. *Exceptional Children, 53*(4), 325–326.

Lilly, M. S. (1989). Teacher preparation. In D. K. Lipsky & A. Gartner (Eds.), *Beyond separate education: Quality education for all* (pp. 143–157). Baltimore: Paul H. Brookes.

Lincoln, Y. S. (Ed.). (1985). *Organizational theory and inquiry: The paradigm revolution.* Beverly Hills, CA: Sage.

Lincoln, Y. S., & Guba, E. G. (1985). *Naturalistic inquiry.* Beverly Hills, CA: Sage.

Lipsky, D. K., & Gartner, A. (1987). Capable of achievement and worthy of respect: Education for handicapped students as if they were full-fledged human beings. *Exceptional Children, 54*(1), 69–74.

Lipsky, D. K., & Gartner, A. (Eds.). (1989a). *Beyond separate education: Quality education for all.* Baltimore: Paul H. Brookes.

Lipsky, D. K., & Gartner, A. (1989b). School administration and financial arrangements. In S. Stainback, W. Stainback, & M. Forest (Eds.), *Educating all students in the mainstream of regular education* (pp. 105–120). Baltimore: Paul H. Brookes.

Lipsky, M. (1975). Toward a theory of street-level bureaucracy. In W. D. Hawley, M. Lipsky, S. B. Greenberg, J. D. Greenstone, I. Katznelson, K. Orren, P. E. Peterson, M. Shefter, & D. Yates (Eds.), *Theoretical perspectives on urban politics* (pp. 196–213). Englewood Cliffs, NJ: Prentice-Hall.

Lloyd, J. W., Crowley, E. P., Kohler, F. W., & Strain, P. S. (1988). Redefining the applied research agenda: Cooperative learning, prereferral, teacher consultation, and peer-mediated interventions. *Journal of Learning Disabilities, 21*(1), 43–52.

Lortie, D. C. (1975). *Schoolteacher: A sociological study.* Chicago: University of Chicago Press.

Lortie, D. C. (1978). Some reflections on renegotiation. In M. C. Reynolds (Ed.), *Futures of education for exceptional students: Emerging structures* (pp. 235–243). Reston, VA: Council for Exceptional Children.

Lyotard, J. F. (1984). *The postmodern condition: A report on knowledge.* Minneapolis: University of Minnesota Press. (Original work published 1979)

MacMillan, D. L. (1971). Special education for the mildly retarded: Servant or savant? *Focus on Exceptional Children, 2*(9), 1–11.

MacMillan, D. L., & Semmel, M. I. (1977). Evaluation of mainstreaming programs. *Focus on Exceptional Children, 9*(4), 1–14.

March, J. G., & Olsen, J. P. (1976). *Ambiguity and choice in organizations.* Bergen, Norway: Universitetsforlaget.

Martin, E. (1978). Preface. In M. C. Reynolds (Ed.), *Futures of education for exceptional students* (pp. iii–vi). Reston, VA: Council for Exceptional Children.

McDonnell, L. M., & McLaughlin, M. W. (1982). *Education policy and the role of the states.* Santa Monica, CA: Rand.

McKinney, J. D., & Hocutt, A. M. (1988). The need for policy analysis in evaluating the regular education initiative. *Journal of Learning Disabilities, 21*(1), 12–18.

McNeil, L. M. (1986). *Contradictions of control: School structure and school knowledge.* New York: Methuen/Routledge & Kegan Paul.

Meier, D. (1984). "Getting tough" in the schools. *Dissent, 31,* 61–70.

Mercer, J. (1973). *Labeling the mentally retarded: Clinical and social system perspectives on mental retardation.* Berkeley: University of California Press.

Mesinger, J. F. (1985). Commentary on "A rationale for the merger of special and regular education." *Exceptional Children, 5*(6), 510–512.

Meyer, J. W., & Rowan, B. (1977). Institutionalized organizations: Formal structure as myth and ceremony. *American Journal of Sociology, 83,* 340–363.

Meyer, J. W., & Rowan, B. (1978). The structure of educational organizations. In M. W. Meyer (Ed.), *Environments and organizations* (pp. 78–109). San Francisco: Jossey-Bass.

Meyer, J. W., & Scott, W. R. (1983). *Organizational environments: Ritual and rationality.* Beverly Hills, CA, Sage.

Meyer, M. W. (1979). Organizational structure as signaling. *Pacific Sociological Review, 22* (4), 481–500.

Miller, D., & Mintzberg, H. (1983). The case for configuration. In G. Morgan (Ed.), *Beyond method: Strategies for social research* (pp. 57–73). Beverly Hills, CA: Sage.

Mintzberg, H. (1979). *The structuring of organizations.* Englewood Cliffs, NJ: Prentice-Hall.

Mitroff, I. I., & Pondy, L. R. (1974, September/October). On the organization of inquiry: A comparison of some radically different approaches to policy analysis. *Public Administration Review,* pp. 471–479.

Mommsen, W. J. (1974). *The age of bureaucracy: Perspectives on the political sociology of Max Weber.* New York: Harper & Row.

Morgan, G. (Ed.). (1983). *Beyond method: Strategies for social research.* Beverly Hills, CA: Sage.

Murphy, J. T. (1989). The paradox of decentralizing schools: Lessons from business, government, and the Catholic Church. *Phi Delta Kappan, 70*(10), 808–812.

Naisbitt, J., & Aburdene, P. (1985). *Re-inventing the corporation.* New York: Warner Books.

National Advisory Committee on the Education of the Handicapped (1976). Subcommittee on Education of the Committee on Labor and public welfare. Washington, DC: U.S. Government Printing Office.

National Commission on Excellence in Education. (1983). *A nation at risk: The imperative for educational reform.* Washington, DC: Government Printing Office.

Noel, M. M., & Fuller, B. C. (1985). The social policy construction of special education: The impact of state characteristics on identification and integration of handicapped children. *Remedial and Special Education, 6*(3), 27–35.

Oakes, J. (1985). *Keeping track: How schools structure inequality.* New Haven, CT: Yale University Press.

Oakes, J. (1986a). Keeping track, Part 1: The policy and practice of curriculum inequality. *Phi Delta Kappan, 68*(1), 12–17.

Oakes, J. (1986b). Keeping track, Part 2: Curriculum inequality and school reform. *Phi Delta Kappan, 68*(2), 148–154.

Patrick, J., & Reschly, D. (1982). Relationship of state educational criteria and demographic variables to school-system prevalence of mental retardation. *American Journal of Mental Retardation, 86,* 351–360.

Perrow, C. (1970). *Organizational analysis: A sociological review.* Belmont, CA: Wadsworth.

Perrow, C. (1978). Demystifying organizations. In R. C. Sarri & Y. Hasenfeld (Eds.), *The management of human services* (pp. 105–120). New York: Columbia University Press.

Pettigrew, A. (1979). On studying organizational cultures. *Administrative Science Quarterly, 24*(4), 570–581.

Pfeffer, J. (1982). *Organizations and organization theory.* Marshfield, MA: Pitman Publishing.

Philip, M. (1985). Michel Foucault. In Q. Skinner (Ed.), *The return of grand theory in the human sciences* (pp. 65–81). Cambridge, UK: Cambridge University Press.

Poplin, M. S. (1987). Self-imposed blindness: The scientific method in education. *Remedial and Special Education, 8*(6), 31–37.

Pugach, M. (1988). The consulting teacher in the context of educational reform. *Exceptional Children, 55*(3), 266–277.

Pugach, M., & Lilly, M. S. (1984). Reconceptualizing support services for classroom teachers: Implications for teacher education. *Journal of Teacher Education, 35*(5), 48–55.

Pugach, M., & Sapon-Shevin, M. (1987). New agendas for special education policy: What the regular education reports haven't said. *Exceptional Children, 53*(4), 295–299.

Pugh, D. S., Hickson, D. J., Hinnings, C. R., MacDonald, K. M., Turner, C., & Lupton, T. (1963). A conceptual scheme for organizational analysis. *Administrative Science Quarterly, 8*(4), 289–315.

Reich, R. B. (1983). *The next American frontier.* New York: Penguin.

Reich, R. B. (1990). Education and the next economy. In S. B. Bacharach (Ed.), *Education reform: Making sense of it all* (pp. 194–212). Boston: Allyn & Bacon.

Resnick, D., & Resnick, L. (1985). Standards, curriculum, and performance: Historical and comparative perspectives. *Educational Researcher, 14*(4), 5–20.

Reynolds, M. C. (1962). A framework for considering some issues in special education. *Exceptional Children, 28*(5), 367–370.

Reynolds, M. C. (1976, November 22–23). *New perspectives on the instructional cascade.* Paper presented at the conference "The Least Restrictive Alternatives: A Partnership of General and Special Education," sponsored by Minneapolis Public Schools, Special Education Division.

Reynolds, M. C. (1988). A reaction to the JLD special series on the regular education initiative. *Journal of Learning Disabilities, 21*(6), 352–356.

Reynolds, M. C., & Birch, J. W. (1977). *Teaching exceptional children in all America's schools.* Reston, VA: Council for Exceptional Children.

Reynolds, M. C., & Lakin, K. C. (1987). Noncategorical special education: Models for research and practice. In M. C. Wang, M. C. Reynolds, & H. J. Walberg (Eds.), *Handbook of special education: Research and practice: Vol. 1. Learner characteristics and adaptive education* (pp. 331–356). Oxford, UK: Pergamon Press.

Reynolds, M. C., & Rosen, S. W. (1976, May). Special education: Past, present, and future. *Education Forum,* pp. 3–9.

Reynolds, M. C., & Wang, M. C. (1981, October). *Restructuring "special" school programs: A position paper.* Paper presented at National Invitational Conference on Public Policy and the Special Education Task of the 1980s, Racine, WI.

Reynolds, M. C., & Wang, M. C. (1983). Restructuring "special" school programs: A position paper. *Policy Studies Review, 2*(1), 189–212.

Reynolds, M. C., Wang, M. C., & Walberg, H. J. (1987). The necessary restructuring of special and general education. *Exceptional Children, 53*(5), 391–398.

Rhodes, W. C. (1970). A community participation analysis of emotional disturbance. *Exceptional Children, 36,* 306–314.

Ricoeur, P. (1981). *Paul Ricoeur: Hermeneutics and the human sciences* (J. B. Thompson, Ed. & Trans.). Cambridge, UK: Cambridge University Press.

Rist, R., & Harrell, J. (1982). Labeling and the learning disabled child: The social ecology of educational practice. *American Journal of Orthopsychiatry, 52*(1), 146–160.

Ritzer, G. (1980). *Sociology: A multiple paradigm science.* Boston: Allyn & Bacon.

Ritzer, G. (1983). *Sociological theory.* New York: Alfred A. Knopf.

Romzek, B. S., & Dubnick, M. J. (1987). Accountability in the public sector: Lessons from the Challenger tragedy. *Public Administration Review, 47*(3), 227–238.

Rorty, R. (1979). *Philosophy and the mirror of nature.* Princeton, NJ: Princeton University Press.

Rorty, R. (1982). *Consequences of pragmatism.* Minneapolis: University of Minnesota Press.

Rorty, R. (1989). *Contingency, irony, and solidarity.* Cambridge, UK: Cambridge University Press.

Ross, A. O. (1980). *Psychological disorders of children.* New York: McGraw-Hill.

Rounds, J. (1979). *Social theory, public policy and social order.* Unpublished doctoral dissertation, University of California, Los Angeles.

Rounds, J. (1981). *Information and ambiguity in organizational change.* Paper presented at Carnegie-Mellon Symposium on Information Processing in Organizations, Carnegie–Mellon University, Pittsburgh.

Rowan, B. (1980). *Organizational structure and the institutional environment: The case of public schools.* Unpublished manuscript, Texas Christian University, Fort Worth.

Ryan, M. (1982). *Marxism and deconstruction.* Baltimore: Johns Hopkins Press.

Sailor, W., & Guess, D. (1983). *Severely handicapped students: An instructional design.* Boston: Houghton Mifflin.

Sailor, W., Halvorsen, A., Anderson, J., Goetz, L., Gee, K., Doering, K., & Hunt, P. (1986). Community intensive instruction. In R. Horner, L. Meyer, & H. Fredericks (Eds.), *Education of learners with severe handicaps* (pp. 251–288). Baltimore: Paul H. Brookes.

Sapon-Shevin, M. (1987). The national education reports and special education: Implications for students. *Exceptional Children, 53*(4), 300–307.

Sapon-Shevin, M. (1988). Working towards merger together: Seeing beyond distrust and fear. *Teacher Education and Special Education, 11*(3), 103–110.

Sarason, S. B. (1971/1982). *The culture of the school and the problem of change* (orig. ed. 1971; rev. ed. 1982). Boston: Allyn & Bacon.

Sarason, S. B., & Doris, J. (1979). *Educational handicap, public policy, and social history.* New York: Free Press.

Schein, E. H. (1972). *Professional education.* New York: McGraw-Hill.

Schenck, S. J. (1980). The diagnostic/instructional link in individualized education programs. *Journal of Special Education, 14*(3), 337–345.

Schenck, S. J., & Levy, W. K. (1979, April). *IEPS: The state of the art—1978.* Paper presented at annual meeting of American Educational Research Association, San Francisco.

Schön, D. A. (1983). *The reflective practitioner: How professionals think in action.* New York: Basic Books.

Schön, D. A. (1987). *Educating the reflective practitioner: Toward a design for teaching and learning in the professions.* San Francisco: Jossey-Bass.

Schön, D. A. (1988). Coaching reflective practice. In P. Grimmett & G. Erickson (Eds.), *Reflection in teacher education.* New York: Teachers College Press.

Schön, D. A. (1989). Professional knowledge and reflective practice. In T. Sergiovanni & J. Moore (Eds.), *Schooling for tomorrow: Directing reforms to issues that count.* Boston: Allyn & Bacon.

Schrag, P., & Divorky, D. (1975). *The myth of the hyperactive child.* New York: Pantheon.

Schroyer, T. (1973). *The critique of domination.* Boston: Beacon Press.

Schumaker, J. B., & Deshler, D. D. (1988). Implementing the regular education initiative in secondary schools: A different ball game. *Journal of Learning Disabilities, 21*(l), 36–42.

Schwartz, P., & Ogilvy, J. (1979). *The emergent paradigm: Changing patterns of thought and belief.* Menlo Park, CA: SRI International.

Scott, R. W. (1981). *Organizations: Rational, natural, and open systems.* Englewood Cliffs, NJ: Prentice-Hall.

Segal, M. (1974). Organization and environment: A typology of adaptability and structure. *Public Administration Review, 34*(3), 212–220.

Sergiovanni, T. J., & Moore, J. H. (Eds.). (1989). *Schooling for tomorrow.* Boston: Allyn & Bacon.

Shepard, L. A. (1987). The new push for excellence: Widening the schism between regular and special education. *Exceptional Children, 53*(4), 327–329.

Simon, H. A. (1977). *The new science of management decision.* Englewood Cliffs, NJ: Prentice- Hall.

Singer, J. D., & Butler, J. A. (1987). The Education for All Handicapped Children Act: Schools as agents of social reform. *Harvard Educational Review, 57*(2), 125–152.

Sirotnik, K. A., & Oakes, J. (1986). *Critical perspectives on the organization and improvement of schooling.* Boston: Kluwer–Nijhoff Publishing.

Sizer, T. R. (1984). *Horace's compromise: The dilemma of the American high school.* Boston: Houghton Mifflin.

Skinner, Q. (Ed.). (1985). *The return of grand theory in the human sciences.* Cambridge, UK: Cambridge University Press.

Skrtic, T. M. (1986). The crisis in special education knowledge: A perspective on perspective. *Focus on Exceptional Children, 18*(7), 1–16.

Skrtic, T. M. (1987a). An organizational analysis of special education reform. *Counterpoint, 8*(2), 15–19.

Skrtic, T. M. (1987b). The national inquiry into the future of education for students with special needs. *Counterpoint, 7*(4), 6.

Skrtic, T. M. (1988a). The crisis in special education knowledge. In E. L. Meyen & T. M. Skrtic (Eds.), *Exceptional children and youth: An introduction* (pp. 415–447). Denver: Love.

Skrtic, T. M. (1988b). The organizational context of special education. In E. L. Meyen & T. M. Skrtic (Eds.), *Exceptional children and youth: An introduction* (pp. 479–517). Denver: Love.

Skrtic, T.M. (1990a, August 10–14). *School psychology and the revolution in modern knowledge.* Paper presented at American Psychology Association Convention, Boston.

Skrtic, T. M. (1990b). Social accommodation: Toward a dialogical discourse in educational inquiry. In E. G. Guba (Ed.), *The paradigm dialog: Options for inquiry in the social sciences* (pp. 125–135). Beverly Hills, CA: Sage.

Skrtic, T. M. (1991a). *Behind special education: A critical analysis of professional knowledge and school organization.* Denver: Love.

Skrtic, T. M. (1991b). Students with special educational needs: Artifacts of the traditional curriculum. In M. Ainscow (Ed.), *Effective schools for all* (pp. 20–42). London: David Fulton Publishers.

Skrtic, T. M., Guba, E. G., & Knowlton, H. E. (1985). *Interorganizational special education programming in rural areas: Technical report on the multisite naturalistic field study.* Washington, DC: National Institute of Education.

Skrtic, T. M., & Ware, L. P. (1992). Reflective teaching and the problem of school organization. In E. W. Ross, G. McCutcheon, & J. Cornett (Eds.), *Teacher personal theorizing: Connecting curriculum practice, theory, and research.* Albany, New York: State University of New York Press (pgs. 207–218. 298–303).

Slavin, R. E. (1989). PET and the pendulum: Faddism in education and how to stop it. *Phi Delta Kappan, 70*(10), 752–758.

Spring, J. (1980). *Educating the worker-citizen: The social, economic, and political foundations of education.* New York: Longman.

Stainback, S., & Stainback, W. (1984). A rationale for the merger of special and regular education. *Exceptional Children, 51*(2), 102–111.

Stainback, S., & Stainback, W. (1985a). *Integration of students with severe handicaps into regular schools.* Reston, VA: Council for Exceptional Children.

Stainback, S., & Stainback, W. (1985b). The merger of special and regular education: Can it be done? A response to Lieberman and Mesinger. *Exceptional Children, 51*(6), 517–521.

Stainback, S., & Stainback, W. (1987a). Facilitating merger through personnel preparation. *Teacher Education and Special Education, 10*(4), 185–190.

Stainback, S., & Stainback, W. (1987b). Integration versus cooperation: A commentary on educating children with learning problems: A shared responsibility. *Exceptional Children, 54*(1), 66–68.

Stainback, S., & Stainback, W. (1989). Integration of students with mild and moderate handicaps. In D. K. Lipsky & A. Gartner (Eds.), *Beyond separate education: Quality education for all* (pp. 41–52). Baltimore: Paul H. Brookes.

Stainback, S., Stainback, W., & Forest, M. (Eds.). (1989). *Educating all students in the mainstream of regular education.* Baltimore: Paul H. Brookes.

Stainback, W., Stainback, S., Courtnage, L., & Jaben, T. (1985). Facilitating mainstreaming by modifying the mainstream. *Exceptional Children, 52*(2), 144–152.

Stedman, L. C. (1987). It's time we changed the effective schools formula. *Phi Delta Kappan, 69*(3), 215–224.

Swap, S. (1978). The ecological model of emotional disturbance in children: A status report and proposed synthesis. *Behavioral Disorders, 3*(3), 156–186.

Teacher Education Division of the Council for Exceptional Children. (1986, October). *Message to all TED members concerning The National Inquiry into the Future of Education for Students with Special Needs.* Reston, VA: Author.

Teacher Education Division, Council for Exceptional Children. (1987). The regular education initiative: A statement by the Teacher Education Division, Council for Exceptional Children. *Journal of Learning Disabilities, 20*(5), 289–293.

Thompson, J. D. (1967). *Organizations in action.* New York: McGraw-Hill.

Thousand, J. S. (1990). Organizational perspectives on teacher education and school renewal: A conversation with Tom Skrtic. *Teacher Education and Special Education, 13*(1), 30–35.

Thousand, J. S., Fox, T., Reid, R., Godek, J., & Williams, W. (1986). *The homecoming model: Educating students who present intensive educational challenges within regular education environments* (Monograph No. 7–1). Burlington: University of Vermont, Center for Developmental Disabilities.

Thousand, J. S., & Villa, R. A. (1988). *Enhancing success in heterogeneous classrooms and schools* (Monograph 8–1). Burlington: University of Vermont, Center for Developmental Disabilities.

Thousand, J. S., & Villa, R. A. (1989). Enhancing success in heterogeneous schools. In S. Stainback, W. Stainback, & M. Forest (Eds.), *Educating all students in the mainstream of regular education.* Baltimore: Paul H. Brookes.

Timar, T. B., & Kirp, D. L. (1988). *Managing educational excellence.* New York: Falmer Press.

Timar, T. B., & Kirp, D. L. (1989). Education reforms in the 1980's: Lessons from the states. *Phi Delta Kappan, 70*(7), 504–511.

Toffler, A. (1970). *Future shock.* New York: Bantam Books.

Tomlinson, S. (1982). *A sociology of special education.* Boston: Routledge and Kegan Paul.

Tye, K. A., & Tye, B. B. (1984). Teacher isolation and school reform. *Phi Delta Kappan, 65*(5), 319–322.

U.S. Department of Education, Office of Special Education and Rehabilitative Services. (1988). *Annual report to Congress on the implementation of the Education for all Handicapped Children Act.* Washington, DC: Government Printing Office.

Vergason, G. A., & Anderegg, M. L. (1989). Save the baby! A response to Integrating the Children of the Second System. *Phi Delta Kappan, 71*(1), 61–63.

Walberg, H. J., & Wang, M. C. (1987). Effective educational practices and provisions for individual differences. In M. C. Wang, M. C. Reynolds, & H. J. Walberg (Eds.), *Handbook of special education: Research and practice. Vol. 1: Learner characteristics and adaptive education* (pp. 113–128). Oxford, UK: Pergamon Press.

Walker, L. J. (1987). Procedural rights in the wrong system: Special education is not enough. In A. Gartner & T. Joe (Eds.), *Images of the disabled/disabling images.* New York: Praeger.

Wang, M. C. (1981). Mainstreaming exceptional children: Some instructional design and implementation considerations. *Elementary School Journal, 81,* 195–221.

Wang, M. C. (1988, May 4). A promising approach for reforming special education. *Education Week,* pp. 36, 28.

Wang, M. C. (1989a). Accommodating student diversity through adaptive instruction. In S. Stainback, W. Stainback, & M. Forest (Eds.), *Educating all students in the mainstream of regular education* (pp. 183–197). Baltimore: Paul H. Brookes.

Wang, M. C. (1989b). Adaptive instruction: An alternative for accommodating student diversity through the curriculum. In D. K. Lipsky & A. Gartner (Eds.), *Beyond separate education: Quality education for all* (pp. 99–119). Baltimore: Paul H. Brookes.

Wang, M. C., & Reynolds, M. C. (1985). Avoiding the "catch-22" in special education reform. *Exceptional Children, 51*(6), 497–502.

Wang, M. C., & Reynolds, M. C. (1986). "Catch 22 and disabling help": A reply to Alan Gartner. *Exceptional Children, 53*(1), 77–79.

Wang, M. C., Reynolds, M. C., & Walberg, H. J. (1985, December 5–7). *Rethinking special education.* Paper presented at Wingspread Conference on the Education of Students with Special Needs: Research Findings and Implications for Policy and Practice, Racine, WI.

Wang, M. C., Reynolds, M. C., & Walberg, H. J. (1986). Rethinking special education. *Educational Leadership, 44*(1), 26–31.

Wang, M. C., Reynolds, M. C., & Walberg, H. J. (Eds.). (1987a). *Handbook of special education: Research and practice: Vol. 1. Learner characteristics and adaptive education.* Oxford, UK: Pergamon Press.

Wang, M. C., Reynolds, M. C., & Walberg, H. J. (1987b, October 1–3). *Repairing the second system for students with special needs.* Paper presented at Wingspread Conference on the Education of Children with Special Needs: Gearing Up to Meet the Challenges of the 1990s, Racine, WI.

Wang, M. C., Reynolds, M. C., & Walberg, H. J. (1988). Integrating the children of the second system. *Phi Delta Kappan, 70*(3), 248–251.

Wang, M. C., Reynolds, M. C., & Walberg, H. J. (1989). Who benefits from segregation and murky water? *Phi Delta Kappan, 7*(1), 64–67.

Wang, M. C., & Walberg, H. J. (1988). Four fallacies of segregationism. *Exceptional Children, 55*(2), 128–137.

Weatherley, R. (1979). *Reforming special education: Policy implementation from state level to street level.* Cambridge, MA: MIT Press.

Weatherley, R., & Lipsky, M. (1977). Street-level bureaucrats and institutional innovation: Implementing special education reform. *Harvard Educational Review, 47*(2), 171–203.

Weber, M. (1946). Politics as a vocation. In H. H. Gerth & C. W. Mills (Eds. & Trans.), *From Max Weber: Essays in sociology* (pp. 77–128). Oxford, UK: Oxford University Press. (Original work published 1919)

Weber, M. (1949). "Objectivity" in social science and social policy. In E. A. Shils & H. A. Finch (Eds. & Trans.), *The methodology of the social sciences.* New York: Free Press. (Original work published 1904)

Weber, M. (1978). *Economy and society* (G. Roth & C. Wittich, Eds.; E. Fischoll et al., Trans.) (2 vols.). Berkeley: University of California Press. (Original work published 1922)

Weick, K. E. (1976). Educational organizations as loosely coupled systems. *Administrative Science Quarterly, 21*(1), 1–19.

Weick, K. E. (1979). Cognitive processes in organization. In B. M. Staw (Ed.), *Research in organizational behavior* (Vol. 1, pp. 41–74). Greenwich, CT: JAI Press.

Weick, K. E. (1982). Administering education in loosely coupled schools. *Phi Delta Kappan, 63*(10), 673–676.

Weick, K. E. (1985). Sources of order in underorganized systems. In Y. S. Lincoln (Ed.), *Organizational theory and inquiry: The paradigm revolution* (pp. 106–136). Beverly Hills, CA: Sage.

Weintraub, F. J. (1977). Editorial comment. *Exceptional Children, 44*(2), 114.

White, R., & Calhoun, M. L. (1987). From referral to placement: Teachers' perceptions of their responsibilities. *Exceptional Children, 53*(5), 460-468.

Will, M. C. (1984). Let us pause and reflect—But not too long. *Exceptional Children, 51*(1), 11–16.

Will, M. C. (1985, December). *Educating children with learning problems: A shared responsibility.* Paper presented at Wingspread Conference on the Education of Special Needs Students: Research Findings and Implications for Policy and Practice, Racine, WI.

Will, M. C. (1986a). Educating children with learning problems: A shared responsibility. *Exceptional Children, 52*(5), 411–416.

Will, M. C. (1986b). *Educating children with learning problems: A shared responsibility.* A report to the Secretary. Washington, DC: U.S. Department of Education.

Wise, A. E. (1988). The two conflicting trends in school reform: Legislated learning revisited. *Phi Delta Kappan, 69*(5), 328–333.

Wolcott, H. F. (1977). *Teachers versus technocrats: An educational innovation in anthropological perspective.* Eugene, OR: Center for Educational Policy and Management.

Woodward, J. (1965). *Industrial organizations: Theory and practice.* Oxford, UK: Oxford University Press.

Wright, A. R., Cooperstein, R. A., Renneker, E. G., & Padilla, C. (1982). *Local implementation of P.L. 94–142: Final report of a longitudinal study.* Menlo Park, CA: SRI International.

Wright, J. S. (1967). *Hobson vs. Hansen: Opinion by Honorable Skelly Wright, Judge, United States Court of Appeals for the District of Columbia.* Washington, DC: West Publishing.

Ysseldyke, J., Thurlow, M., Graden, S., Wesson, C., Algozzine, B., & Deno, S. (1983). Generalization from five years of research on assessment and decision-making: The University of Minnesota Institute. *Exceptional Education Quarterly, 4,* 75–93.

Zucker, L. G. (1977). The role of institutionalization in cultural persistence. *American Sociological Review 42,* 726–743.

Zucker, L. G. (1981). Institutional structure and organizational processes: The role of evaluation units in schools. In A. Bank & R. C. Williams (Eds.), *Evaluation and decision making* (CSE Monograph Series No. 10). Los Angeles: UCLA Center for the Study of Evaluation.

Note

1. Max Weber was one of the greatest and most original social science philosophers of the early twentieth century. Drawing on his idealist background, beginning with the concept of "verstehen," Weber attempted to distinguish the social sciences from the natural sciences. Specifically, he sought to locate a middle ground between empiricism and interpretation as a means for studying the social world. Quote from Max Weber is taken from "Politics as a Vocation," published first in 1919 and translated in 1946 by H. H. Gerth and C. W. Mills (Editors) in the book *Max Weber: Essays in Sociology* (p. 117) (Oxford, England: Oxford University Press).

2. Although the special education community responded favorably to the "school restructuring phase" (see Elmore, 1987; notes 8 and 56) of the excellence movement, the push for higher standardized test scores during the early phase of the excellence movement (see Wise, 1988) was viewed negatively (see Pugach & Sapon–Shevin, 1987; Shepard, 1987).

3. Developments in the social disciplines include the general trend away from objectivism and toward subjectivism (see, e.g., Bernstein, 1976; Schwartz & Ogilvy, 1979) and, more important, the reemergence of antifoundationalism (see, e.g., Bernstein, 1983; Lyotard, 1979/1984; Skinner, 1985). Whereas social inquiry historically has been dominated by the objectivist conceptualization of science and the foundational view of knowledge, and thus by a monological quest for the truth about the social world, contemporary scholars began calling for dialogical social analysis—an antifoundational discourse open to multiple interpretations of social life (see, e.g., Bernstein, 1983; Rorty, 1979; Ricoeur, 1981). The reemergence of antifoundationalism has led to a revival of interest in philosophical pragmatism, particularly in the work of John Dewey (see Antonio, 1989; Kloppenberg, 1986) and his contemporary appropriators (e.g., Rorty, 1979, 1982), as well as increased attention to the work of contemporary Continental philosophers such as Derrida (1972/1982a) and Foucault (1980).

   An important methodological outcome of these developments has been the emergence of new antifoundational methodologies and the reappropriation of older ones (see notes 4, 5, 7, and 9). A second important outcome has been the emergence of the text as a metaphor for social life (Geertz, 1983), which implies a mode of social analysis that views human and institutional practices as discursive formations that can be read or interpreted in many ways, none of which is correct in a foundational sense but each of which carries with it a particular set of moral and political implications. Among other things, social analysis under the text metaphor studies that which conditions, limits, and institutionalizes discursive formations; it asks how power comes to be concentrated in the hands of those who have the right to interpret reality and define normality (Dreyfus & Rabinow, 1983; see notes 4, 5, 7, and 9).

4. My version of critical pragmatism uses four antifoundational methodologies (see note 3): two reappropriated ones, immanent critique and ideal type (note 5), and two newer ones, deconstruction (note 7) and genealogy (note 9). Given its grounding in philosophical pragmatism, critical pragmatism does not seek

"truth" in the foundational sense; it is, rather, a form of edification (see Cherryholmes, 1988; Rorty, 1979). As used here, it is a mode of inquiry that, by forcing us to acknowledge that what we think, do, say, write, and read as professionals is shaped by convention, helps us avoid the delusion that we can know ourselves, our profession, our clients, "or anything else,' except under optional descriptions" (Rorty, 1979, p. 379). Critical pragmatism is "the same as the 'method' of utopian politics or revolutionary science (as opposed to parliamentary politics or normal science). The method is to redescribe lots and lots of things in new ways, until you . . . tempt the rising generation to . . . look for . . . new scientific equipment or new social institutions" (Rorty, 1989, p. 9). For an extended discussion of my version of critical pragmatism, see Skrtic (1991a). For a somewhat different version, see Cherryholmes (1988).

5. Immanent critique is more than a method of analysis. Historically, from Hegel and Marx to more contemporary emancipation theorists in the social disciplines (e.g., Horkheimer, 1974) and education (e.g., Giroux, 1981), it has been understood as the driving force behind social progress and change, a process driven by the affinity of humans for attempting to reconcile their claims about themselves (appearances) with their actual social conditions (reality) (Hegel, 1807/1977; Kojeve, 1969). It is an emancipatory form of analysis in that it is intended to free us from our unquestioned assumptions about ourselves and our social practices, assumptions that prevent us from doing what we believe is right (Antonio, 1981; Schroyer, 1973). As a method, however, immanent critique does not on its own provide a way of identifying the ideals or actual conditions of social phenomena. For this, I will use Max Weber's (1904/1949) method of ideal types.

   The ideal-typical analytic is premised on the idea that the meaning of social phenomena derives from the cultural significance (value orientation) behind human and institutional action. As such, ideal types are exaggerated mental constructs (developed from empirical and theoretical knowledge) for analyzing social phenomena in terms of their value orientation. They are not "true" in a foundational sense; they are mental constructions used as expository devices (Dallmayr & McCarthy, 1977; Mommsen, 1974; Ritzer, 1983). I use ideal types extensively here to draw out and emphasize the explicit and implicit value orientations in the discourses and practices considered, particularly in the characterizations of school organization that are used in the second half of the chapter (see notes 38 and 39).

6. I use the term "educational administration" in both a narrow sense (to refer to the field and practice of educational administration) and a broad sense (to refer to the fields and practices of educational policy and educational change, or school improvement or educational reform), inclusive of the role played by persons in the fields of educational administration (narrow sense), including special education administration. By the discourse on school organization and adaptability, I mean the discourse on these topics in the field of educational administration (both senses), as well as in the broader discourse on organization and change in the multidisciplinary field of organization analysis (see Scott, 1981; notes 34 and 37). I use "school organization and adaptability" rather than "school

organization and change" to refer to this discourse because I am interested in the capacity for change at both the microscopic level of the individual professional and the macroscopic level of the entire organization (see notes 35 and 36).

7. Deconstruction is Derrida's (1972/1982a,b) method of reading texts by focusing on their margins (silences, contradictions, inconsistencies, and incompleteness) rather than on their central ideas or arguments. Although Derrida deconstructs philosophical texts, the method of deconstruction has been applied broadly to the texts of the social sciences and professions, including professional, institutional, and social practices and discourses (see Cherryholmes, 1988; Hoy, 1985; Ryan, 1982; Rorty, 1989). Whereas traditional analyses purport to enable us to read or interpret a text, discourse, or practice (as an accurate or true representation of the world), deconstruction tries to show that interpretation is a distinctively human process in which no single interpretation ever has enough cognitive authority to privilege it over another (see Derrida, 1972/1982a).

8. I use terms such as *general education, regular education,* and *regular classroom* in reference to the typical kindergarten through 12th-grade program within public education. Although I recognize that these terms often carry "decidedly neutral or even negative connotations" (Lilly, 1989, p. 143) for professional educators outside the field of special education, I use them for ease of presentation only, particularly where clarity demands that I distinguish between general education and special education professionals, practices, and discourses, as well as between education in a broad sense (the entire field or institution of education) and education in a narrow sense (the kindergarten through 12th-grade program).

   Although I use the term *special education* in the narrow sense of the professional field (or institutional practice) of special education, the implications of much of what I have to say in the first half of the chapter apply equally well to students in the other special needs programs (e.g., compensatory, remedial, and bilingual education), as well as students who are tracked in one way or another within the general education program (see note 12).

   In the second half of the chapter, I make explicit the references to the other special needs programs and tracking practices in general education. By "the discourse on educational excellence" in the field of general education, I mean what general educators think, do, say, read, and write about educational excellence, a discourse that can be understood in terms of two related debates: what I refer to as the "effective schools" and "school restructuring" debates (see note 56). Although it plays a key role in special education classification practices under the EHA, I have not included the field of school psychology in the present analysis. For a separate treatment, see Skrtic (1990a).

9. Genealogy is Foucault's (1980, 1983) approach for analyzing what conditions, limits, and institutionalizes social practices and discourses. He used genealogy to study "the way modern societies control and discipline their populations by sanctioning the knowledge claims and practices of the human sciences: medicine, psychiatry, psychology, criminology, sociology and so on" (Philip, 1985, P. 67; Foucault, 1961/1973, 1963/1975, 1975/1979). The key difference between genealogy and traditional historical analysis is that the genealogist is far less

interested in the events of history than in the "norms, constraints, conditions, conventions, and so on" (Dreyfus & Rabinow, 1983, p.108) that produced them.

10. My use of the qualifiers "explicit" and "implicit" here is a bit misleading. It is more accurate to think of all three discourses as being grounded in unquestioned presuppositions. "Explicit" here refers to the idea that certain presuppositions are an explicit part of the profession's knowledge tradition relative to other ones that are merely implicit norms in society. This problem will come up again (see note 19) because the degree of implicitness and explicitness of guiding assumptions is a key part of the subject matter of this type of inquiry (see notes 4, 5, 7, and 9).

Although one could argue that the field of educational administration implicitly assumes that school failure is pathological on the grounds that historically it has avoided topics on school effects and student outcomes (Bridges, 1982; Erickson, 1979), human pathology is explicit in the conceptualization of administration that grounds the field. The Getzels-Guba model of administration (Getzels & Guba, 1957), "the most successful theory in educational administration" (Griffiths, 1979, p. 50), is, in part, an extension of Barnard's (1938) conceptualization of administration (Campbell, Fleming, Newell, & Bennion, 1987), which assumes a cooperative (rational) organization in which uncooperativeness is pathological (Burrell & Morgan, 1979).

11. The same assumptions in the language of the general education and educational administration discourses are that: (a) school failure is a (psychologically or sociologically) pathological condition that students have, (b) differential diagnosis (identification by ability, need, and/or interest) is objective and useful, (c) special programming (homogeneous grouping in general education tracks and segregated and pull-out classrooms in special, compensatory, gifted, and remedial education) is a rationally conceived and coordinated system of practices and programs that benefits diagnosed students, and (d) progress in education (increases in academic achievement and efficiency) results from incremental technological improvements in differential, diagnosis and intervention practices and programs (see Bridges, 1982; Cherryholmes, 1988; Erickson, 1979; McNeil, 1986; Oakes, 1985, 1986a,b; Sirotnik & Oakes, 1986; Spring, 1980).

12. Although I am emphasizing the institutional practice of special education here, we will see in subsequent sections that, from an organizational perspective, practices that group or track students in general education (e.g., in-class ability grouping, curriculum tracking), as well as the other institutional practices that remove students from the general program (e.g., compensatory, gifted, remedial education), are artifacts of functionalist assumptions about organizational rationality and human and social pathology.

13. Although the introductory discussion dichotomized the mainstreaming debate and the REI debate as if there were a period between them when the field was completely certain about the adequacy of mainstreaming and the EHA, it is more accurate to think of the field of special education as being in a more or less constant state of self-criticism since the early 1960s. Criticism subsided somewhat during the period shortly before and after enactment of the EHA, but it did not disappear (see, e.g., Keogh & Levitt, 1976; MacMillan & Semmel, 1977;

Reynolds, 1976; Reynolds & Birch, 1977). The field of educational administration (narrow sense) has been in a constant state of self-criticism since at least the early 1950s (Clark, 1985; Cunningham, Hack, & Nystrand, 1977; Griffiths, 1959, 1983, 1988; Halpin, 1970; Halpin & Hayes, 1977; Hayes & Pharis, 1967; Spring, 1980). Driven by the persistent anomaly of little or no substantive change or improvement in public education, the field of educational change or school improvement has been characterized by the same sort of self-criticism since the early 1960s (Elmore & McLaughlin, 1988; House, 1979; Lehming & Kane, 1981; note 36).

14. Hallahan, Kauffman, Lloyd, and McKinney (1988), key opponents of the REI, argued that the concept first appeared in Reynolds and Wang (1981), which, in revised form (Wang, Reynolds, & Walberg, 1985, 1986), subsequently received formal recognition from Madeleine C. Will (1985, 1986a,b), Assistant Secretary for the Office of Special Education and Rehabilitative Services in the Reagan Administration. This is an important connection because, in subsequent criticism of the REI, a major argument has been that it is "entirely consistent with Reagan–Bush policies aimed at decreasing federal support for education, including the education of vulnerable children and youth" (Kauffman, 1989a, p. 7).

Although Wang (Wang & Walberg, 1988), a key proponent of the REI, agrees that Will (1986a) provided the original policy statement for the REI, she contends that the REI itself is grounded in empirical evidence on the inadequacies of the current system contained in Heller, Holtzman, and Messick (1982); Hobbs (1975, 1980); and Wang, Reynolds, and Walberg (1987a). Thus, the REI opponents tend to characterize the REI as a political outcome of conservative ideology, whereas the proponents characterize it as a logical outcome of empirical research.

Nevertheless, it perhaps is more accurate to think of the REI as a logical outcome of Maynard Reynolds's liberal strategy of "progressive inclusion" (Reynolds & Rosen, 1976), the idea that the entire history of special education is or should be one of incremental progress toward more normalized instructional placements. In 1976, Reynolds, one of the architects of the "continuum of placements" model that underwrites mainstreaming (Reynolds, 1962; see also Deno, 1970) and a key REI proponent, rejected the pull-out logic of mainstreaming in favor of making "regular classrooms . . . more diverse educational environments, [thus reducing] the need to . . . use separate . . . educational environments" (Reynolds, 1976, p. 8). He proposed to do this "through the redistribution of resources and energies, through training, and, finally, through the redistribution of students" (1976, p. 18). Thus, although there probably is a moment of truth in both the REI proponents' and the opponents' characterizations of the motivation behind the REI, Reynolds formulated the concept and started the debate before either the empirical data were available or the conservative ideology held much sway in Washington.

15. Besides Will's (1984, 1985, 1986a,b) statements on or related to the REI, and several attempts to place the REI in perspective (e.g., Davis, 1989; Davis & McCaul, 1988; Lieberman, 1984, 1988; Sapon–Shevin, 1988; Skrtic, 1987a,b, 1988b), the vast majority of the literature promoting the REI has been produced by eight

individuals working either alone or in teams of two (or, at times, with other colleagues). I will refer to them as REI proponents according to the following two-person teams: (a) Maynard Reynolds and Margaret Wang (Reynolds, 1988; Reynolds & Wang, 1981, 1983; Reynolds, Wang, & Walberg, 1987; Walberg & Wang, 1987; Wang, 1981, 1988, 1989a,b; Wang & Reynolds, 1985, 1986; Wang, Reynolds, & Walberg, 1985, 1986, 1987a,b, 1988, 1989; Wang & Walberg, 1988); (b) M. Stephen Lilly and Marleen Pugach (Lilly, 1986, 1987, 1989; Pugach & Lilly, 1984); (c) Susan Stainback and William Stainback (Stainback & Stainback, 1984, 1985a,b, 1987a,b, 1989; Stainback, Stainback, Courtnage, & Jaben, 1985; Stainback, Stainback, & Forest, 1989); and (d) Alan Gartner and Dorothy Kerzner Lipsky (Gartner, 1986; Gartner & Lipsky, 1987, 1989; Lipsky & Gartner, 1987, 1989a,b). The analysis of the REI proponents' arguments against the EHA and for their REI proposals is based on virtually all of the literature cited in (a) through (d), above, as well as some additional related work done by these authors and others, as noted.

16. In their criticism of the current system of special education, all four teams of REI proponents referred, more or less, to a common body of EHA implementation research, virtually all of which was reviewed or cited in Wang, Reynolds, and Walberg (1987a) and Gartner and Lipsky (1987). The 4.5 million figure represents an increase of about 20 percent in the number of students identified as handicapped since 1976–1977, much of which resulted from increases in the number of students identified as having learning disabilities, a classification that in the late 1980's represented more than 43 percent of all students identified as "handicapped" and that, despite attempts to tighten eligibility criteria, increased more than 140 percent since 1977 (U.S. Department of Education, 1988; Gerber & Levine-Donnerstein, 1989).

    In addition to these three classifications, the "mildly handicapped" designation includes students with mild forms of speech and language problems and students with physical and sensory impairments that are not accompanied by other severely disabling conditions, such as severe mental retardation (Reynolds & Lakin, 1987). When these additional students were included in the count, estimates of the proportion of students considered mildly handicapped ranged from 75 to 90 percent of students classified as handicapped in school (Algozzine & Korinek, 1985; Shepard, 1987; Wang, Reynolds, & Walberg, 1989).

17. The first published reactions to the REI (Lieberman, 1985; Mesinger, 1985) were decidedly negative but focused exclusively on Stainback and Stainback (1984). These were followed by reactions from three subgroups within the field that, although sensitive to the prevailing problems and generally supportive of reform, merely called for more information (Teacher Education Division, Council for Exceptional Children, 1986, 1987), proposed a mechanism for interpreting information and building a consensus (Skrtic, 1987b) or specified several preconditions of reform (Heller & Schilit, 1987).

    Neither these reactions nor those of other critics of the REI in part (e.g., Davis, 1989; Davis & McCaul, 1988; Lieberman, 1984, 1988; Sapon–Shevin, 1988; Skrtic, 1987a, 1988b) or in whole (e.g., Vergason & Anderegg, 1989) have had much impact on the course of events.

The controversy over the REI began with the publication of a special issue of the *Journal of Learning Disabilities (JLD)* in 1988 and was sustained by several subsequent articles written by some of the same authors. Together, the *JLD* articles and these other pieces include: (a) Braaten, Kauffman, Braaten, Polsgrove, & Nelson (1988); (b) Bryan, Bay, & Donahue (1988); (c) Council for Children with Behavioral Disorders (1989); (d) Gerber (1988a, 1988b); (e) Hallahan, Kauffman, Lloyd, and McKinney (1988); (f) Hallahan, Keller, McKinney, Lloyd, and Bryan (1988); (g) Kauffman (1988, 1989a,b); (h) Kauffman, Gerber, and Semmel (1988); (i) Keogh (1988); (j) Lloyd, Crowley, Kohler, and Strain (1988); (k) McKinney and Hocutt (1988); and (l) Schumaker and Deshler (1988). My analysis of the REI opponents' assessment of the adequacy of the prevailing system of special education and their criticism of the REI proponents' proposals for reform is drawn from the literature cited in (a) through (j), above, as well as from some additional work by these authors and others, as noted.

18. The controversial nature of the REI debate and the degree to which it has divided the field is clear in some of the more recent encounters in the literature. In these pieces the REI advocates characterized the opponents as segregationists (Wang & Walberg, 1988) and compared the prevailing system of special education to slavery (Stainback & Stainback, 1987b) and apartheid (Lipsky & Gartner, 1987), whereas the REI opponents characterized the proponents as politically naive liberals and the REI as the Reagan-Bush "trickle-down theory of education of the hard-to-teach" (Kauffman, 1989b, p. 256).

19. There is no argument that most disabilities in the severe to profound range are associated with observable patterns of biological symptoms or syndromes, and thus are comprehensible under the pathological model (Mercer, 1973). In any event, the issue relative to these students, as in the case of the students identified as "mildly handicapped," is whether they are being served adequately and ethically under the system as it exists (see note 25). In most cases, students who were classified as mildly handicapped, and particularly those classified as learning disabled, emotionally disturbed, and mildly mentally retarded, did not show biological signs of pathology (Algozzine, 1976, 1977; Apter, 1982; Hobbs, 1975; Mercer, 1973; Rhodes, 1970; Rist & Harrell, 1982; Ross, 1980; Schrag & Divorky, 1975; Skrtic, 1988b; Swap, 1978).

The participants in the REI debate clearly were not speaking explicitly to the four assumptions (see note 10). Indeed, that is the problem with the debate, as noted. Thus, from this point on (including endnotes), I will at times omit the qualifiers "implicit" and explicit" when discussing the implications of REI proponents' and opponents' arguments for the four grounding assumptions, particularly when including them is cumbersome, as it is in this section because the discussion includes two other levels of implicitness.

First, there is the nature of agreement (implicit or explicit) between the REI proponents' and opponents' assessments of existing practices, a level I will retain in text. Second, there is the nature of the unquestioned presuppositions that ground the field (explicit in the professional knowledge tradition or an implicit social norm) (see note 10), which I will not retain in text. So, when I say that the REI proponents or opponents "reject" or "retain" an assumption or presupposition, it should be understood that they do so implicitly. The same holds true (relative to the four assumptions) for the arguments of participants in the effective schools and school restructuring debates in general education, which will be addressed in subsequent sections (see notes 8 and 56). In all cases in which it seems necessary for clarity, however, I use the qualifiers in the text or in a note.

20. A further argument of the REI proponents relative to the nonadaptability of the general education system is that the existence of the special education system is a barrier to development of a responsive capacity within general education, both in public schools and in teacher education (Lilly, 1986, 1989; Pugach, 1988; Pugach & Lilly, 1984; Reynolds, 1988). This assertion relative to public schools is addressed extensively in subsequent sections from an organizational perspective (see also Skrtic & Ware, 1992). For my position on this assertion relative to teacher education, see Thousand (1990).

    On the related matter of the attribution of student failure, both the REI opponents and proponents alike agree that an exclusively student-deficit orientation is inappropriate. Although some of the REI opponents have argued that the proponents lean too far toward an exclusively teacher-deficit orientation (Kauffman, Gerber, & Semmel, 1988; Keogh, 1988), the REI proponents have clearly recognized the student's responsibility in the learning process (Gartner, 1986; Walberg & Wang, 1987; Wang, 1989b).

21. The only REI opponent who made a case for the potential instructional relevance of differential diagnosis considers it to be an empirical question that, if answered in the negative, should signal the discontinuance of the practice of differential diagnosis and the categorical approach to special education (Keogh, 1988). Although Bryan, Bay, and Donahue (1988, p. 25) did not make an explicit argument for the instructional relevance of differential diagnosis, by arguing that "one cannot assume that any two learning disabled children would be any more similar than a learning disabled child and a normally achieving child, or a normally achieving child and an underachieving child," they actually made an implicit argument against the instructional utility of differential diagnosis, and thus implicitly agreed with the REI proponents' position that all students have unique learning needs and interests, even those within the traditional categories of mild disability.

22. Although the REI opponents generally have agreed that the instructional effectiveness of special education interventions has not been demonstrated, they put forth two arguments in favor of instruction delivered in special education settings. The first is that teachers in general education are unable to meet the diverse needs of students with learning disabilities in their classrooms (Bryan, Bay, & Donahue 1988). The second argument rests on the speculation that more powerful instructional techniques might be more easily implemented in special education settings than in regular classrooms (Hallahan, Keller, McKinney, Lloyd, & Bryan 1988; see also Hallahan & Keller, 1986).

23. The argument that the prevailing system is politically rational cannot be divorced from the argument that progress is rational–technical because, although targeting students for services that are instructionally ineffective but

will be rendered effective in the future might be politically justifiable, targeting them for ineffective services that will not be rendered effective in the future is not justifiable, politically or ethically (see note 33).

As to the question of whether special education is a rationally coordinated system of services, the REI proponents argue that it is coordinated with neither the general education system nor with the other special needs programs. They characterize the entire special needs enterprise, including the special education system, in terms of disjointed incrementalism—a collection of disjointed programs, each with its own clients, personnel, administrators, budget, and regulations, which have been added to schools incrementally over time (Reynolds & Birch, 1977; Reynolds & Wang, 1983; Reynolds, Wang, & Walberg, 1987; Wang, Reynolds, & Walberg, 1985, 1986). Although the REI opponents have been generally silent on the issue of coordination, Kauffman, Gerber, and Semmel (1988) responded by linking it to their argument for the political rationality of the prevailing system. Although they recognized the lack of coordination, they considered it to be an unavoidable consequence of the politically rational targeting function of the EHA, a function that is fundamental to the very notion of categorical programs.

24. Although she was a major figure in the REI debate, Will (1985, 1986a, 1986b) did not offer a specific proposal as such (see notes 14, 15, 27, and 28).

25. This issue actually separates the four teams of REI advocates into two camps. The Gartner and Lipsky and the Stainback and Stainback teams distanced themselves from the other two teams and from the REI itself, noting that, though it has resulted in some positive momentum for reform, ultimately it is merely "blending at the margin" (Lipsky & Gartner, 1989a, p. 271) because it maintains two separate systems. For Stainback and Stainback (1989, p. 43), the REI concept is too restrictive because it "does not address the need to include in regular classrooms and regular education those students labeled severely and profoundly handicapped" (see also notes 19 and 27).

26. The Lilly and Pugach proposal excluded students classified as "mildly handicapped" who have developmental learning disabilities (Pugach & Lilly, 1984, p. 53)—that is, learning disabilities presumed to be pathological (Kirk & Chalfant, 1983).

27. Reynolds and Wang reserved the option of separate settings in the belief that "surely there will be occasions to remove some students for instruction in special settings" (Wang, Reynolds, & Walberg, 1985, p. 13). Will's (1986a) position in this regard was similar to those of Lilly and Pugach and Reynolds and Wang, in that her version of a restructured system continued to rely on separate instructional settings for some students, a position that was criticized by Stainback and Stainback (1987b) and Gartner and Lipsky (1987, p. 385) as perpetuating "a dual system approach for a smaller (more severely impaired) population."

28. Each team of REI proponents, as well as Will (1986a,b), took a unique stance on this point, both in terms of the degree to which general and special education should be merged and the level or levels of the institution of public education at which merger should take place. Although neither Will nor any of the four teams of proponents spoke to each of the following levels, taken together they

addressed changes at or had implications for: (a) the U.S. Department of Education, (b) research and development centers, (c) teacher education programs, (d) local education agencies, (e) school buildings, and (f) classrooms. Though she was somewhat contradictory on the matter (see Gartner & Lipsky, 1987; Stainback & Stainback, 1987b; note 27), Will (1986a, p. 415) called for enhanced component parts, better cooperation, and shared responsibility between the two systems at all levels, particularly at levels (a) and (c); she did not, however, call for outright merger of the two systems at any level. In the analysis of these proposals in text, the notion of merger was addressed at the building and classroom levels only (see notes 29 and 30).

29. Above the regular classroom teachers and generic specialists, Reynolds and Wang (1983) proposed a merger of district-level consultants who would provide the classroom teachers and generic specialists with consultation and training on generic topics (Wang, Reynolds, & Walberg, 1985).

30. In addition to merging special and remedial education at the building level, the Lilly and Pugach plan (Pugach & Lilly, 1984, p. 54) proposed a merger at the level of teacher education. Their plan would merge "what is now special education for the mildly handicapped [in departments of special education] with what are currently departments of elementary and secondary education or curriculum and instruction" (p. 53) for the purpose of "providing instruction of the highest quality . . . for advanced preparation of support services specialists at the graduate level" (p. 54), as well as undergraduate instruction for persons in preparation for the role of regular classroom teacher.

31. Other than the recommended use of more powerful instructional technologies such as cooperative learning, curriculum-based assessment, and peer tutoring (Lloyd, Crowley, Kohler, & Strain, 1988; Thousand & Villa, 1988, 1989) and professional problem-solving mechanisms such as teacher assistance teams (Chalfant, Pysh, & Moultrie, 1979) and collaborative consultation (e.g., Pugach, 1988), the primary difference at the classroom level was that students who would have been removed under the existing system would remain in the classroom on a full-time basis where they, their teachers, and any other students needing assistance would be provided with in-class support services.

32. Drawing on the work of Edmonds (1979), Gilhool (1976, 1989), Allington and McGill-Franzen (1989), and Lezotte (1989), Gartner and Lipsky argued that (a) all students, including those with special needs, can learn effectively from the same pedagogy; (b) this generic pedagogy is known and available in the principles and practices contained in the effective schools research; and (c) these principles and practices are replicable through school improvement programs. Ironically, although they argued that effective education for students labeled as "handicapped" is a matter of will and commitment on the part of teachers and schools, Gartner and Lipsky called for reformulating the EHA into a new mandate "that requires a unitary system [that] is 'special' for all students." That is, they called for transforming the EHA into "an effective schools act for all students" (1989, p. 282).

33. The explicit historical and political arguments against the possibility of change presented in Council for Children with Behavioral Disorders (1989), Kauffman

(1988), and Kauffman, Gerber, and Semmel (1988) contradicted the implicit arguments for the possibility of incremental change through research and development presented in Braaten, Kauffman, Braaten, Polsgrove, and Nelson (1988); Bryan, Bay, and Donahue (1988); Council for Children with Behavioral Disorders (1989); Hallahan, Keller, McKinney, Lloyd, and Bryan (1988); Kauffman (1988); Kauffman, Gerber, and Semmel (1988); Keogh (1988); and Lloyd, Crowley, Kohler, and Strain (1988). It is obvious that by contradicting their position on the possibility of rational–technical change, the REI opponents reversed their position on the fourth assumption. This also reversed their position on the third assumption because, on political and ethical grounds, their position on the third and fourth assumptions could not be separated (see note 23).

34. In the mid-1950s there was an attempt to ground educational administration (narrow sense) in the theoretical discourse of the social sciences (Griffiths, 1959; Hayes & Pharis, 1967), but it failed (Cunningham, Hack, & Nystrand, 1977; Halpin, 1970; Halpin & Hayes, 1977). As a result, the field came to be grounded in the prescriptive discourse of scientific management (Clark, 1985; Griffiths, 1983; Spring, 1980). Although some people in the field (e.g., Clark, 1985) and others (e.g., Spring, 1980) have criticized this orientation, and arguments from within the field for a critical orientation emerged (e.g., Bates, 1980, 1987; Foster, 1986), the field has continued to be dominated by the prescriptive discourse of scientific management and by functionalist conceptualizations of organization, administration, and inquiry (Clark, 1985; Griffiths, 1988; Lincoln, 1985).

35. These modes of theorizing can be understood in terms of two dimensions of metatheoretical assumptions: (a) an objectivism–subjectivism dimension that corresponds to various presuppositions about the nature of science, and (b) a microscopic–macroscopic dimension that reflects various presuppositions about the nature of society. Counterposing the two dimensions forms four modes of theorizing or paradigms of social scientific thought: (a) functionalism (micro-objectivist), the dominant mode in the West; (b) interpretivism (micro-subjectivist); (c) structuralism (macro-objectivist); and (d) humanism (macro-subjectivist) (Burrell & Morgan, 1979; Ritzer, 1980, 1983). Each paradigm represents a unique way to understand the social world, including organization and change (Burrell & Morgan, 1979; Morgan, 1983).

    In terms of the theoretical discourse in the field of organization analysis, the objectivism–subjectivism dimension corresponds to assumptions about the nature of action in organizations, ranging from the objectivist notion of rational action to the subjectivist notion of nonrational action. The microscopic–macroscopic dimension corresponds to assumptions about the level at which organizational activity is most appropriately analyzed, ranging from theories that emphasize organizing processes at the micro-level of individuals and small groups to those that emphasize organization structure at the macro-level of total organizations (Pfeffer, 1982; Scott, 1981).

36. One major development has been a series of paradigm shifts. Referring to the four-paradigm matrix in note 35, the three shifts are: (a) one in the 1960s from the micro-objectivist to the macro-objectivist paradigm, (b) one in the 1970s at the microscopic level of analysis from the micro-objectivist to the micro-subjec-

tivist paradigm, and (c) one in the 1980s at the macroscopic level of analysis from the macro-objectivist to the macro-subjectivist paradigm (Burrell & Morgan, 1979; Pfeffer, 1982; Scott, 1981). A related development has been the emergence of several theories that implicitly or explicitly bridge paradigms (see Skrtic, 1988b, 1991), each of which facilitates the integration of theoretical insights from two or more paradigms (see note 38).

Although educational administration (narrow sense) continues to be dominated by the rational–technical perspective on organization and change, the field of educational change has shifted from the rational–technical to the non-rational–cultural perspective on change (House, 1979). This shift has been driven since the late 1950's by uncertainty surrounding the apparent inability to actually bring about meaningful change in school organizations (Boyd & Crowson, 1981; Cuban, 1989; Elmore & McLaughlin, 1988; Lehming & Kane, 1981; Wise, 1988). As a result, the nonrational-cultural perspective increasingly has become the favored outlook on change (e.g., Goodlad, 1975; House, 1979; Sarason, 1971/1982; Sirotnik & Oakes, 1986; notes 37 and 38).

37. In the interest of space, I conduct my deconstruction of the discourse on school organization and adaptability in the field of educational administration indirectly. That is, I spend most of the available space in this section on the antifoundational interpretation of school organization and adaptability that I will use in subsequent sections to deconstruct the institutional practice of special education, the discourse on school failure, and the institution of public education. Nevertheless, virtually everything that is presented in this section and the ones to follow can be read as a deconstruction of the discourse on school organization and adaptability in the field of educational administration because it delegitimizes the presupposition of organizational rationality, the explicit grounding of the field of educational administration. For a more direct deconstruction of the discourse on school organization and adaptability in the field of educational administration, see Skrtic (1988b, 1991). For additional critical analyses that can be read as deconstructions, see Bates (1980, 1987), Foster (1986), House (1979), and Sirotnik and Oakes (1986).

38. The structural and cultural frames of reference do not correspond to the rational–technical and nonrational–cultural perspectives (see notes 35 and 36). Indeed, the particular combination of theories in each frame of reference was selected to avoid this dichotomy, as well as those between objectivism–subjectivism and microscopic–macroscopic. This is the sense in which the present analysis is antifoundational and dialogical. Such an analysis gives a voice to a variety of perspectives while recognizing that none of the perspectives, including its own, are "true" in a foundational sense (see Skrtic, 1988b, 1991, 1992).

39. Throughout this section all of the material relative to configuration theory (e.g., nature of work, division of labor, coordination of work, interdependency or coupling among workers) is drawn from Mintzberg (1979) and Miller and Mintzberg (1983), except where noted otherwise. All of the material relative to institutionalization theory (e.g., material and normative structures, decoupled structures and subunits, and myth, symbol, and ceremony) is drawn from Meyer and Rowan (1977, 1978) and Meyer and Scott (1983), except where noted otherwise.

Within both the structural and the cultural frames of reference, I treat each theory and the images of organization and change that emerge from them (and from combining them) as ideal types (see note 5), as exaggerated mental constructs for analyzing traditional school organization in terms of its value orientation. My aim in the discussion here is to combine these ideal types to form two larger ideal types—one structural and one cultural. In subsequent sections I combine the structural and cultural ideal types into a larger ideal type and use it to carry out my deconstruction and reconstruction of public education.

40. The process of organizational change from this perspective is similar to a Kuhnian (1970) paradigm shift: long periods of stability that are maintained by the self-reinforcing nature of the organization's current paradigm (what Kuhn would call the long period of normal science) and occasional periods of change in which unreconcilable anomalies eventually destroy the prevailing paradigm (what Kuhn would call revolutionary science and the shift to a new paradigm).

41. Other than a few citations that clarify and extend my theoretical arguments on organization and change, virtually all of the citations in this section refer to empirical and interpretive evidence that supports the theoretical claims made in text.

42. For empirical evidence that teachers rarely view their instructional practices as a potential source of the problem in special education referrals, and that the special education referral and classification process is oriented to place the blame for failure on the student rather than on the standard programs in use, see Bennett and Ragosta (1984), Sarason and Doris (1979), White and Calhoun (1987), and Ysseldyke et al. (1983).

43. For historical evidence on the conditions under which the special classroom emerged, see Lazerson (1983) and Sarason and Doris (1979). For empirical evidence on the disjunction between the special classroom and the rest of the school enterprise, see Deno (1970), Dunn (1968), Johnson (1962), and Reynolds (1962). See Chandler and Plakos (1969), MacMillan (1971), Wright (1967), and Mercer (1973) for empirical evidence on the overrepresentation of students from minority groups in segregated special classrooms after *Brown v. Board of Education* (1954), which is another example of the use of the special classroom to protect legitimacy.

Indeed, the organizational isolation of the special classroom and the overrepresentation of students from minority groups in these classrooms were two of the major arguments for the EHA (Christophos & Renz, 1969; Deno, 1970; Dunn, 1968; Johnson, 1962). From an organizational perspective, the problem of overrepresentation of students from minority groups in special education classrooms and programs, both before (e.g., Christophos & Renz, 1969; Dunn, 1968) and after the EHA (e.g., Heller, Holtzman, & Messick, 1982), can be understood as school organizations using an existing decoupled subunit to maintain legitimacy in the face of failing to meet the needs of disproportionate numbers of these students in general education classrooms.

44. In organizational terms, although special education is a nonrational system, it is a politically rational system in two opposite senses: (a) It protects students from the nonadaptability of school organizations, in the REI opponents' sense; and (b)

it protects school organizations from the uncertainty of student diversity, in the sense developed here. I will return to these ideas, and particularly to the moment of truth in the REI opponents' political justification for special education, in subsequent sections.

45. Recognition of the adhocratic configuration, or what were called "organic" organizations, occurred in the 1960s (Pugh et al., 1963). Because these organizations operated in dynamic, uncertain environments, where innovation and adaptation were necessary for survival, they configured themselves as the inverse of the bureaucratic form (Burns & Stalker, 1966; Woodward, 1965). Mintzberg (1979) called them adhocracies following Toffler (1970), who popularized the term in the book *Future Shock*.

46. Although I will not pursue the issue of accountability in any great depth here, the mode of accountability that emerges in the adhocracy represents an alternative to the two extreme positions on accountability that have shaped the debate on school restructuring, what Timar and Kirp (1988, p. 130) called the "romantic decentralist" (i.e., professional) and the "hyperrationalist" (i.e., bureaucratic) modes of accountability (see also Murphy, 1989; Timar & Kirp, 1989), as well as Conley's (1990, p. 317) middle-ground "constrained decision-maker" position.

Modes of accountability are shaped by the logic of the division of labor, means of coordination, and form of interdependency in organizations. There is no way out of the professional–bureaucratic dilemma as long as schools are configured as professional bureaucracies. The constrained decision-maker position merely tries to strike a balance between the two extremes while leaving the existing configuration of schools intact. The key to accountability in the adhocracy is that it avoids all three positions by assigning responsibility to groups of professionals, thereby politicizing discretion within a discourse among professionals and client constituencies. For a somewhat more extended treatment of this topic, see Kiel and Skrtic (1988) and Skrtic (1991); see also note 58.

47. The EHA is completely consistent with the third and fourth assumptions; it is a rational–technical mechanism for change that assumes that schools are machine bureaucracies—that is, organizations in which worker behavior is controlled by procedural rules and thus subject to modification through revision and extension of formalization and supervision (see Elmore & McLaughlin, 1982). Its requirements for classification, parent participation, individualized education programs, and least restrictive environment placements are perceived to be new technologies for diagnosis and intervention. Moreover, its requirement for a comprehensive system of personnel development, what Gilhool (1989, p. 247) called "probably the most important provision of the act," assumes that "there [are] known procedures for effectively educating disabled children," and that the problem is simply that "the knowledge of how to do so [is] not widely distributed." This, of course, assumes the possibility of rational–technical change through dissemination of practices and training (see notes 35 and 36).

48. For empirical and interpretive evidence on the degree to which the EHA has resulted in an increase in political clashes, a decrease in collaboration, and an

increase in the number of students identified as "handicapped," see note 15 and Bogdan (1983); Lortie (1978); Martin (1978); Patrick and Reschly (1982); Singer and Butler (1987); Skrtic, Guba, and Knowlton (1985); and Weatherley (1979).

For empirical and interpretive evidence that the EHA's adhocratic goal of personalized instruction contradicts its bureaucratic means of uniform procedures, see Singer and Butler (1987); Skrtic, Guba, and Knowlton (1985); and Wright, Cooperstein, Renneker, and Padilla (1982). For empirical and interpretive evidence that special education has itself conformed to the two-structure, machine-professional bureaucracy configuration to deal with this contradiction, see Singer and Butler (1987); Skrtic, Guba, and Knowlton (1985); and Weatherley (1979). As Singer and Butler noted, the EHA "has created a dual locus of organizational control," an arrangement in which information necessary for "legal or monitoring purposes, quick-turnaround defense of special education priorities . . . or public relations in the wider community" are managed centrally in the office of the special education director; whereas instructional decisions "have become or have remained more decentralized" in the hands of professionals (p. 139).

49. On the rational–technical nature of the excellence movement (note 56), see Bacharach (1990), Cuban (1983), Meier (1984), Resnick and Resnick (1985), and Wise (1988). For example, Wise (1988, p. 329) characterized it generally as "state control, with its emphasis on producing standardized results through regulated teaching." See Cuban (1989) on the relationship among school reform, the at-risk category, and the graded school, "the core processes" of which are "labeling, segregating, and eliminating those who do not fit" (p. 784). The graded school, of course, is the traditional school organization—that is, the actual case of the idealized professional bureaucracy configuration presented here.

50. The degree of decoupling, as well as the availability of the requisite personnel, depends in large measure on the local history of special education services, which reflects the value orientation embedded in political cultures at the state, local, and school organization levels. For empirical and interpretive evidence on this point, see McDonnell and McLaughlin (1982); Skrtic, Guba, and Knowlton (1985); Noel and Fuller (1985); and Biklen (1985). Although there are exceptions (Biklen, 1985; Thousand, Fox, Reid, Godek, & Williams, 1986), students classified as having severe and profound disabilities and the professionals who serve them are located in segregated classrooms, a matter of great concern in the work of Stainback and Stainback (see note 15) and others (e.g., Biklen, 1985; Thousand et al., 1986). When these classrooms are located in regular school buildings, they follow the organizational form of the traditional decoupled subunit, which historically has existed as an adhocratic space outside of the bureaucratic configuration of general education.

The needs of the students in these programs typically are so variable that the notion of a standard program is virtually precluded. Moreover, the complexity of the diagnostic and instructional problems is so great that interdisciplinary collaboration is essential. Given the extreme ambiguity and complexity of the work in these programs, the fact that they are decoupled from the machine bureaucracy structure, and the degree to which collaboration, mutual adjustment, and discursive coupling characterize the work (see Sailor & Guess, 1983), these programs are prototypical of the adhocratic form in public education. See Skrtic (1991) for an extended discussion of this point.

51. Although the EHA requires regular classroom placement for students to the maximum extent possible, they are identified as "handicapped" because they cannot be accommodated within existing standard programs, in particular regular classrooms (Skrtic, Guba, & Knowlton, 1985, Walker, 1987). As such, depending on the degree to which the particular school is more adhocratically or bureaucratically oriented, mainstreaming for these students more or less represents symbolic integration, primarily in nonacademic classrooms and activities. For empirical and interpretive evidence on this point, see Biklen (1985); Carlberg and Kavale (1980); Skrtic, Guba, and Knowlton (1985); and Wright, Cooperstein, Renneker, and Padilla (1982).

52. In principle, teachers working collaboratively in the interest of a single student for whom they share responsibility violates the logic of loose coupling and the sensibility of the professional culture (Bidwell, 1965; Mintzberg, 1979; Weick, 1976) and thus, in principle, collaboration should not be expected to any meaningful degree in professional bureaucracies. At a minimum, mainstreaming and the resource room model require reciprocal coupling (Thompson, 1967), which is not the type of interdependency that specialization and professionalization yield. For empirical evidence that collaboration among regular teachers and between regular and special education teachers has been rare, fleeting, and idiosyncratic in the professional bureaucracy, see Bishop (1977); Lortie (1975, 1978); Skrtic, Guba, and Knowlton (1985); Tye and Tye (1984); and notes 48 and 53.

53. Although the adhocratic ends of the EHA are distorted because of the bureaucratic nature of the law and its implementation context, schools seem to have complied with its procedural requirements because of the adoption of practices that, although they may be well-intended and in some respects actually might result in positive outcomes, serve largely to symbolize (e.g., IEPs and resource rooms) and ceremonialize (e.g., IEP staffings and mainstreaming) compliance with the letter of the law rather than conformance with its spirit.

For empirical evidence on the symbolic and ceremonial nature of the IEP document and staffing process, resource room programs, and mainstreaming, see Carlberg and Kavale (1980); Gerardi, Grohe, Benedict, and Coolidge (1984); Schenck (1980); Schenk and Levy (1979); Ysseldyke et al. (1983); and notes 51 and 48. Moreover, from a policy perspective, symbolic compliance with procedural requirements can lead monitors and implementation researchers to faulty conclusions. For example, Singer and Butler (1987, p. 151) observed that "federal demands have equilibrated rapidly with local capacity to respond," and thus concluded that the EHA demonstrates that "a federal initiative can result in significant social reform at the local level." Although they are correct in asserting that such equilibration has resulted in "a basically workable system" (p. 151), they failed to recognize that equilibration is largely a process of institutionalizing the necessary symbols and ceremonies of compliance (Rowan, 1980; Zucker, 1977, 1981), which, given the contradiction between their bureaucratic orientation and the EHA's adhocratic ends, renders the system workable for school organizations but not necessarily for the intended beneficiaries of the federal initiative.

54. Citations for the proposals of the four teams of REI proponents have been omitted in this section. The proposals analyzed here are those described in the section "on Special Education as a Professional Practice" and its corresponding notes. The same format is followed in the remainder of the article for references to the REI proponents' and opponents' arguments for and against the REI and the current system of special education, as well as for the REI proponents' reform proposals.

55. For empirical evidence that the excellence movement has resulted largely in extensions of rationalization and formalization, see Clark and Astuto (1988), Timar and Kirp (1988), and note 49. For empirical evidence that the excellence movement, in general, and the effective schools movement (see note 56), in particular, have increased ritualization and professionalization and decreased personalization, see Cuban (1983, 1989), Slavin (1989), Stedman (1987), and Wise (1988). For example, Cuban noted that, under the effective schools formula, curriculum and instruction in many schools have become more standardized and thus less personalized.

   The problem is that advocates of effective schools, although well meaning, "seldom [question] the core structures of the graded schools within which they [work]. Their passion was (and is) for making those structures more efficient" (Cuban, 1989, p. 784).

56. By the "effective schools" debate, I mean the earlier phase of the excellence movement, which was shaped by the thinking in *A Nation at Risk* (National Commission on Excellence in Education, 1983) and generally seeks excellence through means that are quantitative and top-down; quantitative in that they simply call for more of the existing school practices; top-down in that their bureaucratic value orientation turns the goal of higher standards into more standardization for producing standardized results (e.g., Wise, 1988; notes 49 and 55). The proponents of this approach do not question traditional school organization, they simply want to make it more efficient (e.g., Cuban, 1989; notes 49 and 55).

   By the "school restructuring" debate I mean the more recent phase of the excellence movement, which was shaped by the thinking in books such as *High School* (Boyer, 1983), *A Place Called School* (Goodlad, 1984), *and Horace's Compromise* (Sizer, 1984). The participants in this debate (see, e.g., Bacharach, 1990; Clark, Lotto, & Astuto, 1984; Cuban, 1983, 1989; Elmore, 1987; Elmore & McLaughlin, 1988; Lieberman & Miller, 1984; McNeil, 1986; Oakes, 1985; Sergiovanni & Moore, 1989; Sirotnik & Oakes, 1986; Wise, 1988) generally seek excellence through means that are qualitative and bottom-up: qualitative in that they call for fundamental changes in the structure of school organizations; bottom-up in that they call for an increase in professional discretion, adult-adult collaboration, and personalization of instruction.

57. Although tracking as such is criticized, neither students labeled "handicapped" nor special education as an institutional practice have received much attention in the restructuring debate or the effective schools debate (Lilly, 1987; Pugach & Sapon–Shevin, 1987; Shepard, 1987).

58. The best articulation of this position within the restructuring debate is Schön's (1983, 1987, 1988, 1989) argument for developing reflective practitioners by eliminating the "normal bureaucratic emphasis on technical rationality" (Schön, 1983, p. 338) in schools and thus permitting teachers to become "builders of repertoire rather than accumulators of procedures and methods" (1988, p. 26). Although Schön clearly recognized that the reflective practitioner requires a reflective organization (Schön, 1983, 1988), he conceptualized the reflective practitioner as an individual professional engaged in a monological discourse with a problem situation, rather than a team of professionals engaged reflectively in a dialogical discourse with one another. As such, Schön retained the structural contingencies of specialization and professionalization and thus the professional bureaucracy configuration. For a deconstruction of Schön's notion of the reflective practitioner, see Skrtic (1991).

    Beyond the problem of innovation, eliminating rationalization and formalization while retaining specialization and professionalization creates a professional mode of accountability, which places virtually all decisions about the adequacy of practice in the hands of individual professionals. From an organizational perspective, this is a problem in a structural sense because the convergent thinking and deductive reasoning of professionals and professions means that they tend to see the needs of their clients in terms of the skills professionals have to offer the client (Mintzberg, 1979; Perrow, 1970; Segal, 1974). In a cultural sense, professionals and professions tend to distort negative information about their paradigms to make it consistent with their prevailing paradigms of practice (see, e.g., Brown, 1978; Rounds, 1979, 1981; Weatherley & Lipsky, 1977; Weick, 1985; see also note 46).

59. For genealogies (note 9) of special education's professional knowledge, practice, and value orientation, see Skrtic (1986, 1988a, 1991). For histories of special education see, for example, Lazerson (1983), and Sarason and Doris (1979).

60. For evidence on the ethics and efficacy of special education practices before the EHA, see note 43. For evidence on these practices after the EHA, see notes 15, 17, 48, 51, and 53.

61. See Cherryholmes (1988) for a discussion of critical pragmatism (note 4) as a mode of professional practice and discourse in public education. See Skrtic (1991) for a discussion of it as a means of developing and sustaining an adhocratic professional culture. Critical practice is "continual movement between construction of a practice . . . and deconstruction of that practice, "which shows its incompleteness and contradictions. Critical discourse is continual movement between the constitution of a methodology designed to [construct, deconstruct, and reconstruct practices] and subsequent criticism of that approach" (Cherryholmes, 1988, pp. 96–97). The goal of critical pragmatism is education or self-formation (Gadamer, 1975), a pedagogical process of remaking ourselves as we think, write, read, and talk more about our practices and discourses.

62. For the negative evidence on educational excellence, equity, and adaptability see, for example, Cuban (1979), Edgar (1987), Elmore and McLaughlin (1988), Goodlad (1984), Lehming and Kane (1981), McNeil (1986), Oakes (1985), Sizer (1984), and note 15. For empirical and interpretive evidence that some schools

are more effective, equitable, and adaptable than others, as well as discussions of contributing factors, see Berman and McLaughlin (1974–1978); Brophy (1983); Clark, Lotto, and Astuto (1984); Goodlad (1975); Lieberman and Miller (1984); McNeil (1986); and note 63. For the same type of evidence and discussions relative to the EHA and mainstreaming, see Biklen (1985); Skrtic, Guba, and Knowlton (1985); Thousand, Fox, Reid, Godek, and Williams (1986); Wright, Cooperstein, Renneker, and Padilla (1982); and note 63.

63. For empirical and interpretive evidence on the place of human agency in successful schools, see Biklen (1985); Brophy (1983); Clark, Lotto, and Astuto (1984); Lieberman and Miller (1984); McNeil (1986); Singer and Butler (1987); Skrtic, Guba, and Knowlton (1985); and Thousand, Fox, Reid, Godek, and Williams (1986).

I would like to thank Dwight Kiel and Linda Ware for their helpful comments on an earlier draft of the original article.

PART TWO

Personal Journeys

Chapters

From Creative Discontent Toward Epistemological Freedom in Special Education: Reflections on a 25-year Journey

Lous Heshusius

Thus I learn from life itself.
—Helen Keller, 1903 , p. 28
Discontent is the means to freedom ...(is) the very flame of inquiry.
—Jiddu Krishnamurti, 1953, pp. 42, 43

At least in the beginning of this chapter, I might give the impression, that I see the world in two mutually exclusive categories: the disabled and, therefore, as primary background, the nondisabled, or the abled. This may give the impression that the latter, the abled, need no examination. This impression exists initially because this chapter reflects the history of discontent with precisely this dichotomy, a dichotomy that harbors able-ist metaphors, conceptualizations, institutions, and pedagogical and research practices. As the story of discontent moves into the present, and into Chapter 8 of this book, it becomes clear that at the core of these chapters is the quest to dissolve this dichotomy into the difficult, but I believe evolutionary, task of living and learning together, honoring all diversity as "modes of expression—a phrase I borrow from Frazee (2000, p. 43).

One bright morning in the mid-1970s, I woke up early, and had, what then was for me, an astounding insight: I was soon to embark on a dissertation, probably in the area of mental retardation, would have a Ph.D. in special education, take a promising job, perhaps as an assistant professor teaching courses in mental retardation, or as an administrator or researcher in a school or institutional system, and I had *no idea* what those we labeled "mentally retarded" are like as people. I did not know them as human beings. I had no real sense of what their lives were like, and what their social status, or lack thereof, meant to them. I did not know what they thought about, worried about, were happy about. I did not know what they wanted for their own lives. I only "knew" them as profiles of test scores, as correlations, as "mental ages," as IQ scores, as frequency counts of desired, or, more to the point, of undesired behaviors to be respectively reinforced or extinguished—all this knowledge obtained by, I was taught to believe, accurate application of methodology. That is how I knew them. *Method* was the secret to knowing. I soon would be certified to teach about "them," to make decisions about "them," and to publish about "them"— all this because of my method-obtained state of knowing, which had put them and their lives into my little method boxes.

Once this realization had sunk in, my next thought was: How would I dare to do so and not know them as people? Not know them in the ways that we human beings get to know each other—through listening, through exchanging stories, by doing things together, by learning together, by knowing each other over time. *What* had I been learning all these years in graduate school? *How* had I been taught to know those who are different than most of us in some aspect or other? And how had I *not* been allowed to know them? What did I *not* know about them?

The answers to these sudden questions came as fast and as clearly as the questions had: "Little, really" and "in humanly incorrect ways" were the answers to the first two questions. "In direct human ways" and "a whole lot" were the answers to the last two questions. My years in graduate school (a master's degree in educational psychology, doctoral work in special education) suddenly seemed unimpressive to me. Useless really. Worse, in fact. Because the courses I had taken had not just bored me; they had tried to convince me that I could not learn from life itself.

I was being indoctrinated into "methodolatry," that worshipping of method as if it were a divine intervention, lifted over and above life itself. I was being taught that I could not validly know anything about others by using my own mind and humanness, my listening and interactive abilities, my observational and reflective abilities. It was not just "them" who had been put into little method boxes. I had been placed into them myself.

Had I conducted a standard dissertation in the late 1970s, undoubtedly I would have *run* an experiment *on* "my subjects," who would have been subjected to my wishes. I would have ordered them to do certain tasks, or engage in certain behaviors. I would have counted their behaviors, measuring and ranking them on scales of some kind or another, analyzing the outcomes only in terms of my intervention and in terms of statistical processes. I would have been measuring the "impact of my interventions" (Sugai, 1998, p.171), the quintessential task of inquiry for positivists and behaviorists. I would have been in their "presence" only in the "see–touch measuring realm" meaning of the word, the realm of the natural sciences. But I would not have been in *their* presence, I would not have been listening to who they were as human beings. I would not have learned how they learn by attentively being with them, as I have learned how my own children learn by being with them—without having to statistically process data that I gathered by putting them through an experimental design. And that was it precisely: I would not have been allowed to be *with* them. Neither they nor I were allowed a presence in the deeper sense of that word.

Elsewhere (Heshusius, 1981, 1996a) I have recounted how I came to do a qualitative, participant observation study instead, relying directly on normal human interactions, the kind of study of which there are plenty of these days, and are even considered traditional, given more recent approaches to research. But in the 1970s such a study was foreign to special education. Most departments of special education would not have allowed it to count as research.[1]

My answer to our editor's question then—What made me begin reading philosophy and epistemology outside of the field of special education—goes back to the realization that dawned upon me that early morning, still half asleep, now some 25 years ago. That insight crystalized for me the vague feeling of discomfort that had been with me from the beginning of graduate studies when taking 101 in statistics and in behavioral methods, and reading the first research articles I was required to read, all using experimental methods. I never felt quite at ease. In fact, I always felt distinctively dis-eased. The courses in measurement and statistics were difficult enough, but I was bored with them. They were life-less. They cheated me out of life. They cheated me out of myself. All they asked of me was to superimpose formulas and rules onto others, as well as onto myself—but this I did not understand back then. I came to this insight only much later, as I finally came to see that one cannot define another without defining one's self, in what may seem to be an opposite way, but which at a deeper level occurs by exactly the same dynamics and values. It is in defining the self in a certain way (however subconsciously this might be happening) that the other is simultaneously constructed as a necessary background to the particular self-definition. I attempt to write about this complex process in this chapter in relation to disability and special education.

The courses in behavioral theory and research I had to take also were based entirely on the application of control techniques and formulas to people. The reductionistic simplicity that characterized what I had to learn in these theories astonished me. I could not believe that academics actually used these methods, which, after all, were taken directly from experiments with laboratory animals (which is not the same as "animals." They are two different species. No self-respecting rats or pigeons would voluntarily—out of *self-organization*—engage in what their laboratory counterparts, half-starved and isolated, can be "taught" to do).

I had taught both regular and special education (ED and LD) for 7 years, largely in the Netherlands, my home country, prior to entering graduate school in the United States, and I had realized early on that the challenge and secret in education was not to reduce human phenomena to simple mechanisms that one thinks one can control but instead to honor their complexity and diversity, and thus to honor and, as Helen Keller said, learn from life itself.[2] My own work as a teacher had been so much richer than anything I learned in my graduate courses. Had I been using the teaching procedures I had to study in these courses, I would have been a greatly reduced teacher.

Fortunately, I turned that experience of deep boredom and irrelevancy into acts of "creative discontent" rather than suppress them or let myself be made subservient to them. By "creative discontent" I do not mean mere expression of negative reactions, which dulls the mind and the emotions and kills the creative potential of genuine discontent. Rather, I mean the creative effort to go outside the prescribed parameters and see what lies beyond that might free the mind and the heart to see the object of one's discontent anew and within a larger reality.

By freedom I do not mean doing whatever one pleases. As Jiddu Krishnamurti (1972) states:

> Freedom is not licentiousness, doing what you like—freedom demands tremendous discipline... not the discipline of suppression, of conformity...The word "discipline" means "to learn"...the very learning is discipline; not [that] you discipline yourself first and then learn. The very act of learning *is* discipline, which brings about freedom from all suppression, from all imitation. (p. 34)

This was the kind of disciplined freedom to think and study that I needed but that I was not allowed to have. This meaning of freedom necessitates that one does not harbor fear for anticipated responses to one's work. Fear, by definition, is in anticipation of response. Any such fear will hinder new perception. I will return to this important point when discussing the review process.

Everything I have written, ever, has germinated in actual experience. When I could not reconcile what I had to study and how I had to teach with how I saw my own children learn, with my memory of my own schooling, with how I learned, with common sense, I started to rely on other sources that provided food for thought and action: novels, stories, parents' experiences, my own observations, philosophical and literary essays, and scholarship in other fields. For what I was expected to believe within the world of special education was not humanly meaningful for me, and one has to make meaning in one's life to keep one's sanity.

Publishing To Stay Sane

The first article I published (1982a) that was critical of the status quo of special education was written to make sense of the "Why" of what I learned in graduate school, as well as with how I was required to teach youth with learning disabilities. At the time of the writing, holding my first academic position in the United States, I was both a university professor and a public school special education teacher in my dual role at a University Laboratory School. I based the article directly on my experiences in my function as a public school teacher. As any other teacher, I had to adhere to behavioristic principles that Public Law 92–142 had legalized. I abhorred the way I was supposed to teach (test, program and reinforce; test, program and reinforce), and I refused to do so, which got me routinely into trouble with the local state supervisor—but never with the children (see also Heshusius, 1984a, 1996a).

Why, the question was for me, had I been forced to learn what were to me unacceptable ways of knowing by otherwise seemingly rational and good people? I wrote about what I had come to understand regarding the paradigmatic basis of all knowledge by reading history and philosophy of science. I had read and re-read classics at the time such as von Bertalanffy (1968), Bronowski (1956), Bohm (1980), Jantsch (1980), and Kuhn (1970). I then critically framed the demands that were placed on my role as a teacher of "special needs" learners within that knowledge base.

Reading this 1982a article now, it does not seem to be much of an act of creative discontent compared to what is written today, but at the time it was. During my studies I had not encountered a single publication within the special education literature that addressed the paradigmatic parameters of special education's understanding of "science" and of its particular epistemology. In preparing the 1982a article, I conducted an extensive literature review, which rendered only two references in special education that touched on concerns similar to mine (Fisher & Rizzo, 1974; Mann & Phillips, 1967).

I experienced writing the article as a creative act because, by making new connections, I could transform for myself what I perceived as far too simple and inadequate theorizing, research, and assessment/instructional special education practices, practices I was required to partake in. Writing the article helped me to deal creatively with the despair I often felt, for it meant going into unknown and freeing territory, into a level of study that went outside of the parameters within which I was supposed to stay, parameters of which I found the inner logic deeply flawed. It felt creative, because from that new place I could cast a very different lens on what I was supposed to believe in and how I was supposed to teach. I started to understand the latter in terms of the *underlying* values and presuppositions of the prevailing mechanistic paradigm and positivist epistemologies. It stunned me to realize that no graduate course in the special education department had taught us what those underlying values and assumptions were. We had been taught the How, not the Why of the how, nor whose How and whose Why it really was.

I used the article then to tell others what I had learned: that there was a specific set of historically shaped human values behind all the rules of theorizing, research, and practice, and that one's own mind can discover and understand why and when and by whose authority these rules came into being—and that one does *not* have to believe their adequacy, their universality, their authority, or trust their values. Moreover, I wanted to show that there were completely different, noncompatible ways of drawing the parameters of knowledge, which I saw as far more adequate in terms of the complexities of teaching and learning. It was important to stress that these different ways were not compatible. Too easily, deeply different and incompatible paradigmatic meanings get (mis)appropriated by existing theories, which is exactly what several critics did with some of my work.[3] In the very process of such misappropriation, meanings become completely distorted (for an excellent discussion of this process see Smith, 1997. For specific examples of it in special education, see Heshusius, 1989b).

The Early Reviews

As paradigmatic analyses were practically unheard of in special education, it was no wonder that one of the reviews of the 1982a article I received stated: "Very esoteric, but seems important." Unfortunately, I do not remember other specifics, for I did not keep the reviews. The comment I just quoted is the only one I clearly remember. Had I only known that keeping reviews would come in handy 20 years later! I also threw away reviews of most other articles during my many moves, in trying to clean out files. I do remember that I had to make some changes in my writing style to the 1982a article. I initially had used a more narrative style, and I was asked to use a more standard academic style. Narrative inquiry was still a long way off.

Perhaps I was just lucky that my first critical piece was accepted readily. Perhaps the editor at that time happened to be courageous. Perhaps my paper was seen as an interesting curiosity—something off the beaten path. Perhaps it was used to show the world that the journal could be broad-minded. Perhaps the editor had some personal explicit or intuitive doubts about the prevailing and near-exclusive monopoly of behaviorist and positivist thought in special education. And a single voice is not threatening: If necessary, it can easily be silenced. This is just what critics (Ulman & Rosenberg, 1986) tried to do, critics who really should not have tried, in that they did not have any background in dealing with the analysis I had offered (see my rejoinder of 1986).

Although I can't recall further specifics about the review process of the 1982a article, what I *do* remember is the reception it received within the special education faculty of the university where I was teaching real-life children in the university's laboratory school, which was housed in a different department. At the same time, I was associated with the special education department. After the article came out, I was told through the grapevine, that almost an entire faculty meeting had been devoted to damning me: How had I dared to write the piece?! I remember being flabbergasted. It always had been—and it still is—my understanding of scholarship that one does not attack an individual, and that the business of scholarship is to think critically and explore and study widely. I had never considered that anyone would be upset. But many were. Yet, no one in the department came directly to me to discuss my ideas and tell me why they seemed wrong to them.

About a dozen years after the 1982a article was published, I did receive a letter from colleagues from that time, who invited me to write a chapter for a book, saying that they regretted that we never had really talked back then. As well, a few years ago I received an invitation to apply for the position of chair of the department. Change, indeed, is always in the air, somehow, somewhere.

That first article did elicit a stream of letters. One came from two well known special educators, whom I saw as relatively traditional, and from whom I never would have expected a favorable response, saying essentially how worthwhile they found the article. Another well known special educator, whom I also saw as relatively traditional, wrote me that he had found the piece "insightful" and had made it required reading in his courses. A superintendent of special education wrote me and requested 50 copies to give to her teachers, for, she said, I had articulated what they were perpetually complaining about. I received a poem from a speech pathologist addressing the same sentiments and understandings. A program coordinator of special education in Los Angeles recommended it to all her principals, consultants, assistant superintendents, in all some 40 folks. Another special educator called me and said, "I wish I had written it—it's exactly what I have always felt but couldn't say."

It was particularly gratifying to receive such positive feedback from people in the field—for my own need to write the article had most immediately emerged from my actual work as a special education teacher. I received these reactions, of course, happily, but somehow they did not really surprise me. It felt normal that my analysis, which had emerged from years of experience and study, would touch some hearts out there. I knew that I was not insane. If I experienced and understood my scholarly and teaching life in the manner I did, surely there had to be others who did similarly.

I believe I have been a late bloomer in life in many ways. Perhaps for once, I was just a little ahead of my time in writing this particular article (allow me my little vanity here!). In all frankness, I am actually convinced that had I been born and been "trained" as a teacher in the United States at that particular time, I would not have thought anything was strange. It was a certain timing and background, resulting in a culture shock when I came to the United States and started studying in the early 1970s, landing at the height of behaviorism and positivism, that caused my early awareness of and objection to the strangeness of what I was being taught.[4]

Characteristics of the Reviews

I did keep reviews of the article published in 1989a, appearing here as Chapter 2, and one of the reviews of the 1991 article. I kept the latter, a review of 15 single-spaced pages, as it was a fascinating review, paradigmatically speaking. The editor at the time told me it was a historical record with regard to length. More on that review later.

For other publications, two clear characteristics of the collective reviews come to mind:

1. It is fair to estimate, in retrospect, that the greater number of reviews were uninformed and lacked the paradigmatic knowledge to judge the manuscript, though certainly some did reflect familiarity with the ideas I had expressed and the literature I had used.

2. Reviews for any particular article were a number of times contradictory in the extreme, from perhaps one being positive and two others dismissive and at times ridiculing. Among the dismissive ones were some that consisted of no more than one paragraph, merely stating in essence: This is nonsense. This is bad because I say it is bad. I still wonder how such reviewers got away with doing so little, so poorly.

The fate of one submission is worth telling in detail as the initial reception of the manuscript was both thoroughly uninformed and dismissive, yet the process ended happily. As it happens to be the case, this befell the article that became what is Chapter 2 in this book. In 1987, I initially submitted the manuscript to a mainstream special education journal. The previous editor had asked me to write my views for this journal a year earlier. We had just debated each other as panel members at a conference in the area of learning disabilities regarding the proper research methods for the field of special education, and he had completely disagreed with my views. In a pleasant conversation afterward, however, he told me that, regardless of his disagreements, he thought these issues should be aired in the open. I was excited and started on it right away. But there was so much to say—as I intended to write a broad paradigmatic discussion and critique of the existing epistemological underpinnings of research and theories in the field of special education, and to outline different possibilities—that by the time I finished, the editorship had changed.

The new editor sent back the manuscript without delay, stating that—and I am quoting: "The writing style is often awkward and difficult to follow." And further:

> I think you are trying to say that approaches to special education need to follow a steady transition from theory formulation to model building to basic research to test the model to applied research to test for practicality and applicability to practice. This point, the major point of the paper, is not well articulated.

This person further suggested that I look up an article written by this person and a colleague, which would help "clarify your thoughts."

How anyone on the planet could possibly interpret my article to say that I was proposing the traditional trajectory from theory formulation, through model building and basic research to testing for practicality, is a puzzle over which I still shake my head in disbelief. But, then, I should not. There is a clear paradigmatic explanation for such blindness: When solidly caught within only one particular paradigm, *everything* gets constructed by its beliefs, as no other sense-making frames are available to the thinker's consciousness. It was a splendid example of the constructing force that paradigms can assert.

The article had not been sent out for review. The editor had rejected it personally, out of hand. I wrote back to the editor, stating that the misunderstanding of my paper was not caused by my awkward writing style but rather, by this person's uninformed state of mind. I noted my regret that the journal had closed off its open attitude under new editorship.

I immediately sent the exact same manuscript to the *Journal of Learning Disabilities,* and it was sent to five reviewers. It has been the only time in my experience that more than three or four reviewers have been involved. As I noted in my cover letter to the editor, reviewers' comments were more contradictory among each other than I had ever experienced, and no item of critique was shared by all five. In this case, however, none of the reviews was merely dismissive.

Two reviewers recommended acceptance, with no more than minor suggestions. It was indeed time for the LD field to attend to the ideas in the paper, one reviewer said, as the paper raised the question of paradigmatic bias to a level of discourse not seen in any of the LD journals. The other said I had written an excellent argument for embracing holistic principles, but the reviewer saw some possible problems with my theory-versus-paradigm distinction and with my view that behaviorism locates the problem (whatever the problem is) within the child. (See my rejoinder, 1989b, for my response to these perceived problems, with which I had to disagree.) One of these reviewers ended by saying: " I have little doubt that [the holistic paradigm] is the correct one. We *have* failed miserably by using both the ontology and the epistemology of prior paradigms. I'd be surprised if anyone could mount a convincing argument to the contrary." This reviewer also agreed that my citations "supported that current paradigms are failing all over the place in other fields, not just in special education. Several of my colleagues in an interdisciplinary department that includes the so-called "harder" sciences...also report this." This person ended with an important comment:

> Most of us raised in the mechanistic tradition will have a great deal of trouble (as Heshusius indicates we already have) picturing the alternative ways of knowing (let alone teaching); but that's our trouble.

The reviewer went on to say that the "holists" (and by implication all other views alternative to positivism/mechanistic thought, I would assume) need to get on with demonstrating how this will work—*to their own satisfaction, not necessarily ours..."* (emphasis mine). This reviewer understood that asking for "proof" or "evidence" that holistic principles "work," as some of the other reviewers who criticized the manuscript did, is a paradigmatic mistake: That is, "what works," *and* therefore the criteria used to decide it does, *is* paradigmatically dependent. This makes this entire debate so difficult. The positivist will never agree that alternatives "work," because these alternatives do not "work" according to positivist criteria and measurements. Neither I, nor anyone else, will be able to "prove" that alternative thought "works" as well as or better than positivist thought, nor would we want to, or possibly consider trying. To do so, we would have to adopt and "incorporate" (which means, making part of its body) into the alternative position the positivist criteria for what it means to say that a theory or paradigm works. In trying to do so, one would no longer offer an alternative paradigmatic perspective.

Conceptualizations of criteria (what they are, on what basis one needs them, how one is allowed to meet them, for what reason, who is in charge of setting them) are woven into and through all the other dimensions of a particular paradigmatic framework and are inextricable from them. To try to superimpose a particular paradigm's set of criteria onto an alternative one is, in essence, to demand that the other move back into the earlier paradigm. The particular story of paradigmatic discontent told here thus also holds that positivist notions and criteria for what "works," along with the entire paradigm, are lacking and are in need of fundamental, paradigmatic reconstruction.

I no longer have the fifth reviewer's formal review sheet but do have the review itself. He or she said that the manuscript "deserves publication," and "some version of it should be published" but argued that the existing paradigm was not as bad as I made it out to be, and that I had not shown clearly enough why the paradigm I advocated was "better." I thus explained in greater detail in the final version why I thought that was in fact so, without having to fall back on positivist criteria.

In the rewrite, which became the final version, I elaborated on the *paradigm-as-metaphor* and attempted to make the important distinction between paradigm-as-metaphor and theory clearer than I had in my original submission. These reviewers also wanted me to indicate the "specific impacts or techniques" of the paradigmatic views I was advocating. I tried to make clear that holistic principles are not a set of techniques or strategies but instead a different way of looking at relations that make up life and learning, and out of which different educational practices, relations, and pedagogies emerge. Although observable outcomes will become different, of course, they are not a *direct* target for change, to be accomplished piece by piece by cause–effect assumptions. One perhaps can draw a direct parallel with the differences between traditional medicine, with its focus on intervention and dealing with specific symptoms typically in isolation from the rest of the patient's life on the one hand, and holistic medicine on the other hand, which heals, rather than treats symptoms, while in the healing the symptoms are also "treated."[5]

What was so positive about this particular review process, then, was that all five reviewers had seriously engaged my writings. I could use many of their comments to further clarify what I was saying. The editor accepted the rewrite and suggested making it into a feature article to which others would respond.[6] The review process of this particular submission then showed that two special education journals, both under the same ownership umbrella, and the two editors could not possibly have been more differentially informed and unimaginably contradictory in their evaluation of the manuscript: outright rejection without review, and feature article.

Subsequently, I wrote a letter to the powers that were, stating my objection, not to the fact that a journal under their umbrella had rejected something I wrote, but that it had not been sent out for review because of the editor's unacceptable state of mind and lack of scholarly wisdom and knowledge. It goes to show how acceptance or rejection of a manuscript is far from a neutral, "scientific" decision, and how crucially important editors and editorial boards are. This is analogous to the paradigmatic stance that no way of knowing is not also deeply personal (and therefore also emotive and somatic), social, and political. The claim to neutrality is a ventriloquist trick, a mode of speaking in which the real voice is smartly hidden, so smartly that the reader/listener is made to believe it comes from somewhere else. The personal and the scholarly do not have the neat, sharp boundaries that traditionalists assume. This is not to suggest deliberate bias. It is, however, to honor the power of the situatedness and embeddedness of knowledge in all dimensions of human life.

Critique of CBA

The 15-page, single-spaced, review of the 1991 critique of CBA (by which I meant both the curriculum based assessment (CBA) and the direct instruction movements) was fascinating for a number of reasons. The manuscript had been sent to three people, all of whom believed in the very thing I was critiquing. Two reviews were purely dismissive, though I can't recall the details. The review of 15 single pages I kept—not because of its unusual length but, rather, because of its unusual passion and its genuine effort to understand what I was saying, though I was seen as arrogant, harsh, outrageous, argumentative and offensive. This review was, in some ways, the fairest ever. Even though the person expressed his or her outraged emotions about what I said, he or she also doggedly worked through each point, lashing out, then giving me the benefit of the doubt, then rejecting it, then accepting some of it.

On and on, this reviewer said, in effect: I am outraged by what you are saying, but there is some validity to what you are saying, at least in published literature; but curriculum based assessment and direct instruction do not have to be that way; it is unfortunate that what you say can be applied to too many, but it does not have to be that way . . . and so forth. More than 20 statements said: What you are saying is ridiculous, but you may be right, at least in some cases. . . . For example, what I wrote, said the reviewer "reveals some level of ignorance. On the other hand, it *is* quite true that many of the published applications of CBA *can* be criticized for many of the problems the author raises"; and, "The notion that "one-size-fits-all" curricula are fundamental to CBA is silly. . . . Still, there is an element of validity in your statement. . . ."

Further, "That people [those who believe in CBA and DI] are overlooking many of the considerations raised by the author is, in my opinion, a legitimate concern. . . . However, the argument that people *must* overlook those considerations if they use CBA is, also in my opinion, an indefensible position." This comment made me explain in my final version (1991, p. 319) the reasons why I believe it is, indeed, a defensible position.

"I *struggled*" said this reviewer, "to see beyond my initial rage. . . ." And in directly showing her or his struggle in the review, and in providing some examples as to how he or she went about teaching, I felt the person behind the words and was struck again by how disembodied is the field's literature that relies on positivist rules, how ventriloquist its tone. Here, clearly, was a person who was deeply and personally committed to the educational needs of youngsters, in a manner that never could show itself within the prescribed rules of CBA processes and research reports. The harm done by methodolatry was, to me, written all over this review.

This reviewer recommended publication, as the manuscript was "thought provoking in the extreme," and "reinforced many of my own concerns." Yet, many, many times the review stated I was wrong. It is in this internally contradictory and conflicting review that I saw the power of conflicting paradigms poignantly illustrated: in this case, the conscious professional beliefs of the mechanistic paradigm, in conflict with the more tacit knowledge of personal/social experience that is crucial to holistic relations. (This is, of course, my interpretation, with which the reviewer might not agree.)

"Real" and "Meaningful"

One of the major paradigm conflicts that played itself out in the reviews of my submissions to special education journals is the contradictory understanding of the notions of "real" and "meaningful." These words mean incompatible things to the differing paradigmatic understandings. This reviewer, too, struggled with, and paradigmatically misinterpreted, my reference to these notions. "Meaning" here, too, was taken to mean no more than "individualizing" tasks. The words "real" and "meaningful" within positivist thought are seen as subservient to the task and the curriculum materials presented, the nature of which is, in turn, subservient to demands for their measurability.

The prescribed tasks and curriculum materials, then, *in reaction to which* youngsters' performances are measured, come first. Then, "meaning" and "real life purpose" are "added" to them. As this reviewer conceded, many special educators are remiss in not even trying to do that. But can it even be done? Speaking paradigmatically, to "add" real-life meaning to predetermined and programmed tasks is not possible. First comes real-life meaning, and learning engagements *emerge* from that. One cannot "add" real-life meaning, or it will not quite stay real-life meaning. It actually will become a plastic kind of meaning. In my rejoinder (1989b, pp. 597–598) to Licht and Torgeson's similar positivist's misappropriation of my discussion of "real-life meaning," I make this very clear, by exposing the specific "plastic" content of examples they referred to but did not describe. Anne Sullivan's understanding of her work with Helen Keller (1903, p. 382; see also footnote 2) comes to mind:

> I have tried from the beginning to talk naturally to Helen and to teach her to tell me only things that interest her and ask questions only for the sake of finding out what she wants to know. When I see that she is eager to tell me something, but is hampered because she does not know the words, I supply them and the necessary idioms, and we get along finely.

And further:

> I am beginning to suspect all elaborate and special systems of education. They seem to be built upon the supposition that every child is a kind of idiot who must be taught to think. . . . Let [the child] come and go freely, let him touch real things and combine his impressions for himself, instead of sitting indoors at a little round table, while a sweet-voiced teacher suggests that he build a stone wall with his wooden blocks, or make a rainbow out of stripes of coloured paper, or plant straw trees in a bead flower pot. Such teaching fills the mind with artificial associations that must be got rid of, before the child can develop independent ideas out of actual experience. (in Keller, 1903, p. 319)

Said this particular reviewer:

> I found your use of the term "real" very confusing. After much consideration (and rereading many portions of the manuscript), I finally concluded that by "real" you probably mean "meaningful and believable."

And I had taken for granted that that was obvious. Paradigmatic images, meanings, and dictates run always deeper than we think. Nevertheless, I was honored with this passionate and thoughtful review. The reviewer had struggled hard to see my position, which was so critical of this person's own views, and in doing so had helped me to think deeper about what I was writing about.

The Hegemony of Positivism and Behaviorism

Of all the manuscripts I ever submitted to special education refereed journals, not counting rejoinders, the review process was difficult for three submissions (1988, 1989a, 1991), with one or more poorly informed or dismissive reviews requiring a lot of effort to respond to them. It is very telling that these three difficult submissions all directly and extensively called into question the hegemony of positivism and behaviorism in special education. Of other, easily accepted submissions, two did the same, but one of those (1984a) was a submission to *The Learning Disability Quarterly,* where at that time a kindred soul, Mary Poplin, was the editor. The first (1982a) article was somehow miraculously accepted without the request for major revisions.

Other easily accepted submissions to special education journals addressed different ways of knowing, but in doing so only implicitly critiqued positivist doctrine such that it probably was invisible for those who did not wish to deal with the issue. One article, for instance—an interview with a learning disabled adult—was accepted under the rubric of "Perspective" (1984b), seen as the kind of personal knowledge that might be interesting and helpful but that did not count as "real" knowledge. Another easily accepted piece was published in *Mental Retardation* (1982b). This journal seems always to have been extremely broad-minded, and from early on has welcomed a wide range of approaches to scholarship.

All manuscripts of articles I have submitted to special education journals were, in the end accepted. But I did not realize, until I started to submit manuscripts of similar paradigmatic nature to journals outside of special education, how much work I typically had to do for special education journals by having to respond to misunderstandings by reviewers. Reviews received from journals outside of special education were distinctly better informed about the paradigmatic issues. Also, it is fair to say that the enormous contradictions in reviews relative to a specific special education submission have not been characteristic of the reviews from outside of special education. The latter have been far more balanced and consistent with one another. Last, I have not received any purely dismissive/ridiculing reviews anywhere else, ever. Special education may not be the only narrowly defined field of study within the broader field of education, but, it surely must be one of the most restricted ones.

"Portraits"

One other submission beautifully illustrates the traditionally narrow, disembodied notion of what constitutes helpful knowledge for our profession. In the mid-1980s, I sent a manuscript to some 10 publishers of special education-related professional books and journals. The manuscript was a translation from the original Dutch of a series of "portraits" of people with disabilities and retardation, abused and neglected youngsters, people with mental disturbance, and otherwise mistreated or forgotten people. Each portrait is about a real person and an actual situation. "I can take your hand and introduce you to each of them," Lize Stilma, the writer, told me. Stilma met the people she writes about in her work in Dutch institutions, and she won a prestigious Dutch cultural award for her publications. Her "portraits" move through and beyond the intellect, through and beyond rules and institutions, research, and regulations, and then reattach all of these to a deeper human impulse, outside of the grasp of traditional rationalities. Below is one of these portraits, chosen almost at random, as it was not possible to choose a "representative" one, as the uniqueness of each defies such artificial notion.

Lydia

People in the neighborhood were used to the evening breeze
bringing Lydia's calling into their homes.
Everyone in the little town knew what would happen at the end of the day.
As soon as twilight came, crazy Lydia would sit on her decrepit porch and call, for at least fifteen minutes, "Isabel...Isabel...come here..."

No one heard the despair in her voice any longer.
No one felt pity any more.
Lydia had been crying her evening cries for so many years!
It had become as insignificant as the yapping of a farmyard dog.
Children and strangers would sometimes ask the meaning of her calling.
Then the tale was told with words long drained of empathy.
They would explain that crazy Lydia had had a baby, many years ago.
Just imagine, Lydia a baby!
The authorities, of course, decided that it could not be tolerated.
A civil servant and a nurse had placed the orange crate in which Lydia had carefully tucked in her little daughter on the back seat, and had driven away.
The only thing to do, people said.
Nobody had ever told Lydia where the official car had gone.
And that was a good thing, too, people said.

In this town lived many mothers who had a baby to cherish.
Lydia could only cry a name in the twilight.
For years.

And always in vain.
No one ever opened the gate to chat a bit.
Not until twenty years of pleading had passed.
On a fine summer's evening someone, out of the blue, joined Lydia on the porch, said "Hello," and filled his pipe.

Lydia did not answer his greeting; she didn't know how, for no one had every greeted
   her before.

The man told her a short and simple tale.

But Lydia must have thought it a most wonderful story.

He said, "Because of my work, I got to know your daughter Isabel.

And now listen carefully, Lydia.

She always had enough to eat.

Always enough clothes.

And every night she slept in a warm bed with blankets.

Then she got sick one day. She had no pain, but lives no more."

"That's nice," said Lydia, as if she had received a gift.

"That's nice," she said once more.

And she sat motionless on her porch.

As deeply peaceful as a person can be when a wall of loneliness has been removed.

After that evening the little town said,

"Lydia is crazier than ever.

No, she doesn't cry any more, not that.

But do you know what she does now?

She waves at the clouds.

And laughs!"

The man who filled his pipe was Lize Stilma's father, a social worker.
Understanding Lydia to be an equal human being, he spoke truth.

Every single review of this manuscript went on at length about how
beautiful these portraits were, how the editorial staff had been moved, at
times to tears, how insightful they were, how they reflected what was wrong
with society in relation to people with disabilities. But they did not think
there would be enough of a "market" for them. They were too different from
what was normally published. We subsequently went to a Canadian publisher
of artistic work who loved and published them (see Heshusius & Peetoom,
1986). Given today's rapidly changing notions of what constitutes knowledge, how it is constructed, and how it can be expressed, one could characterize Stilma's work as narrative, interpretive, and poetic knowledge (though
Stilma says, "I don't write poetry; I just write down what I see"). Perhaps
some publishers who focus on disability and special education concerns
might have been interested in them now.

Some Insights

On several occasions I have been asked how I managed to get published in special education journals so early on, given the critical nature of my thinking.

I am not sure. Luck must be part of it, especially in the sense that I must have had mostly good luck with who happened to be the editors at the time of submission. As the story about what happened to the submission of the article printed in this book as Chapter 3 shows, the editor can be a decisive factor. Another reason is my persistent confidence that what I think is not irrational or without merit. This, combined with my passion about what I think, feel, and write, can make me most persistent. This often has meant spending extraordinary amounts of time and effort going over all reviewers' comments, one by one, and writing letters in response to reviews. I made an extensive analysis of them, even color-coding the various objections across reviews to see more readily where they might overlap or contradict. I then responded to each and every item in the most scholarly way I could. I gave the critical comments the benefit of the doubt, often going back to the books to check the accuracy of my own understanding in the matter, read more, double-checked references, concepts, and so forth.[7] In reworking the manuscript, I then outlined carefully which objections I could respond to and which ones I could not because the reviewer had misunderstood what I said, and I would explain why. I marked the parts in the reworked manuscript where I had incorporated the reviewers' comments by often working preventively. That is, in cases of reviewers' misunderstandings, I expressed what I had stated in the first submission and then added, "This is not to say . . . ," followed by the misunderstanding the reviewer had exhibited. This works very well. It helps the reader to know how not to understand my words. In that sense, I always consider reviews as potential reader reactions. If a reviewer totally misunderstands what I say, many readers likely will do so as well. While I tried to work preventively, I can say that not once did I change the substance of what I wanted to say in responding to the reviews. Needless to say, some of these cover letters became lengthy epistles on their own account (some as long as nine pages single-spaced) and I expended a huge amount of effort to write them.

The most crucial attitude to take when responding to critical comments, I believe, is never to see them as personal attacks but instead as scholarly challenges. I never was much interested in whom the reviewer might have been, and I still cannot easily remember who wrote against me in formal publications. Frankly, it does not matter to me. What matters are the ideas, for ideas, as someone said, have consequences. And ideas that are not dangerous, said Oscar Wilde, are not worthy to be called ideas. By "dangerous" he meant that which challenges rusty rules, outdated frames, and narrow constructs.

I mention some of the above to signal to young academics and graduate students that scholarship comes first, second, third, and last. I have been quite unhappy with having listened to far too many academics or aspiring academics who have expressed fear that if they don't do their research the way the mainstream does it, they will not get a job, lose their job, not finish their dissertation, not get funding, and all the rest of it. The very evening I am writing this (October 24, 2000) believe it or not, I spoke in the afternoon with two brand new Ph.Ds (not in special education) who had submitted an article, had responded to requests for revisions, and had received word from the editor that he had now accepted it and that it probably would appear in issue number such and so.

The submitters heard nothing for a while. Upon inquiring, they learned that the editorship had changed, and they received a letter from the new editor that she had sent it out for review again, and it was rejected. They asked my advice. I responded with indignation at the new editor's unjust action and told them to demand that the initial acceptance be honored, or else take it all the way up to wherever that might lead. Said one of the authors, "But as young academics, couldn't she hurt our future?"

I do, and do not, understand this fear of personal vendettas. Rarely, for that matter, have I seen any such vendettas carried out in the face of good scholarly work, though, of course, it does happen. In my own case, had I had that kind of fear, I never would have written that first 1982a article, given that I was associated with a department of special education that at the time was completely on the behaviorist track and did not acknowledge that any other ways of knowing could possibly exist. I never would have spoken up in many places of scholarly gatherings as I have. The idea here is not to deliberately present opposing views but, instead, to study well. Do your homework well, and then say what you need to say. I don't know why anyone would want to become an academic and engage in scholarly endeavors if it were not for this reason. What it takes not to be captured by this fear of repercussions I do not know.

Publishing Alternative Views Within Special Education: Toward an Easier Present?

In some ways, things might have slowly improved in terms of outlets for our writings. Among the journals that now address special education-related areas deliberately devoted to many ways of knowing are *The International Journal of Special Education; Disability and Society; Disability, Handicap & Society; Disability Studies Quarterly;* and a new journal, *Disability, Culture, and Education.* And as mentioned already, *Mental Retardation* has been open to various lenses cast on the phenomena of mental retardation.

On the other hand, a backlash seems to have arisen in the major special education journals. These journals have "behaved" in what seems, at the

surface, erratically, accepting articles from an alternative paradigmatic perspective at certain times, even making them into feature articles, while rejecting articles of the same nature at other times. But there probably is nothing
erratic about it. It can be understood in terms of the extraordinary need for
mainstream special education leaders to retain the positivist and behaviorist
status quo in the field.

Colleagues' Experiences

In speaking to seven special education colleagues I know personally, and
whose work I know well and see as most appropriate contributions to the discussions on the nature of science and knowledge in special education, I
learned the following about their recent experiences with the review process
of mainstream special education journals. I did not include Tom Skrtic and
Richard Iano, as they are telling their own stories in this volume. Many others I do not know personally, but, having read some of their work, might well
have similar stories to tell were not contacted. This personal "survey" is, of
course, not a systematic study, but it perhaps could be a stimulus for conceiving such a study—perhaps someone's dissertation project?

Four of the seven colleagues told me that they have not submitted anything to special education journals. One, because she refuses to submit work
to journals whose editors and reviewers likely will not understand the manuscript and will dismiss it without an informed consideration. The other three
decided to submit to journals in the area of disability studies or to general
education journals to bring the issues to the broader readership in education
and other social sciences.

The other three of the seven colleagues, all well published scholars,
have run into problems similar to, or perhaps even worse than, the problems
I recounted with my own submissions. The following, with their permission, is what they told me. Brantlinger (1997) sent her paper first to
Exceptional Children, where it was rejected, and then had it accepted by the
Review of Educational Research. One of *Exceptional Children's* co-editors,
at the time of the initial submission, had reacted favorably to the manuscript
and had shared some of Brantlinger's concerns about the exclusionary
nature of special education positivist scholarship expressed in her paper.
Brantlinger's paper critiqued the positivist/empiricist position for denying
its own particular ideology in relation to the role of research in the inclusion
debate (even more specifically, for denying that it could be based on any
ideology at all). The editor had referred to it as "thought-provoking" and
"extremely interesting." The paper, however, was too long. By the time the
paper was reworked, the co-editor rejected it, saw the piece as "inflamma-
tory," and objected to the fact that it was not "data-based." This editor

suggested that Brantlinger should first engage in a data-based analysis so it would be "scientific."

Here, too, as I discussed at greater length in my rejoinder (1989b) to the reactions to the article printed here as Chapter 2, the positivist and behaviorist ideologies hold tight to the notion that all we can rely on are "data-driven theories," whereas almost everywhere else in scholarship, it is clearly understood that the only "empirical" knowledge humans can construct is theory-driven. Paradigmatic and theoretical ideas and beliefs come first—not last—as they actually decide what can even count as "data" in the first place. The theory-as-data-driven stance, which conceives of "data" only in the limited positivist/empiricist construction of the concept (for it *is* a concept), allowing only numerical and statistical manipulation of information obtained through external lenses to count as "data," is choking the field.

Another article by Brantlinger (1994), submitted to the three journals *Remedial and Special Education, Journal of Special Education,* and *Exceptional Children*, was rejected by all (one of the editors overruled two of three positive reviews) and then was published by the *Journal of Adolescent Research*. This paper addressed high- and low-income students' differing views of the special education they received. The latter, who are far more likely to be placed in special education classes, saw special education as a negative, stigmatizing experience.

Another of my colleagues, Scot Danforth, routinely sends everything he writes to special education journals first, though he knows it probably will be rejected. I am quoting from his e-mail response to my inquiry:

> My goal all along has been to write for a special education audience. Generally, each article that I have published was rejected harshly at two other places before it found a home. At first, I was naive enough to think that such journals as *Behavioral Disorders, the Journal of Learning Disability, and Exceptional Children* would appreciate alternative perspectives. After I realized that they didn't, I made a point of continuing to send my manuscripts to them. I knew that the papers would get rejected, but I wanted the editors to know that I and others were doing alternative work. I have wanted them to know that their rejections on ideological grounds would not halt the development of non-positivist and non-traditional theories. They cannot force consensus on the field. It is obviously terrible for these journals to squelch work from alternative perspectives. But it would be even worse if these editors and reviewers were to come to the misguided conclusion that the small circle of ideas they support are the only ideas going on in the field. Of course, [the rejections] annoy me, but I feel it is important to [send manuscripts first to special education journals].

Examples of articles first rejected by special education journals and then accepted elsewhere include a paper linking resistance theories to behavior disorders as defined by schools, providing a class and race analysis of the politics of oppositional behavior. The paper discusses well known qualitative research studies by critical ethnographers on the nature of students' resistance to traditional schooling processes and applies this discussion to the area of behavior disorders. Danforth sent it first to *Behavioral Disorders*, where it was rejected based on the view that resistance could be explained by way of "functional behavioral assessments." Again, this illustrates the ideology that one can only know validly and reliably by use of behavioral methods; otherwise, one cannot know anything at all. The paper subsequently was accepted by *Multiple Voices,* a CEC journal for the multicultural division, the reviewers of whom loved the piece (see Danforth, 2000). One wonders, in despair really, how artificially fragmented the journals of any one particular association can be—and how contradictory in the extreme editors and reviewers can be.

A second example is a paper on John Dewey and pragmatism, an area of knowledge in which Danforth is well versed, relating Dewey's views to the field of special education. He sent the paper first to *The Journal of Learning Disabilities,* then to *Remedial and Special Education.* In both cases it was rejected *without review. RASE* noted that the journal does not publish "first-person essays," which I take to mean writings that are not based on positivist definitions of "data." In that interpretation, even Dewey himself has nothing to contribute because his writings were not data-based, and therefore were only "first-person essays," merely "personal experience" or "personal testimony," to use Kauffman's phrasing. The paper subsequently was accepted by *Disability and Society* (see Danforth, 1999), an excellent journal based in England—but, unfortunately, a journal that not many special educators in North America read.

Still another submission was first rejected by *Exceptional Children* but subsequently accepted by *Anthropology and Education Quarterly.* The article discussed a social construction (rather than a medical and psychometric) approach to attention deficit disorders (see Danforth & Navarro, 2000).

Still another paper that Danforth submitted to *Exceptional Children*, discussing the now infamous Kauffman and Brigham (1999) editorial in *Behavioral Disorders,* also was rejected. Most of the paper addressed the question of how Dewey would have responded to the editorial. "Dewey and democracy," Danforth said in his e-mail to me, "how can anyone object?" But reviewers did, though they did not point to any passage in which Danforth might, according to them, be misrepresenting positivism, or any passage in which he might, according to them, be misrepresenting Dewey. The ideas in the paper themselves were not engaged. The reviewers essentially said that positivism is beyond critique. As I understand this statement, then, positivism is a divine intervention.

Another interesting rejection relates to a 1997 submission by Deborah Gallagher to the *Journal of Learning Disabilities*. Her paper questioned the notion of "science" in positivist special education scholarship. One reviewer saw the paper as a "manifesto" and saw "implicit Marxism" in it. Another one dismissed it as "psychobabble," and parenthetically also included Tom Skrtic and Mary Poplin in this characterization by referring to them as the "usual suspects." "Of what," asked Gallagher in a letter back to the editor, "are they suspected other than expressing views contrary to those of the reviewer?" One wonders why these reviewers are still being used. Interestingly, Gallagher's paper was published by *Exceptional Children* (see Gallagher, 1998).

Another paper by Gallagher (2001), providing an explanation why the very claim to neutrality is itself a moral stance (though this is denied by positivist thought), referencing philosophers such as Gadamer and Taylor, was rejected by *Exceptional Children*. The main reason provided by one reviewer was that the manuscript said what had been said already. And rejected. But the latter is never added to the argument: It has already been said, and we rejected it. Once is enough. We are the authorities. The reviewer ended her or his dismissive review, noting that, if published, the readers would say, "Oh, no, not this again." (The argument that an alternative position has already been offered, and that enough is enough, is frequently given by reviewers who reject alternative positions. I do not understand their logic: The positivist position can be repeated again and again, for years, for decades, but other positions can be offered only once?) Other reasons for the rejection were: Its "hard-line, anti-empirical position" does not do justice to science, and in fact "abuses science." One reviewer further referred to the paper as "fashionable nonsense" (borrowing the title of a book), which is "incoherent" and "fails to discriminate sense from nonsense." The paper then is cast into the metaphors of "fundamentalism, demagoguery, and totalitarianism."

Mainstream special education journals, I believe, have become even more conservative and narrowly focused in recent years, in an effort to keep out anything that challenges the status quo. Remarkably, many graduate students and young academics are finding their way outside of these parameters nevertheless, and are engaging in alternative work, welcoming multiple ways of knowing.

My "survey" of seven colleagues—and adding to these Skrtic's and Iano's accounts—raises the question of how many manuscripts submitted by many others may be routinely rejected by special education editors/reviewers because the latter do not have sufficient knowledge about the content of the submission, or simply want to maintain the power of their own stances.

For all we know, the work of many new academics who have written excellent dissertations from alternative perspectives (and many are being written) is rejected by the very journals that are supposed to represent the broad range of knowledge of the field. Or, well aware of the likely rejection, how many don't even bother, and go elsewhere?

Clearly, special education at present has no such thing as a review process that accesses and fairly represents a broad base of the relevant discussions in contemporary scholarship, not even with regard to scholarship within the special education community, which is much broader-based than the positivist editors want to admit.

It seems to me that executive board members of special education associations should be far more mindful in their choices of editors, and in making such choices, they should be wary of appointing the same individual again and again. I don't mean this literally, of course, but in terms of editors' orientations to scholarship. At risk is a field that is closing in on itself, closing itself off from the rest of academia, and from many of the younger and upcoming thinkers and researchers in special education.

I should stress here that my references to colleagues' work does not necessarily indicate agreement with everything they say. But *that is not necessary*. Even where I might disagree with specifics, with parts of their account, or even with their epistemological stance, their writings force my mind and emotions to ask new questions, to consider very different epistemological, methodological, and even ontological considerations, therefore asking of me to consider very different relations between myself and knowledge, between myself and a different "special needs" other. In doing so, I deepen or revise my own lenses through which I look. This openness to critically consider the most basic of what we do and believe is precisely what is not allowed within positivist frameworks. Yet, for a field of study to become a true discipline, it must be free of suppression. It must allow the freedom to see, to learn, and to look through different lenses.

Teacher Education

Regarding teacher education programs in special education, there continue to be far too many special education departments where the voices of discontent are carefully ignored or, when they somehow do show up, are dismissed. As a result, undergraduate students and graduate students still are receiving exclusive "training" in behaviorism, standard diagnostic assessment instruments, and positivist notions of research (see also Gabel, 2001; Ware, 2001). By way of anecdotal evidence: I learned from someone who was there that, at a certain well known department of special education, a student in a graduate class had brought in my article (now Chapter 2 of this book) and wanted to discuss it. The professor, a well known positivist thinker, and an influential figure in editorial circles, said: "Why do persons with strange names write strange things?" He refused to deal with the article any further.

At an AREA conference in the mid 1990s, a graduate student from a special education department somewhere approached me and told me that in her graduate class the professor had used only the first few pages of my 1991 article, which provides an overview of the CBA movement, leading into a critique thereof. He had considered the overview to be excellent. When students had said, "But she doesn't agree with it!" he had gestured the remainder of the article away, saying that my critique was irrelevant and had refused to deal with it.

Four or five years ago a graduate student from a U.S. university contacted me for an interview. She was conducting interviews for her dissertation with a number of special educators who had critiqued the hegemony of positivist methodology and argued for acceptance of qualitative inquiry. She recounted her rather serious struggles with the faculty from her department, before she was allowed to do this study, and told me about a number of demands from her committee that were inappropriate in that they came from a positivist, quantitative research understanding of research. She cheerfully straightened it all out by sheer persistence, but it meant having to engage in a serious struggle. I, too, have been asked to "straighten out" a "messy" committee situation, for instance, where the same was happening; the student was "allowed" to do a qualitative study but was told to meet positivist demands.

I stress that these examples are *not* just the usual disagreements about specifics of methodology. They constitute a much deeper struggle about incompatible paradigms, and the student all too often gets caught unfairly in the middle. My advice to graduate students I teach is invariably: Pick your committee carefully![8] I have received letters over the years asking me: Please tell me how to deal with my dissertation supervisor! I want to do a narrative study, and I am not allowed to. How do I deal with this?

This saddens me because, after so many years of struggle to open up the narrow parameters of research in special education, it should not be happening anymore. Students who wish to explore alternatives should not to have to fight these obstacles. Thus, while more and more academics and graduate students in special education seek out a wide range of modes of inquiry and have access to a huge literature in this regard (also within the broader field of education), too many departments of special education continue to draw the parameters very close to the bone of positivism and behaviorism.

Of course, there are many exceptions. In my own department at York University, as one example, the knowledge base to understand diversity in ability is broad in scope and distinctly non-positivist. Syracuse University has a longstanding tradition of alternative perspectives. At the University of

South Florida, the doctoral program in special education offers courses in the philosophical basis of inquiry, broadening the base of inquiry and encouraging doctoral work that includes research of a wide range of paradigmatic perspectives (Paul & Marfo, 2001). And, of course, alternative thinkers in special education across the United States teach their views in their own courses and work with their own graduate students across special education departments and integrated departments at many universities.

With regard to the most recent backlash from editors and reviewers, I have noticed two interesting broad strategies that are applied to writings that are not appreciated and are seen to be in need of silencing. One is that of lumping all alternative voices together, no matter how distinct they are from one another, and assigning them a bad name, such as "Marxist" or "postmodern," without an adequate effort to define this labeling. Published examples of this can be found, for instance, in Kavale and Forness (1998), who lump together constructivists, resistance theorists, holists, and sociological and social thinkers and refer to them collectively as "Marxist." They devote one page to what they see as Marxist ideology in education, to be followed by more than nine pages to "LD: Marxist Views," in which widely diverse thinkers in special education are combined under the label "Marxist," which clearly is meant as a negative accusation (though they never explain why Marxism is so bad).

The mere reference to notions such as "social construction," "sociocultural understandings," "social justice," and "forms of resistance" are enough for Kavale and Forness to trigger the Marxist threat. I think I am asked to believe that *anything* that differs from positivist and behaviorist thought is Marxist and, therefore, terrible and wrong. In various places we are all seen as "dangerous." One of my surveyed colleagues, too, received a review that called her work "Marxist," though she did not have a Marxist reference or concept in her paper.

Others have lumped together various alternative views under the label "postmodern" and dismissed them summarily. Gerber (1994), for instance, lumps together constructivism and holism and calls them "postmodern"— which is inaccurate and a major oversimplification; Gerber's paper does not begin to describe holism or constructivism or postmodernism (see also footnote 10). Likewise, Sasso (2001, p. 178) sees just about everything that is not positivist as "postmodern" and goes so far as to attribute postmodern tenets to whole-language theory and inclusion movements; then Sasso (2001, p. 10) characterizes all of that as "decidedly leftist" and also implies Marxism. See also the special issue of *Behavioral Disorders* (volume 23, issue 3) on postmodernism, in which postmodern thought is dealt with inadequately in a remarkable manner, particularly distorted, then damned by all special educators in that issue, who lumped together any and every position that is not clearly positivist or behaviorist and dismissed them as "postmodern."

Quoting Jim Paul (personal communication, 1999, with permission), who wrote a letter of objection to the editors, extensively detailing the inadequacy of the (mis)treatment of postmodernism: "The account of postmodern thought in the special issue was not accurate. We would not accept a doctoral student's dissertation with a distorted or unfair description of a philosophical position." (The editors' brief response to Paul's letter was a nonresponse. They misstated what Paul had said, and essentially indicated that their response to his letter signaled the end of the discussion.) Nor, I would like to add, would we accept a dissertation with the kind of commentary we have seen in some of the writings of late.

I cannot even imagine, for instance, that it would be acceptable in a dissertation to characterize a position that the candidate disagrees with or those who hold that position as "mules" and "mulish," as "shamelessly egocentric" (Kauffman, 1999a, pp. 265, 266); as "possessing a significant ego preserve," "resembling a cult of ambiguity" (Kavale and Forness, 2000, pp. 280, 288); as "chutzpah," "charlatans," "scam-artists," "pied pipers," "peddling junk science and other frauds," and as an array of additional explosives (Kauffman, 1999b, p. 248, 249, 250); as "sham inquiry," "propaganda," "revenge," "payback," and so forth. (Sasso, 2001, pp. 182, 183, 184), and as "PD lingo" in regard to postmodernism, also seen as a "foil," engaging only in "what feels good" (Walker et al., 1998). These writers see all of these "scam artists" as "dangerous." I am not clear why that is.

If our views are as foolish as all that, why would anyone with a rational mind care? Do positivist thinkers really think that so many people out there will be seduced by true foolishness and irrationality (assuming, just for a moment, for the sake of argument only, that our views could be so characterized)? Couldn't it be that many people out there choose a different kind of rationality, when the old kind has become too restrictive and lacking further promise? When it has become clear that in today's world, epistemological and methodological single explanations no longer match the complexity that has become apparent everywhere?

What is disturbing is that journal editors are complicit in publishing this kind of lashing-out attacks—attacks on character, which are not within the parameters of scholarly dialogue. These do not qualify as analysis. It also is peculiar in the light of these writers' many claims to possessing an ability to know "objectively" and maintain a stance of "neutrality." Perhaps it would be a good idea if we all would think of ourselves as doctoral students, writing our dissertations, when engaging the work of those with whom we disagree.

A second strategy to silence dissenters is to call them "anti-science," " incoherent," "fashionable nonsense," "anti-empiricist," "non-legitimate," and so forth—accusations that are rampant in positivist reactions, both in formal publications and in manuscript reviews that dismiss alternative ways of knowing. The telling story here is that these characterizations say what they dismiss is *not*. In essence, the message is: This is not what *we* are about. We make sense. We are coherent. We are legitimate. Anyone who does not think as we do is *not*. These are defensive reactions that do not come from an informed position.

One of the journals that has participated a great deal in this dismissive and less-than-civil reacting to new voices, *Behavioral Disorders,* did publish alternative approaches in earlier years (see, e.g., Danforth, 1995; Duplass & Smith, 1995). It initially surprised me somewhat, for Kauffman, for instance, expressed interest in my work at one time. And, as my colleague in this volume, Richard Iano recounts, it was Kauffman who was instrumental in publishing his article that is included as Chapter 3. It is anyone's guess why seemingly broad-minded attitudes turn into narrow and exclusionary ones. As noted earlier, perhaps the initial openness on the part of some traditional special education editors was an expression of wanting to publish something controversial, to get some sparks going, but something easily put down if necessary, not to be taken really seriously, something not really threatening.

I wonder if there was actually any threat at all in our early critiques of the positivist position, because the system then was so certain of itself, so closed, and so sure it was right, so in equilibrium, that any "strange" point of view could not possibly make a dent. That started changing, I think, in the late 1980s. The critiques of our work became a bit more carefully stated, with some sort of grudgingly granted respect (in my own case, see for example, Licht & Torgeson, 1989). Rather than merely dismissing and ridiculing, critics tried to say at least something positive while, of course, still dismissing it, though a bit more politely—as did the completely uninformed earlier critics such as Ulman and Rosenberg (1986).

But the system of special education inquiry is no longer in equilibrium, no longer stable, and strange voices are not very strange anymore: They come from everywhere, from the social sciences and philosophy at large, from education in general, and, in ever greater numbers, from within the special education community. And as open-system theory explains with regard to a system "far from equilibrium," even minor input can bring about major upheavals and transformations (Prigogine & Stengers, 1984; and in education, see, for example, (Doll, 1993; Davis, Sumara, & Luce–Kapler, 2000).

Witness further the more recent debate, if not fury, regarding editorial policies set by editors of *Behavioral Disorders* (Kauffman & Brigham, 1999, 2000). The 1999 editorial spurred a series of exchanges between special educators working hard to broaden the field of inquiry for special education and positivist-oriented editors who have the power to set editorial standards. The editors set an exclusionary policy, stating that only "scientific and positivistic" work with a "sound empirical base" will be published. The editors promised "to discriminate legitimate from nonlegitimate claims," a way of making decisions that privileges the "incremental" build-up with "reliable and replicable findings" that can be verified, often beginning with "the homeliest of topics." All this will lead to "scientific understanding" and "scientific truth" (Kauffman & Brigham, 1999, p. 5). Thus, much is excluded, including narrative inquiry, interpretive inquiry, empowerment approaches to research, poststructuralist analysis, and sociological revisitations of difference. This must be so, say Kauffman and Brigham (1999, p. 7) because "some claims to truth cannot be taken seriously as part of the scientific understanding of things."

Data that live up to their demands can be quantitative or qualitative. Thus, qualitative inquiry of "sound empirical base" is accepted, but this is the soft positivist kind of qualitative inquiry that imitates positivist rules: incremental, reliable, replicable, verifiable, and so on. I am *not* arguing that such approach to qualitative inquiry cannot render helpful information. It is to say that soft positivist qualitative work, or what some have referred to as "clandestine positivism" (in Ballard, 1994a, p. 303), is acceptable by Kauffman and Brigham because it also can be subjected to parallel positivist notions of objectivity, neutrality, and reliability—though some other names might be used to indicate essentially the same concepts (for further discussion of this appropriating phenomenon in regard to the taking ownership over qualitative research by positivist thinkers, see, (e.g. Ballard, 1994a; Ferguson, Ferguson, & Taylor, 1992; Smith, 1997; Smith & Heshusius, 1986). This stance leaves many other forms of qualitative inquiry excluded.

The debates surrounding this event, including a number of e-mail exchanges to which I have been privy, show, in my view, a forceful attempt to close doors to anyone who does not agree with the status quo. I have been stunned by this development. And yet, in many, if not all, ways it is a sign of success on the part of alternative thinkers. For one major difference with the early 1980s is that then there were only a few explicit alternative thinkers. Now there are many, which poses a much more serious threat to established ways of thinking. Several of those who signed a formal objection, as well as those who have engaged in personal e-mail exchanges with the editorial powers that be, have been special educators whom I would see as "middle of the road." These are folks who are not necessarily against positivist research but who simply want the inquiry base broadened, as there are in the world of scholarship now many formally acknowledged ways of knowing for inquiry.

The extraordinary resistance in special education to this timely request makes no other sense, I believe, than to see it as a nervousness about our collective strength. Sadly, then, these responses to the more recent request to broaden the base for inquiry are, in my view, not nearly as sophisticated and interested in a good-faith discussion as at least some of the responses to the same request we received in the late 1980s and early 1990s. Traditionalists seem to be getting severely nervous about what they always have proclaimed to be their natural privileged status.

In May 2000 I wrote a letter to the president of CCBD in relation to the now infamous Kauffman/Brigham (1999) editorial, suggesting that the major voices on all sides peacefully come together, *not* to argue about who is right and who is wrong but, rather, to patiently listen to each other's ways of making sense. I further suggested to have a moderator who would see to it that the dialogue would stay at the scholarly level. To date (almost Christmas), I am still waiting for a response. Listening to those with whom we disagree may indeed be the most difficult thing in our scholarship, as in life, but it must be done if we are going to be a discipline. As Paul stated in his letter to the editors of *Behavioral Disorders*, uninformed and dismissive responses to new ways of thinking "truncate a serious scholarly debate" in which the focus is on "silencing the dissenters." He further stated:

> If...we come to believe we only need more of what we know and our established methods for knowing stand above critique, then we expose ourselves to political assaults not only on the relative efficacy...of our practices, but charges of arrogance, rigidity, and philosophical inadequacies of an area of applied professional practice trying—but failing—to be a discipline.

It is difficult to read the words of those who are dismissive of alternative voices while at the same time stating that they want to work on collaboration, if not integration of the positivist and alternative perspectives. For instance, Kauffman, Forness, and Carnine (and possibly others whose recent work I am not familiar with) all have their name as authors on a statement issued by the Shaklee Institute for Improving Special Education (Andrews, Carnine, Coutinho, Edgar, Forness, Fuchs, Jordan, Kauffman, Patton, Paul, Rosell, Rueda, Schiller, Skrtic, and Wong, 2000), which outlines the traditionalist positivist perspective (called the "incrementalist" perspective) and the alternative perspectives (which include the social constructivists, system thinkers, and alternative research methods perspectives). The concluding statement indicates that the authors think that collaboration, reconciliation, if not integration, while difficult given the fundamentally different perspectives, is possible and must happen. Yet, in the exact same issue, Kavale and Forness (2000) state a number of times that only, and only, an "empirical research foundation" can render "rational" knowledge. Lumped together are qualitative research and postmodern thought (as if these are the same) because they use a form of "discourse" that offers "no insight into the worth of the arguments presented" (p. 288). Alternative forms of inquiry are seen as "ideology buttressed by anecdotal case studies and testimonials" (p. 289) that "evade the truth" (p. 280). Kauffman and Carnine, both also signers of the Shaklee statement, have, of course, stated the same on many occasions.

If these authors had last expressed their utter disagreement, and at times undisguised anger with alternative thinkers, half a dozen years ago or more, one could believe that they had genuinely changed their minds and given up on claiming their beliefs as the only ones that can render knowledge that one can trust, and thus make collaboration perhaps possible. But in the same issue as the "let's collaborate statement"? Or only one or two years earlier (Kauffman, 1998, 1999a, 1999b; Kauffman & Forness in Walker et al., 1998; Kauffman & Brigham, 1999; Carnine, in Kauffman, 1999a, p. 268, 1999)? The question is which of their statements to believe. What is this all about?

Responding to our editor's query as to what we see happening in the future, I am convinced, at this point, that the only way a genuine form of dialogue can take place (not to even think of integration at this point) is for positivist and empiricist thinkers to acknowledge that their position is also ideological, that they adhere to an ideology of objectivity and neutrality—but an ideology nevertheless (hundreds of volumes in both the history and the philosophy of science have traced why this is so, and several are referenced in this book). That might open a way to engage in dialogue. As long as the positivists see only their view as real and trustworthy, as not ideological, as rendering truth, and all others as non-truth, as ideology, as only personal testimony, and all the rest of it, how possibly could genuine dialogue and collaboration occur? In no time at all, the conversation would turn into still another argument about who is and is not "ideological," and so forth.

I stress here that I am not at all suggesting that the conflicting statements between one article and another are deliberately made in bad faith. Rather, I think that the deep paradigmatic conflicts, if not well understood, or if treated defensively, confuse the mind. The authors might not even be aware that they have deeply contradicted themselves within weeks or months. Everyone, of course, has the need to see himself or herself as rational, by which I mean here as *making sense*. Or, stated otherwise, one must see oneself not as irrational, as not making sense.[9] The problem is that traditional positivists and behaviorists see themselves as owning the only kind of rationality, the only kind of sense-making that they believe is correct. Everyone else is just babbling, is merely personal, is nonlegitimate, speaks non-truths.

As Waugh (1989, p. 32) states, "The [euro-centric] rational self finds itself unable to make sense out of a world in which the consensus about what constitutes rationality has broken down." "Reality," says Anderson (1990) with gentle irony, "isn't what it used to be." This, indeed, is exciting news for all those who were forced to believe in only one reality, one rationality, constituted on someone else's restrictive terms, by which to define the world, the self, social life, and learning. Eurocentric masculine rationality is now seen as only one kind of rationality, with no inherent superiority and no claim to universality. This, I believe, is at the heart of the matter: The traditionalists in special education cannot bear to have lost their claim to an exclusively rational, universal, and superior way of knowing.

At a deeper level still, it is the forgetting that the roots of one's epistemological claims are lodged in the individual and collective consciousness, in the very creative metaphors and images through which our relations to others and to knowledge (and to one's self, as I will argue later) come into being, a forgetting that has to be brought to awareness again. In his discussion of Owen Barfield's influential book, *Saving the Appearances—A Study in Idolatry,* Jones (1982, p. 5), a physicist himself, points to the deceptiveness involved in people's understanding of science, which we can only recognize, he says, in realizing that:

> When metaphors become crystallized and abstract, cut off from their roots in consciousness, and forgotten by their creators, they become idols. For an idolater is not so much one who creates idols, [as] one who worships them. This failure to recognize the central role of consciousness in reality...has been a chronic problem throughout the modern era of scientific discovery, since the Renaissance and the Enlightenment.

It is at this level of our consciousness, from which the very impulses and metaphors that shape epistemologies and methodologies—and thus our relations with others—arise, that the problems we face in our field must be seen and understood. Elsewhere (1994, 1996b; Heshusius and Ballard, 1996) I have tried to engage this level of discussion in relation to special education, and I do so as well in the second chapter in this book.

Reception by the field

Our editor asked us to share the reception our work has received in the field after publication. As far as negative characterizations are concerned in published critiques of which I am aware, my writings have been characterized as "superstitious," "dangerous," and "mystifying" (Ulman & Rosenberg, 1986), as "a campaign" and "metaphysical" (Dixon & Carnine, 1992, pp. 461, 462), as "Marxist," "riling," and "dangerous," engaging in a "healthy dose of victimology" (Kavale & Forness, 1998, pp. 263, 264), as suggesting a "political and ideological agenda," "inviting irrationalities" (Gerber, 1994, p. 377), and as "polemical" (Gersten, 1992, p. 467).[10] I did not do a library search on this, so there might well be more. Informally, my work has been referred to, I have been told, as "touchy-feely," "feminine," "unscientific," and "radical." Combining formal and informal negative reactions, I am riling unscientific, dangerous, superstitious, touchy-feely, polemic, mystifyingly feminine radical Marxist, who engages in metaphysical campaigns, suffers from victimology, and invites irrationalities. I did not know that I am such an interesting person!

When people react in directly personal and emotional, nonscholarly ways, I shrug my shoulders. A close colleague told me recently that she had been to a special education conference and my name had come up. "People either love or hate what you write," she said. These comments take me by surprise, then ebb away. I did not set out to be loved or hated. I simply want to engage in an exchange of scholarly ideas, preferably without being either loved or hated, for such reactions stand in the way of clear thinking and scholarly debate. Positive references by special educators to my writings have also appeared (e.g., Hammil, 1993), and I have noticed many positive uses of my writings by others. As well, a few serious discussions have been published (e.g., Warner, 1993, who also discussed Poplin's and Iano's work, though part of his interpretation of holism engages some common misunderstandings).[11]

In terms of what actually happened to my career as a result of my struggle for epistemological freedom, all has been happily most positive. I can't think of one thing that was not. I have received far more invitations for speaking and writing engagements than I can handle, many invitations for visiting professorships, as well as attractive jobs offers, including an endowed chair position. I can't help but be bemused a bit as to what the traditional thinkers in special education, who see my 'kind' as superstitious and babbling, think of our successful careers *and* what they must think of the many who hire and invite us.

A Very Rational Present:
The Call for Open Inquiry

In response to our editor's question—what do I think of the present and future—I recounted my thoughts when presenting at the 1999 TASH international conference in Chicago, for a symposium organized by Scot Danforth, titled, "100 Ways of Constructing Lives and Disabilities: The Case for Open Inquiry." I had been immediately struck by the term "open" because it *felt* so right. It was the exact term to signal what was needed in special education. I started to think about why that was so. My first thought was that "open inquiry" is such an accurately chosen term because it *implies* the nature of what we have felt restricted by—namely its opposite, *closed* inquiry. And feeling "closed in" was what I had experienced, back in graduate school, when being trained in the methods of positivism and behaviorism, being given no freedom to think for myself.

In graduate school I had felt simultaneously closed off from real life and closed into a series of often mind-boggling procedures and formulas, which very few *really* understood and most just learned to apply. Nor did we have an idea where these rules and procedures had really come from and who had put them together, when, and why. Yet no one seemed to question these procedures and formulas while they nevertheless dictated how we were allowed—and not allowed—to come to know other persons. There was a mysterious tone to the whole thing—as if we were entering a secret kind of society, where one simply obeys the rules unquestioningly.

In preparing for the symposium presentation, I started to think about the meaning of "closed." My dictionary lists, as synonyms: end, conclude, finish, complete, terminate, to bring or come to a stopping point or limit. The synonym "end," my dictionary states, conveys a strong idea of "finality" and refers to a "form of progress or development that has been carried through." The synonym "terminate" implies the "setting of a limit in time or space," and "conclude" applies to "transactions and proceedings that have a formal ending." "Yes, yes" I thought. Precisely. These synonyms provide the *feel* and the *ambience* of traditional inquiry. There is a finality to the procedures, a sameness, for they have to be followed just so. They have a distinct beginning and a distinct end, superimposing a "limit in time and space."

The study's design is under the detached control and direction of the researcher, who sees to it that the study " has been carried through." You "run" a study, or have someone else "run" the study for you. These methods, supposedly, have no *inherent, necessary* relationship to the researcher, or to the one "being researched," or, presumably, to any other human relationship or human meaning. This is believed to be so because the methods are presented as *in*dependent of human thought and emotion. Taking courses 101 and 201 in research design and statistical analysis confers the privileged status of being able to lock one's embodied self—one's values, culture, race, gender, abledness—outside of the methodological parameters.

The meanings that my good old Webster dictionary ascribes to the word "closed" resonate deeply with my feelings and thoughts about the methods I had to learn back then. These methods do, of course, offer *some* kind of knowledge, but mediated by an exclusive Western rationality of method, looking through external lenses only, they miss the core of human meaning-making, though they render a form of knowledge that may, here and there, for particular purposes, at times, be useful. What is objected to is the privileged status claimed for them.

Then I turned my dictionary's pages to the meanings of "open," and I read an entirely different set of meanings: not impeding or preventing passage; not shut up; affording free ingress or egress (entrance or exit); not covered over; free to be entered, visited, or used; without restrictions as to the participants; free to avail oneself of; the invitation is still open; empty, or nearly so, of obstruction to passage or view; undefended by military forces; not secret or disguised; revealed; public; without reserve or pretense; not closed against appeals; accessible; responsive; amenable; to keep one's mind open, hence generous; to expand or enlarge; to begin. I could not have provided a better description of what "open inquiry" meant to us. Every one of these synonyms speaks directly to the need to transform research in special education. Open inquiry (in the forms of qualitative research, in-depth interviewing, interpretive research, narrative inquiry, biographical and autobiographical work, action research, critical work, participatory research, empowerment research, post-structuralist analysis, or a combination of these, or other forms I have not yet encountered) *should not* impede or prevent passage; should not shut anybody up; should afford entrances and exits; should be free to avail oneself of; should be an ongoing invitation (to participate, modify, elaborate, ask, question, contradict, revisit, reflect); should not be secret or disguised; should not be militaristic; should not contain reserve or pretense; should not be closed against appeals; should be accessible, responsive, amenable; should keep one's mind open; and hence, should be generous. It should enlighten, expand, enlarge. It should give access. It should begin.

Open inquiry always should begin, in the sense of always being open to revisiting, to refeeling and rethinking, to looking anew, and anew again—because values inspire one to do so, or reflection, or experience, or discussion, or new personal interactions, or insights one did not have before. One should not have to wait for a statistical analysis to rethink and refeel one's knowledge about human behavior. The notion of "beginning" must be understood properly. It is not a formulaic beginning, because in open inquiry there is no conceptual, formal start or end to a research study. Beginning or ending a study happens for practical reasons from the perspective of the day-to-day life of the people involved (of time, energy, funds, and the like), but never conceptual or in terms of method. One does not "run" a study. No methodology dictates that now it starts, now it is over. Life is not subservient to method. Method must be subservient to life. And life's processes are always already there, always already present, always already continuing. Says Nobel Laureate poet Wislawa Szymborska (1995, p. 199): "Every beginning is only a sequel, after all, and the book of events is always open halfway through."

I wish to stress that I am not saying that traditional researchers are mean-spirited, that they do not care about what happens to learners in their lives. But

they have to make these human commitments *subservient to their methods* and to what their methods can address. Within traditional special education, method, not human discussions of the values themselves, decides how values must, or must not, translate into consequences. It is this attempt to lift method above life, above social relations, above the self, and thus above values, that is the essential meaning of the concept of methodolatry. To use the word "privilege," then, in relation to relying on method over life itself refers to the assumption that some know more than others, in the first place, by virtue of knowing a specific methodology and not, in the first place, by virtue of anything else or, in the first place, by virtue of who they are as human beings. That is, if they wouldn't be excellent methodologists, their status as scholars would be inferior.

The very claim that it is even possible to escape from life and from all the dimensions of the self when we make knowledge claims is a peculiar human emotion indeed. As Berman (1989) notes, detachment, and its need to think of oneself as objective and neutral, is a very definite emotion, a way of participating in an underhanded manner, of participating through forcing, and then attempting to control what appears as, a psychic distance. This need was not present in the ages before the scientific revolution, and indeed was created in the birth of the latter. The triumph, says Berman of the scientific revolution, meant that "things must never be examined except from the outside" (p. 114). Such forcing of the "outer" from the "inner" was entirely new to the human race. It allowed for the new idea of mastery and control over something as a definition of knowledge of that something. Methodological orthodoxy, or methodolatry, was born. Says Berman (1989):

> It is not that the emotional life got repressed [during the scientific revolution and all its consequences], but that one particular emotion triumphed above all the rest. "Emotionless" activity, e.g., scientific or academic detachments, is driven by a very definite emotion, viz., the craving for psychological and existential security. (pp. 112, 113)

In this regard, I refer once more to the article by Kauffman (1999a), not to hammer away at his thinking but, rather, because it provides such a clear example of what Berman is saying. Kauffman states here again that positivist science alone can validly and reliably show anything at all. If one does not know by positivist methods, one does not know. All other knowledge claims, he says, are merely "personal experience" and "personal testimony," which are "idiosyncratic" and reflect only what a person *believes* to be true, not what *is true* (p. 268); (see also Walker et al. 1998, p. 11, and just about all other positivist writings noted in this chapter).

One ponders that those who hold on to this perspective also should understand their *own* personal experience (in any dimension of life one wants to consider) as not really true. For, in terms of consistency and integrity regarding their own epistemological conviction, though they may, of course, *believe* their very own personal experience to be true, it cannot *actually* be true—at least not until such time, if it were to come, that empirical science would determine that their personal experience is "found" to be true. Thus, if empiricist positivist science does not make our experience its object of scientific investigation, hopefully (or perhaps not, whatever the case may be) determining for us that our experience is as true as we believed it was—we never will really know if we were actually true, if we were who we thought we were.

Relatedly, Kauffman (1999a, p. 268) states that gender, class, or race, and by implication psychological, cultural and social needs, have nothing to do with science as a way of knowing—a view that is highly contested everywhere.[12] I never can follow this argument. The procedures of science were not divine intervention. No God wrote them down for us on stones. Nor were they constructed during the scientific revolution by indigenous peoples, by persons with disability, by slaves, by females, by children, or by poor or uneducated men and women—though thinkers such as Kauffman deny that this has anything to do with anything. It does not matter, they say, who originally thought of this particular approach to claiming knowledge. I thus imagine a cosmic vacuum from which positivist rules rained down on us, with no possibility to trace back who was responsible for thinking them up (and find out whose values, culture, race, class, gender, and psychological and emotional needs had shaped the ideas involved). Instead, positivist thought renames the very specific socially/culturally embedded origin of the values involved in the development of the scientific method as rendering "common" and "universal" knowledge (Kauffman, 1999a, p.268; see also Walker et al., 1998, p. 11) (This belief pervades all positivist writings). Given the large percentage of people who had no part in developing the values and procedures of the scientific method, I would rather see this paradigm as rendering uncommon knowledge. Using the reference "common knowledge" allows positivists, they think, to then see alternative perspectives as "merely personal" and "divisive."

They *have to* argue in this manner to imagine their claim to neutrality. If they were to acknowledge that it does matter that very particular humans (and thus not others) constructed these ways of thinking about knowledge, this would mean at least four interdependent acknowledgements:

1. They would have to acknowledge the racial and gender and class heritage of the very *impulses* for the birth of the scientific method.
2. They would have to acknowledge the particular—and many now say, the peculiar—meaning of "science"—that is, the equation of knowing with detachment, with quantifying, with mastering, with controlling.

3. They would have to acknowledge that there are other ways of understanding what it means to come to know.

4. They would have to acknowledge that most alternative epistemological and methodological voices, initially, and still, come precisely from those who were not involved, back then, in developing the scientific method and do not see it as a divine intervention but, instead, as a historically and socially embedded construction.

To try to make their argument stick, positivist thinkers need to make us believe that "personal experience" and "personal testimony" can never, under any circumstances, claim valid and reliable knowledge—that only science can do so, for otherwise their claim to epistemological universality would fall apart. Significantly, Kauffman (1999a), as is characteristic of positivist thinkers (in special education, see also Walker et al., 1998), refers to "personal" experience, and "personal" testimony, and "personal preference" (p. 268) as determiners of knowledge that cannot be trusted, but not to *social* experience and social testimony, and social preferences. To do the latter would not be so "easy"; it would actually be explosive. (From a scholarly perspective, it is not at all "easy," of course, as the positivist mind thinks it is, to deny the truth of personal experience.) Yet, the personal and the social are inextricably interdependent, and alternative ways of knowing often emerge from differing social, cultural, class, and gender experience. Ways of knowing other than positivism and empiricism often are articulated by voices from groups characterized by race, gender, class, or ability different from those of the fathers of positivism and empiricism. These are groups that have increasingly come to refuse to be made subservient to positivist doctrines, because their epistemologies, methodologies, understanding of language, metaphors, and for some, even their very cosmologies, differ. What traditional science has said about them has all too frequently not only been disempowering but also not true.[13] For positivism reduces everything it touches. It turns formulaic everything it reduces. Although doing this could be useful at times, for specific circumstances, as an epistemological "universal" stance it is deeply unacceptable, and plainly mistaken.

A rational present that calls for open inquiry, then, does not place a privileged methodology over and above life. We can only fall back on ourselves. Though we may use methods, we cannot hide behind them. We are present, in our inquiries, in flesh and bones, so to speak, just as in our day-to-day lives. An important outcome of open inquiry is that it calls forth many previously unheard voices that were not counted as worthy enough to listen carefully to on their own terms, as they were seen as "personal experience/ testimony" only, as "idiosyncratic," as "merely" subjective. If

I were to use that same sentiment, that of a subjective–objective oppositionality as the *only* two choices available to characterize research, one could say that we have reached a point now at which we can see traditional research as merely objective. But such forced oppositional dualism as providing the only two possible choices is not at all adequate. The objective–subjective characterization leaves out the far more complex understanding of knowledge as participatory, which effaces the subjectivity–objectivity dichotomy and engenders an entirely different set of understandings of how knowledge emerges (see Heshusius, 1994, for further discussion and further references.)

From Discontent Toward Freedom

I understand open inquiry, at its best, as an epistemological and methodological civil rights movement. It is a call for freedom and participation of everyone's mind, heart, and social and cultural situation. The call for open inquiry in special education goes a long way back and has appeared and reappeared in several waves over time, waves of explicit discontent. By my unscientific count, there have been at least four such waves over the last three decades. I will briefly indicate when they started (and all continue to be important), as well as some of the people who brought them about. The boundaries in time that I draw here are, of course, created to some extent as a result of whom I happen to be most familiar with. That is, others might draw them a bit differently and group them in three, five, or six "waves." Nor am I providing an exhaustive list of contributors by any means, only an illustrative list. As my task for this chapter is to render a personal account, I am relating my own experience of this journey, noting those whom I know best, who have influenced my own thinking, and who in many cases I have met personally or worked with.

It is important, I think, that newcomers to the call for open inquiry, and particularly those who are shielded from it by their studies in traditional departments of special education, know that this history exists. They need to know that what they might read today are not the voices of some sporadic radical folks. There is a clear movement here, which has evolved for many years and shows an ever expanding force, with the present often made up of thinkers of all waves coming together in interesting and powerful ways, as boundaries are crossed, alliances are formed, and differences debated, contested, respected, or blurred. Regardless of their differences—and there are some important ones—what they all have in common is the rejection of closed inquiry, the rejection of the positivists' and empiricists' claim to the exclusive path to knowledge about how things "really" are.

The First Wave

The first major wave of writings that explicitly contested the "science" of traditional special education started in the mid- and late-1970s. This first wave of creative discontent is what influenced me deeply in my own thinking. It was spearheaded by Burton Blatt and his colleagues who are still going strong, Robert Bogdan and Douglas Biklen. This is not to say that discontent had not been expressed earlier. Burton Blatt himself, for one, had been doing a great amount of "discontent work" with his advocacy, his institutional reform work, and his reformulation of the concept of intelligence. And Robert Edgerton (1967), an anthropologist, had published his *Cloak of Competence,* which focused on the real day-to-day meaning-making in the lives of mentally retarded persons. It was the only qualitative ethnographic study that existed during my graduate-student years, and it inspired me to do a qualitative dissertation myself.

In terms of explicitly challenging the "science" in special education research, some of the chapters in *An Alternative Textbook in Special Education* (Blatt, Biklen, & Bogdan, 1977) were what launched a focused critique of what Blatt referred to as the "triviality" of the scientific method in special education when he said, "The dominant research strategy in our culture virtually guarantees the triviality of our research" (p. 16). Time has borne out the appropriateness of his early critique. For me, the work by Blatt, Biklen, and Bogdan sparked the earliest, and therefore perhaps the most influential, impulse toward new insights. Their sociological and phenomenological lenses offered a relief from the positivist and behaviorist overload I suffered from. They let me breathe again, freed my mind, and helped me along on this difficult path of creative discontent.[14]

I still remember my reaction to Burton Blatt's sudden death in the mid-1980s. I felt that the father of creative discontent in special education, the voice that had spoken so passionately and eloquently for the dispossessed and had so unapologetically critiqued positivist research, had died. I also vividly remember what a prominent positivist researcher in special education had said to me only a year or so earlier—and I am paraphrasing: "Burt is a really nice man—he was just not bright enough to do the research methods courses well in graduate school. But he has done a lot of good." In other words, Burt was a good man, meant well, worked hard for the unfortunate among us, but a scholar—no. At that time I did not have the intellectual knowledge to counter this person, but my gut level understood the arrogance and blindness behind this statement, and the positivist self-appointed and self-congratulatory superiority it emerged from, and I have never forgotten it.

Also during this period of the 1970s, Gerald Coles (1978; see also 1987) published his influential article taking on the many problems with the test batteries used to "identify" learning disabilities, signaling the critique of positivism in the area of assessment. William Rhodes (Rhodes & Tracy, 1974, and in a set of subsequent volumes) reconceptualized the phenomena of emotional disturbances from an ecological perspective, steering away from medical and personal-affliction models that placed the "disturbance" inside the individual. In doing so, he helped to set the stage for the development of holistic principles, and for alernative understandings for special education to which he has also contributed (e.g., Danforth, Rhodes, & Smith, 1995).

The Second Wave

The second wave of discontent, starting in the early and mid-1980s, was made up largely of constructivists and explorers of holistic principles, such as Richard Iano, Mary Poplin, and myself, who directly and in greater detail objected to positivist ideologies and the presumably neutral procedures involved in the scientific method. Collectively, we proposed more complex notions of how knowledge is constructed, pointing to constructivism, to holistic principles, and to the construct of complexity. We discussed how the configurations among what appear to be parts and wholes on the surface (that is, from an outsider's, see–touch reductionist realm) are actually dynamically, relationally constituted interdependencies, always emergent, and constituted by *the system itself* and influenced by perception of meaning and always purposeful and immanent meaning-making (see also Heshusius, 1982a, 1986, 1996b; Iano, 1986, 1990, Poplin, 1987, 1988a, 1988b).[15]

During these years, James Carrier (1983), Christine Sleeter (1986), and Sally Tomlinson (1982) offered us powerful sociological analyses of the phenomena in special education, drawing attention to the intersection of race, gender, class, and both the representation and the treatment of "special needs" learners. In doing so, these authors critiqued the supposedly neutral measurement and ranking notion of knowledge that denies the significance of social and cultural influences in deciding who is and who is not designated as "a special education student," and pointed to a very different way upon which to base our epistemologies. Relatedly, critical ethnography entered special education with, for instance, the work by Mehan, Hertweck, and Meihls (1986), describing how processes of decision making about special education placements worked in real life settings. Their analysis reflected a qualitative, critical sociological framing, pointing to social stratification in how decisions about handicapping conditions are made, and likewise calling into question the efficacy of "scientific reasoning" (p. 165) in the formalized assessment procedures used in schools.

The Third Wave

The third wave in my story of discontent came with the writings in the early and mid-1990s, and into the late 1990s, by scholars from England such as Mike Oliver (1992), that looked at special education and disability issues from a materialist perspective. They pointed out that dominant epistemologies have failed to improve the day-to-day lives of disabled people and have not done them any good. They demanded a dialectic approach to inquiry, whereby people with disabilities take charge of all aspects of research and academic researchers put their skills at their disposal.

The voice of postmodernism came on the scene when Tom Skrtic published his well known book in 1991, in which he extensively critiqued positivist and behaviorist frames (he referred to these as the functionalist paradigm) and analysed special education as an ad hoc phenomenon, designed to cover up the failure of regular education to live up to its promises of democracy for all. But of course, Tom is telling his story in this volume himself.

And Phillip and Dianne Ferguson and Steven Taylor (1992) reinforced the significance of narrative and interpretive research in the study of special education, as did others (Reid, 1996; Ballard, 1994b). As well, the 1990s saw several attempts to bring Piagetian and Vygotskian understandings of learning to special education. Although these theories did not necessarily directly address the notion of science, they did provide major theoretical alternatives to behavioral views on learning. Kim Reid (1998) has provided an excellent overview of these attempts in special education and of the unfortunate (mis)appropriation of them by behaviorism.

The Fourth Wave

In the late 1990s, the fourth wave in this journey of discontent exploded on the scene. I believe the present stage is characterized by the rather sudden and rapidly emerging field of *disability studies* (DS), to which various insights of previous waves have contributed, but which also has a trust all of its own. Borrowing from the AERA–Disability Studies Special Interest Group statement, and from the Society for Disability Studies, DS is an emerging interdisciplinary field of scholarship that emerges from, supports, and goes beyond disability rights movements. It critically examines issues related to the dynamic interplays between disability and various aspects of society, infusing analyses of disability throughout all forms of educational research and teacher education. DS represents a shift from a prevention/ treatment/remediation/measurement understanding of disability (however disability is seen to be manifested) to a social/cultural/political understanding. DS does not deny the presence of impairments, is not a rejection of the potential utility of intervention, but it disentangles impairments from the myth and stigma that influence social statuses and social policy.

At the core of DS scholarship is a large body of work by scholars who themselves have disabilities, have children with disabilities, or are otherwise intimately familiar with the story of lives and social conditions that give rise to disabling and undemocratic educational settings and practices, including those pertaining to research and its underlying epistemologies. For the first time in history, a substantial number of academic theorists and researchers themselves have disabilities, and this makes for a deeply significant impact in the way scholarship in special education is now being reconceived.[16] In many ways DS can be compared to areas of scholarship such as women studies, black studies, and indigenous studies. There is a major focus on unequal power relations that make up social, political, and policy relations and also relations in research, academic scholarship, and epistemology and methodology. These unequal relations shape the very identities that everyone involved acquires along the way.

The New York Times ("Ideas and Trends: A New Culture Moves on Campus; Viewing Ahab and Barbie Through the Lens of Disability," 2000) cites DS as possibly the most powerful movement to date, as disability crosses all other categories of human lives. Theoretical and research studies that bring DS to bear on education, educational research, and special education include, among many others, the work by Keith Ballard (1999), Michael Berube (1996), Scott Danforth (1997), Nirmalla Erevelles (2000), Susan Gabel (2001) Roger Slee (1997), Linda Ware (1999). I have noted only one publication by each of these prolific authors, to illustrate.

I reiterate here, that the foregoing is a personal account of the movement of discontent in our field. As such, it is an illustrative account that did not set out to provide exhaustive coverage. A more formally researched account might be an excellent project to pursue—perhaps for still another dissertation?

The sheer number of alternative thinkers in special education and overlapping areas such as disability studies is now so large that I can no longer say, as I have always thought I could: I know most of them. And that is an exhilarating realization. The waves have become more like an ocean, with waters deep enough so that all need to respect its powers. My reading of the present is that discontent with the past hegemony of positivism no longer need be the main driving force, because the collective mind is strong and large enough, laying out its own perspectives, needs, and goals, and in the process redefining what it means to engage in rigorous scholarship. Much work is to be done, but the research and theorizing mind is now free in the sense I defined the notion of "freedom" at the beginning of this chapter: a disciplined freedom to learn, to study, and to critically understand a field of inquiry, a disciplined freedom that is not repressed by forced methodology.

Closing Thoughts: This Problem of Measuring, This Problem of Diversity

From time to time, I walk in the woods and think about what has been the core problem with the positivist, empiricist, and behaviorist traditions. At various times I come up with various answers that are, nevertheless, deeply interrelated: the need to reduce all complexity to simple units of measurement; the need to reduce wholes to no more than the sum of parts, and no matter how sophisticated the design and statistical analysis, it misses the self-organizing, forever emergent whole/part interdependencies; the deep need to see the act of knowing as identical to the act of control; the need to see oneself as being a privileged knower and the prestige that comes with it; the fact that it is easier—that is, no matter how difficult and complicated the designs, the analyses, the formation and testing of hypotheses, it is still easier, I firmly believe, than facing knowledge as a direct involvement in the human experience, which is typically difficult, complex, confusing, and involves the self as much as it does the other.

These days, on my walks in the woods, I find myself pondering about the identicalness of the measuring and ranking acts, acts that are always central to the other core problems I see with the positivist tradition as noted above. In special education, the obsession with measurement is the key to its very existence. Without it, special education would not exist as we know it. To measure allows one to *feel* that one has reached an explicit and objective state of knowing (the feeling is as important as what one tells himself or herself cognitively). When one knows exactly where Annie "is" in relation to Johnny on some measurement or other, the illusion enters that one "knows" both Annie and Johnny.

This illusion further results in a related illusion—that of the ability to predict and control, all through further measurement and ranking. This process (measurement, predications, stating we need more—and better—measurements, more measurement, more predications, more statements stating, more, more, more . . .) never ends. And the norms against which Annie is ranked are most often set by those in charge. In cases where Annie is measured against herself—that is, against a previous or a future desired individual performance—ranking obviously is also at the heart of this measurement exercise. The focus of the educator, the researcher, and in due time of Annie herself, is always *away* from attention to the meaning of the embodied present. The present is important only in relation to the measured past or the imagined measured future, thereby always creating the conditions for remembering past failure or for fear of continued and future failure.

Whatever the goals for performance are, the core *intention* is to measure/rank. Everything is predicated on this. Even among the critics of traditional special education, I do not always read an awareness of the dilemmas brought on by this most deeply ingrained ranking need that is hidden in the measuring act. The need to rank is prior to and informs the need to measure.

In his great book, *Physics as Metaphor,* Jones (1982, p. 11) writes: "We shall see that the celebrated ability to quantify the world is no guarantee of objectivity and that measurement itself is a value judgment created by the human mind." He then sets out to argue his case beautifully, addressing measurements involved in the intricacies of physics all the way to those involved in the mundane task of measuring the kitchen table. In doing so, he shows what he refers to as the imaginative and metaphorical nature of our knowledge claims (including by those who deny such metaphorical basis for their claims), which break down "false subject–object barriers." Similarly, metaphor, says Corradi-Fiumara (1995), is more than just a linguistic phenomena. It is an interactive, interpersonal *process* that fundamentally shapes our ways of reasoning and our experience of the world. It is a process in which our rationality and affectual experience are intertwined (see also, e.g., Lakoff & Johnson, 1980; Polanyi, 1964; Cousins, 1985). "[O]ur idol of objectivity" Jones (1982, p. 14) says, sustained by the "dominance of quantitative description in our scientized lives...keeps us from an intimate participation in our world." That intimate participation in our world is what underlies all knowledge claims, all our epistemologies, all our methods, and our consciousness, everything that my chapters here are all about.

The measuring/ranking obsession is informed by the belief that failure is intrinsic to learning. The measuring/ranking act would have no point if it were not for the *idea,* and therefore the perceived possibility, of failure. The sorting impulse through the act of ranking is instinctive to it. The idea of failure is made concrete differently across different contexts and cultures. In our system the act of quantitative measurement is what makes the idea of failure seem concrete. Again, formalized method is the arbiter. To call the need to measure and rank "scientific"is to blind oneself to the deeply *human* need to rank that hides behind it.

A particularly sad dilemma involved is that the perceived obligation to measure, and thus rank, often flies in the face of the rhetoric everywhere in education, also within traditional special education, of "honoring diversity." Diversity and ranking are singularly incompatible. You *cannot* measure and rank diversity; doing so flattens and thus kills it. Diversity is flattened and disappears in the very act of being measured and ranked. When those referred to as "diverse" in ability (by those who probably consider themselves as belonging to the norm, or at least to know the norm) are measured against a desired goal or standard, the goals and standards are always less diverse than diversity itself, and thus reduce diversity to the limited diversity *allowed* by the standards and the measurement devices.

At the heart of this matter is the question: By whom, how, and guided by what epistemological ideology are the standards set and the measurements conceptualized and carried out? At this point the "politics of the self" enter. Or, as Berube (1996, p. 209) says: "How you carve up these differences depends largely on who and where you are." Differences are not to be denied and are precisely what constitutes diversity, but it is the carving up of them into categories and other boxes that is the entry place for values, both personal and social. Here the question of who, and how, and on what basis becomes of central importance.

This is not an argument against measurement in all cases. Nor is this a "touchy–feely" sentiment. It is a conceptual explanation that indicates how fragile is the concept of "diversity" in our educational system, how meaningless in the face of the ever increasing political need to measure and rank, how empty it is in many cases, and how easily it is (and I believe already has become) coopted by traditional educational and political framings. When measuring and ranking is the habit, diversity always will remain the problem. In relation to assessment, these problems, of course, are the prominent feature. Special education has looked almost exclusively through the "lens view of reality" (a term used by Pibram, 1981, p. 149, in his discussion of David Bohm's work, on what is the alternative construct, that of "implicate order"). But as alternative thought shows, there are other ways of conceptualizing and carrying out assessment of learning (see particularly the literature on alternative, holistic, context-based assessment).

An excellent example of the differences between the "lens view" of reality, and the "implicate order view" (Pibram, 1981, p. 149) in education is Anne Sullivan's view on learning, teaching, and assessing what Helen Keller needed, as referred to earlier. Another example in direct relation to "special needs" learners is reflected in Berube's story. Berube (1996), himself a scholar and the father of a son with Down syndrome, while not denying that his son has impairments that need special attention, shows in detail the differences between the "lens view" of his son's accomplishments as measured by the world of special education and what I think we indeed can call the "implicate order" view that focuses on the real-life embedded accomplishments of his son in day-to-day purposeful interactions and activities as observed in his ongoing life with his son. I deliberately phrase this in the manner I do, for it is not correct to speak of assessment by saying: "What his son can and cannot do," as special education assessment procedures typically state. For the latter precisely deny that which is compelling *to the learner,* because personal and social purposes in ongoing real-life settings can make a tremendous difference in how a learner "performs," in what a learner can and cannot do, will and will not do. "Measurement," then, is a highly problematic, contested, and social–political construct, and its meaning cannot be taken for granted.

Open inquiry at its best has no need to measure and rank using the positivist "external lens view." My hope is that open inquiry will go back to the root meaning of the word "to measure." As I noted in Chapter 2 of this book, and I think it is important to repeat here, to measure something before the rise of 17th-century's view of science meant to understand the totality of inner proportions, of a complex order that constituted an understanding of "its innermost being." As Bohm (1980, pp. 21–22) states, a measure was a form of insight and a person's actions following such insight would bring about forms of harmonious living, in terms of physical health and social and mental harmony. Importantly, such insight was *not* gained by conforming to external standards, which are always involved in today's notion of the measuring/ranking act, but instead by creative insight into the deeper meaning of what one wanted to understand. Only since the rise of 17th-century science, says Bohm, has measurement come to mean comparison to an external standard only, and has become routinized, habitual, and relatively mechanical.

One can trace the complex notion of implicate order back at least as far as the notion of science in ancient Greece. It involves an understanding of order that does not draw dichotomous separations between what one can directly observe and place into one's measurement categories, and what one can not directly perceive and observe—a dichotomy that would become the doctrine of the scientific revolution. Says Hardison (1981, p. 11), "In its dominant mode, Greek science was the study of the...harmonious order of the world—an order that is in the world whether it is perceived or not." It is deeply deceptive, then, to believe that "measurement" has always meant what it has come to mean now. Its present meaning is rather new to the scene of human evolution. My trust in the promise of open inquiry, in its many forms, is based on this need to incorporate the original meaning of the word "to measure" and transform the field of (special) education into welcoming a sense of order that is not merely the "lens view of reality" but, rather, welcomes an "implicate order" (Bohm, 1980) that does not force mechanical separations between "inner" and "outer," "personal" and "common," dismissing the former and proclaiming the latter as superior.

This 30-year path from being subservient to methodolatry, to creative discontent, and into epistemological freedom in how we allow each other to make knowledge claims, is not over. Another major stage on this difficult path, I am convinced, has to do with how we understand the idea of the "self." For this stage of the journey, I am thinking here foremost of the self of the nondisabled person, because that is the self I know. Scholarship in special education has always been about the other—about the differing other, about the other that needs to be measured, ranked, segregated or integrated, remediated, or adjusted to. Or, within the various waves of discontent, it has been about the actual personal, social, and political experience of disability in day-to-day life, about society, institutions, and discriminatory practices and power relations. All of these are immensely important.

One dimension, however, keeps slipping through the cracks of our attention, because it is, I believe, the most difficult dimension yet. I believe that within academic scholarship, as elsewhere, few have entered the difficult stage of looking at persons with disabilities as if we are looking in the mirror and see ourselves—and then observe what happens. Doing so enters the dimension of the inner images that make up the "self," images that always stretch outward, beyond the skin, to construct one's relations with others, and to be constructed oneself by these relations. And constructing these evolving, self–other relations is also what all research does, including all traditional forms of research, even though its adherents implicitly and explicitly deny it. They proclaim instead to be "finding" things, "finding" facts, "finding" data—a process from which supposedly the self is absent. But we don't find anything. In research, as in life, all our actions construct relations between self and other, between other and self, relations that emerge not through the methods we use in the first instance, but at a deeper and more powerful level, by the human needs and values that gave rise to these methods. The methods are the concretizations of these values. Says Sir Arthur Eddington (in Jones, 1982, p. 5), "The footprint we have discovered on the shores of the unknown is our own."

Borrowing Brantlinger's (1997) phrase, the attempt (however brought about by unconscious needs and emotions) to hide one's self is "a case of non-recognition" of the politics and values of the self. It is thus that millions of hours of measuring and ranking people in the history of traditional special education inquiry has been informed largely by the self's (and thus also by society's) need to rank, predict, and control. There are ways of assessing students' learning in deeply contextual, meaningful, and life-oriented settings, where self-organization, holistic principles, and voice are honored. But that rarely has been the way in which mainstream special education has done its epistemological and methodological business.

Only if we can enter this difficult realm of the self, I am convinced, will a way of living together become possible, in which all the ways by which life expresses itself, are, to borrow a phrase by Frazee (2000, p. 43), a "mode of expression," not a series of comparative and competitive rankings. Modes of expression do not have to be ranked. They have to be appreciated.

Catherine Frazee, former Ontario Human Rights Commission Chief, herself a disabled "flaccid paralytic, suffering from a genetic mutation that causes profound and progressive wasting of the skeletal muscle" (p. 41), relates the story of her lifelong wish to be able to walk, to the dissolving of that wish into the desire to "assume (her) place in the cosmos—no more, no less" (p. 43). Frazee leads us into a stunning piece of writing. It took my breath away. Directly or indirectly, it touches on personal tragedy models of disability, on medical models, psychological models, measurement/ranking models, exclusion models, adaption models, behavior models, stoic-acceptance models, dignity models, technological models, stigma models, sociological models, integration models, empowerment models, political models, advocacy models, and social-movement models, all of which have characterized the evolutionary journey of "abled" and "disabled" persons inhabiting life in each other's company—or refusing to do so—and then moves straight into the core of existence, where she says she will stay "when I know that I have every right to be here" (p. 43).

Supposedly not being a disabled person, I cannot assume my place in the cosmos and stay there because I belong—until I can look in that mirror that is the disabled other—see me, and let the one I see and the one I now am, be "modes of expression," living and learning in each other's company. Only then will I, too, have the right to be there. It is to this difficult step in our evolution of living and learning together that I will attempt to feel and think about in my other contribution to this book.

References

Adelman, H. (1989). Paradigm accountability (Reaction paper to Heshusius' "The Newtonian Mechanistic . . ."). *Journal of Learning Disabilities, 22*(10), 419–421.

Anderson, W. T. (1990). *Reality isn't what it used to be: Theatrical politics, ready-to-wear religion, global myths, primitive chic, and other wonders of the postmodern world.* New York: Harper and Row.

Andrews, J., Carnine, D. W., Coutinho, M. J., Edgar, E. B., Forness, S. R., Fuchs, L. S., Jordan, D., Kauffman, J. M., Patton, J. M., Paul, J. M., Rosell, J., Rueda, R., Schiller, E., Skrtic, T. M., and Wong, J. (2000). Bridging the special education divide. *Remedial and Special Education, 21*(5), 258–267.

Ballard, K. (Ed.). (1994a). Research, stories and action. In K. Ballard (Ed.). *Disability, family, whanau and society,* pp. 293–314. Palmerston, New Zealand: Dunmore Press.

Ballard, K. (Ed.). (1994b). *Disability, family, whanau and society.* Palmerston, New Zealand: Dunmore Press.

Ballard, K. (Ed.). (1999). *Inclusive education: International voices on disability and justice.* Philadelphia: Falmer Press.

Barton, L. (Ed.). (1987). *The politics of special education needs.* Lewis: Falmer Press.

Barfield, O. (1965). *Saving the appearances: A study of idolatry.* New York: Harcourt, Brace and World.

Berman, M. (1989). *Coming to our senses: Body and spirit in the hidden history of the west.* New York: Simon and Schuster.

Berube, M. (1996). *Life as we know it: A father, a family, and an exceptional child.* New York: Pantheon Books.

Biklen, D. (1985). *Achieving the complete school: Strategies for effective mainstreaming.* New York: Teachers College Press.

Blatt, B. (1970). *Exodus from pandemonium: Human abuse and a reformation of public policy.* Boston: Allyn & Bacon.

Blatt, B. (1973). *Souls inextremis.* Boston: Allyn & Bacon.

Blatt, B., Biklen, D., & Bogdan, R. (Eds.). (1977). *An alternative textbook in special education.* Denver: Love.

Bogdan, R., & Biklen, S. (1975). *Qualitative research for education: Introduction to theory and method.* Boston: Allyn & Bacon.

Bogdan, R. & Taylor, S. (1976). The judged, not the judges: An insider's view of mental retardation. *American Psychologist, 31*(1), 47–52.

Bohm, D. (1980). *Wholeness and the implicate order.* Boston: Routledge & Kegan Paul

Bohm, D., & Peat, D. (2000). *Science, order, and creativity* (2d ed.). London: Routledge.

Brantlinger, E. (1994). High-income and low-income adolescents' views of special education. *Journal of Adolescent Research, 9*(3), 384–407.

Brantlinger, E. (1997). Using ideology: Cases of nonrecognition of the politics of research and practice in special education. *Review of Educational Research, 67*(4), 425–459.

Bronowski, J. (1956). *Science and human values.* New York: Harper & Row.

Brown, P. L. (2000, August 20). Ideas and trends: A new culture moves on campus; Viewing Ahab and Barbie through the lens of disability. *New York Times,* Week in Review: Section 4, p. 3.

Carnine, D. W. (1999). Campaigns for moving research into practice. *Remedial & Special Education, 20*(1), 2–6, 35.

Carrier, J. G. (1983). Masking the social in educational knowledge: The case of learning disability theory. *American Journal of Sociology, 88,* 948–974.

Coles, G. S. (1978). "The learning-disabilities" test battery: Empirical and social issues," *Harvard Educational Review, 48*(7), 321–340.

Coles, G. (1987). *The learning mystique: A critical look at "learning disabilities."* New York: Pantheon Books.

Cousins, N. (Ed.). (1985). *Nobel prize conversations.* New York: Saybrook.

Corradi–Fiumara, G. (1995). *The metaphoric process: Connections between language and life.* New York: Routledge.

Danforth, S. (1995). Toward a critical theory approach to lives considered emotionally disturbed. *Behavioral Disorders, 20*(2), 136–143.

Danforth, S. (1997). On what basis hope? Modern progress and postmodern alternatives. *Mental Retardation, 35*(2), 93–106.

Danforth, S. (1999). Pragmatism and the scientific validation of professional practices in American special education. *Disability and Society, 14*(6), pp. 733–752.

Danforth, S. (2000). *Resistance theories: Exploring the politics of oppositional behavior. Multiple Voices for Ethnically Diverse Learners,* pp. 13–29.

Danforth, S., & Navarro, V. (2000). Hyper talk: Sampling the social construction of ADHD in everyday language. *Anthropology and Education Quarterly, 32*(2), 167–190.

Danforth, S., Rhodes, W., & Smith, T. (1995). Inventing the future: Postmodern challenges in educational reform. In J. Paul, H. Rossellli, & D. Evans (1995). *Integrating school restructuring and special education reform* (pp. 214–236). Fort Worth: Harcourt Brace College Publishers.

Davis, B., Sumara, D., & Luce–Kapler, R. (2000). *Engaging minds: Learning and teaching in a complex world.* Mahwah, NJ: Lawrence Erlbaum Associates.

Dixon, R. C., & Carnine, D. W. (1992). A response to Heshusius' "Curriculum-based assessment and direct instruction: Critical reflections on fundamental assumptions." *Exceptional Children, 58*(5), 46–463.

Doll, W. E. (1993). *A post-modern perspective on curriculum.* New York: Teachers College Press.

Duplass, D., & Smith, T. (1995). Hearing Dennis through his own voice: A redefinition. *Behavioral Disorders, 20*(2), 144–148.

Edgerton, R.B. (1967). *The cloak of competence: Stigma in the lives of the mentally retarded.* Berkeley: University of California Press.

Erevelles, N. (2000). Educating unruly bodies: Critical pedagogy, disability studies, and the politics of schooling. *Educational Theory, 50*(1), 25–47.

Ferguson, P. M., Ferguson, D. L., & Taylor, S. J. (1992). Interpretivism and disability studies. In P. M. Ferguson, D. L. Ferguson, & S. J. Taylor (Eds). *Interpreting disability: A qualitative reader.* (pp. 1–11) New York: Teachers College Press.

Fisher, C. T., & Rizzo, A. A. (1974). A paradigm for humanizing special education. *Journal of Special Education, 8,* 321–329.

Frazee, C. (2000). Body politics. *Saturday Night Magazine,* Sept. 2., pp. 41–43.

Gabel, S. (2001). "I wash my face with dirty water": Narratives of disability and pedagogy. *Journal of Teacher Education, 52*(1), 32–48.

Gallagher, D. J. (1998). The scientific knowledge base of special education: Do we know what we think we know? *Exceptional Children, 64*(4), 493–502.

Gallagher, D. J. (2001). Neutrality as a moral standpoint, conceptual confusion, and the full inclusion debate. *Disability and Society, 16*(5), 637–654.

Gerber, M. (1994). Postmodernism in special education. *Journal of Special Education, 28*(3), 368–378.

Gersten, R. (1992). Passion and precision: Response to "Curriculum based assessment and direct instruction: Critical reflections on fundamental assumptions." *Exceptional Children, 58*(5), 464–467.

Hammill, D. D. (1993). A brief look at the learning disabilities movement in the United States. *Journal of Learning Disabilities, 26*(5), 295–310.

Hardison, O. (1989). *Disappearing through the skylight: Culture and technology in the twentieth century.* New York: Viking.

Heshusius, L. (1981). *Meaning in life as experienced by persons labeled retarded in a group: A participant observation study.* Springfield, IL: Charles C Thomas.

Heshusius, L. (1982a). At the heart of the advocacy dilemma: A mechanistic worldview. *Exceptional Children, 49*(1), 6–13.

Heshusius, L. (1982b). Sexuality, intimacy, and persons we label retarded: What they think—what we think. *Mental Retardation, 20*(4), 164–168.

Heshusius, L. (1984a). Why would they and I want to do it? A phenomenological–theoretical view. *Learning Disability Quarterly, 7*(4), 363–368.

Heshusius, L. (1984b). The survival story of a non-reader: An interview. *Journal of Learning Disabilities, 17*(8), 472–476.

Heshusius, L. (1986). Paradigm shifts and special education: A response to Ulman and Rosenberg. *Exceptional Children, 52*(5), 461–465.

Heshusius, L. (1988). The arts, science, and the study of exceptionality. *Exceptional Children, 55*(1), 60–65.

Heshusius, L. (1989a). The Newtonian mechanistic paradigm, special education, and contours of alternatives: An overview. *Journal of Learning Disabilities, 22*(7), 403–415.

Heshusius, L. (1989b). Holistic principles: Not enhancing the old but seeing a-new: A rejoinder. *Journal of Learning Disabilities, 22*(10), 595–602.

Heshusius, L. (1991). Curriculum based assessment and direct instruction: Critical reflections on fundamental assumptions. *Exceptional Children, 57*(4), 315–328.

Heshusius, L. (1994). Freeing ourselves from objectivity: Managing subjectivity, or turning toward a participatory mode of consciousness? *Educational Researcher, 23*(3), 15–22.

Heshusius, L. (1996a). Of life real and unreal. In L. Heshusius & K. Ballard (Eds.), *From positivism to interpretivism and beyond: Tales of transformation in educational and social research (the mind–body connection)* (pp. 50–55). New York: Teachers College Press.

Heshusius, L. (1996b). Modes of consciousness and the self in learning disabilities research: Considering past and future. In D. K. Reid, W. P. Hresko, & H. L. Swanson (Eds.), *Cognitive approaches to learning disabilities* (pp. 617–651). Austin, TX: Pro–Ed.

Heshusius, L. & Ballard, K. (Eds.). (1996). *From positivism to interpretivism and beyond: Tales of transformation in educational and social research. (The body–mind connection).* New York: Teachers College Press.

Heshusius, L., & Peetoom, A. (Trans.) (1986). *Portraits.* Oakville, Ontario: Mosaic Press.

Iano, R. (1986). The study and development of teaching: With implications for the advancement of special education. *Remedial and Special Education, 7*(5), 50–61.

Iano, R. (1989). Comments related to Professor Heshusius' application of paradigm change to special education. *Journal of Learning Disabilities, 22*(10), 416–417.

Iano, R. (1990). Special education teachers: Technicians or educators? *Journal of Learning Disabilities, 23,* 462–465.

Isaacson, S. L. (1993). Open systems as seen on the street and from the fourteenth floor. *Journal of Learning Disabilities, 26*(5), 326–329.

Jantsch, E. (1980). *The self-organizing universe: Scientific and human implications of the emerging paradigm of evolution.* Oxford, UK: Pergamon Press.

Jones, R. S. (1982). *Physics as metaphor.* Minneapolis: University of Minnesota Press.

Kavale, K. A., & Forness, S. R. (1998). The politics of learning disabilities. *Learning Disability Quarterly, 21,* 245–273.

Kavale, K. A., & Forness, S. R. (2000). History, rhetoric, and reality: Analysis of the inclusion debate. *Remedial and Special Education, 21*(5), 279–296.

Kauffman, J. M. (1998). Are we all postmodern now? *Behavioral Disorders, 23*(3), 149–152.

Kauffman, J. M. (1999a). The role of science in behavioral disorders. *Behavioral Disorders, 24*(4), 265–272.

Kauffman, J. M. (1999b). Commentary: Today's special education and its messages for tomorrow. *Journal of Special Education, 32*(4), 244–254.

Kauffman, J. M., & Brigham, F. J. (1999). Editorial. *Behavioral Disorders, 25*(1), 5–8.

Kauffman, J. M., & Brigham, F. J. (2000). An apology and—we hope—a clarification. *Behavioral Disorders, 25*(3), 167.

Keller, H. (1903). *The story of my life.* New York: Doubleday & Page.

Krishnamurti, J. (1953). *Education and the significance of life.* New York: Harper & Row.

Krishnamurti, J. (1972). *You are the world.* New York: Harper & Row.

Kuhn, T. S. (1970). *The structure of scientific revolutions.* Chicago: University of Chicago Press.

Lakoff, G., & Johnson, M. (1980). *Metaphors we live by.* Chicago: University of Chicago Press.

Licht, B., & Torgeson, J. (1989). Natural science approaches to questions of subjectivity. *Journal of Learning Disabilities, 22*(10), 418–419.

Mann, L., & Phillips, W. A. (1967). Fractional practices in special education: A critique, *Exceptional Children, 33,* 311–317.

Mehan, H, Hertweck, A., & Meihls, J. L. (1986). *Handicapping the handicapped: Decision making in students' educational careers.* Stanford, CA: Stanford University Press.

Oliver, M. (1987). Re-defining disability: Some issues for research. *Research, Policy and Planning, 5,* 9–13.

Oliver, M. (1992). Changing the social relations of research production? *Disability, Handicap & Society, 7*(2), 101–114.

Paul, J. L., & Marfo, K. (2001). Preparation of educational researchers in philosophical foundations of inquiry. *Review of Educational Research, 71*(4), 525–547.

Pibram, K. H. (1981). Behaviorism, phenomenology, and holism in psychology. A scientific analysis. In R. S. Valle & R. von Eckartsberg (Eds.), *The metaphors of consciousness,* (pp. 141–151). New York: Plenum.

Polanyi, M. (1964). *Personal knowledge: Towards a postcritical philosophy.* New York: Harper & Row.

Prigogine, I., & Stengers, I. (1984). *Order out of chaos. Man's new dialogue with nature.* New York: Bantam Books.

Poplin, M. (1987). Self-imposed blindness: The scientific method in education. *Remedial and Special Education, 8*(6), 31–37.

Poplin, M. S. (1988a). The reductionist fallacy in learning disabilities: Replicating the past by reducing the present. *Journal of Learning Disabilities, 21*(7), 389–400.

Poplin, M. S. (1988b). Holistic/constructivist principles of the teaching/learning process: Implications for the field of learning disabilities. *Journal of Learning Disabilities, 21*(7), 401–416.

Reid, D. K. (1996). Narrative knowing: Basis for a partnership on language diversity. *Learning Disability Quarterly, 19,* 138–151.

Reid, D. K. (1998). Scaffolding: A broader view. *Journal of Learning Disabilities, 31*(4), 386–396.

Rhodes, W., & Tracy, M. (Eds.). (1974). *A study of child variance: Vol. 1. Conceptual model.* Ann Arbor: University of Michigan Press.

Sasso, G. M. (2001). The retreat from inquiry and knowledge in special education. *Journal of Special Education, 34,* 178–193.

Scheurich, J. J., & Young, M. D. (1997). Coloring epistemologies: Are our research epistemologies racially based? *Educational Researcher, 12*(4), 4–16.

Skrtic, T. M. (1991). *Behind special education: A critical analysis of professional culture and school organization.* Denver: Love.

Slee, R. (1997). Imported or important theory? Sociological interrogations of disablement and special education. *British Journal of Sociology of Education, 18*(3), 407–419.

Sleeter, C. E. (1986). Learning disabilities: The social construction of a special education category. *Exceptional Children, 53*, 46–54.

Smith, J. K. (1997). The stories educational researchers tell about themselves. *Educational Researcher, 26*(5), 4–11.

Smith, J. K., & Heshusius, L. (1986). Closing down the conversation: The end of the quantiative–qualitative debate among educational researchers. *Educational Researcher, 15*(1), 4–12.

Sugai, G. (1998). Postmodernism and emotional and behavioral disorders: Distraction or advancement? *Behavioral Disorders, 23*(3), 171–177.

Szymborska, W. (1993). *View with a grain of sand: Selected poems.* New York: Harcourt Brace.

Tomlinson, S. (1982). *A sociology of special education.* London: Routledge & Kegan Paul.

Ulman, J. D. & Rosenberg, M. S. (1986). Science and superstition in special education. *Exceptional Children, 52*, 459–460.

van Pareren, C. P. (1984). *Ontwikkelend onderwijs.* Amersfoort, Netherlands: Acco.

Von Bertalanffy, L. (1968). *General systems theory.* New York: George Braziller.

Walker, H. M., Forness, S. R., Kauffman, J. M., Epstein, M. H., Gresham, F. M., Nelson, C. M., & Strain, P. S. (1998). Macro-social validation: Referencing outcomes in behavioral disorders to societal issues and problems. *Behavioral Disorders, 24*(1), 7–18.

Ware, L. (1999). My kid, and kids kinda like him. In K. Ballard & T. McDonald (Eds.), *Inclusive education: International voices on disability and justice.* London: Falmer Press.

Ware, L. (2001). Writing, identity, and the other: Dare we do disability studies? *Journal of Teacher Education, 52*(2), 107–123.

Warner, M M. (1993). Objectivity and emancipation in learning disabilities: Holism from the perspective of critical realism. *Journal of Learning Disabilities, 26*(5), 311–325.

Waugh, E. (1989). *Feminine fictions: Revisiting the postmodern.* New York: Routledge.

Notes

1. I acknowledge my debt to one of the very few professors who actually brought the meaning of real life into his courses, Dr. Samuel Guskin, who was the supervisor of my dissertation. He introduced us to ethnographic, qualitative work by Robert Edgerton (1967), the first ethnographic study in the area of mental retardation, the study that enabled me to conceive of the possibility of doing a very different, qualitative dissertation. In a course in a different department, I was introduced to the work of Ludwig von Bertalanffy, the father of General Systems Theory, which opened my mind to paradigmatic thinking, to complexity, and provided me with a solid critique of behaviorism. These are really the only two courses during graduate school that addressed ways of knowing not anchored in positivism and behaviorism.

2. I can't but fear what would have become of Helen Keller had she been "programmed" by behaviorist methods. The eminent Dutch scholar Carl van Pareren

(1984) pointed out to me the differences between what Itard accomplished with the wild boy of Aveyron and what Anne Sullivan accomplished as Helen Keller's teacher (see Keller, 1903; the comparison I draw here is not absolute, as the two children involved were completely different. That is, I am not implying that the wild boy of Aveyron would have necessarily learned what Helen Keller learned had he only been under Sullivan's care. I am saying that Helen Keller most likely would not have learned as splendidly as she did had she been under Itard's care).

Itard, a physician, practiced ways of teaching that reflected what would come to be known as *behavior modification.* He followed the mechanistic conception of what it means to be scientific. Itard broke down language into what was seen as its smallest components before handing these to Victor: (a) speech sounds for speaking, and (b) isolated letters and words for reading. Although Victor learned to master some isolated pieces of "language," they never were "generalized," that is, they never were incorporated into communicative abilities.

For Helen Keller, who was blind, deaf, and mute, the "problem of generalization" never occurred. This is because the idea of generalization is a byproduct of conditions constructed by mechanistic, behaviorist, and positivist thought, in which evaluation of achievement on predetermined tasks occurs under controlled conditions in the form of quantitative measures—conditions that do not resemble real life. Only when things are taught/trained in isolation does "generalization" arise as an idea.

Anne Sullivan never concerned herself with "generalization." She did not concern herself with the teaching of isolated words or sounds. She used complete phrases and sentences that were directly related to what she and Helen were doing. Helen's mind never became confused about what her learning was for, or what she was supposed to "generalize" to. Teacher and student were simply always engaged in real-life, worthwhile activities. Learning (not the artificial construct of generalization) was always happening. In their book on wholeness, dialogue, creativity, and scientific thought, Bohm and Peat (2000), refer to Anne Sullivan's teaching as exemplary in the understanding of genuine communication and creative perception, of passion and insight, as the basis for genuine learning and, they say, for science itself.

3. See my rejoinder (1989b, p. 597) to Licht and Torgeson, for example, that explains this appropriating phenomenon—or the "we-are-already-doing-this" phenomenon—in regard to their claim that positivism too, attends to "personal experience," a claim I show to be deeply distorted.

4. My own teacher education program in the Netherlands surely had not been perfect either, but at least we were not indoctrinated into one theoretical and methodological approach as I would have been in the United States in the 1970s. I had been exposed to many different ways of thinking about special education, including approaches by the Waldorff schools, Piagetian theory, and a deeply ingrained humanistic approach to dealing with diversity in ability. The love affair with behaviorism and positivism in special education never caught on in the Netherlands and other parts of Western Europe to the extent it did in the United States.

5. Perhaps I can best illustrate my comments in this section by referring to a publication by Walker, Forness, Kauffman, Epstein, Gresham, Nelson, and Strain (1998). They, too, state that only positivism can help us. Rarely do positivists actually say what accomplishments positivism has achieved. That question is a contested matter, even within positivist circles where some acknowledge that the successes have not been all that grand. At times, both positions—we have grand accomplishments but, then, they are not all that grand—seemed to be held simultaneously. For instance, in their conclusion, Walker et al. (p. 16) speak of positivist/ empiricist methods having "revolutionized practices and dramatically improved the quality of life of thousands of individuals and their families." Yet, earlier in the same article they state (p. 13):

> *We have tended to pursue a relatively narrow, insular agenda of topics and outcome measures in our research activities. We select goals, intervention procedures, and outcome measures that make sense to us, that show some sensitivity or responsiveness to our intervention attempts. . . . We impress ourselves and our immediate constituencies with the changes we produce on such measures as out-of–seat behavior and talk-outs, academic engagement levels [what this translates into is time-on-task], number of words read correctly and math problems solved per minute, or our ability to reduce the number of times aggressive students hit each other at recess. These are useful achievements . . . however, they do not serve to capture public attention, nor do they effectively address major issues confronting society.*

Indeed, these piecemeal accomplishments do not mount a convincing argument that positivist research has been as grand as often claimed. As well, the phrase "We select goals, intervention procedures, and outcomes measures that make sense to us" is significantly misleading, for the fact is that positivist researchers *cannot freely select* their goals: Their prescriptive methods do not allow them to select anything else but a narrow, insular agenda of topics and outcome measures. Holistic educational approaches bring about changes in pedagogical relations that also result in less "out of seat behavior," or "more time on task"—*except* that this will not be stated that way, or conceived of that way, or measured that way, not thought of that way, not cared about that way. "Out of seat behavior" or "time on task" as piecemeal "variables" to be measured *for their own sake*, as prestipulated goals all by themselves, do not exist within holistic and other alternative visions for education.

This is *not* to imply the opposite: that holistic thinkers would not care if youngsters are running all over the place or are not academically engaged (which, I must note, is very different from 'time-on-task'). Alternative approaches offer just that: a different vision, and in carrying out that vision, youngsters, apart from many other engagements, also will be more academically engaged and have less inclination to run around. Thus, the question can never be "who is more successful in having youngsters stay in their seats, behaviorally conceived and measured approaches to education, or holistic ones?" Paradigmatically, alternatives do not conceive of posing the question of effective education in the manner of isolated behavioral measurements (see also Smith, 1997).

6. The responses were by Adelman (1989), Iano (1989), and Licht and Torgeson.

7. The one clear mistake I engaged in, as far as I know, regarded my 1991 article critiquing CBA. I had paraphrased Thompson and Gickling as advocating sorting children into various groups according to levels of accomplishments, whereas they actually had been disagreeing with it. Afterward I could see why I had inadvertently misunderstood their argument, and felt badly about it.

8. I tell students that the decision as to who supervises and who is on their committee is in their power to decide—at least at all universities where I have taught or have been involved in dissertation work. I strongly suggest that they interview faculty members before they commit themselves. I stress that they are not obliged to ask faculty members just because they have taken courses with them, because professors have "been good" to them, because, because. . . . I stress that just because a faculty member knows about her or his topic is not necessarily a good reason to ask that person, for he or she might think from within an inquiry paradigm that is not compatible with the kind of inquiry the student wants to pursue. I often have been amazed by how relieved students are when I stress these matters. Often, the formal policies are not explained properly to students, or noted clearly in departmental handbooks. I am dismayed by the pressure that can be put on students to choose certain people as their thesis supervisors, for whatever reasons this is done.

9. Besides the rational (that is, the traditional understanding of rational as resulting exclusively from the logical workings of the mind, which are seen to function separately from the emotions and from the body), and besides the irrational (that is, the traditional notion of irrationality, that which is seen outside of the rational, and therefore as unreliable, emotional, not trustworthy), there are the emotive and somatic ways of knowing, the artistic and the intuitive, the personal, and the political. These ways of knowing are perfectly rational in their own right. We all use them (whether we acknowledge so or not), they are deeply human, and they should never be denied (see Heshusius & Ballard, 1996, for an extensive discussion and further references on these ways of knowing in relation to both research and practice, also in special education.)

10. Gerber (1994) starts out with what seems at first to be a serious discussion of our work, citing in his references several of Poplin's, Skrtic's and my own publications, as if these are actually discussed, but they aren't. He moves quickly into dismissing this collective work in a broad sweep, as postmodern, political, ideological, and so on. For Gerber, too, only two choices are available: positivist/empiricist or ideological and inviting irrationalities. The only specific reference in the text to our work is a brief quote taken from a large section in my 1991 article, in which I discuss the inadequacies of Newtonian principles for the study of human behavior. In reaction to the quote, Gerber states that Newtonian understandings are just fine, and "work very well—thank you very much—in a good game of billiard" (Gerber, 1994, p. 369).

    Using examples from the non-human domain to argue that positivism and empiricism work for the human domain is a very common but very wrong strategy. None of us ever argued that Newtonian principles do not work for a billiard game, or for putting a person on the moon. What Gerber misses is the crucial difference between human and non-human domains, though I call careful attention to this in various publications, including the 1991 article. Other major problems are Gerber's incorrect use of quotes by Charlene Spretnak and Stephen Gould. Spretnak is quoted as if she were in agreement with the positivist tradition. But the work quoted from ("States of Grace: The Recovery of Meaning in the Postmodern Age") is, as is all her work, deeply holistic and even spiritual. Spretnak was merely providing a parody of how the modern mind is reacting to postmodern thinking, not an agreement with the modern mind at all, but Gerber does not make this clear. Instead, agreement is implied.

Gould, in the quote that Gerber (1994, p. 369) uses, refers to notions of "complex, contingent, interactive" (constructs that are all directly or indirectly implied in our work) as "different rationalities," not as "inviting irrationalities" that cannot be known, as Gerber cast the quote to mean. The notion that alternative perspectives hold that things cannot be known, because we supposedly preach "transcendence" that denies the "material world" as Gerber interprets us to do, is a bizarre interpretation of our work and misses the crucial point that we argue, among other differing paradigmatic meanings, for a *different* referencing of material reality, not for a denial of it. For any dialogue to take place, it would be helpful if positivist critics would actually look at our work more carefully and in detail before trying to formulate what they see as a counter-argument. It is not that our work is above critique but instead that broad dismissals, misconstrued and out-of-context quotes are less than helpful and stagnate an important conversation.

11. For instance, Warner (1993, p. 321) attributes to holistic principles a dualistic choice between cultural characterizations, on the one hand, and biological dimensions of learning disabilities on the other hand (holism supposedly favoring the former and denying the latter), which is a misunderstanding of whole–part relations within holistic principles, and of their emergent organization *in relation to each* other. Neither cultural nor biological characteristics and determinants are denied. One of the core principles of holism is missed—namely, that "wholes" and "parts" are actually ongoing *relationships* among what appear, from an external perspective, to be independent wholes and independent parts.

Even in the description of holism that says that the whole is both more than and different from the sum of the parts (and, as such, generates its own emergent properties that cannot be reduced to its parts), this is *not* the same as saying that whole and parts are separate and unrelated, which then could make it possible to ignore one or the other, or to say that one must choose between them. Within holism, one never could just attend to the whole and not to the parts (although many misunderstand this to be the case), nor only to the parts and not to the whole. To say that the whole is both more than and different from the sum of its parts is not to separate them but, rather, to point to the *simultaneous nature* of the existence of every entity as *both* being a whole in itself *and* being a part of another whole, and to the ongoing simultaneous relations between them that make it impossible to separate them into a dualistic frame. See also footnote 15. (This particular misunderstanding of whole–part relations within holism is, unfortunately, common—within special education, see also, for instance, Isaacson, 1993, p. 329, and Kauffmann, 1999b, p. 250). Relatedly, Warner (1993) incorrectly attributes a subjectivity position to my description of holistic principles and misses the distinction between subjective knowing (as an oppositional position to objectivity—neither one I claim for holism) and a participatory knowing which I do claim (see Heshusius, 1994, 1996ab).

12. Kauffman (1999a, p. 268) states that science, rather than having its roots in race and gender values orientations, has, in fact, exposed sexism, racism, and the like. Combining this claim with his claim that all other forms of knowledge except science are only "personal experience" and "personal testimony," and therefore neither valid nor reliable, I can only draw the logical conclusion (if I were to believe him) that sexism, racism, disabled-ism, and so on, as personally experienced, are not to be trusted. For only science offers a path to truth claims—thus, also for the valid and reliable exposure of racism, sexism, and the rest. For how could blacks, women, and the others validly and reliably know their own human condition? Only empiricist science can.

Thus, it must follow that only science can be the liberator of oppressed people. I must see this implication as offensive to those oppressed, past or present— to the untold numbers of race minorities and women all over the world who themselves resist their oppression and demand a voice, often at great cost. And to the indigenous peoples who, by their own and only their own, tenacity and faith, survived as a race, and to many others. *None* needed science to inform them that they were oppressed or wrongly depicted. None waited for science to liberate them from false characterizations. All this extends to people with disabilities, regarding any kind of disability one wants to think of.

This is not to say that positivist social science cannot, at times, for some, provide helpful information for problems the humans experience. It is to say that positivist social science has no special privilege to helping or liberating people. If we ever get to a place where genuine diversity of ability, genuine helpful education, and genuine equality is valued, it won't be in the first place because of the kind of science that Kauffman and his colleagues tell us we must be subservient to.

That science has come up with information here and there that supports the uncovering of prejudice (Kauffman, 1999a, p. 268) is nice but does not make for Kauffman's argument. Science also has sincerely supported and contributed numerous times to discriminating and prejudiced beliefs. *Not*, as Kauffman (p. 1999a, p. 268) states, only because of the making of "false claims," engaged in by "individuals," resulting in the "misapplication of science" (though that surely has also happened) but, rather, because science *believed* it, and had "evidence" for it, obtained by its supposedly neutral methods untainted by humans' deeper needs. Here, Kauffman would say: Just hang in there. Because science's procedures are "self-corrective" (p. 268), science will correct whatever unfortunately might have been "found" by incorrect application of method, or by method still insufficiently developed. Science, his argument goes, surely will correct itself at some point if its findings are now wrong. For it is not the scientists themselves who were at fault, not their own prejudices and beliefs, not their own upbringing, not the values of their gender, race, class, ability, and historical era, nor the essential tenets of their methods, but only the underdevelopment of their procedures or the unfortunate poor application of them. So, just wait, all you people who think you are portrayed falsely, science will come to your rescue to confirm *if* you are right, for you cannot know that yourself, as "personal experience" and "personal testimony" are neither valid nor reliable and cannot be trusted to correspond to reality. Besides, your own language (narrative, testimonials, and so on.) is inadequate to express truth claims, as it is merely personal. Blacks, women, indigenous peoples, those with disabilities—all would still be waiting.

If all this sounds absurd, I agree. But I can't come to any other sensible conclusion about what is said while it is not said in these sorts of arguments. They are so penetratingly disembodied in denying the truth value of personal and social experience, the methodolatry in it so blinding, and leading to such convoluted argumentation, that I think of thinkers who hold to these ideas as living in a world of blinding abstraction. Some years ago the Science Center in Toronto held an exhibition called "This Question of Truth." This Science Center is world-renowned. One of its exhibitions featured a display of many of the most important scientists from several hundred years up to the present, all white males, citing "evidence" that they had "found" about people different from themselves—that is, about other races, about the poor, and about females—that make the claim by Kauffman, that science renders knowledge obtained without reference to the genetic and racial heritage of the investigator, sound surreal.

Within special education, Jim Paul (personal communication, 1999) states similarly that readers who believe that "these leaders (special education leaders) in the field—unlike others—somehow stand above implicit gendered or cultural bias, appreciate neither the critiques of knowledge nor even the cultural assessments of the complexity of bias still operating in our theories, data, and practices in special education." Further, see Scheurich and Young (1997) for an excellent discussion on the various levels of race-based epistemologies (in addition to personal, institutional, and societal race-based levels) and, by implication, gender-based, abled-based, and other dimensions of human life-based epistemologies and how they play themselves out in educational research. It is here that the Kauffman and Brigham (1999) statements surrounding the editorial controversy also miss the mark, in that they do not recognize, and in fact would deny (see Kauffman,1999a) that *epistemologies themselves* are embedded in cultural, race, ableist, class and gender values. If my rendering here of the positivist positions held by Kauffman and others is mistaken, I look forward to a clearer explanation on their part as to what was meant instead.

13. As I have related elsewhere, and what bears repeating here—several of the Maori peoples, for instance, are now refusing to be researched and have taken control over all aspects of research that affects them. When outside researchers are used, it is only in complete accordance with Maori life and protocols of behavior and tradition, and thus completely under their cultural, and therefore under their metaphorical, epistemological, language, and methodological, control. See Ballard (1994b) for instance, as a research example of this understanding of

what it means to construct knowledge that focuses on disability issues among Maori peoples. There is, of course, resistance everywhere to "being researched" on terms set by academic researchers. The study of disability (as is the case with much of womens studies, black studies, indigenous studies) is an example of this reappropriation of ownership over research in relation to disability.

14. Always on my bookshelves will remain some of their many earlier publications, including Blatt (1970, 1973), Biklen (1985), Bogdan and Taylor (1976), and Bogdan and Biklen (1975). Bogdan and Biklen (1975), the first textbook in qualitative methods for educational research, now several editions later, is a book that I still often use in courses I teach in qualitative methods. How it is possible that people obtain degrees in special education without any exposure to these important and widely published voices, I cannot fathom, but it still happens.

15. A from-the-outside-perspective only, which is by definition positivist and behaviorist perspectives, functioning exclusively in the see–touch realm, will always miss what is happening on an ongoing basis. This is so because it superimposes constraints and mathematical frames *onto* living systems, trying to "freeze" them, believing that to do so is possible, and then believing that "complexity" is left intact (it is also at this point that the idea about the "problem of generalization" is born). But complexity in living systems, which, of course, includes every and all reference to human life, is characterized by self-organizing—that is, innately active emergence of life's properties. The (incorrect) belief that complexity does not disappear when trying to capture it piecemeal from an external perspective, is what reductionism is all about. Von Bertalanffy (1968, p. 55) refers to this belief as the "summative" notion of knowledge about systems. Living systems, however, cannot be so understood. The understanding of the always emergent nature of the reality of living systems, which relates to the whole being more than the sum of its parts, he referred to as "constitutive" whole–part relations. Complexity theory further has supported these understandings. When the word "science" is used in traditional special education and other social sciences, what invariably is referred to are concepts of accumulating science, the summative understanding that can address only the see–touch, "external lense" realm, and thus misses the constitutive, emergent nature of reality. New modes of the sciences of complexity understand the nature of reality in fluid, complex, and, in part, interior ways. Says the publisher's introduction to the second edition of David Bohm's and David Peat's (2000) book:

> Where does reality lie? In the equations of physics? In scientific theories or the creative imagination? In wholes or fragments? In meaning or mechanics? In *Science, Order, and Creativity,* David Bohm and David Peat argue that science must go beyond the narrow and fragmented view of nature and embrace a wider holistic view that restores the importance of creativity and communication for all humanity—not just for science.

In part, what this means is that there must be a focus on, and trust in, precisely what traditional special education academics dismiss—that is, personal and social experience and testimony as fully dynamic dimensions of valid knowledge claims. What was considered "merely" inner experience or "mere" personal experience (soft, decorative, personally interesting perhaps, but not valid or reliable) is again seen as one of the forces that lie at the core of knowledge. The boundaries of what was seen as "inner" and "outer" now are blurred and are understood to have been a result of the forced dualisms of mechanistic conceptions of science. In education, Davis, Sumara, and Luce-Kapler (2000) offer an extensive discussion of the science of complexity and how it translate into pedagogy.

16. Witness, for instance, the new Disability Studies in Education–Special Interest Group (SIG) of the American Educational Research Association (AERA), which was formed at the 2000 AERA annual conference. The SIG was organized by a group of scholars, many of whom are well known special educators. Thus, this group is not separate from special education, as disability rights groups in the first instance often have been, but includes a direct focus on matters of special education. Another example of the interface between disability studies and education is the October 2000 conference "Desegregating Disability Studies: An Interdisciplinary Discussion," held at Syracuse University, Department of Educational Foundations. Further, a conference was in June 2001 on the Chicago campus of the National-Louis University, called "Critical Reflections on Special Education," the First Annual Second City Conference on Disability Studies and Education, which explored the interplay between disability and special education.

The Tale of a Reluctant Empiricist

Richard P. Iano

My interest in philosophy, and particularly in epistemology, without doubt accounts for the way I departed from most of my colleagues in the way that I thought about and understood education and teaching. I found myself drawn to philosophy early on, during my undergraduate years. At the time I was a psychology major but took as many philosophy courses as I was allowed under program requirements. The contrast between my psychology and philosophy courses and the way they were taught was itself instructive and telling.

I found the philosophy courses to be educational and their influence on me to be deep and lifelong. The psychology courses and their teaching were more contemporary in style, and the textbooks used were specially designed for students and courses. These textbooks tended to smooth down the most interesting and jagged features of the discipline, presenting compilations of studies, findings, theories, and personalities. They played down ambiguities and confusions, and presented the debates among leading theorists in synoptic form, emphasizing conclusions reached rather than the struggle and steps taken in building to a position, or the assumptions and values that drove researchers and theorists and constituted their commitments.

The philosophy course readings, by contrast, were almost always challenging and personally engaging, primarily because we students so often were expected to go to the original works of the philosophers themselves rather than to textbook presentations of their writings. A common undergraduate experience is the reading and discussion of Plato's *Dialogues*. Many people I have talked with say they have rather vivid memories of the experience. This is because the *Dialogues* personally engage us, they invite us in and ask us to participate, enticing us to try out our own response to Socrates's questions before we read the response of the protagonist and Socrates's subsequent comments and probing questions. This kind of reading is educative in that it teaches us to move out of our own contemporary sphere into that of a time, place, and company of people who are distant from us and who think and live very differently than we do. This reading teaches us to search for other possibilities, thereby broadening and deepening how we think about and see our own lives. With the example of the constant questioning of Socrates, the dialogues teach us how, through reflection, reasoning, and the imagination, we can go beyond the everyday and taken-for-granted and achieve a more comprehensive and deeper understanding of our lives and what we truly would like to become.

The British Empiricists

Equal to the *Dialogues* in being engaging and educational, although in a different way, was the experience of having to go to the original works of Lucretuis, Descartes, and the British empiricists John Locke, George Berkeley, and David Hume. In the first place, the style and usage of the writing itself presents a challenge to a 20th-century undergraduate and demands effort in reading. Approaching the works in the right spirit, however, can be somewhat like the experience we often get of entering another world when we read a novel that captures us. In entering any of these works, we know right away that the writer is engaged in life-important questions: What is this world I find myself in? What is this "thinking" I do? What has my inner, personal experience to do with that other, "outside" world? How can I understand this sense of a self that persists over time and place? As we enter into works like this, if we do so with a sympathetic spirit, we find, whether we agree or disagree with the writer, that some kind of sense has been made and at the very least the ideas, questions, and arguments must be taken seriously. And in seeing how the writer makes sense, we also begin to see how we can add to and enlarge our own thinking.

But it was in encountering Berkeley's works that I first experienced the exhilaration of becoming truly active and critical in my reading. In building on Locke's empiricism, Berkeley was critical of Locke's inconsistent application of his empiricist method of analysis. Berkeley applied Locke's own principles and arguments and convincingly showed that Locke's distinction between primary and secondary qualities did not hold. That is, if we accept Locke's argument that the qualities of color, sound, taste, and so on are secondary and subjective or mind-dependent rather than existing materially and independently of our mind, then, by the very same argument, everything we perceive, including qualities such as extension and shape (which Locke classifies as primary), also must be regarded as subjective and mind-dependent.

It seemed to me, though, that Berkeley departed from his own empiricism when, to account for the perceptions we have that are independent of our will, he posited as their cause an independent spirit who is God. It also seemed to me that, to assert the real existence of minds and mental events, Berkeley implicitly relied on the notion of an independently existing material world.

Altogether, the experience of reading Berkeley and other great philosophers showed me that I could continually develop my ideas and questions by reading challenging and serious works. Later, after I entered the field of education and also after I began teaching, I found that I constantly went to the literature of education, philosophy, and philosophy of science in my attempt to understand the conceptual difficulties and questions I faced.

Entry Into Education

After I graduated with an A. B. and a major in psychology from Syracuse University, I found the then recently established special education center headed by William Cruickshank, G. Orville Johnson, and Louis DiCarlo. The time was 1954, and this center was one of the early, pioneering departments of special education. It was part of the post-war push to expand special education, prepare an army of certified special education teachers to teach in the rapidly forming special education classes, and develop the new "leaders" of special education. These leaders would administer and direct the public school special education programs, prepare special education teachers in the colleges and universities, and become scientific researchers needed to develop the special education field.

Because of my major in psychology, I was steered to G. Orville Johnson, who directed a most interesting two-track program. One track emphasized preparing to teach students with mental disabilities and the other, preparing for school psychology, but there was considerable overlap in courses and experiences between the two tracks. Because I had majored in psychology, I was advised to go into the school psychology track. It was fortunate for me that this track required courses in education and even some student teaching, because it gave me the chance to see that I was far more interested in education and teaching than I was in school psychology. I had a friend who had graduated and was working in the schools as a school psychologist. Almost all her work involved testing children for placement into special education classes, which did not at all appeal to me. But the education courses and the student teaching did introduce me to the richness of the education field and the exciting challenges of classroom teaching.

Beginning Teaching and Some Important Educational Works

At the start of my teaching career, two educational works were particularly important to me: the text by Kirk and Johnson, *Educating the Retarded Child* (1951), and John Dewey's *Democracy and Education* (1916). These two texts worked together in influencing my development as an educator and teacher. The Kirk and Johnson text, I believe, was far superior to the texts that later supplanted it for use in teacher preparation courses. Subsequent texts on educating students with mental retardation narrowed their base and depended increasingly upon fashionable psychological theory rather than drawing on educational models and theories. The Kirk and Johnson book had a long, detailed section on earlier developments in educating "the retarded," and the entire text was informed by historical and contemporary educational principles and thinking.

For my own teaching, I drew on the Kirk and Johnson text itself and also, following the pattern I had learned already for my philosophy courses, I tracked down the original works of a number of the educators whose programs were summarized in the text, including the works of Itard, Seguin, Montessori, and Ingram. Each of these works helped me in different ways and inspired me in my teaching, especially the works of Montessori and Ingram.

Dewey's Democracy and Education

The special education program at Syracuse University required dual certification in elementary and special education. The elementary education staff members at Syracuse University styled themselves as progressive educators who followed John Dewey's educational theories. Curiously, they never assigned us any of Dewey's works, but after hearing his name invoked in class a number of times, I decided to read Dewey firsthand and bought a copy of his *Democracy and Education* (1916). I studied the book thoroughly, and from that time onward I was very much influenced by Dewey.

I then combined the pragmatism of Dewey and William James so that the empiricist influences from my earlier, undergraduate studies of Locke, Berkeley, and Hume were modified. In the late 1950s I also combined Dewey and Ingram (1960) in working out the "experience units" in my teaching of children classified as "educable mentally retarded." Dewey provided me with the theoretical underpinnings, and from Ingram I took practical examples of the kinds of experience units that could be created with the children I was teaching.

The Subject–Object Divide

Another benefit I derived from Dewey's *Democracy and Education* was further insight into Berkeley's difficulties, which then generalized to include a better understanding of the subjective–objective opposition and separation embedded in Western thought. Dewey attacked various related oppositions, which he characterized as representing dualistic thinking, and convincingly showed how such thinking leads to difficulties. Prominent among the oppositions Dewey examined were subjective and objective, interest and effort, individual and society, conservatism and progressivism, theory and practice, and means and ends.

Dewey argued that the polar ends of each of these oppositions are actually dependent on one another and, though they might be abstractly separated for one purpose or another, they nevertheless form a unity. Then I could see that Berkeley's mistake had been a consequence of starting out by making a radical separation between the knower or perceiver and the known or perceived, meanwhile forgetting or failing to recognize that the knower and the known are always an interdependent and interacting unity. Once Berkeley made the radical separation between the subjective and the objective, the only way he could see to bring them together again was as a unity within the mind, thereby effectively eliminating the objective. I later found that dualistic thinking undermined much of the theory, research, and practice in special education.

Early Teaching Years and Graduate Study

During the mid- to late-1950s, I was both teaching and taking graduate, post-master's-degree courses in education and special education. During this time I began to see how much of the theoretical and research literature in education failed to address the classroom life of public school teaching and learning. As one example, a favorite assignment of both of my professors in philosophy of education and theories of learning was for the students to choose one philosophy or learning theory and work out its implications for the students' classroom teaching. Although I enjoyed these exercises as a challenge to my logical and imaginative capabilities, I found them to be artificial, in that the philosophies or theories never seemed to fully touch classroom life and the students I worked with, although at the time I could not clearly comprehend the limits in the assumptions behind such assignments. I did begin to see more clearly, however, that my professors could not and did not know as much as I did about my classroom work.

One incident particularly exemplifies a turning point in my attitude and thinking. I had been acceding much to the authority of my university professors. Some of the special education faculty members were urging us to use the subtest scores of the Stanford Binet Intelligence Test as a basis for educational programming for our students with mental retardation. The practice at the time was to provide special-class teachers with the complete test results for each student in the class. I wanted to follow the recommendation but found that I was unable to determine how to do it. I assumed that something was missing, so I asked one of my professors, Dr. S., if he would show me how to program for one of my students by using the test scores. He gladly agreed to do so. I brought the student's test scores to Dr. S., and he went through the test and made program suggestions for the student. As Dr. S proceeded, I suddenly began to see the absurdity of my expectation that, through test scores, he could tell me how or what to teach a student he had never met, a student I knew well from everyday observation, interaction, and teaching in the classroom. When Dr. S. finished, I thanked him for the demonstration, and from then on relied primarily on the authority of my firsthand experience in the classroom.

What Dr. S.'s approach in the late 1950s represented was the beginning of a growing dependence in special education on the use of cognitive and perceptual, or "process," categories, which soon served as the basis for the new learning disability category.

Introduction to Logical Positivism

Sometime close to 1960, while browsing in a bookstore, I found a small paperback with an intriguing title. The book was A. J. Ayer's (1946) *Language, Truth and Logic*. This book introduced me to the logical positivist movement. I did not know that the book had become a contemporary classic and that the logical positivist movement already was beginning to lose its dominance in Anglo–American philosophy and also was very much on the defensive. In any case, I was strongly attracted to the writing style and presentation and to the subject matter itself. I immediately saw the connection, in many sections of Ayer's book, to the writings of the earlier British empiricists. The writing style and approach, including Ayer's confident and dogmatic rejection of all metaphysics, are reminiscent of Hume's work.

I was very much taken with Ayer's book, and reading it reinforced my empiricist tendencies. Yet I did not quite become a full-fledged positivist, probably because of the continuing influence that the ideas of Dewey and James had on me. In fact, I gave my own peculiar interpretation to the principle of verification, an early keystone of the positivist edifice. I mistakenly saw verificationism as a sort of extension or refinement of James's pragmatism, thereby softening its thrust and limiting its application in ways that positivists probably would find distorting or even corrupting.

Objectivism and the Behaviorist Movement

At about the same time, near the end of the 1950s, programming, programmed learning, teaching machines, and behavioral objectives were making their way into education and for awhile became quite the fashion. Later, during the 1960s, special educators took up and further developed programming, behavioral objectives, and then task analysis, long after they went out of fashion in general education. I became temporarily interested in programming and behavioral objectives, which I found, in working at them, to afford a gamelike pleasure.

Interesting though the procedures of programming, task analysis, and behavioral objectives initially were to me, I soon began to see their severely limiting consequences for educational practices. These procedures increasingly were raised to the status of overall theory, especially in special education, and they often were promoted as the sole basis for teaching method and curriculum development. The urge for objectification that drove these procedures encouraged the separation of subject from object, of knower from the known, and of means from ends—the very dualisms Dewey had criticized in earlier approaches to curriculum formulation and teaching method. Ignored or overlooked, or perhaps even suppressed, were the considerations that Ingram and Dewey had given to tasks such as how teachers might connect with the emerging and growing capabilities, interests, and tendencies of their students so as to create worthwhile educational projects and experiences.

Programming, task analysis, and behavioral objectives are grounded in the same objectivitist urges as the logical positivists' programs of operational definition and verification. They all share in the reductionism which, in special education, was critically challenged by Heshusius (1982) and Poplin

(1984). Thus, according to logical positivists, through operational definition and verification, all scientific concepts, theories, and laws are reducible to empirical events, measurables, and observables. Similarly, through the objectivist procedures of programming, task analyses, and behavioral objectives, all general educational goals and all complex performances are reducible to observables, measurables, or smaller steps or parts.

These objectivist procedures and their radical dualism resulted in separation of the curriculum from the learner and often from the teacher as well. If the teacher prepares the curriculum, the emphasis is placed on preplanning, with an initial laying out of "terminal" or behavioral objectives in as much specificity and detail as possible. Although it is taken for granted that the teacher will adjust and adapt to the learners along the way, the emphasis nevertheless is on a detailed scripting of the lessons and program beforehand. The curriculum, however, can as well be prescribed and developed apart from the teachers who are to carry it out.

Prescripting of educational programs by experts, distant from learners and teachers, is only a further extension and elaboration of a practice that had begun in early 1900s of having experts distant from classrooms, teachers, and learners construct educational materials. These materials, in the form of textbooks, workbooks, teacher manuals, basal readers, kits, and so on, varied in the degree to which they invited or encouraged teachers and students to take an active part in the construction of activities and objectives rather than only following what was scripted. The primary thrust of programmed learning materials, task analyses, and behavioral objectives listings, however, was to be as complete and self-contained as possible. By the 1970s school districts could even buy, from "banks," ready-made lists of behavioral objectives and task analyses representing a wide variety of subject matter and skills areas.

Programmed learning and task analysis do lend themselves to certain, limited kinds of practices that are technical, routinelike, and relatively closed-ended, such as tying knots, buttoning shirts, washing clothes, and operating machines. But programmed learning and task analysis do not have much to offer for most of the educational curriculum, which consists of knowledge and skills that open up new possibilities for learners, transform how they experience and understand their lives, demand interpretation from learners, and tend to relate to broad cultural values.

These objectifying procedures turned attention away from how teachers and students together might find purpose in their classroom activities and projects, how objectives might emerge, turn, or become clarified through ongoing activities, and how teachers might attempt to relate students' interests, questions, or experiences to the standard curriculum. These procedures could not be of much help to educators in understanding how valued cultural traditions might be assimilated and re-created by particular classroom groups of students within particular communities.

Another way objectivist procedures in education paralleled the program of the logical positivist is in their "quest for certainty" (Dewey, 1929/1960), in their desire for an undoubtable and absolute foundation. The foundation is derived from the empiricist notion that all complex and general ideas are composed of or built up from lower-order and simpler elements, such as simple stimulus elements, or sensations, or immediate observables. Thus, logical positivist philosophers of science talked about the "soil" of observations from which scientific laws, constructs, and theories are built up and the same soil of observations that serve to verify the hypotheses, laws, constructs, and theories. Or logical positivists talked about "anchoring" theories and constructs in observations.

Similarly, objectivist educators talked of building up general knowledge and understanding out of the elements of immediately observed performance, and of reducing subjectively and vaguely stated general aims to clear and objectively stated behaviors. In each case, observables or "raw" data are considered capable of serving as the foundation because they are neutral, objective, or given to us in their concrete immediacy rather than being subjectively constructed or interpreted.

This empiricist approach reduces the entire meaning and significance of any abstract and general concept to some limited set of observables. The meaning of a general concept supposedly is entirely captured and exhausted in the set of observables or empirical instances that have been designated. The empirical instances or observables supposedly are given to us immediately, without subjective interpretation, so that they are neutral, objective, and foundational, and therefore they are given priority and reality over the abstract and general. Scientific theories, laws, and constructs are conceived of as mere conveniences or summaries of concrete instances or designated observables, just as general educational aims and concepts are mere conveniences or summaries of observable and measurable instances of behavior or performance.

Consequently, the open-textured feature of general concepts and theories is obviated, the feature that is basic to their generative power in applying to new instances, in entering into discovery and inquiry, and in furthering the development of understanding. Moreover, the empiricist reduction fails to account for how, at the start, we are able to identify the particular data, empirical instances, or observables that we do, as they are never simply or immediately given to us but, rather, we construct them using one or another interpretive framework, theory, or general scheme. In short, the empiricist dualism supports the illusion that the objective can clearly, and with certainty, be separated from the subjective and interpretive.

Cognitivism and the Construction of Learning Disabilities

During the 1960s, another movement, which I will call "cognitive," took hold in special education. The cognitive movement eventually became the basis for the new category of learning disabilities in special education. Although many of the special educators within the cognitive school rejected the behaviorists' strict limitation to immediately observable behaviors, the cognitive school was not really a fundamental departure from objectivism and a strong attachment to empiricist and logical positivist principles. Also, the dualisms mentioned earlier were retained: subject from object, knower from known, and means from ends. As one aspect of dualism, behaviorists radically separate the inner, subjective experience and thought from the outer, objective world of observable behaviors and events, insisting that educational researchers and teachers should restrict themselves to the outer, objective world of observables.

The cognitivists retained this radical dualism but insisted that it was legitimate to infer inner processes or mental events, such as auditory and visual perceptions and associations, memory recall, and auditory and visual sequencing and integration. Nevertheless, inner, inferred processes, perceptions, or cognitions were anchored to outer observables. Usually, the cognitive models developed were represented in standardized tests so that the empirical anchoring was in the test items and the related recordings of testee responses to those items.

The inner processes or mental events the cognitivists posit become the abilities and disabilities that compose the various models for learning disabilities. Abilities and disabilities are radically separated from the outer world and are conceived as entities located within individuals. These inner entities are further conceived of as, through diagnosis, separately identifiable from each other and from social and cultural contexts. The special education classification of learning disabilities, then, has become an essential part of what Skrtic (1991) has referred to as one of special education's grounding assumptions, the assumption that "disabilities are pathological conditions that students *have*" (emphasis mine). Once we conceive of abilities and disabilities as conditions that students have, as separate entities located within students, it is impossible to account for the way students typically behave in an organized fashion, integrating various abilities, interests, emotions, and dispositions in their activities and projects. It also is impossible to account for the way by which abilities and disabilities are linked to and embedded within the contexts of particular cultural and social practices.

This dualistic conception has become central to the learning disabilities classification in special education. From the early 1960s to the present day

(Kavale & Forness, 1998), a major problem for learning disabilities professionals has been how to define learning disabilities with such objectivity that a student's learning disability could be identified and described as distinct and apart from particular cultural contexts and social practices and as distinct and apart from the student's other personal traits and characteristics. The search for a definition of learning disabilities that would objectively set learning disabilities apart from all contextual and particular environmental settings and from all personal characteristics is a fruitless search, moving endlessly from a "now this and now that" focus in an attempt to find a scientifically objective starting point and foundation: from positing physiological–neurological events to psychological processes constructed from statistical manipulations.

Northrup and Piaget

To further my understanding of how cultural and social practices, as well as the contingent circumstances of particular, local situations, relate to teaching and education, I had to search outside the special education literature. The works of Dewey and Ingram continued to be major inspirations for me during the early 1960s. Furthermore, as I already described, whether of the behaviorist or cognitive and process schools, special educators generally followed the empiricist procedure of operationalizing and reducing general theories to limited sets of observables. Therefore, I also had to search outside the special education literature to further my understanding of the role of general theories, beliefs, concepts, goals, and values for teaching, curriculum development, educational theory, and educational research. Two sources that I found to be particularly helpful in the early 1960s were Northrup's (1959) *The Logic of the Sciences and the Humanities* and Piaget's (1952/1963) *The Origin of Intelligence in Children.*

The works of both Northrup and Piaget showed me how general and abstract concepts and theories, far from being mere conveniences or summaries, provide significance and meaning to particular observations, can generate new data and also new hypotheses and possibilities, and how concepts and theories are essential for constructing observations or data. These ideas influenced the way I conceived of theory and research in education and also the way I viewed teaching, teaching methods, and curricular development.

Post-Empiricist Philosophy of Science

Through the 1960s and 1970s I read a wide number of post-empiricist approaches to the philosophy of science, including the works of Hanson

(1958/1972), Harris (1970), Kuhn (1970), Polanyi (1958/1964), Popper (1962/1968, 1972), and Taylor (1964). Although Popper often has been classified as a positivist, he has denied that he is one, and I found that many of his ideas break with the standard positivist position. It is true that Popper's concern with "demarcating" the disciplines of science from disciplines that are not science and his "falsifiability" thesis are certainly in line with the positivist program. Nevertheless, Popper definitely moves beyond positivism in his insistence that our knowledge has no ultimate source or authority whether in observation or in reason (1962/1968, pp. 3–30), that all observation involves interpretation in the light of theory (1972, p. 295), and that observation is always preceded by something theoretical—by a question, a problem, an anticipation, or an interest (1972, pp. 342–343).

Charles Taylor's book was most enlightening in its critique of behaviorist and stimulus–response learning theory and research, in which I had been immersed as a graduate student during the late 1950s. Taylor used the S–R researchers' own reports to show how the behaviors of the animals in their experiments, behaviors that they explained mechanistically, could be reinterpreted and more convincingly and economically explained as purposive, adaptive, and inventive.

Harris, Hanson, and Kuhn each effectively argue the inseparability of theory from observation or data, the dependence of all data construction on theory, and the creative and inventive power of theory. Harris uses a series of case studies of the researches and theories of famous scientists to show how reason combines theory and data in the construction of new explanations and understandings.

Polanyi

Polanyi's work had a truly profound effect on me. Like Dewey's work, and to some extent that of a number of the post-positivist philosophers of science, Polanyi embraces ordinary, everyday knowing as well as scientific knowing, and he shows the continuities between the two. Thus, as I studied Polanyi's *Personal Knowledge* (1958/1964), I constantly found that I could apply his arguments and insights to questions of teaching and education: how learners participate in their own educational development, how teachers and learners jointly pursue ends not yet fully known or understood, and how educational growth is driven by a desire to make sense of things and achieve self-made standards.

Polanyi also opened up the significance of the tacit component of knowledge and skills, how complex skills and practices are achieved "by the observance of a set of rules which are not known as such to the person following them" (Polanyi, 1958/1964), how in our explicit knowledge we always rely on a wider, more fundamental ground of tacit knowledge, and how our formal instruments of thought rely on our pervasive personal participation and our essentially inarticulate intelligence. Closely related to these ideas is Polanyi's explication of how complex practices, skills, and traditions, including scientific practices, are passed on and learned through the apprenticing of novices to experts or masters. I found Polanyi's insights to have striking implications for teaching and learning and for the direction the study of teaching might take.

Jackson and Lightfoot Studies

In the early 1970s I encountered the reports of two studies that opened new possibilities for how educational research might be done. One of the studies was by Philip Jackson (1968). He selected 10 individuals who were considered to be good teachers, observed their teaching, and interviewed them. Jackson captured the experience of teaching, I found, in a way the conventional research of the time had been unable to.

The second study was by Sarah Lawrence Lightfoot (1973), who, like Jackson, used intensive observation and interview as her main methods. Lightfoot selected for her study two classrooms of black children. The teacher of each class had a political ideology that contrasted with the other. Lightfoot showed how the contrasting political philosophies of the two teachers resulted in very different classroom practices and in very different patterns of learning and development for the children within each of the two classrooms.

In subsequent years I pointed a number of my students to these works as models and inspirations for their doctoral dissertations. A series of original and interesting dissertation studies, mostly of special education teachers followed, demonstrating in various ways how teachers' actions and decisions in the classroom and their planning related to their personal philosophies, beliefs, and skills, combined with the particular circumstances and events of the classroom and also the characteristics and behaviors of the students.

The difficult part of bringing these kinds of dissertations to a successful conclusion was not with the students but, rather, with my faculty colleagues, nearly all of whom during the early and mid–1970s were committed to conventional research relying on statistical measurements and operationalized variables. I learned that it was necessary that my student and myself had first gotten far enough along in planning the study so that members joining the committee would in effect have accepted the alternative approach from the start.

The Education for All Handicapped Children Act and the IEP

In the late 1970s, the objectivist procedures that I described previously were played out in the way the individualized education program (IEP) provision of PL 94–142 was interpreted and implemented by state and local education agencies across the country. I wrote a critique of the objectivist models of IEPs and submitted it to *Exceptional Children.* All three reviewers rejected my manuscript. The reviewers were indignant that I would criticize the IEP procedure in the face of wide consensus that the procedure represented a progressive advancement for special education.

Soon after *Exceptional Children* had rejected my IEP critique, a former doctoral student of mine, Nancy Safer, who at that time was a researcher for the Bureau of Education for the Handicapped (BEH), suggested that I submit a prospectus to BEH, based on my critique, for an IEP project. BEH was commissioning papers to examine the implementation of the individualized education programs provision of PL 94–142. I doubted that my approach would hold any interest for the directors of the project, but Nancy urged me to submit a prospectus and insisted that the directors were interested in diversity among the papers to be developed. I submitted a prospectus, and to my surprise it was accepted. As the work was required to be submitted in stages, at each new stage I expected that the directors would drop me from the project, but they didn't and BEH published my paper along with the three others that were commissioned.

BEH asked each of us who were commissioned to develop position papers on developing criteria by which the quality of IEPs and progress toward their implementation could be evaluated by local education agencies (LEAs). In the first section of my paper, I rewrote and elaborated on my critique that *Exceptional Children* had rejected. I included detailed criticisms of prevailing prescriptive approaches to teaching and the type of educational evaluations generally associated with these approaches. In the second section of the paper, drawing primarily on Dewey's works (Dewey, 1916, Archambault, 1964), I proposed an approach to evaluating IEPs that required, first, that the emphasis be placed on the actual program as carried out rather than what is written down beforehand. Second, means and ends or objectives are to be evaluated holistically and in their intimate relationship with one another. Third, I proposed five criteria or standards for determining the value of educational experiences and activities.

Dewey's *Quest for Certainty*

At about the time I was studying the works of Popper, Polanyi, Northrup, and Taylor, I also read John Dewey's *Quest for Certainty* (1929/1960) and found this latter writing to dovetail remarkably well with the former, more contemporary writers, including the work of Kuhn, which I read somewhat later. Similar to Popper, Polanyi, and Kuhn, Dewey stressed the real existence of qualitative wholes and the power of general knowledge and concepts to generate ideas, apply to new phenomena, and lead to discovery.

Dewey was particularly helpful to me in making clear how we can use our intelligence and judgment in our practical activities, particularly those of teaching, as we encounter the individually unique, the particular, the novel, and the contingent. Dewey revealed the fallacy in the positivist notion that, through scientific research, fixed laws, relationships, or rules might be established for teachers to follow.

Kuhn's *The Structure of Scientific Revolutions*

Sometime after reading Polanyi, I was introduced to Kuhn's (1970) impressive *The Structure of Scientific Revolutions* by a friend and colleague who worked in philosophy of education. Like Popper, Polanyi, Dewey, Piaget, and Northrup, Kuhn showed how mistaken was the empiricist notion that observations serve as a foundation for science, or that they serve as a last court of appeal when disputes arise about laws, constructs, or theories, or that observations are neutral and independent checks on our theories, hypotheses, speculations, and explanations. Through a historical recounting of the actual theoretical and experimental work of several scientists, Kuhn demonstrated that concepts, theories, and frameworks are intimately implicated in all scientific observation and data construction so that observations are always, from the start, "theory-laden," and also that the observations and data of scientists represent highly sophisticated achievements or constructions.

It can be seen that the empiricist program of highly detailed and reductive behaviorist objectives for educational programming is also mistaken. The idea is that by reducing a teacher's vague, subjective, and general objectives to specific and behavioral ones, they would thereby be so objectified that anyone could easily understand the teacher's purposes and program. Moreover, it is believed that, through such objectification, the educational program or experience is easily evaluated, simply by testing the extent to which students' performances at the conclusion of the program match the prescribed objectives.

This reductive empiricist scheme denies that larger wholes, in the form of experiences, projects, activities, and aims, have meaning beyond the reductively stated objectives. Similarly it is denied that to understand or evaluate a teacher's purposes and program, one would have to know the larger context of the teaching–learning situation, the nature of the activities and subject matter, and the students and their histories. Thus, just as Kuhn and others demonstrated the error in the positivist proposal for objectifying science through a foundation of observables, so the empiricist proposal for objectifying teaching and learning through specification of behavioral objectives may be seen to be an error.

Kuhn, Popper, and Polanyi reject the empiricist notion of scientific objectivity based upon neutral data or observations and provide an alternative explanation for the objectivity and progressivity of science. Each stresses that scientists publicly expose to the scientific community their findings, theories, explanations, and questions for review, critical scrutiny, and testing and to engage in the collaborative development of ideas. Polanyi and Kuhn rely heavily on the concept of apprenticing to account for how novices are inducted into the sciences. Kuhn also uses the concept of exemplars, to account for how novices learn to do science, and also as a partial explanation for how scientists achieve objectivity and progressivity. Taken together, these ideas suggest how teaching might achieve a degree of objectivity and progressivity in ways other than through attempting to imitate outworn, positivist models of science.

Teaching, which is a practice and not a science or a discipline, is embedded within a complex structure of moral, social, political, and cultural structures. That web is a constitutive part of the practice of teaching, so that teaching cannot be separated or walled off from those structures in the way the sciences and disciplines are walled off from wider structures, especially in their methods and goals. Nevertheless, teachers could systematically submit their projections and visions to public scrutiny and exemplars of teaching and educational programs could be published in films and in written narratives, both for critical review and for inspiring new possibilities.

Hermeneutics

Sometime in the early 1980s, I encountered hermeneutic theory in the works of Gadamar (1975), Habermas (1971), and Taylor (1971). Hermeneutics introduced me to a whole new way of conceiving the human sciences and thereby a new way of conceiving the scientific study of teaching. From this literature I also found many suggestions for viewing teaching as a practice.

Gadamer's *Truth and Method* (1975) made an impression on me comparable to that of the works of Dewey and Polanyi. I had to struggle to understand many parts of the book, whether because of a poor translation or because of my lack of knowledge about many of the writers and schools of thought that Gadamer brought into his discussions. Nevertheless, I worked on the book because of the many new insights I found in it. Gadamer shows how growth in understanding involves changes in the self and therefore makes it clear that educational growth is a self-formation and a self-transformation, in contrast to a mere mechanical adding on of skills and pieces of knowledge. Also, this work made clear to me just why technicist approaches narrow and degrade teaching by ignoring larger moral and cultural contexts and the constant necessity in teaching for making sensitive judgments and interpretations.

As I continued to teach, prepare teachers, and work with graduate students, teaching assistants, and supervisors of practica, I increasingly realized the truth of Dewey's idea that a significant educational experience involves a transformation of experience. I saw in various ways how genuine learning involves an appropriation to and change in one's self and how teaching itself often demands a reformulation of the teacher's self-understanding. Gadamer's (1975) *Truth and Method* and Polanyi's (1964) *Personal Knowledge* helped me to appreciate more fully these complex aspects of education and teaching.

During those years I almost entirely ignored the special education literature, finding it insulated from the dramatic and exciting changes that were occurring, in postpositivist philosophy of science, anti-foundationalist epistemology, hermeneutic theory, and critical theory, among others. This literature was a source of inspiration for myself and for my students.

Return to the Special Education Literature

In the mid-1980s I wrote an article, "The Study and Development of Teaching" (Iano, 1986), which eventually became the version used in Chapter 3 of this book. Believing there wasn't much sympathy or interest in special education for the ideas I was proposing, I initially wrote the article for a general education audience and planned to submit it to a general education journal. Before submitting the manuscript to a journal, I gave copies to a number of colleagues for comments and suggestions. I sent one of the copies to an old friend, Donald Hammill. Hammill called, and I was surprised when he urged me to add some sections referring to special education and submit it to the chief editor of *Remedial and Special Education,* James Kauffman. I doubted that Kauffman would like the article, but Hammill seemed to think Kauffman was interested in getting "controversial" pieces, so I added some sections on special education and sent the manuscript to Kauffman.

Kauffman wrote back that he was interested in the manuscript and that he would give copies to three reviewers. Later, Kauffman sent me the comments from the three reviewers. Two of the reviewers recommended rejection and the third recommended provisional acceptance, but only with major changes in the manuscript. Yet, in Kauffman's letter accompanying the reviews, he stated that he wanted to publish the manuscript and make it the lead article in a two-issue debate. I was delighted with the idea.

I was disappointed with the level of the responses to my article. Naturally, knowing the deep commitment of most special educators to the ideas I was criticizing, I expected the responders to be critical of my ideas. I was surprised, however—and perhaps I was naive to be—with the degree to which the responders failed to address the substance of the article. Skrtic (1991, pp. 117–118, 120) characterized this kind of response to my critique and to other similar critiques of special education as "completely understandable" and a consequence of such "alternative theoretical discourse" being "noncomprehensible to the field." Nevertheless, I was pleased to have a forum in a leading special education journal and the opportunity to have the "last word" in my rejoinder.

In my rejoinder, I decided to give the most space and attention to the longest of the three responses. The authors of this response claimed to find "a great deal to agree with" (Forness & Kavale, 1987, p. 47) in my article, and in their stated intention to elaborate on my position they produced a response that essentially represented an illustration of the very position that I had criticized. Therefore, I devoted most of my rejoinder to their response, using it as a foil for reinforcing and elaborating my own position.

A major benefit from having these articles published in a special education journal was learning about the writings of Poplin and Heshusius. As I had lost interest in the special education literature, I was unaware that a small but significant critical literature had begun to appear within the larger literature of special education. Following the publication of the above described article, I received a telephone call from Lous Heshusius, and from that call I learned about the writings of Heshusius and Poplin. It was a pleasure and inspiration to read their writings, and I began to use these works in my courses and to direct my students to them. Shortly afterward I discovered the unusual and creative writings of Skrtic, which I also brought to my special education students.

In recent years these critical writings and their alternative positions, along with the inclusion movement, seem to me to have made some permanent mark on special education. It seems fair to say, though, that most of the special education literature remains hostile to genuine alternative approaches to education and teaching, with most of the accepted innovations being elaborations on the basic technicist framework that has taken hold in the last decades. It also seems fair to say that most special educators regard broad educational reform as a threat rather than an opportunity.

References

Archambault, R. (1964). *John Dewey on education: Selected writings.* Chicago: University of Chicago Press.

Ayer, A. J. (1946). *Language, truth and logic* (2d ed.). London: Feigel & Brodbeck.

Dewey, J. (1916). *Democracy and education.* New York: Macmillan.

Dewey, J. (1960). *The quest for certainty: A study of the relation of knowledge and action.* New York: Capricorn Books. (Original work published in 1929 by G. P. Putnam & Sons, New York)

Forness, S. R., & Kavale, K. A. (1987). Holistic inquiry and the scientific challenge in special education: A reply to Iano. *Remedial and Special Education, 8*(1), 47–51.

Gadamer, H. G. (1975). *Truth and method.* New York: Seabury Press.

Habermas, J. (1971). *Knowledge and human interests.* Boston: Beacon Press.

Hanson, N. R. (1972). *Patterns of discovery: An inquiry into the foundations of science.* New York: Cambridge University Press. (Original work published in 1958)

Harris, E. (1970). *Hypothesis and perception: The roots of scientific method.* New York: Humanities Press.

Heshusius, L. (1982). At the heart of the advocacy dilemma: A mechanistic world view. *Exceptional Children, 49*(1), 6–13.

Iano, R. P. (1986). The study and development of teaching: With implications for the advancement of special education. *Remedial and Special Education, 7*(5), 50–61.

Ingram, C. P. (1960). *Education of the slow-learning child* (3d ed.). New York: Ronald Press.

Jackson, P. (1968). *Life in classrooms.* New York: Holt, Rinehart and Winston.

Kavale, K. A., & Forness, S. R. (1998). The politics of learning disabilities. *Learning Disabilities Quarterly, 21,* 245–273.

Kirk, S., & Johnson, G. O. (1951). *Educating the retarded child.* Cambridge, MA: Riverside Press.

Kuhn, T. S. (1970). *The structure of scientific revolutions* (2d ed.). Chicago: University of Chicago Press.

Lightfoot, S. L. (1973). Politics and reasoning: Through the eyes of teachers and children. *Harvard Educational Review, 43*(2), 197–244.

Northrop, F. S. C. (1959). *The logic of the sciences and the humanities.* New York: Meridian Books.

Piaget, J. (1963). *The origins of intelligence in children.* New York: Norton. (Original work published in 1952)

Polanyi, M. (1964). *Personal knowledge: Towards a post-critical philosophy.* New York: Harper & Row. (Original work published in 1958)

Poplin, M. S. (1984). Toward a holistic view of persons with learning disabilities. *Learning Disabilities Quarterly, 7*(4), 290–294.

Popper, K. R. (1968). *Conjectures and refutations: The growth of scientific knowledge.* New York: Harper & Row. (Original work published in 1962)

Popper, K. R. (1972). *Objective knowledge: An evolutionary approach.* New York: Oxford University Press.

Skrtic, T. M. (1991). *Behind special education: A critical analysis of professional culture and school organization.* Denver: Love.

Taylor, C. (1964). *The explanation of behavior.* New York: Humanities Press.

Taylor, C. (1971). Interpretation and the sciences of man. *Review of Metaphysics, 25,* 3–34.

Accidental Tourist and Deliberate Seeker: Two True Stories

Thomas M. Skrtic

When asked how I came to choose special education as a career, and why my work in the field has taken such a divergent path, I tell two different but interrelated stories. In the first story I am an accidental tourist, one whose journey into and through special education was shaped by a series of largely fortuitous events that found their final expression in my teaching and writing. In the second story I am a deliberate seeker of knowledge and meaning, one whose teaching and writing reflect a purposeful attempt to develop a deeper and broader understanding of disability and special education, first personally and professionally, then intellectually and politically. Both stories are true, more or less.

An Accident Waiting to Happen

I began my college career at California State College, a former teachers' college in California, Pennsylvania. When I arrived at CSC in the fall of 1964, I had no interest in becoming a teacher, and during that year I had no contact with education or special education. In fact, although I claimed to be a math major, I had little contact with the math department, or with much else at CSC that was academic. At best, I was an ambivalent student; at worst, I was resistant to anything that had to do with formal schooling, just as I was during my high school days in McKeesport, Pennsylvania. Things might have been different had I been a better student in high school, but, as it turned out, I was completely unprepared for academic life. Like most working-class kids, I didn't think of myself as "college material," and neither did my high school guidance counselor who, correctly projecting that I would graduate in the bottom fifth of my class, had gently tried to steer me in a different direction.

The summer after my freshman year, I went to Los Angeles with two hometown friends who were moving there. My plan was to return to CSC for my sophomore year, but the excitement of the LA scene in 1965 was too much to resist, and I decided to stay, at which point I got a part-time job and enrolled for my second year of college at Los Angeles Harbor Junior College in Wilmington, California. I changed at LA Harbor. Maybe it was because I was working and (barely) supporting myself, or because there was little in the way of campus life to distract me, or because I was just growing up. Whatever it was, I became a more responsible person than I had been previously and, in turn, a somewhat more serious student. By this time I had lost interest in mathematics, but I can remember being interested in most of my liberal arts courses at LA Harbor, especially psychology and geology, and even English, to a point.

Having gained some confidence in myself as a student, I planned to apply to one of the four-year schools in the Cal State system for my junior year. Toward the end of 1965–66, however, my transplanted LA friends decided to move to Las Vegas, which meant that I might not be able to afford to live in LA. Purely as a back-up, I reapplied to CSC and, when it became clear that I would have to return there for my junior year, asked a friend to enroll me in whatever courses he was taking the next fall. When I reconnected with him back in McKeesport at the end of the summer, I learned that I was signed up for Physical Education, Senior Life Saving, and a special education course he called "Secondary MR Methods." Although landing in this course was an accident, my family history had a lot to do with why I stayed in it, and ultimately with why I completed the special education degree and certification program at CSC and went on to become a special education teacher.

Disability always had been part of my life because my younger sister, who had experienced brain trauma at birth, had been in special education for most of her school career. By conventional standards, Cathy has a mild developmental disability in conjunction with some specific and unique learning disabilities. Had she been born in 1970 rather than 1950, she would have been placed in a regular classroom with special education resource room services. Having had a relatively standard school experience, she no doubt would have had a relatively typical life after leaving school. She would have gone on to a job, I'm sure, and most likely to what my parents and I would have considered a fairly typical adult life in McKeesport, including marriage and probably a family of her own. Also, had my parents known more about the true nature and extent of Cathy's disability, they might have reacted differently to it and to her, and especially to the dire prognosis and inappropriate placement recommendation they were to receive when she was in second grade.

Before Cathy started school, her disability didn't seem to make that much of a difference. Even when she entered first grade at the same Catholic school I attended, she was pretty much a "regular" kid. Her first-grade teacher accommodated her needs quite well as a matter of course in the regular classroom, and she adjusted well to first grade and even liked school. Unfortunately, Cathy's second-grade teacher was unable or unwilling to accommodate her needs and clearly didn't want her in the classroom. Cathy sensed her teacher's disdain, of course, and early in the school year developed an acute case of school phobia. My most salient memories of that year are of Cathy crying uncontrollably and vomiting each morning before school and, most days, in her classroom as well.

In relatively short order, the teacher referred her for testing at the Catholic Diocese in Pittsburgh, and when Cathy scored below the cutoff point on the Stanford-Binet (in those days, 1 standard deviation below the mean), she was labeled "mentally retarded" and removed from her second-grade classroom. Furthermore, as incredible as it may sound, especially for a child who had successfully completed first grade, the Diocese's psychologist assured my parents that the best thing they could do for Cathy (and themselves) would be to put her in a nearby "home for the mentally retarded."

Not knowing any better, and certainly not up to questioning a professional or, God forbid, the Catholic Diocese, my parents accepted the psychologist's diagnosis and made arrangements to visit "the home." I remember driving to this place in the country and waiting in the car while my parents took Cathy inside the main building. They were not gone long when, suddenly, they burst back through the front doors and hurried down the steps. As they approached the car, I could see that my mother and Cathy were crying and, by the time my father pulled our 1950 Ford back out onto the highway, so was he. That was the first time I had seen my parents frightened, but it wasn't the last. Over the next few weeks, fear and apprehension overtook our home as my parents frantically searched for an alternative to "the home" for Cathy.

Basically, there were two choices back then, both of which were self-contained special classrooms in McKeesport. One of the classrooms was in a public school in the poorest part of town, which my parents rejected out of hand because of the school's unsavory reputation. The other one was in the basement of another Catholic school. Although my parents were concerned when they learned that this special class served students of all ages (roughly 6 to 18) with all types and degrees of disability, they felt far more comfortable with this option, in part, because it appeared to be more orderly and safer than the public school special class. Cathy spent the next decade of her life in this segregated special classroom, with the same teacher and students for the entire time.

Although her teacher, a Franciscan nun, wasn't a special educator or even a certified teacher, she was a very caring person who, from all appearances, came to know and value her students, including Cathy. The worst thing about the arrangement was that Cathy never again had contact with her typical age peers or with the regular school curriculum. The worst thing at home was that my parents accepted the professional assessment of Cathy's ability and treated her accordingly. Looking back, by accepting and acting upon an inappropriate underestimation of her capacity and potential, my parents and I—and, by extension, our relatives, family friends, and neighbors — unwittingly restricted Cathy's development and ultimately constructed her as someone less capable than she would have been otherwise.

Until I accidentally enrolled in my first special education course at CSC, I associated most things about my sister's disability with the same fear and apprehension that I sensed at home. And, while I also was apprehensive about taking the class, it turned out to be the start of a 30-year process in which I developed an entirely different understanding of disability and, in the end, a fundamentally different view of the world. The course was taught by Dr. Dave Dickie, a young, enthusiastic professor who seemed to be committed to his field and genuinely concerned about people with disabilities and about people in general. The most important thing I learned that semester was that there are different degrees of mental retardation (the only type of disability covered), and that, with the right kind of education, people with mental retardation can learn, become independent, and lead happy and fulfilling lives. Because this was a different view of disability than I had lived with at home, I came away from the course with far less apprehension about my sister's situation and, more important, with a sense of optimism about her future, which I immediately began to share with Cathy and my parents.

As a result of this experience, I continued in the program, and when I graduated in January 1969, with a Bachelor's degree and certification in Secondary Mental Retardation, I felt that I finally understood disability for what it was, and that, as a special educator, I was embarking on a career of service to help people like my sister lead happy and fulfilling lives. Dr. Dickie and my other special education professors at CSC taught me that special education is a valued service for students with disabilities and their families, and that special educators are to provide and advocate for the best possible professional services for their students. This and the other special education courses I took at CSC changed my life and, over the years, also changed the lives of my sister and parents.

Insecurity and Doubt

My first teaching position was at an urban elementary school in a racially segregated section of Pittsburgh. Virtually all of the students who attended the school were African American, as were all of my special education students. I taught in one of two self-contained special classrooms for the "educable mentally retarded" located in the basement of the run-down and unruly building. Actually, to say that I taught is an overstatement, in part, because the school was almost completely out of control in terms of discipline, but more significantly because, having been trained as a secondary work–study teacher, I was insecure about my ability to teach the academic subjects, especially reading. The best I could do, it seemed, was to keep my students occupied with what I hoped were at least interesting, if not completely sound, instructional activities.

What was even more troubling was that my obvious lack of academic teaching skills didn't seem to matter to my superiors. Clearly, my main job was to control my students' behavior, or at least to keep them in my classroom, which raised doubts in my mind about what I had been taught about special education and my role as a professional. And although I lasted only 2 months in this position, it was long enough to raise even greater doubts about disability and the function of special education in schools. Whereas all of my students had learning and behavior problems, as I got to know them socially and academically, only a few seemed to have mental retardation.

I left this teaching job for a permanent substitute position at a special day school, one of five such segregated facilities in Allegheny County to which were bused all of the public school students with disabilities from the districts surrounding Pittsburgh. The school was named Mon Valley High School, but it actually served a K–12 population, and once again I was assigned an elementary classroom for students labeled "educable mentally retarded." This meant that I still had to deal with my insecurities about teaching young children, but now I had a plan, which was one of several reasons for my switching jobs.

Because Mon Valley was a special education school, I knew that all of my colleagues would be special educators, and my plan was to draw upon them to learn to teach reading, which at that point I saw as a simple matter of learning the right techniques. Moreover, as a special education school, I assumed that Mon Valley would embody what I had been taught about special education and my role as a professional, and that, at a minimum, my superiors would care about the quality of my teaching. This turned out to be true, but my plan backfired.

Before I had a chance to learn the "right techniques," the County Office sent a special education supervisor out to Mon Valley to evaluate my teaching. Although the supervisor was very professional, I will never forget the professional devastation and personal embarrassment I felt when she delivered her blistering criticism of my teaching to me and my principal. I felt more insecure than ever, of course, but right there in the principal's office I vowed that this would never happen to me again, that I would learn to teach reading once and for all.

Another reason for switching jobs was that I assumed that at a special education school I finally would get to work with the type of student I had learned about in college, but this did not turn out to be the case. About half of the students at Mon Valley and in my class were African American and, like my first group of students, most of them didn't fit the definition of "educable mentally retarded." Moreover, only a few of my white students fit the label, and though all of my kids had academic or behavior problems, or both, what the majority of them seemed to have in common was the fact that they were poor. Finally, I went to Mon Valley because, at my urging, the previous fall my parents had transferred my sister there for her last 2 years of high school. This had been traumatic for them because Mon Valley turned out to be a pretty tough school, especially compared to the relatively sheltered existence Cathy had experienced over the past 10 years. I felt responsible for my parents' anxiety and thought that by being a teacher at the same school, I could at least calm their fears about Cathy's safety.

My job at Mon Valley High ended with the close of the 1968–69 school year, at which point I went back to southern California, where I landed my third teaching position, this time as a secondary work–study coordinator at Magnolia High School in Anaheim. Maybe because I was sensitive to the issue, the first thing I noticed was that many students in my mostly Latino class were not "mentally retarded," even though they all had learning or behavior problems. The reason why they were placed in special education was something of an enigma to me.

During my 2 years at Magnolia, I ran a decent work–study program and managed to place and keep most of my students in jobs. I even had a fair amount of success at integrating some of them into regular art, music, home economics, and physical education classes. I can't say that the regular education teachers and I worked "hand-in glove" along these lines, but I did manage to keep my students in their classrooms and to keep the peace, so to speak. Furthermore, from my experiences at Magnolia, I realized that many of my students were victims of poor instruction earlier in their school life, and that, with effective remedial instruction (especially in reading and language arts) and better attitudes and some training for general education teachers, they could have been integrated into many academic classes as well. This realization led me directly back to the issue of pedagogy.

Back to the Well

During my 2 years at Magnolia High School, I worked on my Master's degree at California State University at Long Beach. Technically, the degree program was in Educational Psychology, but within Ed Psych one could choose to major in one of three special education categorical areas: elementary mental retardation, secondary mental retardation, or learning disabilities, the latter of which had just emerged as a disability category and area of teacher preparation. Nominally, I was in the secondary mental retardation track, but I'd already taken most of the required courses as an undergraduate, so I had quite a bit of flexibility in creating my own "blended" or—to use a term that would become common some years later—"cross-categorical" program of study.

Because of my insecurity about teaching and my doubts about the nature of mental retardation, I took the characteristics, methods, and practicum courses in both the elementary mental retardation and learning disabilities tracks, and repeated some of the secondary mental retardation courses that I had taken as an undergraduate back in Pennsylvania. Given my shaky start as a teacher, and especially the vow I had made to myself back at Mon Valley, I was a serious student at Cal State Long Beach, which my professors Al Lazar, Chuck Kokaska, and Al Schmidt recognized and rewarded by offering me a 1-year Bureau of Education for the Handicapped fellowship. I accepted their offer and, as a full-time student, was able to complete my Master's degree by the end of the 1971–72 academic year.

In my Master's program I learned a great deal about teaching and, most important, about why many of my students in Pittsburgh and Anaheim had not fit the traditional definition of mental retardation. By taking courses in mental retardation and learning disabilities simultaneously, I learned that most of my former students probably had learning disabilities rather than mental retardation, and that some of them probably had both. I also learned that these disability labels made little difference in terms of instruction, and that students with either label could benefit from many of the same methods. More significantly, from class readings and discussions on two important

California court cases—*Diana* v. *Board of Education* and *Larry P.* v. *Riles*—I realized that the overidentification of minority students in special education was a widespread problem stemming from, among other things, the racially and ethnically biased tests that were used in the identification process.

Finally, I learned that segregated special classes themselves could be socially and academically debilitating for students with special needs, and that there were alternatives, such as the resource room model that had emerged with the rise of the learning disabilities classification. This last lesson was particularly troubling for me as I thought about my sister, who by this time had graduated from Mon Valley High and was sitting at home with no friends, no job, and no prospects. From my perspective, Cathy was leading a lonely and isolated life, an outcome, I concluded, that had more to do with her segregated special education experience than with her disability.

At the urging of my Long Beach professors, I applied for and was accepted into the special education doctoral program at the University of Iowa. Though I was slated to begin the program in 1972–73, I delayed my entry for a year to take another teaching job in Fountain Valley, an innovative school district in southern California that was experimenting with what today would be called inclusive education. I was drawn to Fountain Valley because of what had happened to my sister as a result of her segregated special education experience. It was clear to me by this point that the segregated special classroom was entirely inappropriate for kids like Cathy and most of the students I had taught. I spent the 1972–73 school year working as a cross-categorical middle school resource teacher. The school had no separate special education classrooms or even resource rooms; all students with disabilities were placed in regular classrooms, and the other special educators and I simply worked in common learning centers and in the regular classrooms with any student who needed help. To say the least, my year at Fountain Valley was an enlightening and exciting experience.

When I arrived in Iowa City for the 1973–74 school year, I still was intensely interested in learning more about teaching methodology and mild disabilities. Given my personal and professional experiences to that point, including my year at Fountain Valley, I had developed a new passion for what, in retrospect, I would call special education policy design and implementation. Although my advisor, Professor Alan Frank, specialized in mental retardation, I chose to major in the combined behavioral disorders/learning disabilities doctoral program, in part because of what I believed were clear advantages of the cross-categorical approach, and also because it would give me advanced training in behavioral disorders, a third mild disability area that, as a relatively new categorical area, had not been available to me during my undergraduate or Master's degree programs. I also took courses in special education administration, from Professor Clifford Howe, with the hope of learning more about special education policy, including the relative advantages of the various service delivery models under which I had worked—a special day school, full-time and part-time special classrooms in regular schools, and the inclusive education program at Fountain Valley.

Taking advanced courses in learning disabilities and behavioral disorders reinforced what I had learned earlier about the similarities and differences among the mild disability classifications, including the questionable significance of these distinctions when it came to instruction. Moreover, given the flood of special education court cases and legislation in the early 1970s, my special education administration courses became arenas for highly charged legal, moral, and political debates on virtually every aspect of special education programming, both before and after Public Law 94–142, the Education for All Handicapped Children Act of 1975, was signed into law at the start of my third year at Iowa. New concepts and procedures such as "the right to education and treatment," "least restrictive environment," "individualized education programs," "nondiscriminatory evaluation," "parent participation," "mainstreaming," and "continuum of services" occupied our attention and stimulated our thinking during those heady days.

Something important was happening in and to special education. It was changing and, based on my professional and personal experiences, it was changing in the right direction. Given my collective professional and personal experiences, I was heavily invested in these debates. These questions mattered deeply to me, and I had plenty to say about them. After all, I had seen the negative effects of traditional special education on my sister and family, had witnessed the overrepresentation problem firsthand, and had worked under three of the service delivery approaches at the core of the new "continuum of services" model, as well as one approach that wouldn't become generally available for more than a decade. Given my interest in special education policy design and implementation, my dissertation research focused on implementation of PL 94–142 and mainstreaming through inservice training of general and special educators.

I also chose to minor in the psychology of reading, which at first I saw as the final installment on my vow to become a better teacher. I had come a long way in this regard at Cal State Long Beach, but I wanted more. I wanted an in-depth understanding of reading, which I had come to see as the most important academic subject, especially for students with mild to moderate disabilities under the mainstreaming model. Although I had learned many of the "right techniques" in my Master's program, I wanted to understand the theory behind the techniques. As it turned out, my work in the psychology of reading was even more valuable and stimulating than my work in special education. This was so because, under the guidance of my minor advisor, Professor Joyce Hood, my fellow graduate students and I studied and applied every known approach to reading instruction, from synthetic phonics to whole-language reading, and related each to its respective learning theory and presumed psychological processes, and ultimately to the types of learner attributes for which each was best suited. Until then, I had been content to learn techniques, but now I began to see the relationship between theory and practice. This gave me an entirely different perspective on learning and teaching and also provided me with my first exposure to epistemological frameworks and metatheoretical paradigms—terms that I wouldn't be exposed to and actually use for another few years. My work in the psychology of reading at Iowa was the tacit beginning of a more articulated conceptual shift that was to come later at the University of Kansas.

Deliberately Seeking Meaning

As my doctoral program came to a close in the summer of 1976, I accepted a newly created position at the University of Kansas, which, in all respects but one, seemed to have been written just for me. Ed Meyen and Dale Scannell, Chair of Special Education and Dean of Education, respectively, had structured the position as a joint appointment in the Departments of Special Education and Curriculum and Instruction, and they had done so specifically to address the personnel preparation implications of PL 94–142 and mainstreaming. On the special education side of the appointment, I was to become the School's point person on preparing general educators for their new roles with regard to students with disabilities. I was ready for this, given my cross-categorical training in the mild disability categories, my dissertation research, and my minor in psychology of reading.

The only problem was that the general education side of the appointment called for me to teach in the area of elementary mathematics, not in reading. The Curriculum and Instruction department at KU had a full stable of reading instructors at the time but needed another person in mathematics education, which I agreed to learn on the job as a condition of employment. My subsequent interest in philosophy and organization, and eventually in critical social theory, developed out of a convergence of two sequences of fortuitous events at KU, both of which arose from the practical demands of my new faculty position.

Linking Reading and Math

I set out to become proficient in mathematics education by devising a retooling plan with Professor Lelon Capps and his graduate teaching assistant, who together comprised the elementary mathematics education faculty. During the first year of the plan, I attended a large-group lecture taught by Lee Capps, and two of the three small-group math labs taught by his graduate assistant, and then, based on this and some additional reading and preparation, taught a fourth lab session on my own. The next year I taught the large-group lecture and one math lab, and from the third year foreword I alternated between teaching the lecture course and a graduate course in remedial math. Although at first I assumed that my investment in reading at Iowa was simply a lost cause, this was anything but the case.

Linking Theory and Practice

As it turned out, Lee Capps's math education program was based upon a cognitive approach to mathematics instruction called "meaningful math," which, like "constructivist math" today, stressed understanding and appreciation of mathematical concepts and principles rather than simply math facts and mastery of algorithms. This approach made perfect sense to me, of course, because I already had been exposed to cognitive theories of learning and development with respect to whole-language reading instruction. Through exposure to a second academic subject that drew upon many of the same theories, I came to understand and appreciate my training in the psychology of reading even more.

On one level, I had undergone a constructivist shift in reading instruction at Iowa, and now I was immersed in the same kind of epistemological shift in mathematics instruction. Far more important, however, I had been exposed, albeit implicitly, to the idea that theory matters, that there are different theoretical frameworks upon which to base practice, and, further, that one can and should choose theory in a purposeful way. With this insight, I began to see that teacher education tended only to scratch the surface in pedagogy, and that much of the controversy over "best practice," including the predictable pendulum swings from one pedagogical extreme to another, stemmed from this narrow, largely atheoretical understanding of teaching and learning. I still didn't recognize the broader social and philosophical implications of these insights, but at least pedagogy began to make sense to me.

My appreciation of the link between theory and practice was only one of many incremental gains in a long line of conceptual breakthroughs that were to come. Having begun to resolve some of the pedagogical challenges that had gnawed at me, I felt fairly satisfied with the direction I was going. But my sense of satisfaction was short lived because of new questions that had begun to occupy my attention, substantive and methodological questions that were raised by three related experiences in educational reform.

Kicking a 40-Foot Sponge

Prior to the creation of my joint appointment, the KU School of Education had begun to address the challenge of preparing general educators for PL 94–142 and mainstreaming. The Department of Special Education had done so in the early 1970s by creating the "Special Education Area of Emphasis," an elective program to prepare undergraduate teacher education students for teaching students with disabilities in general education classrooms. The School addressed the problem by securing a federally funded Dean's Grant project in 1975, which, like the national network of such projects, was designed to achieve the same goal on a much broader scale—by revising the entire teacher education curriculum. In effect, my joint special education/general education position was a capstone on these efforts. Upon my arrival at KU, I became the coordinator of the Special Education Area of Emphasis program and an active member of the Dean's Grant steering committee.

Dean's Grant

Although the Area of Emphasis and Dean's Grant project had the same ultimate goal, they approached the problem in completely different ways. The Area of Emphasis was a separate, 12-credit-hour add-on to the regular teacher education program, whereas the Dean's Grant project was designed to reform the program itself by infusing special education content into the teacher education curriculum. Although the Area of Emphasis was highly regarded among teacher education students, we agreed to discontinue it as a separate program and, in the spirit of mainstreaming, to infuse its special education objectives and content into existing teacher education courses.

After distributing the special education objectives across the entire teacher education curriculum, we developed a multi-volume set of published materials that contained virtually everything instructors would need to teach the content, including student and instructor readings, lecture notes, class assignments, exam items with answers, and overhead transparency masters. In addition, to facilitate implementation, I served as "resource professor" to my general education colleagues, a role in which, upon request, I taught the special education content for the first time in their courses.

Initially everything seemed to be going as planned, but before too long we realized that most general education faculty members simply allowed the infused content to drift off. Although some continued to teach it, most gave it less and less attention over time. Some recommended selected readings to students, but most didn't incorporate them into class lectures or discussions. By the time our Dean's Grant funding ended in the mid-1980s, virtually no one was teaching the infused content in any meaningful way. To say the least,

I was discouraged and puzzled by this turn of events. Why would good instructors and dedicated colleagues fail to follow through on something we all thought was so worthy and that we had worked so hard to accomplish? Searching for an answer to this question played a major part in shaping the next phase of my career in higher education.

REGI Grants

Whereas initially I had focused my efforts on reforming the preservice teacher education curriculum, in 1979 I also began to address inservice education through a series of federal grants funded under what was called the Regular Education Inservice or REGI program. Our design was quite unique for the times (Skrtic, Knowlton, & Clark, 1979). Drawing on adult learning theory, which itself tends to draw most heavily upon cognitive theories of learning and development, we began by turning inservice education into a problem of curriculum development to be solved by building-based teams of practicing professionals. From there, we used a fairly typical curriculum development model to show local educators how to design, develop, and deliver their own staff development programs. We showed them how to identify their training needs, write and validate training objectives with their colleagues, design learning activities to achieve the objectives, and deliver and evaluate their staff development curriculum, feeding the results back into the curriculum development cycle.

At first, the creative and enthusiastic involvement of project participants was impressive and encouraging. There was a tremendous espirit de corp among participants and their colleagues as they worked together to identify and address their own professional development needs. When the grants ended at the various participating schools, however, so did the change process. In the end, it seemed that nothing had really changed. The project effects quickly dissipated; years of effort had produced little in the way of meaningful and lasting change.

By this point, then, I had witnessed two examples of failed educational reform firsthand—one in teacher education and one in public schools. Both seemed to have produced a good deal of enthusiasm and focused activity at first, only to dissipate and eventually fade away over time.

National Institute of Education Project

My third experience with educational reform was more comprehensive and complex. And because this one involved research on educational change itself, it ultimately, though not directly, helped me understand the lack of meaningful, lasting change in the first two experiences. In the process I also came to understand research differently, particularly the role of theory in disciplined inquiry.

This experience with educational change also began in 1979 when, as a minor player in a department-wide effort to write a proposal for a Regional Resource Center, I was introduced to Egon Guba's monograph, *Toward a Methodology of Naturalistic Inquiry in Educational Evaluation* (Guba, 1978). Gordon Alley, a highly regarded special education colleague to whom our faculty often deferred on methodological questions, brought the paper to the group and recommended that we use "naturalistic inquiry" for the needs assessment and evaluation components of the RRC proposal. Although at the time we didn't refer to colleagues as being either "quantitative" or "qualitative," Gordon was a well established quantitative person, which made his arguments for using a qualitative methodology all the more weighty. Given his stature and methodological credentials, the group adopted his recommendation and submitted the proposal with the naturalistic components.

Through my involvement with the grant application, I became quite familiar with the Guba monograph and, more important, with the frame of reference upon which naturalistic inquiry is premised. Most of my special education colleagues seemed to have more difficulty understanding and accepting naturalistic inquiry, but the method, and particularly its metatheoretical grounding in the interpretivist paradigm, immediately made sense to me because of my prior exposure to this frame of reference through my work in reading and mathematics. At the time, I didn't use terms such as "metatheoretical," "interpretivist," "paradigm," or "constructivist." I hadn't yet begun to think of cognitive theories of learning and development and research methods such as naturalistic inquiry as sharing a common metatheoretical grounding in what I would understand later as the interpretivist paradigm of modern social scientific thought. At this point, however, I began vaguely to see the link between research methodology and what I had learned about pedagogy at Iowa and KU.

Shortly after the RRC proposal was submitted, the now-defunct National Institute of Education (NIE) issued a request-for-proposals for a national study of PL 94–142 implementation in rural schools. Given its longstanding interest in rural education, multidistrict educational service agencies (ESAs), and qualitative research, the NIE wanted a single contractor to mount a qualitative study of the role of ESAs in implementing the law in their member districts. Although I knew little about rural education or ESAs, I immediately was attracted to the qualitative aspect of the RFP because of my exposure to the Guba monograph and the chords it had struck with my understanding of reading and math. Also, given my role in the School of Education and the fact that to this point I had devoted most of my energy to issues of teacher education, I saw the NIE contract as an opportunity to develop a research agenda on special education policy design and implementation, thus pursuing another of my interests while rounding out my work as a faculty member at a research university.

Shortly after we submitted the NIE proposal, I was invited by what was then the Bureau of Education for the Handicapped to review special education grant applications. As luck would have it, during my stay in Washington, DC, I shared a University of Maryland dorm room with John McLaughlin, who, at the time, held a special education faculty position at Virginia Tech. I didn't know John or that he and Egon Guba were good friends. When I told him about the NIE proposal and my plan to use naturalistic inquiry, however, he told me that he had been the best man for Egon's recent marriage to Yvonna Lincoln, who the year before had joined the education faculty at KU. I knew Yvonna to see her but didn't know her personally or that she had any connection to Egon Guba or naturalistic inquiry. When I returned to Lawrence, I immediately contacted her and, through her, spoke to Egon by phone about the possibility of his getting involved in the NIE project if it were funded. He agreed to read the proposal and to come to KU from Indiana University to discuss my offer.

When I met Egon for the first time a week or so later, it was at Yvonna's dining room table, where we discussed the NIE proposal and the possibility of his coming to KU to work on the project. It became clear in the meeting, which in many ways was like a dissertation defense, that Egon didn't like the proposal, especially the way it was almost apologetic about using naturalistic inquiry as the research methodology. Nevertheless, he ultimately agreed to become a member of the research team if we were to win the contract, including taking a sabbatical at KU for part of the project period. In part, Egon came around because I agreed to revise the treatment of naturalistic inquiry in the proposal, but mostly, I suspect, because of the prospect of actually living with his wife for awhile. As it turned out, we won the contract, in no small measure because, in the "best and final offer" phase of the competition, I was able to say that Egon Guba, the person behind the proposed methodology, would join the research team.

After we had won the contract, Egon moved to Lawrence and, together with several of my KU special education colleagues, we conducted in 1980–81 and 1981–82 what became the first national, multisite application of naturalistic inquiry (Skrtic, 1985). When the project began in the fall of 1980, Egon and Yvonna were writing their first book on naturalistic inquiry, *Effective Evaluation: Improving the Usefulness of Evaluation Results Through Responsive and Naturalistic Approaches* (Guba & Lincoln, 1981), which came out the following year. Although much of the theoretical work on naturalistic inquiry had been completed before the NIE project began, most of the procedures for implementing it had not been developed or tried. As such, the project became a vehicle for developing and testing the procedures that eventually came to define naturalistic inquiry in their second book, *Naturalistic Inquiry* (Lincoln & Guba, 1985), throughout which the NIE project serves as the exemplar of naturalistic research.

We began the NIE project with what can only be described as a crash course for project staff on the conceptual foundations of naturalistic inquiry. Looking back 20 years, the concepts we covered seem fundamental, but at the time this was my introduction to philosophy of social science. Most of the training focused on a comparison of the axioms, frames of reference and research postures of the positivist and naturalist paradigms. Although it seemed that my colleagues were having a difficult time with some of these ideas, they all made immediate sense to me, again because of the earlier, but still somewhat tacit, epistemological shift I had undergone in my pedagogical work in reading and mathematics.

What was different this time was that the shift was occurring with respect to research methodology. At this point, I began to see that theory also matters in inquiry, and that one's choice of a grounding theory for research largely shapes what one sees in the object of inquiry. Here again, I began to see that educators only scratch the surface in research methodology, and that much of the controversy over "quantitative versus qualitative methods" that had emerged in the early 1980s stemmed from this narrow take on inquiry and inquiry systems.

In any event, we carried out the NIE study and found that, despite PL 94–142 and its emphasis on nondiscriminatory evaluation, individualized programs, multidisciplinary collaboration, parent participation, and least restrictive placements, special education practice in the five state and 100 or so school districts we studied was pretty much the same as it had been when I began teaching in the late 1960s. Most of the requirements of the law were in place, of course: multiple (though not always nondiscriminatory) measures were being used in the identification process, each identified student had an IEP on file, multidisciplinary IEP staffings were being conducted, and parents were attending and, more or less, participating in the staffings.

Yet, special education students were still largely segregated, minority students were still conspicuously overrepresented in these classrooms, and most students who spent any time at all in general education classrooms were not actually integrated instructionally or socially. The time we spent observing in schools, districts, and ESAs, and the interviews we conducted with professionals, parents, and students made it clear to us that, good intentions and good-faith efforts notwithstanding, the law was not being implemented in any meaningful sense of the word. Just as in my two prior experiences with educational reform, all the trappings of change were present, but below these surface activities was very little that one could point to in the way of meaningful change.

I had gone after the NIE research contract, in part, to learn more about why meaningful educational change is so elusive, but after 2 years in the field, what I got was another, more comprehensive and compelling example of its evanescence. To be sure, studying PL 94–142 implementation naturalistically helped us understand how the law was being implemented in our research sites—in effect, the meaning of change in these particular schools and school systems. It also gave us firsthand knowledge of the many social and procedural barriers to change from the multiple perspectives of our research participants. Like all empirical research, however, it did not tell us why one would find what we had found—why such barriers to change existed in educational organizations.

Although at this point I was more baffled than ever by the process of educational change, Egon was far less surprised by our findings. He expected less in the way of meaningful implementation than the rest of the research team, in part because he had been a student of organization and change for much of his career and was already internationally known for both the Getzels–Guba model of administration (Getzels & Guba, 1957) and the Clark–Guba model of research, development, and diffusion (Clark & Guba, 1967). Drawing on his knowledge of and experience with organization, administration, and the process of organizational change, Egon summarized our collective experiences with PL 94–142 implementation in a single phrase—"Changing schools is like trying to kick a 40-foot sponge."

Although Guba's aphorism captured what we had found in the NIE study, as well as what I had observed in my prior experiences with educational reform, it was not enough to satisfy my curiosity. At that point, understanding why meaningful change was so difficult in schools became my new mission in academic life, just as understanding pedagogy had been my earlier mission. Drawing on my prior experience with pedagogy, though, this time I knew I needed to understand change theoretically.

Getting a Theoretical Life

Funding for the NIE project ended in May of 1982, by which time we had finalized our case studies and drafted the final report. Soon thereafter, Egon went back to Bloomington and the NIE research team more or less dispersed. Although the final report was due in September of that year, I immediately requested the first of what became a series of no-cost extensions that, in the end, delayed the report submission date for 3 years. Getting the first few extensions was fairly easy, in part because of the turmoil at NIE, which at the time was being dismantled by the Reagan Administration, but, more important, because I had convinced my project officer (and myself) that, with additional time, I would produce an explanation for our largely discouraging findings.

According to the terms of the NIE contract, my colleagues and I had read and synthesized what little research was available at the time on PL 94–142

implementation. Although much of this literature could be read as supporting what we had found in the NIE study, like our own implementation
research it offered little in the way of explaining the discouraging results. I
began my search for such an explanation by reading more broadly in the
areas of policy implementation and educational change. I wasn't long into
this reading before realizing that I needed to know much more about schools
as organizations. With this in mind, I turned to the field of educational
administration, which, though largely unfruitful itself, led me to the field of
organization analysis.

Organization Analysis

Although the literature on formal organizations appeared to be potentially
helpful in terms of understanding the findings of the NIE study, at first I
found it difficult to read, not only because of its unfamiliar terms and concepts but also because, taken as a whole, it seemed to be largely self-contra-
dictory. Each new book or article I read seemed to contradict some or all of
what I had read previously. Over time I came to see that this was in part
because of the different basic conceptions of organization reflected in the literature, ranging from what I came to understand as rational–technical (objectivist) to nonrational–cultural (subjectivist) views, which tended to correspond to different methodological perspectives, ranging from positivist to
anti-positivist or constructivist, respectively.

Given my earlier work in reading and mathematics and my more recent
exposure to competing philosophies of science during the NIE study, I took
these epistemological differences more or less in stride. But I was largely
unprepared for two additional sources of variation in the literature on organization, both of which stemmed from the fact that organization analysis is an
interdisciplinary field.

The first source of variation was based on different levels of analysis,
which tended to correspond to different disciplinary perspectives on the
essential nature of social organization and thus on the most appropriate unit
of analysis, ranging from what I came to understand as the microscopic level
of individuals and groups to the macroscopic level of organizations as such,
populations of organizations, and the social context of organizations.

The second source of variation was based on different conceptions of
society, ranging from a view that emphasized the apparent order, inevitability, and legitimacy of the status quo in society, implicitly or explicitly, to one
that emphasized conflict, domination, and exploitation and advocated radical
social change. In addition to being a major turning point in my intellectual
and political development, my exposure to these sources of variation in organization theory led me to the realization that, if I were to take full advantage of

this literature, I would have to deal with its interdisciplinarity by extending my reading to the social disciplines themselves.

Social Disciplines

When I began reading more broadly in the social disciplines, I immediately found that scholars within each discipline characterized the same social phenomena quite differently because they were using different conceptual frameworks to understand and thus interpret their meaning. It was here that I began to understand that, rather than unitary bodies of thought, each of the social science and humanities disciplines is itself composed of multiple frames of reference shaped by metatheoretical presuppositions regarding the nature of science (objectivist–subjectivist) on the one hand, and different conceptions of society (order–conflict) and levels of analysis (microscopic–macroscopic) on the other. Given this realization, I came to understand the field of organization analysis as a multidisciplinary, multiparadigmatic scholarly endeavor, an important insight (for me) that figured prominently in my subsequent attempts to apply what I was learning to special education. Further, this realization was what finally led me to philosophy, the alleged methodological and ethical arbiter of the social sciences and humanities.

Although I had set out to explain the findings of the NIE study, the first thing I found in all of this reading was that, in a sense, there were too many explanations. I came to see social phenomena such as disability, special education, and change as contested concepts and began to realize that understanding them depends on the frame of reference one employs. More important, I began to see that, as a guide to interpretation and action, choosing a frame of reference has profound moral and political implications for individuals and society.

Given my personal and professional experiences with disability and special education, I began to question how these concepts had been framed historically, as well as what the dominant frame of reference had meant for children, families, and society, including especially my sister and my family and the social systems we had encountered and within which I had worked as a special education professional. I also began to question my own doctoral training in special education and that of others who, like me (I had to assume), had not been exposed to the ideas, authors, disciplines, or frames of reference that I had encountered in my reading. What did this mean socially, politically, and morally? How might things have been different for children, families, and society if these alternative frames of reference had been part of special education doctoral training?

The second thing I found in this reading was that the social disciplines and philosophy were in the midst of an intellectual crisis over the very question of frames of reference or paradigms. By this time I had come to expect some intellectual infighting in these fields. Indeed, I had learned that, as a discourse on the transition from traditional to modern society, much of social science is a debate over the best paradigm for theorizing modernity, not unlike the more familiar and related debates over the best paradigm for theorizing pedagogy, inquiry, or organization. In this case, however, the controversy was more fundamental and of far greater consequence. This was so, the argument went, because a series of social and cultural transformations in the late 20th century had changed modernity itself, which in turn marked the opening of a new postmodern period in human history, one that challenged all modern paradigms and, in turn, raised serious questions about the epistemological and moral grounding of modern institutions. This got me thinking about the epistemological and moral grounding of public education—the modern institution I had been trying to understand and, particularly, about the institutional practice of special education and how it might be more productively theorized, intellectually, politically, and practically.

Application to Special Education

By this time, it was late in the spring semester of 1985, and my extensions on the NIE final report finally had run out. The doors were about to close for good at the NIE, and my project officer couldn't wait any longer. I had come a long way (for me) in my reading over the past 3 years and even had written several working papers to help me understand, integrate, and apply what I was reading. And though some of this writing applied to special education and PL 94–142 implementation, I hadn't incorporated very much of it into the NIE final report. Therefore, early that summer, under an ultimatum from my project officer, I submitted virtually the same report that my colleagues and I had drafted in 1982, a four-volume, 800-page tome entitled, "Interorganizational Special Education Programming in Rural Areas: Technical Report on the Multi-site Naturalistic Field Study" (Skrtic, Guba, & Knowlton, 1985). Although the report included an extensive discussion of research methodology and detailed qualitative case accounts of PL 94–142 implementation, it included virtually nothing about what I had learned from my reading in organizational analysis, the social sciences, and philosophy, and thus very little about PL 94–142 implementation from an organizational perspective and nothing about alternative perspectives on special education and disability.

Frustrated that I hadn't included much of my newer thinking in the final report, after it was submitted, I immediately set out to write something definitive that applied what I had been reading over the past 3 years to special education and disability. The writing venue came unexpectedly in the form of an invitation from Ed Meyen to co-edit the third edition of his special education textbook, *Exceptional Children and Youth: An Introduction* (Meyen, 1978,

1982), which was scheduled to appear in 1988. I accepted his offer with the understanding that my contributions to the edition would be based on introducing the idea of alternative perspectives on special education and disability, including the organizational perspective I had begun to develop over the past 3 years. Exactly how these alternative perspectives were to be integrated into an introductory special education textbook was left unspecified, a problem to be worked out later. This was fine with me because I had a bigger problem to solve.

Professorship

Given the amount of reading I had done since 1982, I felt fairly comfortable that I knew enough to get started with my writing. By reading independently, I had exposed myself to several key ideas that I believed had direct application to special education and disability, and had even begun to make such applications in my working papers. At the same time, however, I knew from the start that I would need to know much more than I could ever learn by reading independently. With this in mind, in the fall of 1984, I had applied for what is known at KU as an Intrauniversity Visiting Professorship, a wonderful faculty development opportunity that, at the time, provided recipients with 11 months of paid release time to study and teach in disciplines other than their own.

In the application for the professorship, I recounted my experiences with failed educational reforms and proposed an interdisciplinary project to broaden and deepen my understanding of organization theory and philosophy of science, which in turn I would use as a means to develop a comprehensive, interdisciplinary research agenda on organizational change and policy research. As background for all of this, I proposed to study in the disciplines of philosophy, sociology, and political science, and to team-teach a qualitative research course with Yvonna Lincoln. In late spring of 1985, about the time I was preparing to submit the NIE final report, I was notified that I had won a professorship for the 1985–86 academic year.

Now that I had a way to address my bigger problem during the next academic year, I spent the summer of 1985 drafting the material that eventually became my contribution to the Meyen and Skrtic textbook. In the process, I decided that the only way to present this material in an introductory text was to divide the book into two parts, one on conventional perspectives on special education and disability, to include state-of-the-art chapters by leading special education authorities (which had been the format of the previous editions), and one part on alternative perspectives, to include the material I was working on, as well as that of other authors writing from unconventional perspectives.

I proposed this format to Ed Meyen and the publisher, Stan Love of Love Publishing. With their approval, I went back to writing my chapters and identifying the other authors I needed to round out the second part of the book. As it turned out, the alternative perspectives part of the book included four chapters—one by myself on what I characterized as an epistemological crisis in special education knowledge (Skrtic, 1988a), which set the stage for three additional chapters that, respectively, reinterpreted special education and disability from the perspectives of society (Bogdan & Knoll, 1988), culture (Janesick, 1988), and organization (Skrtic, 1988b).

In the fall of 1985, the first semester of my professorship, I team-taught with Yvonna Lincoln in her course, Naturalistic Inquiry in Educational Policy and Administration. We taught the course under a format in which she presented the epistemological grounding and methodological principles and postures of naturalistic inquiry and I illustrated these ideas and practices by showing our students how they were actualized in the NIE project. This was a productive experience for me in that it extended my understanding of naturalistic inquiry and qualitative research generally, and prepared me to teach the course myself—which I have done ever since, given that Yvonna left KU the following year.

That semester I also took courses in philosophy of science and sociology of organization and participated in a seminar on political economy, the former to pursue the plan of study I had proposed and the latter because of its interdisciplinarity and macroscopic/conflict outlook. As the most macroscopic perspective in the social disciplines, political economy often represents the most radical perspective on social organization. Exposure to this view was important for me, I believe, because of my prior grounding in psychology and pedagogy, which, of course, tend to see things from the microscopic/order perspective.

I also used the fall 1985 semester to survey the KU social science and humanities faculty in search of additional mentors. I knew I wanted to study in the disciplines of philosophy, sociology, and political science but, given what I had been reading in these and other disciplines, not just any philosopher, sociologist, or political scientist would do. For starters, my mentors in sociology and political science had to be theorists, which, to my surprise, was a tall order, in that the vast majority of faculty in both disciplines at KU and elsewhere are systematic empiricists, quantitative or qualitative, not social or political theorists.

Moreover, as social and political theorists, I wanted mentors who were comfortable working within and across the various social science and humanities disciplines and paradigms. In effect, I was searching for a team of metatheorists, interdisciplinary scholars critically versed in the multiple paradigms of modern social thought and the emerging claims of postmodern theorizing. This was an even taller order, but eventually I found my way to three KU professors who fit the bill better than I ever could have imagined—Gary Shapiro, an internationally renowned Continental philosopher; Bob Antonio, an equally renowned social theorist; and Dwight Kiel, a relatively young but equally talented and insightful political theorist.

In the spring of 1986, I took a course from each of my social science and humanities mentors, which, together, both integrated and consolidated many of the themes I had been pursuing independently and introduced me to a number of important new ideas and areas of study. Overall, during the professorship and the next 5 years, I took 21 courses, seminars, and directed-reading experiences from my mentors and others, including the course Democracy in America, from Bob Kent, an incredibly talented and insightful social historian teaching part-time in the American Studies program. I mention this course in particular because, although I didn't fully recognize it at the time, it had a major impact on my thinking, starting me down a path that eventually shaped my current interests (see chapter 10).

In any regard, the point to be made here is that the professorship and the work that followed it became a major influence on my intellectual and political development and my academic career. This was so not only because of what I learned about philosophy of science and organization theory but, more important, because I developed a broader interest in critical social theory, which over time evolved into an interest in a particular approach to critical social theory grounded in the work of John Dewey and the social philosophy of American pragmatism.

Getting the Word Out

Over the 6-year period during and after my professorship, I published two books and a number of articles and chapters in which I used my emerging understanding of critical social theory to question the conventional understanding of disability and special education policy and practice, organization and administration, and professional education. Two early articles were of particular strategic importance because they opened new avenues for disseminating my work that otherwise may not have been available to me. Again, luck and timing were everything.

The first article, "The Crisis in Special Education Knowledge: A Perspective on Perspective," appeared in *Focus on Exceptional Children* in 1986. After reading a draft of my first chapter for the Meyen and Skrtic book, Stan Love, publisher of *Focus* and the book, and Ed Meyen, co-editor of the book and editorial board member of *Focus,* asked me to submit it to the *Focus* editorial board for consideration as an invited essay. I agreed, of course, and in the fall of 1985 submitted an article-length version of the chapter that would be published the following spring.

After reading the *Focus* article, Judy Smith–Davis, an influential figure in the Teacher Education Division (TED) of the Council for Exceptional Children (CEC), asked me to present my ideas about special education and disability at the annual TED meeting the following November. Judy extended the invitation because she believed that what I had to say was relevant to the regular education initiative (REI) debate, which eventually became the debate over inclusive education that has dominated discourse and politics in the field of special education ever since.

Although my presentation was to be based on the ideas in the *Focus* article, I also used the TED conference to introduce my organizational analysis of special education and disability, which had not been included in the article and, though already written as my second chapter in the Meyen and Skrtic book, was not slated to be published until 1988. After hearing my TED presentation, Judy Smith–Davis extended a second invitation, this time to publish the organizational analysis part of the presentation in *Counterpoint,* which she edited. With permission from Love Publishing, I accepted her invitation, and shortly thereafter an article-length version of the yet-to-be published chapter appeared as "An Organizational Analysis of Special Education Reform" (Skrtic, 1987). Even though *Counterpoint* was not a leading special education journal, I accepted the invitation because it was widely read in the field at the time, in part because of the controversy over the REI and inclusive education.

Had the *Focus* and *Counterpoint* articles appeared in the 1970s or even the early 1980s, I doubt if they would have received much attention in the special education professional community. By the mid-1980s, however, the REI debate had created enough confusion and uncertainty in the field for them to attract far more attention than they would have otherwise. Under the rubric of the REI, leading special educators and key government officials, in effect, were criticizing PL 94–142 and mainstreaming for creating virtually the same problems as the special classroom model, which is precisely what my colleagues and I had found in the NIE study.

Based on what I had learned in my reading following the NIE project, however, what concerned me was that the REI debate focused exclusively on the ethics and efficacy of special education models and practices rather than their grounding assumptions and theories. As I argued in the 1986 and 1987 papers and at the TED conference, the danger here was that, like the earlier round of criticism that led to PL 94-142 and mainstreaming, the current one would merely reproduce the problems of special education practice rather than resolve them. Moreover, I argued that, given the epistemological crisis in philosophy and the social disciplines, the infighting we were experiencing with the REI debate was nothing compared to the external criticism that was sure to follow. What we needed in special education, I proposed, was a critical discourse that, although ultimately concerned with models and practices, is carried out at the level of grounding theories and paradigms.

Apparently these arguments attracted the attention of several people in leadership positions at CEC. Not long after the TED conference, I was invited to present my ideas about special education and disability at a CEC-sponsored invitational conference on the future of special education, which was held in Orlando, Florida, in late 1987. In turn, the Orlando presentation and publication of the Meyen and Skrtic book *Exceptional Children and Youth: An Introduction* (Meyen & Skrtic, 1988) a month or so later led to another invitation from CEC, this time to organize the preconvention program at its annual meeting in 1989. I accepted the invitation with the proviso that, although the program would address the question of the ethics and efficacy of special education models and practices, it would do so from a critical perspective—that is, from the perspective of the field's largely unquestioned theoretical and paradigmatic grounding.

Based on my reading in the early 1980s, I was quite familiar with the small body of critical work on special education and disability in the social sciences. While searching for authors for my part of the Meyen and Skrtic book, however, I had discovered an emerging body of critical work by several authors in or associated with the field of special education. I turned to this group for help in organizing the CEC preconvention program. Drawing on those whose work I believe represented the most accessible theoretical criticism of special education, I assembled a small work group that, over the course of several months in 1988, produced a program entitled Exploring the Theory/Practice Link in Special Education. As the program began to take shape, some of the staff at CEC became increasingly concerned that its critical theoretical bent would dissuade participation and thus fail to attract the customary 100 or so preconvention participants. Nevertheless, the work group pressed on and subsequently delivered the program to an audience of more than 700 special educators at the 1989 CEC conference in San Francisco.

The exposure that my work had received after the *Focus* and *Counterpoint* articles and the TED and Orlando presentations increased significantly after publication of the Meyen and Skrtic book in 1988 and especially after the CEC preconvention program in 1989, after which I received dozens of national and international invitations to speak, write, and consult on the topics of alternative interpretations of disability and special education reform. A particularly important invitation with respect to international exposure was one to deliver a keynote address at the International Special Education Congress in Cardiff, Wales, in July 1989. The Cardiff presentation and its subsequent publication as "Students with Special Educational Needs:

Artifacts of the Traditional Curriculum" (Skrtic, 1990), in Mel Ainscow's widely read book *Effective Schools for All,* were important stepping stones to further international speaking, publishing, and consulting opportunities, which disseminated my work to an even broader international audience.

Based on positive reactions to the alternative perspectives part of the Meyen and Skrtic book, Stan Love asked me to develop a new book focused exclusively on alternative perspectives on special education and disability. I had accepted the earlier invitation to publish my work in what became the 1988 Meyen and Skrtic book rather than to write a book of my own, because I knew that stand-alone critical treatments of special education and disability had had little effect on thinking or practice in the field. Nevertheless, I accepted the offer to write a stand-alone book in the late 1980s because, given the REI controversy and the unexpected interest in the CEC preconvention program, I believed that the timing for such a book was perhaps as right as it ever was going to be. Also, writing the book gave me an opportunity to expand upon what I had written for the Meyen and Skrtic book and in the 1986 and 1987 articles by incorporating more of what I had learned during and after my professorship. Much of what appeared in these early works had been written in the summer and fall of 1985, before my interest in critical social theory had begun to take shape. Drawing on the more expressly critical interdisciplinary thinking I had been exposed to during and after the spring of 1986, I wrote *Behind Special Education: A Critical Analysis of Professional Culture and School Organization* (Skrtic, 1991a), which more fully reflected my understanding of critical social theory and dealt specifically with the issues that had emerged in the REI debate.

As I was writing the book, I accepted an invitation from the editorial board of *Harvard Educational Review* to write an essay review of *Beyond Separate Education: Quality Education for All* (Lipsky & Gartner, 1989), the first book-length treatment of the issues surrounding the REI debate and the emerging inclusive education movement. When I submitted the review, however, the editorial board asked me to expand and resubmit it for consideration as a regular article. Writing the review had already delayed publication of the *Behind Special Education* book by at least 6 months, and the offer to resubmit would delay it even further. Nevertheless, I agreed to do the review because an article-length treatment more than doubled the number of pages with which I had to work, giving me the space I needed for a more extensive critical organizational analysis of special education and disability, including an analysis of the REI debate itself and of the several reform proposals that REI proponents had offered. The expanded manuscript was accepted for publication and subsequently appeared as "The Special Education Paradox: Equity As the Way to Excellence" (Skrtic, 1991), included as Chapter 4 in this book.

Finally, the invitation to organize the preconvention program initially included an offer by CEC to publish the resulting papers as a book or monograph. But as the REI debate devolved into a full-blown political crisis, the leadership at CEC changed and, for reasons about which I can only speculate, nearly a year after the San Francisco convention, CEC finally decided to withdraw its offer to publish the preconvention papers. Later that year I submitted the papers to Teachers College Press, which accepted it for publication and, on the recommendation of two anonymous reviewers and the TCP editor, requested that I expand the manuscript by linking the political and epistemological crisis in special education to the broader question of educational reform and democratic social renewal.

Drawing upon my evolving understanding of critical social theory, I carried out the requested expansion by revising my original papers and writing two additional chapters. The resulting edited volume, *Disability and Democracy: Reconstructing (Special) Education for Postmodernity* (Skrtic, 1995), didn't appear until 1995, the same year that the fourth edition of the Meyen and Skrtic text, renamed *Special Education and Student Disability: Traditional, Emerging, and Alternative Perspectives* (Meyen & Skrtic, 1995), was published.

In part, the delay resulted from the change of heart at CEC and the fact that I was working on two books at the same time. More significantly, however, after completing *Behind Special Education* and the *Harvard Educational Review* article, I realized that I had gone about as far as I could on the basis of what I had learned during and after my professorship. I had achieved an important goal: The work I had published from 1986 to 1991 had attracted far more attention and interest than I had expected. In the process, though, my writing had shown me where I needed to go next, if only dimly, as well as the gaps in my understanding that prevented me from getting there. I realized that advancing this line of inquiry beyond where it had taken me by 1991 would require further study in critical social theory.

With this in mind, I applied for and received a sabbatical leave in 1991–92, which I used to start the additional work I needed to advance my understanding of critical social theory. Without the sabbatical I could not have completed the books that came out in 1995, both of which took my application of critical social theory beyond where it had been in 1991, even though the work I pursued during and after the sabbatical significantly delayed their publication. More important for the long run, however, the people and ideas I was exposed to during and after the sabbatical became yet another formative influence on my intellectual pursuits and academic career. In the early 1990s I developed a new set of interrelated analytical and substantive interests, specifically an interest in history as an indispensable disciplinary perspective for critical social theory, in democratic theory as a normative framework for my overall intellectual project, and, most recently, in disability studies as way to integrate my professional and critical interests.

Although my interest in democracy is apparent in everything I have written since 1986, and even more apparent since 1995, I have only begun to pursue democratic theory and history as an analytic perspective in the depth they deserve. How these interests relate to one another, how they and disability studies relate to my professional and personal commitments to special education and people with disabilities, and what I hope to do about all of this are the topics of Chapter 10.

References

Bogdan, R., & Knoll, J. (1988). The sociology of disability. In E. L. Meyen & T. M. Skrtic (Eds.), *Exceptional children and youth: An introduction* (pp. 449–477). Denver: Love.

Clark, D., & Guba, E. (1967). An examination of potential change roles in education. In *Rational planning in curriculum and instruction* (pp. 117–122). Washington, DC: Center for the Study of Instruction, National Education Association.

Getzels, J. W., & Guba, E. G. (1957). Social behavior and the administrative process. *School Review, 65,* 423–441.

Guba, E. G. (1978). *Toward a methodology of naturalistic inquiry in educational evaluation* (Monograph 8). Los Angeles: Center for the Study of Evaluation, University of California.

Guba, E. G., & Lincoln, Y. (1981) *Effective evaluation: Improving the usefulness of evaluation results through responsive and naturalistic approaches.* San Francisco: Jossey–Bass.

Janesick, V. J. (1988). Our multicultural society. In E. L. Meyen & T. M. Skrtic (Eds.), *Exceptional children and youth: An introduction* (pp. 713–727). Denver: Love.

Lincoln, Y. S., & Guba, E. G. (1985). *Naturalistic inquiry.* Beverly Hills, CA: Sage Publications.

Lipsky, D. K., & Gartner, A. (1989). *Beyond separate education: Quality education for all.* Baltimore: Paul H. Brookes.

Meyen, E. L. (1978). *Exceptional children and youth: An introduction.* Denver: Love.

Meyen, E. L. (1982). *Exceptional children and youth: An introduction* (2d ed.). Denver: Love.

Meyen, E. L., & Skrtic, T. M. (1995). *Special education and student disability: Traditional, emerging, and alternative perspectives.* Denver: Love.

Meyen, E. L., & Skrtic, T. M. (1988). *Exceptional children and youth: An introduction* (3d ed.). Denver: Love.

Skrtic, T. M. (1985). Doing naturalistic research into educational organizations. In Y. S. Lincoln (Ed.), *Organizational theory and inquiry: The paradigm revolution,* pp. 185–220. Beverly Hills, CA: Sage Publishing.

Skrtic, T. M. (1986). The crisis in special education knowledge: A perspective on perspective. *Focus on Exceptional Children, 18*(7), 1–16.

Skrtic, T. M. (1987). An organizational analysis of special education reform. *Counterpoint, 8*(2), 15–19.

Skrtic, T. M. (1988a). The crisis in special education knowledge. In E. L. Meyen & T. M. Skrtic (Eds.), *Exceptional children and youth: An introduction* (3d ed., pp. 415–447). Denver: Love.

Skrtic, T. M. (1988b). The organizational context of special education. In E. Meyen & T. Skrtic (Eds.), *Exceptional children and youth: An introduction* (3d ed., pp. 479–517). Denver: Love.

Skrtic, T. M. (1990). Students with special educational needs: Artifacts of the traditional curriculum. In M. Ainscow (Ed.), *Effective schools for all* (pp. 20–42). London: David Fulton Publications.

Skrtic, T. M. (1991a). *Behind special education: A critical analysis of professional culture and school organization.* Denver: Love.

Skrtic, T. M. (1991b). The special education paradox: Equity as the way to excellence. *Harvard Educational Review, 61*(2), 148–206.

Skrtic, T. M. (1995). *Disability and democracy: Reconstructing (special) education for post-modernity.* New York: Teachers College Press.

Skrtic, T. M., Guba, E. G., & Knowlton, H. E. (1985). *Interorganizational special education programming in rural areas: Technical report on the multi-site naturalistic field study.* Washington, DC: National Institute of Education.

Skrtic, T. M., Knowlton, H. E., & Clark, F. L. (1979). Action versus reaction: A curriculum development approach to inservice education. *Focus on Exceptional Children, 11*(1), 1–16.

PART THREE

Contesting the Present, Envisioning the Future

Chapters

Special Education Knowledges: The Inevitable Struggle With the "Self"

Lous Heshusius

If I am not what I've been told I was, then it means that you're not what you thought you were either. . . . And that is the crisis.

James Baldwin (1988, p.5)

I should let me be us.

University student in Special Education

Fear is at the root of all forms of exclusion just as
trust is at the root of all forms of inclusion.

Jean Vanier (1998, p. 73)

A close colleague, teaching a disability studies course to general education students, called to tell me about an episode with her students. Several disabled speakers had related what it was like to live their lives. My colleague had shown several videos, including the documentary *Selling Murder,* the story of Hitler's careful manipulations to get the German people ready to accept "mercy" killing of people with disabilities. It had been the first time that many of the students had been directly confronted with the lives of disabled people and what can happen to them because of their disabilities. The students had become scared.

"Scared of disabled people?" I asked, not understanding. "No," she said, "scared that *they* would become disabled themselves." An accident perhaps. A disease. Should she try some counseling techniques with them?

I gave a gut-level response and in the next few minutes said more or less the following: No, I would not counsel them on their feelings. If you would do that, they could interpret it as sympathy or empathy, implying agreement that it would be terrible to be disabled. The emphasis would shift toward the comfort level of the abled-bodied again, rather than stay with issues of disability. I would do no more than acknowledge their fears as real, but not as something *you* have to deal with. Just let them sit there with their fears. They will have to become familiar with them. And they have to do it themselves— by looking their fears straight in the eye.

Afterward, I thought long and hard about my response. To become intimately and relentlessly familiar with our fears might be the only way to integrate them into our "selves" by seeing that what we fear, we fear *because* it is part of all our possible selves. Rather than having our fears of different others be pacified and receive sympathy—which would dull them, allowing them to stay hidden and thus keep their power over us—we need to see our fears in all their force and clarity. Perhaps that is what freedom is about—to become intimately familiar with our fears of different others that are indicative of what we consciously or unconsciously try to exclude from that which we construct as desirable for our own "selves."[1]

Constructing the Other, Constructing the Self

The attachments to images we hold as desirable for our selves create fears of others who are different in ways that do not fit these images. And there are many, many such others. Most of us don't mind the thought of having a "self" that is more attractive, smarter, richer, healthier, a self that belongs to a group with desirable status, but not one that would, in our view, reduce us and make us inferior to who we think we now are. Most, even possibly all, of us live comparative lives, which is a cause of much misery and harm. While we talk much about diversity, when it comes to making deep connections and deep friendships, the self typically chooses to do so only with people with whom there is enough overlap and commonality. We keep a safe physical distance, if possible, but certainly a psychological, political, and emotional distance from everyone else. The very need to establish and protect a certain kind of desired self imagines a threatening otherness in those whose lives remind the self of what it does not want for its own. This distancing act can take many forms and many guises. Theorists and researchers, from whatever persuasion, are not exempt from these processes.

Perhaps the most important question is whether one can even *see* this process operating when the self is bent on the act of excluding that which it does not want for its self. Fear and desire blind us from seeing the kind of self we protect, precisely because these processes are not at all necessarily carried out consciously and deliberately. At the center of this chapter's epistemological story is the view that the selves of positivist/empiricist traditions engage in these processes of constructing otherness to protect a certain kind of self in obvious ways, but that alternative approaches to research do not, by definition, make the researcher immune to doing the same. For alternative researchers, too, the act of protecting a certain kind of self is typically hidden from awareness. I further would like to voice the possibility that the very act of seeing oneself as "a researcher" can all too easily, and often does, involve the construction of a certain kind of self that legitimizes to the self and to the world these processes of exclusion in our embodied encounters.

In thinking over the conversation with my colleague about her scared students, I was reminded of another incident that occurred some years ago, when I took a dozen graduate students from York University to the Netherlands, my home country, for a cross-cultural course in special education. We visited the institution De Hartenberg, well known for its embodied approach to being with the severely disabled (Hulsegge & Verheul, 1986). One entire wing of a building is devoted to activities collectively referred to as Snoezelen. This institution is where Snoezelen originated as the brainchild of the artist Ad Verheul. The Dutch word "snoezelen" refers to coziness, to safe snuggling, to being together with someone or something in ways that are soft and pleasant to the senses and to the soul. When one snoezels, there is a total absence of demands, for the need to rank the other or the self for evaluations, or for any other goal-oriented behavior. Snoezelen expresses human warmth, belonging, tenderness, trust, and lots of goodwill.[2]

The Snoezelen wing is an oasis for the senses and for human contact, both physically and emotionally. In the various rooms of the wing, residents and staff can touch soft objects, including walls covered with soft materials, lie on a floor that lights up and warms up when one lies down on it, and smell lovely aromas coming from fancy tubes attached to the wall. In a large room that would be the envy of the well-to-do for its aesthetically inviting and even luxuriously relaxing atmosphere, residents like to linger, following soft lights that move across the walls and ceilings, listening to calming music, being rocked softly by a floor that is essentially a huge, luxurious, leather waterbed that folds into cushionlike forms into which one can cuddle and snoezel, alone or with someone else. Here, the staff lies down with residents, holding them, resting hand in hand or nestled against each other.

The Snoezelen philosophy is revolutionary—that is, revolutionary for those with severe disabilities. For "normal" folks it is straightforwardly human to snoezel with spouses, lovers, one's children, and even one's pets, as a normal expression of good relationships, and most of us reap the emotional and physical benefits from being so together. Typically, people who are disabled or retarded in institutional care are not allowed the expression of this depth of their humanity. In this institution Snoezelen is seen as a profound human right and necessity—never as therapy, never as a measurable "intervention" for academics to focus their research on.

Back in the hotel that evening during our discussion of the day's events, one of the students shared what she had experienced. That morning upon our arrival, one of the handicapped residents had started to touch some of us. This student told us that she had panicked and said to herself, "If he touches me, I'm going to throw up." In her written reflection of the day she wrote:

> I felt this way because I have never experienced a profoundly retarded person as another human being. . . . I was afraid that I myself might look repulsed. . . . The struggle isn't with what I saw/experienced today. *It is with what I have inside* [emphasis added].

She told the class that having seen the staff touch and hold these persons, she could see them for the first time as human beings. They now appeared to her to be more like herself. In her journal she reflected philosophically:

> I should let me be us, and accept us as we have the potential to already be. . . . This may be the weirdest entry you'll ever have to read, but I think I've undergone a break through in a fear block. It's a freeing sensation.

I have always kept a copy of these pages of the student's journal. When I read her words, I knew that her realization that her fear was not with what she saw but instead with something inside of her was a straightforward, yet profound and extremely difficult-to-reach insight. It is not easily reached because of the probably innate human need to maintain the images that create a safe, stable, and socially desirable notion of "self" for ourselves, fearing those selves that threaten those images.

"Scary things not always outside. Most scary things is inside," says a character in Tony Morrison's (1997, p. 39) novel *Paradise*. In speaking about the "Dragon–Princess," the poet Rainer Maria Rilke (in Mood, 1975, p. 99) says, "Has it [the world] terrors, they are *our* terrors; has it abysses, those abysses belong to us." Only someone who is ready for everything,

Rilke (p. 98) says, someone who excludes nothing, will live the relation to another as something alive and will draw exhaustively from his or her own existence.

Ralph Waldo Emerson (in McQuade, 1981, p. 183) speaks of an old man who says to his boys scared by a figure in the dark: "My children, you will never see anything worse than yourselves." Emerson goes on to say about the human being, "He (sic) cleaves to one person and avoids another, according to their likeness or unlikeness to himself." No doubt many more wise thinkers could be found who have spoken of this fear inside, a fear of that, which, in its shadow form, is already part of one's actual or potential self, is what the self does not want and therefore pushes away.

Constructing Separativeness, Entering Trust

Contemporary social inquiry acknowledges that the self is involved in its historical and ideological formations, but rarely do researchers acknowledge—if they are at all aware of this—that the images of what they desire for their *own* self (solidified into a stable notion of self) can function significantly during the actual embodied interaction with the "researched" other. Elsewhere (Heshusius, 1994), I wrote of my work as a researcher many years ago, when I was doing a participant-observation study in a group home for "retarded citizens" and became aware of my own need to distance myself, a distancing act that definitely stood in the way of genuine listening and attending. I wrote:

> I remember distinctly being confronted early on with power and status differences that stood in the way of fully attending. I was forced to recognize my upbringing, values, and related emotions until I finally came to pose the question of merging: Could I imagine such a life for myself? Only when I could start seeing their lives as worthy for myself, or for my children . . . forget the ego concerns that constitute the self, and be fully attentive. . . . I had to completely and non-evaluatively observe my personal reactions and *in* that attentiveness, *dissolve* . . . them, which opened up a mode of access that was not there before. (p. 19)

This personal reflection became an illustration for my discussion of the differences between an alienated and alienating mode of consciousness, which keeps the other at a distance, and a more participatory mode of consciousness within which the constructed separation between other and self begins to blur, as the self begins to consciously lower its boundaries that were constructed to exclude. Then other and self can merge, however briefly, into a mode of attending in which the need to be separative is temporarily dissolved. As the student reflected on her fear of being touched by a severely disabled other: "I should let me be us and accept us as we have the potential to already be."

I use the word "separative" to signal that at the core of exclusionary processes, which erect what appear as distinct boundaries between self and other, lies not a nominal construct, not something that already exists, such as "separation" or "separativeness," but, rather, an agential construct that *achieves* separation each time again. It is not the case that sharp separations and boundaries already exist before our arrival but, rather, that the need to be separative from that which threatens the desired images for the self constructs them each time anew. This process becomes habitual, and it seems that the boundaries between self and other are "real," are already there. But at the deepest level of consciousness, the separation is constructed time and time again, however rapidly this occurs. When attention to this process *as it happens* is *deliberately* slowed down and experienced in slow motion—which can happen only if one is completely attentive and observant and *wants* to see—the habitualness of perceiving boundaries-as-already-existing (instead of realizing that one constructs them anew, again and again) can be broken.

To enter a more participatory, inclusionary mode of awareness, trust, says Vanier (1999, p. 73), rather than fear, must guide the self. In my case, trust took the form of finally finding peace with the notion that if I myself, or my children, would be living a life as theirs, that would be worthy of life nonetheless. Then, and only then, could I enter a mode of awareness and of listening and being with them that was much less guided by exclusionary fears. My reflection also goes to show how deliberately entering a less exclusionary mode of consciousness presents a serious struggle for the self. It shows how the self must be willing, at least potentially, to let go of the images that brings it security (or so it thinks). In my case, to come to that point involved a long struggle with my own attachments to the idea of "normalcy," to desirable status of intelligence, to what appears as attractive, as worthwhile—in short, with a whole array of ego needs. The struggle, as my student wrote, was not in the first instance with what I saw and heard but instead with what I carried inside.

Accepting the possibility of a very different life for oneself as worthwhile, and the related ability to deeply connect with those who are so "other" that the self instinctively wants to exclude them, may well be one of the criteria against which to check the depth of today's discussions about diversity and inclusion. Jean Vanier (1999), co-founder of the now more than 100 L'Arche communities in 30 countries, where intellectually disabled and nondisabled people choose to live together, has this to say about such deeper connections. Using the story of Lazarus as an analogy, he states:

> It is dangerous to enter into a relationship with the Lazaruses of our world. If we do, we risk our lives being changed. All of us are, more or less, locked up in our cultures, in our habits, even in our friendships and places of belonging. If I become the friend of a beggar, I rock the boat. Friends may feel uncomfortable, even threatened. . . . They may become aggressive. . . . I am beginning to discover how fear (of those who are different) is a terrible motivating force in all our lives. . . . Fear is at the root of all forms of exclusion just as trust is at the root of all forms of inclusion. . . . We are all so frightened of losing what is important for us, the things that give us life, security, and status. (pp. 71, 73)

"Where do you want special education to go?" was the question our editor asked us to address. In short, my response is: more and more into a participatory mode of consciousness, in its research, its theorizing, and its pedagogy. Her second question was more difficult to respond to: "What do you see as necessary to get us there?" I would have to say that, if we ever get "there," it will demand hard work in regard to something we are not at all used to focusing on: those inner images that give the self security, safety, and stability but that block participatory attentiveness and, therefore, block participatory knowing and being.

Alternatives to positivist/empiricist traditions acknowledge the power of gender, class, sexual orientation, and race in the making and unmaking of knowledges. These alternatives include the current emphasis on deconstructionist methods that speak of "death of the self." This particular death, this dying of a certain notion of self in deconstructionist thought, however, does not occur in the embodied present. However well theorized, theoretical and historical deaths are not directly at stake in what I am pursuing here. Deconstruction's deaths are not immediately personal enough. They are not embodied, lived deaths. What is needed is an actual lived death to the desired self-images the self harbors, *while* one is in an actual encounter, so one can be free to fully attend. The postmodern deconstructionist theorized "death of the self" does not accomplish this. It is not the case, I believe, that postmodern deconstruction has gone too far, as some critics would have it, but instead that it has not gone far enough. It does not foster an actual ability to die to self-protecting images and desires that are at work *in* actual embodied moments, and that separate and distance.

I think of the students' fears, in my colleague's class, of becoming disabled themselves, which in the first instance had to do with fearing the loss of the desired images for the self they were attached to (of being competent, abled-bodied, strong, and healthy). They could not imagine the death of *that* self while trying to listen to the disabled other. The very confrontation with the possibility that they, too, might have to give up the desired images for themselves someday blocked an ability to fully attend to the different other who possessed characteristics that were undesired and feared for their own selves. I think of the student who felt nauseous at the thought of being touched by one whose life she could not possibly imagine for her self. I think of my own blockages in my actual interactions with residents of a group home for "the retarded," because of my own ego-shaped desired self that I had a hard time dying to.

All these fears were operative in the *present* moment of these actual encounters, not in theoretical reflexivity about representation, language, and power—an important reflexivity, to be sure, but a reflexivity within which one does not necessarily have to *feel and live* one's disgust, fear, jealousy, or whatever, toward another. It is a reflexivity that does not call attention to the feelings, fears, and images of one's own *self-in-action*. To see the historical and structural unfolding of hidden inner exclusionary fears, to see how class, race, gender, disability, sexual orientation, and so forth can be the channel for their materialization and externalization, and to demystify the outcomes of these processes, is extremely important. Doing so, however, should not be equated with a focus on the self in embodied encounters that exist only in the actual present. The scholarly engagements in deconstructing relations of power do not necessarily help to recognize the exclusionary fears within that are operative in actual, embodied moments, fears that construct a threatening otherness. The two modes of knowing involved do not necessarily overlap in one's conscious awareness and can stand in a number of different relations to each other.

The foregoing leads to the view that, in special education theorizing and research, what is at stake in the first instance is not disability, not the "other" in the study of exceptionality, but instead the particular needs of the researching and theorizing self, which in turn decides the parameters by which the other will come to be known or unknown, included or excluded. "Special education" is a process that decides who is "in" and who is "out," who is "regular" and who is "special," who is "abled" and who is "disabled." As many have said, this process is never politically and ideologically free. But neither is it ever an ego-less process from which the embodied self, its life always in the present, is excluded. "There is an endless list of those whom we may exclude," says Vanier (1999, p. 71), and *"every one of us, we may be sure, is on someone's list"* (emphasis mine). All of us are vulnerable to be excluded so that some other self can feel safe and privileged, and all of us are vulnerable to needing to exclude others so we can feel the self of ourselves to be a safe and stable one.

The Refusing Other

When the other refuses to be the "other" the way we need him or her to be so we can be the self we want to be, we are faced with a profound confrontation. As James Baldwin (1988, p. 5) said to the self of the white master: "If I am not what I've been told I was, then it means that you're not what you thought you were either. . . . And that is the crisis." I believe Baldwin's insight holds up for all relationships. When another thinks he or she knows who I am, it is because he or she needs to be a certain self. When I think I know a person, it is because I need to be a certain kind of self when facing that person.

Many groups that have been forced into being known by the selves of researchers are objecting. They refuse to participate in the self–other construction that serves to maintain the researchers' selves. They have taken in their own hands whatever research they deem necessary. This has given rise to much feminist revisionism in epistemology and methodology (Reinhartz, 1992); to post-colonial voices (Sadaawi, 1996); to disability studies (Campbell & Oliver, 1996); to indigenous reappropriations of research methodology into proper indigenous cultural protocols (Bishop, 1998); and to bicultural bilingual research by the deaf community (Lane, 1996). These groups, along with others, have claimed their full right to their own epistemological and methodological story. This poly-voiced chorus of epistemological voices is not always harmonious, and not everyone listens to each other, but it constitutes nothing less than an epistemological civil rights movement.

It therefore is more than disconcerting to still hear positivist/behaviorist voices in major special education journals claim that there is only one way to valid knowledge: theirs (see, e.g., Brigham & Polsgrove, 1998; Kauffman, 1999; Kauffman & Brigham, 1999; Sasso, 2001; Walker et al., 1998). But the easy days in which positivism reigned in special education as the only legitimate voice will not come back. Complex processes, such as the evolution of human knowledges, are not reversible. Time evolves and cannot be reduced to the past (see, e.g., Prigogine & Stengers, 1984). I personally believe that at least some of the positivists in our field who, by virtue of the past still hold political power, know that their privileged status is slipping and giving way to more complex views. But complexity always threatens those who need stable, secure, continuous selves. Their writings have a tone not just of anger but also of despair. Just as important, as noted in Chapter 2, when I listen to graduate students or to new Ph.D.s in special education, I often notice a great appetite for literature in other areas and an excitement to bring differing epistemologies back to their understandings of special education as a social construct.

But it is the self-advocacy movements among the retarded, the deaf, the disabled, the deaf power and disability power movements that most power-fully challenge the traditional world of special education by refusing its aca-demic ownership over them. Special education knows itself now confronted with demands by those it previously did not consider to be competent enough to do what they now do—demanding that their voices count in the deepest epistemological sense possible. For instance, Charlton's (1998) book, a pow-erful account of the "disability-based consciousness and organization" (p. ix) by independent disability groups worldwide, contests any knowledge con-structed about them by others. I mention this book because its title says it all: *Nothing About Us Without Us.*

The contemporary poly-voiced nature of scholarship further challenges the self-assigned superiority of positivism and empiricism by blurring the traditional separations between what traditionally have been considered very different and incompatible ways of knowing. Theoretical knowledge becomes a partner with personal experience; storytelling functions as both deconstruction and reconstruction; advocacy work is written up as disserta-tions; art forms serve for data presentation of formal research; and self-reflexivity has gained the status of formal knowledge. Years ago, in special education, the Blatts, Bogdans, Biklens, and Fergusons of the world started blurring the lines between theory, photography, stories, narrative, and per-sonal experience. Increasingly, others are engaging this blurring of different ways of knowing in creative and often insightful ways, raising new ques-tions, offering more complex pictures of the behavior of all humans involved in this enterprise we still call special education. In another book about the rapidly growing disabled people's movement in Britain, the authors, Campbell and Oliver (1996) state:

> This book is a mixture of social theory, political history, action research, individual biography, and personal experience. We have resisted the temptation (and some academic advice) to separate out these things and treat them as analytically distinct, because we do not regard them as separable. All of the people in this book are, in our own ways, social theorists, political historians, action researchers and personal autobiographers trying to understand our own experiences. To present this in separate academic categories is to fly in the face of reality and to distort our own experiences. (p. 1)

Though I personally believe that academic categories have a place for certain purposes, the blurring of genres surely is a most significant develop-ment that emerges from an awareness of the embodied complexity of all of our lives. It is a complexity and an embodiment that the positivist traditions fear, because complexity and real life cannot be controlled and control is what positivist researchers need above all else to maintain their stable, safe, inner, detached sense of self. As exceptional others refuse to stay in the restricted places that we, as a field of education, needed them to be in so we could be the kind of "selves" we wanted to be, we are not who we thought we were either (expertly in charge, with privileged intellectual status and privileged ways of knowing). And that is, I think, at least one major reason for the tone of despair in today's positivists' defenses of their own position. As the deaf, the retarded, the disabled—by increasingly forming their own organizations and in speaking out on their own—refuse to stay in the places assigned to them by traditional researchers and theorists, the latter no longer can be who they thought they were either. When impairment, disability, deafness, and retardation show their faces as dissent, as action, and as voice, any traditional research approach to those so identified takes on a serious sense of the suspect.

It is in part because of these dynamics, I believe, that the full-inclusion movement is so threatening to traditional special educators, as Brantlinger (1997) has commented on incisively. The "regular" selves—which constructed themselves as "regular" when perceiving differences that were too different for comfort and in doing so constructed the "special needs other" who needed to be excluded from places where the "regular" selves wanted to be alone (physically, emotionally, socially)—now are asked to change who they thought they were, and they do not want to do so. But as the other refuses to occupy the place of the special-needs segregated other, the regular self can't very well stay regular.

The fact remains, however, that many of those placed in segregated settings do not have the freedom to refuse. Elsewhere (Heshusius, 1996, p. 626), I imagine a scenario where special education youngsters take epistemological ownership over the knowledge they construct. They are taking the whole matter of inquiry in their own young hands. What might be the focus of their investigations? Whom would they turn into "subjects" for their studies? Their teachers? Their psychologists? Their researchers? Which settings would they research? Which aspects of curriculum, pedagogy, and instruction would they see as needing to be researched by them? Which outsiders would they invite to be involved in their studies, if any? What approaches to research would they take? Would they even see the need for research? And if not, what kind of actions would take the place of research?

It is relatively easy to continue a critique of positivist and empiricist traditions in the light of my comments so far regarding the need to protect a stable image of the inner self. The measuring and ranking self of the positivist researcher is perhaps the most isolating, insulating, distancing, distanced, and dissociated self the social sciences have known. When we asked

11 educational researchers who had been trained within the positivist/empiri-cist framework, and who had made a paradigmatic transition to interpretive and qualitative perspectives, to tell the personal story of their changing beliefs, they wrote in a strikingly similar way of the estranged self of their positivist period (Heshusius & Ballard, 1996). At the time of their writing, 6 of the 11 contributors had been, or still were, involved in special education. They told of the frustration they experienced, the discomfort, the stress, and even paralysis, and the physical feelings of resistance, fatigue, and nausea they had felt when forced to make their selves invisible, having to repress everything they knew from their own lives, having to deny their emotive, somatic, and real-life knowledges by adopting the measuring and ranking exercises of positivist traditions.

Measuring and ranking are the same movement in one's consciousness. They call each other into being. One necessitates and is implicated in the other. Although positivist thinkers may not explicitly link the two at the level of ideas, the idea that one has the obligation to measure in order to know, seen in positivist traditions as the core obligation, is identical to the idea of need-ing to rank in order to know, for measurement makes the *idea* of failure con-crete. To have the need to rank other folks, one first must construct and adopt the *idea* of failure. Measuring then, is simply the concretization of this idea.

This is not to say that only positivist researchers rank. Youngsters are referred to by teachers who measure and rank all the time. The school sys-tem demands they do so, and so does most of society, and so do we all, in many—I am sure, far too many—aspects of our lives. When researchers measure and rank, however, the ranking act has a extra painful edge to it because they claim that their methods are privileged and render an objective, uncontaminated truth. This hides the reality that the need to measure and rank the other is deeply embedded in the "habits of the heart." As discussed in Chapter 5, some positivist thinkers who are influential in editorial decision making keep insisting that these measuring and ranking practices are, first and foremost, the most fundamental activity of our field. "We must," says Sugai (1998, p. 171) "assume responsibility for measuring and owning the impact of our actions and decisions."

I read Sugai in a literal sense of actual proprietorship. The other is lit-erally owned in an epistemological sense: When one owns the only correct way to know, what results from that process is, by extension, one's episte-mological possession. The object of the measuring act becomes epistemo-logically known precisely, and *only* (positivists believe) because of having been put through the measuring/ranking act. No other ways of knowing (personal, political, cultural, sociological, descriptive, narrative, and know-ing through close interactions in day-to-day living), however interesting perhaps, and possibly informative for informal purposes, are acceptable as formal knowledge claims. (Obviously, I am not eschewing accountability for what we do. I am breaking the particular equation of accountability = measuring/ranking.)

The deepest flaw in the logic of justification that informs this view is a threefold denial:

1. The denial that the self of a human being is deeply involved in these measuring and ranking acts.
2. The denial that such self is shaped by forces of history in all its ideological manifestations.
3. The denial that this self also is fundamentally shaped by self-protecting inner needs and images in actual interactions.

The sadness of the measuring and ranking dictates is that diversity, which the field of education increasingly says it values, does not thrive on ranking. It thrives on being engaged and lived with.

Special Education for Tomorrow: The Continued Struggle With the Self

Researchers engaging in alternative epistemologies and methodologies are not immune from distancing and separative modes of consciousness when they do their work. The inner self of the alternative researcher does not necessarily give up on the need to separate and distance, which, one might argue, constitutes the measuring/ranking act in a different guise. Few, if any, of the alternative approaches to date ask of the researcher to enter the kind of relationship in which the self of the researcher is asked to *deliberately* attend to, and then try to gently set aside, her or his inner protective and separative inner needs that operate in any given actual encounter.

In setting aside positivist dogmas, and by engaging in research in which we interact with and listen to the other in real-life settings, we have made our "knowing selves" certainly somewhat less safe, less stable, and less secure. This helps to create more open and democratic notions of inquiry. We work directly with research participants, face to face, with no instruments between us. Our research encounters become human encounters. A rationality of method has become a human rationality that makes it impossible to play a game of ventriloquism and makes it more difficult to hide our own lives from the impact the contact with the other will have on the self.

Nevertheless, the entire story of the human race illuminates the extraordinary need we have to construct superior, stable, distancing, and safe selves. Changing epistemologies and research methodologies does not release us so easily from this need. As Fine (1994) states, qualitative researchers, too, "speak 'of' and 'for' Others while occluding ourselves and our own investments . . . protecting privilege, securing distance" (pp. 70, 73). Alternative approaches to research ask of researchers to make the self more visible as a location and an agent in the construction of knowledge. This self-positioning typically refers to one's class, race, gender, and any other historically evolved power relation in which one possibly could be found.

However much such reflexivity is needed, I suggest here that its engagement does not necessarily mean that the researcher is free from the need to be separative during the actual research encounter, free from the need to "other" the other because he or she poses a threat to the desired images of the self. That is, there is no necessary relationship between what happens in thinking and writing, however reflexively engaged in, and what happens in one's consciousness *in* any given present vis-à-vis an actual embodied other. It is possible, of course, that scholarly theorizing does create greater awareness of the self's own distancing act during the research encounter. But it would seem equally possible that scholarship can be used, however unconsciously, as a substitute for witnessing one's self engaging in precisely that which one later problematizes in theorizing.

The need of the ego to establish the self as separate, safe, and secure is so great that we find ingenious ways of doing so, even when we set out trying not to. Most researchers (positivist, qualitative, interpretive, ethnographic, action-oriented, deconstuctive, narrative, reflexive, and emancipatory alike) continue to position their researcher's self in some kind of separative manner, in terms of the actual desires, fears, likes, dislikes, judgments, and other such preoccupations that dwell in our consciousness and attentiveness while we are in the actual research encounter, despite a sincere desire to be collaborative. These inner—often subtle—desires, fears, judgments, and preoccupations go well beyond those typically dealt with in the literature (those of race, gender, ethnicity, class, sexual orientation, ability) to include appearance in its many expressions: mannerisms, dress, speech patterns, and so forth. Anything other than what our selves see as desirable can bring about the distancing trick. Or, alternatively, anything that we are embarrassed about or feel guilty about in relation to the "researched other" can do the same.

How do you collaborate equally with those who are many steps down or many steps up the ladder in social status and material well-being? What are the many emotions that present themselves in the presence of research participants who are not nearly as healthy, wealthy, competent, and attractive as we consider ourselves to be? As a friend and colleague who is doing collaborative research with refugee women in Toronto told me, in what was not a detached voice: "Lous, they don't even have money to take the bus, or to buy diapers! I make tons by comparison. . . ."

We did not pursue the anguish that informed the comparison she inevitably had to draw between herself, the researcher, and the refugee women with whom she set out to do collaborative work. I did not ask what, at a deeper level, she did with her comparison, or how her embodied reaction to the poverty of her research participants quite possibly affected the nature of the collaboration in perhaps subtle, but nonetheless important, ways. The very differences that she observed, and that caused her existential guilt, which I am quite certain most of us carry within us, surely must have colored in some way the notion of collaboration and the notion of equality in knowledge construction and created a site of emotional conflict that could be handled only by the distancing impulse.

I am not assigning a moral story to any of this. I am pointing to the inherent contradictions we construct between what we say about collaboration and the need to demystify power relations in our research and theorizing on the one hand and what plays itself out in the embodied encounters at deep personal levels on the other hand, involving contradictions that we don't know how to reconcile.

Research with the "special need others," whose lives we likely would not choose for ourselves or for our children, must be filled for many with deeply personal reactions of all kinds, repressed as soon as they arise, for they call up contradictions with what we say we want our research approach to be like. How does one separate "doing the research" from these gut-level personal reactions to those different others whose lives may shock us at these deeper, self–other constructing levels? By what mechanisms does one do so? Can it be done? And would it not be possible that the very definition of oneself as "a researcher" or "a theorist" actually might continue to facilitate and legitimatize this distancing act, protecting desirable images for the self while pushing away the other, even within what we think of as collaborative and equal research relations? What would my colleague do if she were in a friendship relation with one or more of these refugee women? Knowing her, she would buy them tons of diapers and lots of other things.

The research role does not mean being friends. But what, exactly, does collaboration and equality in the research relationship mean, given the impossibility of separating the researcher from the person?[4] How does one draw the line between equality and collaboration in research and buying badly needed diapers, *if* we take seriously the notion that researcher and person cannot be separated, and that research can be nothing more than just one other voice alongside others in the conversation of humankind? How do I separate the voice of research from the voice of care, friendship, fear, likes and dislikes? Can that really be done in the first place? What does being "a researcher" still privilege us to do or be, or not to do or not to be? What is still the source of such power? I often remind my students: Just because you have taken (or taught, for that matter) course 101 or 201 or whatever in research methods, that does not give you any epistemological or other privileges at all.

It would make for quite a study if someone were to collect the honest feelings—such as my colleague's—of a large number of researchers working with those of both much lower and much higher statuses (of various kinds) in life and trace how the deepest personal reactions to those others might differ from the relationship stipulated by the research in its epistemological and methodological commitments, and, further, to try to understand how the researchers deal with conflicts thus produced. Such a study would address Fine's (1994) "Working the Hyphens" in relation to the inner separative acts, which, too, stand between researcher and researched and keep reproducing power relations.

Can our minds and attentiveness be "uncluttered," asks Vanier (1999, p. 124), of inner needs to feel separate, to be in charge of the self, to feel stable, to feel secure? Uncluttered of the need to protect the desired self? These inner needs, which Vanier (1999, p. 106) refers to as "compulsions deep within us," stand in the way of completely attending to and being with the other, blocking the creation of more inclusive living and learning communities, which we say we want to have. And when our minds and hearts cannot be uncluttered from such needs, when our gaze does not want to go, as my student said, to what is inside, what does that mean for the research we do with "special needs others"?

To be sure, I am not referring to writing audit trails, and to personal reflective journals of one's feelings and emotions during the research process, however helpful these after-the-fact reflections might be in some cases. Rather, what is at stake is the question whether there can be clarity of attention *in* the moment that focuses directly on becoming aware of what, exactly, the self tries to protect as this act of protecting, and therefore of distancing, is occurring. Because the problem is that one can't protect the needs of the self and listen, and be with another, at the same time.

Toward an Epistemologically Listening Self

To do the work required to set aside the separative impulse that has characterized epistemologies and methodologies of social science research, a stance of complete attentiveness and listening, both to the self and to the other, is necessary. Complete attentiveness and listening are difficult for anyone.[5] In special education, positivist researchers, convinced of their duty to measure and rank the other into being, cannot afford to attend and listen in that complete manner, for to do so would threaten the images of the researcher's self as epistemologically and methodologically superior. The positivist self listens in relation to what it has decided it must measure, but it does not listen.

The narrative, action, qualitative, ethnographic, emancipatory, reflective researcher typically is asked to listen carefully, but there is no guarantee that what epistemological and methodological values say should be done, is done. The inner self cannot be told what to do. There is no guarantee at all that adhering to any set of formal values assures that the listening and attention are not shaped by a host of other directives, including those inner needs that want a self that is superior, stable, and safe.

To listen completely, the mind must be silent (as distinct from silenced). And to be thus silent is so difficult, says Corradi (1990), that we are hardly prepared for it. In her influential (and I think brilliant) book, *The Other Side of Language,* Corradi addresses the history and philosophy of the place of silence and listening, which she says are integral to language and to knowledge. But in the development of Western epistemologies, silence has come to be associated with powerlessness.

Within educational research, Scheurich (1997), commenting on the race-based epistemologies in which educational research is grounded, recognizes our inability, as a field of inquiry, to listen. After discussing the "imperial violence" that colors all our notions of validity, Scheurich (1997, p. 90) states that perhaps we ought to be "stunned into silence," into a space that "appropriates no one or no thing to its sameness." But we either fail or fear that space, Scheurich says. The best we can do, he states, is to enter a " polyphonic, tumultuous conversation."

If that, indeed, is all we can do, I must picture a scenario in which everyone speaks but no one listens. For where there is a lack of ability to *voluntarily* enter a state of silence in which one does not appropriate someone or something else to its sameness—that is, a state in which the desired images for the self are temporarily forgotten—the self may hear but cannot listen, can only translate hearing into speaking, and will exclude from attentiveness all that falls outside of the range of its own assertions. The dynamics of fear of that which we do not want for ourselves make our listening not quite listening and keep our politics externalized. There is a world of difference between being "stunned into silence" (which instantly brings about an impulse toward closure, if not a certain kind of paralysis) and being voluntarily silent. Not to be able to self-forget, be voluntarily silent and completely attend is to let "the compulsions deep within us" do their work.

What would it do to our notions of research if all courses in research methodology were to attend to this fundamental need to be completely silent and attentive in the construction of knowledge, and *in* that silence to learn to see what the self is doing? To see what mischief it is up to?[6] What if an entire course would be devoted to that attentive listening to both self and other, to listening as "the other side of language," to borrow Corradi's (1990) phrase, as an integral part of language and knowledge, the way research courses are now devoted to the practice of measuring and ranking the other, the generation of codes and categories about the other, or to the telling of stories about the other?

Researchers, especially from female and feminist perspectives, have written about the shocks, surprises, and confrontations in relation to their understanding of the self during their research activities, surprises, and confrontations that to various degrees bear on the habitual self–other construction discussed in this chapter (see, e.g., Ely, 1991; Reinhartz, 1992). This is difficult, as self-disclosure is inherently involved. Writing publicly what I learned when directing my attentiveness to what I had inside while trying to be a researcher of "retarded citizens," notwithstanding that the recounting was only a few short sentences, I experienced the conflicted emotions that occurred when doing so in a formal publication: Can I really do that? I am not supposed to be that personal. What is the reader going to think? But I came to conclude that it had to be done to stay true to what actually happened in the construction of the knowledge I shared with the reader.

Jean Vanier's work (1999) may well be among the most explicit writings available that illustrate what I am suggesting lies at the core of the politics of ex/inclusion: the need of the inner self to defend its images of what it finds desirable for the self, and thus exclude from participation those who threaten these images. He openly addresses the tremendous difficulties involved in witnessing this process in himself. In January of 2000, the Canadian Broadcast Corporation broadcasted the Massey Lectures of 1999 given by Vanier. Himself a privileged son of Georges Vanier, a former governor general of Canada, Jean Vanier was a philosopher and university scholar before he joined others in living with disabled and retarded people. The CBC program describes Vanier as a social and political thinker. With astonishing honesty, he speaks in these lectures of often wanting to stay distanced from those (the poor, the retarded, the homeless) who threaten his own safe sense of self. Recounting his running away from a woman who had asked him for money as he realized, once he started to talk with her, that she had immense needs, Vanier says, "I was frightened of being swallowed up by her pain and her need." We are frightened, he says, that our hearts will be touched if we enter into a relationship with an other who threatens our own self-safety, for then we have to let the self go. Fear about the safety of the self always seeks, and finds, an object (p. 73). He speaks of his anger and violence at times because of the difficulty in being faced with the intellectual disabilities of those he has chosen to live with. He then says something very important for the entire struggle around the politics of special education:

> In a world of constant, and often quite intense, relationships, you quickly sense your inner limits, fears, and blockages. You can feel the anger rising up in you. When I was tired or preoccupied, my inner pain and anguish rose more quickly to the surface. . . . I have often come head-to-head with my own handicaps, limits, and inner poverty. (pp. 100, 101)

Inclusion in education asks for constant and close relationships, between students and teacher, students and students, and teachers and parents. It does not help to deny or gloss over the idea that the inner selves of many are threatened that they now have to enter into close encounters with those whose lives they would not want for themselves or for their children, which, as I suggest here, triggers the need to distance the other into a threatening otherness—unless one is vigilant and intent enough to *want* to witness this deep compulsion, also within research and theorizing activities, and is capable to look the associated fears straight in the eye, so they might perhaps be set aside.

Another telling account of the self–other construction in the area of disabilities is Beck's (1999) autobiographical story of her initial horror when she discovered that she was pregnant with a Down syndrome child. Beck, too, tells with brutal honesty about her inner needs to protect a desired sense of self, which was all tied up with what others would say about the child, but also about her. Her sudden understanding of the inner fear of a hospital doctor who, accompanied by three medical students, tries to talk her into an abortion, portraying his own images of his desired self, is illuminating of what I have tried to sketch out in this chapter. His fear, she understands, is fear about his own need to avoid being seen, ever, as a failure, and therefore needing to reject and exclude (literally from life) anything that reminds him of the very possibility of failure. As she is struggling with her confusions when this doctor is spending an unusual amount of time and effort trying to gravely convince her to do the "sensible" thing, she suddenly hears the question in her own mind: *Why is he doing this?*

> I looked at Grendel closely, suddenly feeling like an observer rather than a patient . . . this man always made a great show of being too busy even to look at his patients. Why was he spending this inordinate amount of time trying to convince me to abort a child he would probably never even see? . . . I looked at Grendel's face, and there, just behind the tight-stretched skin, I seemed to see another face

appear. . . . This face was terrified. . . . Why should this be? I relaxed
and looked frankly at the second face. . . . The fear in it spoke to me
of a lifetime spent desperately avoiding the stigma of stupidity, of
failure, of not measuring up. (pp. 221–222)

Broun (Broun & Heshusius, in press) provides a deeply striking story of
the self–other construction that goes on in the deep levels where the images
we hold as desirable for the self have taken root. This account is particularly
powerful because, in this case, the self–other construction regards a self and
an other that live in the same body. Broun tells a tale of rejection of disability by a normally walking self that in fact has its home in a body that is disabled. It was the imaged, normally walking self that pictured her disabled
self into the status of other. Broun had focused her research on the question
of educational achievement by disabled women. She chose a life-history
approach to her study and included herself as a participant. She was not prepared for what happened. She could not get through an analysis of the stories because, as she states:

> I did not want to analyze the data because I did not want to analyze
> myself. . . . It was with effort and self-reminders that I wrote "we"
> instead of "they." Although including myself as a participant had
> seemed such a natural thing to do. . . . I thought of my participants
> as other and did not identify myself with them, though I assumed
> that I had. . . . I had been attempting to discuss a group to which I
> often felt I belonged only as a pretender. . . . I had always pictured
> myself as walking without a limp. While I knew that it was not true,
> it was easier for me to get on with my life if I perceived myself as
> walking normally . . . but now, in the video of my mind, I walk with
> a limp and I can't get back my limpless self. . . . I wanted to choose
> the time when I would allow myself to make the switch. I didn't
> want it to come unbidden. I had anticipated that I would make the
> shift to my limping self when I was older. . . . Actually I had planned
> that this shift would occur at the time of menopause, having found
> Greer's (1991) description of the freedom of the invisibility of later
> middle age quite enticing. . . . Now, as a result of my deep engage-
> ment with my research participants, the limp is there and I am no
> longer beautiful to myself. . . . For me, this research has resulted in
> praxis; however, it has been unwelcome and involuntary.

Broun ends by expressing the hope that she will, in the end, emerge more at
peace with herself, no longer having to struggle "to keep the image of the
false (but desired) limpless me at the forefront of my imagination."

Turning one's attentiveness inward to the images that the self holds as desirable while the self is active in relationship, and witnessing how the images stand in the way of relating, has not to do with confessional tales, or with engagement in subjectivity. Nor is it, in the first instance, a moral story. Rather, it points to human impulses that forcefully participate in the construction of knowledge. The important goal of such inward witnessing is not to judge, not to eradicate, but, rather, to become familiar with these forces so one can actually *see* them operate. Otherwise their power cannot be recognized. What is needed to be able to see in that way is a complete, vigilant nonjudging attention to the precise nature of these images as they operate in an actual moment of relation. Only then can they perhaps be gently set aside.[7]

All this was more or less implied when I responded to my colleague who called me to tell that her students had become scared, as recounted at the beginning of this chapter. Through her course, she wanted them to temporarily self-forget—that is, to forget the images they held about their selves as healthy and invulnerable, as able and able-bodied, so they could fully listen to the disabled other, but they were not able to do so. Their fears about their own potential disabled and undesired self kept them from the ability to self-forget and listen.

The Vaniers of the world, who collapse ontology and epistemology—who live as they speak—are intense social and political thinkers. In collapsing their thinking and their living, they engage the most demanding of political undertakings. In doing so, they critique existing conditions of power relations from the inside out. Vanier is not suggesting that we all must sell everything we have and live our day-to-day lives in communities with very different others, though doing so would surely change the face of (special) education overnight. Rather, he is saying, 1 believe, that at any given moment, wherever we happen to be, also as researchers, we must attend to this self–other constructing process and learn to pay vigilant attention to that which, as my student said, we have inside. To engage in such seeing of the inside is a prerequisite for understanding that the inner and outer are one, deeply continuous movement (see also Krishnamurti, 1972, 1993) and, therefore, that inclusion "implies a shift in consciousness" (Vanier, 1999, p. 82).

If we were to imagine that no one in society would get scared at the thought of being disabled, that no one would feel nauseous at the thought of being touched by a severely disabled person, that no one would feel superior in the embodied presence of "retarded citizens," that no one would shy away from forming genuine friendships with them, that no one would have wanted to see herself or himself (and wanted to be seen) as a "regular" learner (which, by definition, requires others who fail in being "regular")—in short, if we were to imagine that no one in society would have any inner fears for those who are very different—social relations would be unrecognizable and a book such as this one would not exist. Power relations in institutions and other established structures must be demystified, but the inner embodied life cannot be exempted from the process. They surely are deeply intertwined. Established structures and institutions that are separative are made by and made up of separative selves.

One might argue that this view is naive and romantic—that every civilization, every culture has its exclusionary practices, that the human self is innately self-protective, that ego needs are part and parcel of being human. It seems clear that this has been the case. But we are evolutionary creatures. Might it thus be that, as Vanier implies, we are not quite human but really are in the process of "becoming human" (the title of his CBC lectures)? Might it be that seeing this very process of other construction within one's self, and doing even the smallest thing toward lessening this distancing act, *is* at the heart of the evolutionary processes of humankind, which, Vanier seems to suggest, is not yet a humankind?

The past few years, when teaching courses in qualitative research methodology, which included students in departments of special education, I make the gist of what I have tried to say here the central principle for the course. I tell the students, and remind them often, that any and every methodological decision they make is first and foremost a decision about the *kind* of relationship they want to enter into with the other, which is determined consciously or—likely far more often—unconsciously by the images they hold for what constitutes a desirable self. Before any research decision is a decision of method, it is a decision about a certain kind of other–self construction. And before that, it is a decision about the kind of self we desire to be.

The message is not that we should no longer do research, as it is, after all, only about the self. The message is that research is in the first instance a construction of an other–self relationship, and precisely in being that, it is a construction of knowledge. Research, and every decision that we make about the process of research, from conceiving the question to the manner in which we write up the study, *is* in the first instance about the images of the self we want to maintain before it is about the other. These images of the self in research will determine what the other is allowed, or is not allowed, to be.

Turning to one of my cherished writers, I open up Ralph Waldo Emerson's essays (in Gilman, 1965, p. 154) and read:

> Do you see that kitten chasing so prettily her own tail? If you could look with her eyes you might see her surrounded with hundreds of figures performing complex dramas . . . long conversations . . . many characters . . . and meantime it is only puss and her tail. How long

before our masquerade will end its noise of tambourines, laughter and shouting, and we shall find it was a solitary performance?

As researchers and theorists, we, too, are like this kitten. We think we catch someone else's tail, but in the first instance it is invariably our own. Everything we say is about this chase. But perhaps we can learn to enter more deliberately into a state where we can tend this process and make the chase less and less self-protective, lessening inner ego needs and entering larger forms of awareness and, therefore, of knowing, both of self and other. "To *attend* means to be present," says Bateson (1994, p. 109); it means to give heed, to be vigilant. The root word of attention means to stretch the mind toward something (Bohm & Edwards, 1991, p. 139). As Bohm and Edwards note, "attention" and "intention" are directly and intimately related; where one's attention goes, one's intention goes, and vice versa. What one attends to, and the quality of such attending, will decide where one's intentions go and to what one's actions are directed. One, therefore, must be careful where one's attention goes.

Even though the many research alternatives we now engage in have opened up in scholarship at least the possibilities to attend to these mirroring processes within ourselves of fear/exclusion, of self/other, of trust/inclusion, much hard work remains to be done. Perhaps this is another way of saying what I hope for the future of education: a stretching of awareness that makes possible a more complete attentiveness to the self-protecting needs of the self as it is engaged with the different other in all matters that relate to what we still refer to as "special education," in its pedagogy, social policy, legislation, research, and theorizing. We must not forget in all of this that self–other constructions, and the morality that such constructions engender, are themselves evolutionary processes. It is precisely in this that hope for the possibility for further emergence of genuine participatory communities lies.

Berube (1996), a scholar in literary theory and father of a Down syndrome son, concludes his insightful—in many ways both deconstructive and embodied—story about being the parent of Jamie, his son, by saying that a crucial question is how we will represent the range of human variation to ourselves. In this chapter I add what I believe is the more primary question of how we represent our desired *self* to ourselves. The question that follows, then, is whether we dare to witness that desired self splashed all over the other in our embodied encounters. The need to develop a more focused attention and vigilance regarding the intensely private site of the self, where exclusionary impulses linger, may well be in the end, and therefore in the beginning, the most intense political dimension that humans face in the difficult struggle around the tensions between exclusion and inclusion.

References

Baldwin, J. (1988). A talk to teachers. In R. Simonsen & S. Walker (Eds.). *The Graywolf annual five: Multicultural literacy* (pp. 3–12). St. Paul, MN: Graywolf Press.

Bateson, M. C. (1994). *Peripheral visions. Learning along the way.* New York: Harper Collins.

Beck, M. (1999). *Expecting Adam.* New York: Random Books.

Berube, M. (1996). *Life as we know it: A father, a family, and an exceptional child.* New York: Panatheon Books.

Bishop, R. (1998). Freeing ourselves from neo-colonial domination in research: A Maori approach to creating knowledge. *Qualitative Studies in Education, 11*(2), 199–219.

Brantlinger, E. (1997). Using ideology: Cases of nonrecognition of the politics of research and practice in special education. *Review of Educational Research, 67*(4), 425–459.

Brigham, F., & Polsgrove, L. (1998). A rumor of paradigm shift in the field of children's emotional and behavioral disorders. *Behavioral Disorders, 23*(3), 166–170.

Broun, L., & Heshusius, L. (in press). Unexpected encounters in participatory research. *Disability, culture, & education.*

Bohm, D., & Edwards, M. (1991). *Changing consciousness: Exploring the hidden source of the social, political, and environmental crisis facing our world.* San Francisco: Harper.

Campbell, J., & Oliver, M. (l996). *Disability politics: Understanding our past, changing our future.* New York: Routledge.

Charlton, J. I. (1998). *Nothing about us without us: Disability oppression and empowerment.* Berkeley: University of California Press.

Corradi, F. G. (1990). *The other side of language: A philosophy of listening.* London: Routledge.

Ely, M. (1991). *Doing qualitative research: Circles within circles.* London: Falmer Press.

Fine, M. (1994). Working the hyphens: Reinventing self and other in qualitative research. In N. K. Denzin & Y. S. Lincoln (Eds.), *Handbook of qualitative research* (pp. 361–376). Newbury Park, CA: Sage.

Gilman, W. H. (Ed.). (1965). *Selected writings of Ralph Waldo Emerson.* New York: New American Library.

Greer, G. (1991). *The change: Women, aging, and the menopause.* New York: Fawcett Columbine.

Heshusius, L. (1994). Freeing ourselves from objectivity: Managing subjectivity or turning toward a participatory mode of consciousness? *Educational Researcher, 23*(3), 15–22.

Heshusius, L. (1996). Modes of consciousness and the self in learning disabilities research: Considering past and future. In D. K. Reid, W. P. Hresko, & H. L. Swanson (Eds.), *A cognitive approach to learning disabilities.* Houston: Pro-Ed.

Heshusius, L., & Ballard, K. (Eds). (1996). *From positivism to interpretivism and beyond. Tales of transformation in educational and social research. (The mind-body connection).* New York: Teachers College Press.

Hulsegge, J., & Verheul, A. (1986). *Snoezelen. Een andere wereld.* Nijkerk, The Netherlands: Intro.

Kalamaras, G. (1994). *Reclaiming the tacit dimension: Symbolic form in the rhetoric of silence.* Albany, NY: State University of New York Press.

Kauffman, J. M. (1999). Commentary: Today's special education and its messages for tomorrow. *Journal of Special Education, 32*(4), 244–254.

Kauffman, J. M., & Brigham, F. J. (1999). Editorial. *Behavioral Disorders, 25*(1), 5–8.

Krishnamurti, J. (1972). *You are the world.* San Francisco: Harper.

Krishnamurti, J. (1993). *On mind and thought.* San Francisco: Harper.

Lane, H. (1996). *A journey into the deaf-world.* San Diego: Dawn Sign Press.

MacMillan, D., Gresham, F., & Forness, S. R. (1996). Full inclusion: An empirical perspective. *Behavioral Disorders, 21*(2), 145–159.

McQuade, D. (Ed.). (1981). *Selected writings of Emerson.* New York: Modern Library.

Mood, J. J. L. (1975). *Rilke on love and other difficulties: Translations and considerations of Rainer Maria Rilke.* New York: W. W. Norton.

Morrison, T. (1997). *Paradise.* New York: Penguin Plume.

Prigogine, I., & Stengers, I. (1984). *Order out of chaos: Man's new dialogue with nature.* New York: Bantam Books.

Reinhartz, S. (1992). *Feminist methods in social research.* New York: Oxford University Press.

Sadaawi, N. E. (1996). Dissidence and creativity. In C. Miller (Ed.), *The dissident word: The Oxford Amnesty Lectures.* New York: Basic Books.

Sasso, G. M. (2001). The retreat from inquiry and knowledge in special education. *Journal of Special Education, 34*(4), 78–193.

Scheurich, J. J. (1997). *Research method in the postmodern.* London: Falmer Press.

Smith, J. K. (1988). The evaluator/researcher as person versus the person as evaluator/researcher. *Educational Researcher, 17*(2), 18–23.

Smith, J. K. (1989). *The nature of social and educational inquiry: Empiricism versus interpretation.* Norwood, NJ: Ablex.

Sugai, G. (1998). Postmodernism and emotional and behavioral disorders: Distraction or advancement? *Behavioral Disorders, 23*(3), 171–177.

Tannen, D. (1986). *That's not what I meant! How conversational style makes or breaks relationships.* New York: Ballantine Books.

Tannen, D. (1990) *You just don't understand: Women and men in conversation.* New York: Ballantine Books.

Vanier, J. (1999). *Becoming human.* Toronto: Anansi.

Varela, F. J., Thompson, E., & Rosch, E. (1993). *The embodied mind: Cognitive science and human experience.* Cambridge, MA: The MIT Press.

Walker, H. M., Forness, S. R., Kauffman, J. M., Epstein, M. H., Gresham, F. M., Nelson, C. M., & Strain, P. S. (1998). Macro-social validation: Referencing outcomes in behavioral disorders to societal issues and problems. *Behavioral Disorders, 24*(1), 7–18.

Notes

1. A previous version of this chapter was presented at the International Colloquium on Inclusive Education: Ideology and the Politics of Inclusion, University of Rochester, New York, June, 1999. In my introductory comments I stressed that I was not suggesting, by choosing my topic, that I considered myself an "inclusive self." To the contrary, I said, this paper had emerged from an ever deepening realization of just how difficult inclusion is. Most of us write not about what we have absorbed but instead about what we are struggling

with. In responding to a question from the audience, asking for an example from day-to-day life, I shared a recent incident as one of many I could have provided, of what I mean by separative and distancing self–other construction based on desired images the self holds for its self.

I recounted how, when strolling leisurely in a city I visited, I noticed a woman who was exotically but poorly dressed, who radiated something that pulled me toward her. I could not make out if she was a homeless person or a mentally ill one, or perhaps both. As I passed, our eyes met and I said, "Hello." We were across from a fancy restaurant, where elegantly dressed people were entering.

She started to talk about the neighborhood, including the museum next to the restaurant, which she obviously had visited and knew a lot about. Then she said about the restaurant, "They have excellent food." I was surprised, as her dress and appearance would not suggest she would eat there. Hesitantly, I asked, "Have you eaten there?" "No," she said, "but they feed me in the kitchen." I told the audience that, had the restaurant been a MacDonald's or some other cheap place, I undoubtedly would have invited her for a meal, as I needed a meal myself and was interested in talking with her further. But now I suddenly saw an uncomfortable picture of the two of us sitting amidst elegantly dressed folks.

I easily could have rationalized, I said in my presentation, that I did not invite her because *she* would have been uncomfortable. But the true observation of my "self" at that moment was that it was my own self, my image of who this self is, what I look like, with whom I socialize, and so forth, that would have been uncomfortable. What would the folks in the restaurant think of *me*?

There it was. Exclusion followed. My decision not to invite the woman was in the first instance not because of her but, rather, because of the images about the self I carried inside. I believe this is a clear example of the separative and exclusionary actions that occur routinely in our day-to-day self-in-action—typically outside of our direct awareness—in regard to those whose lives we do not want for ourselves, including those we place in special education settings.

2. A video in English (1988) of the Hartenberg's approach to Snoezelen is available through Rompa, De Hartenberg, Ede, P.B. 75, 6710 BB, The Netherlands.

3. "Snoezelen" has been transported to North America, and, in the process, unfortunately has been rendered, in all cases I am familiar with, as a "set of pleasant activities" to do for disabled youngsters. Items for a "Snoezelen room" now can be ordered from a catalog, regardless of the originators' legal action to prevent the commercialization of their philosophy. I have nothing against such activities as pleasant activities, but the point is that a philosophy of relations and human intimacy that honored the depth of humanness has been reduced to a set of activities to be scheduled, monitored, programmed, and even IEPd.

4. See Smith (1988, 1989) for excellent discussions on the inseparability of the person as researcher and the researcher as person.

5. This difficulty must be the reason why Deborah Tannen's (1986, 1990) books have been on best-seller lists for years.

6. Eastern spiritual traditions have focused for centuries on the importance of

silence and of attentive observation of the self-in-action as integral to coming to knowledge. Some Western scholars who address the importance of these states of being, drawing directly from Eastern understandings, include Kalamaras, 1994, and Varela, Thomson, and Rosch, 1993.

7. Krishnamurti (1972, 1993) has been particularly lucid about the paradoxically strengthening effect that the acts of evaluating and judging that which one wants to stop doing has on one's ability to let go of the undesired behavior.

Inside the Schools:
Special Education
and Inclusion Reform

Richard P. Iano

arly in her review of special education literature on inclusion Ellen Brantlinger (1997) unambiguously and prominently asserted her full agreement with the belief that "[i]deology is at work in everything we experience as reality" (p. 426). Brantlinger openly informs her readers that her review is based on her own ideological commitments to a critical model of social science and to forms of schooling consistent with John Dewey's ideas about democratic education. On a similar note, Fulcher (1989) asserted that our social practices, including our educational practices, are always politically, morally, and technically informed but that no practice is ever purely technical. In the spirit of Brantlinger, I wish to announce from the onset of this chapter that my support for the inclusion movement in special education, and for broader educational reforms that closely relate to inclusion reform, is based in large part on a view of public schooling growing out of my early study and understanding of Dewey's progressive ideas about democratic education.

As a consequence of my commitment to both special and general education reform, I have been struggling for some time with the following questions:

How did the contemporary system of special education in the public schools, so self-contained and separated from general education, become so well established and deeply entrenched?

And how did many come to see this separate system of special education as so natural, reasonable, even necessary, and rather unremarkable and in little or no need of justification?

And how did the practice of labeling students become so thoroughly entrenched as the basis for determining special education eligibility of students, for organizing separated programs and classrooms, and for certifying and assigning teachers?

How did the various medical–physical–sensory and psychological–behavioral special education labels that have been used, each on its own, come to be looked upon as capable of fulfilling educational purposes, to the extent that students of any given label can be separated from all other students and placed together into one program, classroom, or school and assigned a teacher certified according to that same label?

And how did these medical–physical and psychological–behavioral labels attain quasidisciplinary status among educators to the extent that many special educators have come to be professionally defined by one of more of the labels?

In an attempt to provide some answers to these questions and to related ones, I historically trace, in the pages that follow, how the modern system of public schooling and its subsystem of special education developed together, beginning in the latter half of the 19th century. Along the way I also critique the organization and practices of modern schooling and examine how they have become entrenched. Moreover, I examine how various practices and beliefs continue to mutually support each other and, in combination with certain broad social forces, have helped to maintain the system essentially intact for more than 100 years. In closing the chapter I provide principles or guidelines for successful reform that I have synthesized from numerous studies, examples, and reviews that have been published in the literature since the latter 1980s.

The Development of Modern Public Schooling and Special Education

The ideal of universal public schooling gradually approached reality in practice in the United States over the last half of the 19th century. By that time, most of the states had established compulsory attendance laws that were increasingly taken seriously and enforced. First, the primary and elementary levels of schooling were extended to almost all children of the nation, and the extension of public schooling at the secondary level soon followed. As the nation industrialized and as urban living centers grew in the latter half of the 19th century, the common pattern of schooling changed from the one-room schoolhouse headed by a single teacher of heterogeneously aged children to age-graded public schools with children and teachers assigned to grade levels.

Toward the end of the 19th century, the public schools added the practice of tracking to age-grading, and students were separately grouped or tracked into different classrooms, schools, or programs, usually either according to their actual academic performance or according to their estimated ability to achieve academically. By the early 20th century, tracking and age-grading had become widely established, taken-for-granted, features of schooling as the public schools, particularly the larger schools in urban centers, were transformed into administratively managed and hierarchical bureaucracies. Thus, the major organizational features of modern schooling were well in place by the 20th century.

Extension of the System to Special Education

At the end of the 19th century, public schools initiated special classes and schools separated from other, "regular" classes and schools, and may be considered a rational extension of the practices of age-grading and tracking students. That is, first students are classified and grouped into separate classrooms according to chronological age-level, with each room so classified headed by a single teacher. Then, when tracking is instituted, it is integrated into the already existing age-grading system and students are grouped not only according to age-level but also according to categories of high or low achievement or according to categories of fast or slow progress in learning. When students within an age-graded classroom are placed into separate groups according to their achievement or progress, it typically is called ability grouping, which has become a common practice at the elementary or primary and middle school levels. At the secondary level it has become the common practice to separate or track students into different programs, wherein the high, fast, or college preparatory tracks are composed of students with superior academic achievements and the other students are placed into general, business, or vocational tracks.

Tracking and ability grouping, typically integrated with age-grading, are commonly called homogeneous grouping of students, in contrast to mixing students of various ages or abilities, which is commonly called heterogeneous grouping. Finally, this system of tracking students is extended to provide separate, special education classrooms and schools for special categories of children—those who are especially low in academic performance or especially slow in their progress or learning, or especially uncooperative or disruptive in their behavior, or those having special physical, health, or sensory disabilities.

The practices of age-grading, tracking, ability grouping, and grouping or placement by disability categories are meant to increase the similarities and reduce the range of differences in certain characteristics among students. The support for these practices derives from the belief, which educators widely hold, that through these groupings of students, teaching, learning, and educational programming can be made easier, or more efficient and effective. When combined with other major beliefs and social political forces that have helped to shape modern schooling, these grouping and sorting practices have promoted narrow and restricting views of teaching and learning.

Homogeneous Grouping: Evidence or Ideology?

The belief that teaching and educational programming can be made easier, more efficient, and more effective, and the view of teaching and learning associated with this belief, leads naturally to the expectation that it should be possible to empirically demonstrate the efficacy of tracking and homogeneous grouping through objective standardized achievement testing of students. Despite various kinds of empirical studies conducted throughout the 20th century, convincing evidence supporting the efficacy of homogeneous grouping has not been forthcoming. First, the large number of special education efficacy studies conducted following the mid-century expansion of special education in the public schools generally provided disappointing results (Algozzine, Morsink, & Algozzine, 1986; Gartner & Lipsky, 1987)— that is, disappointing to those many who had hoped or expected that mildly handicapped students separately tracked or placed in special classes headed by special teachers would achieve better than mildly handicapped students who remained in the regular classes.

More recently, syntheses of findings from studies of grouping by ability have been interpreted to indicate that most students, when heterogeneously grouped, achieve at least as well as those who are homogeneously grouped (Anderson & Pavan, 1993; Arnstine, 1995; Braddock & Slavin, 1995; Hill, 1995; Oakes, 1985, 1995). Although occasional studies have found that homogeneously grouping high-ability students results in superior achievement for those students, the larger number of studies suggests that high-ability, like average-ability, students do just as well in heterogeneous groups as in homogeneous groupings. Most striking, however, is the rather consistent finding that lower-ability students generally achieve better when placed in mixed rather than homogeneous groups.

It seems certain that research findings are not what have driven the practices of ability grouping, tracking, and separate special education placements. Rather, these practices have in the first place been promoted by ideology and larger systems of belief about education and teaching. Then, in recent decades, a growing number of educators committed to a different ideology have generated interest in alternatives to these grouping and tracking practices. As I mentioned, tracking, ability grouping, special education classroom or school placements, and age-grading were all instituted about the same time as, or soon after, the transformation of public schooling in the latter half of the 19th century. The way public schooling was organized and structured then was influenced strongly by ideas of Western modernity arising out of the Age of Enlightenment in the 17th century, ideas that Western theorists and philosophers came to seriously challenge only in the mid-20th century (Smith, 1982; Toulmin, 1992).

Enlightenment Beliefs and Roots of Modern Schooling

The broad values and beliefs deriving from the Enlightenment that are of particular relevance to my exploration into the roots of modern schooling are:

1. Modern humans can and should liberate ourselves from the constraints of tradition and from family and religious authority (Kolb, 1986).
2. The physical and social worlds both can be rationally ordered for progressive purposes (Habermas, 1981; Calhoun, 1995; Kolb, 1986).
3. Social, as well as technical and material, progress and the advance of knowledge depend upon application of scientific reason, modeled particularly after the kind of reason exemplified in Newtonian physics (Habermas, 1981; Toulmin, 1992).
4. The objective world is ordered, and, through systematic planning and the application of scientific reasoning, we can achieve power and control over the objective world (Kolb, 1986; Habermas, 1981; Smith, 1982).
5. The key to progressive knowledge, understanding, and control is through developing and applying universal theories and categories and abstract concepts and generalizations, rather than through studying instances and examples of specific practices and contexts (Toulmin, 1992).

In the mid-to-late-19th century, the public schools were transformed into administrative and hierarchically managed bureaucracies for the efficient mass-processing of students (Brown, 1995; Katz, 1971, 1987; Oakes, 1985; Popkewitz, 1991; Tyack & Hansot, 1982). It is easy to see how modernity presumptions and beliefs supported and drove this transformation, as well as related changes in the schools. At the same time that ideas of bureaucratic management were applied to schooling, both "business efficiency" and scientific psychology principles were drawn upon. Thus, concepts and principles of bureaucracy, efficiency management, and scientific psychology were combined to institute the practices of standardizing the curriculum, learning materials, and tests, establishing grade-level measurements for curricular materials and student performances in the subject areas, instituting diagnostic assessment of students, and sorting students by categories of ability and disability. Modernist preferences for theoretical, abstract, and universalizing categories are especially evident in these latter practices of standardizing materials and of separating students by categories.

The practices of age-grading, tracking of students, and grouping of students by ability and disability interlock with the practice of standardizing the curriculum and learning materials, and with the measurement and grading both of curricular or learning materials and of the performance level of students. Moreover, measurement grading by hierarchical levels is the basis for assessing and matching students' performance levels to grade placement, difficulty levels of learning tasks, and materials. Finally, these various standardizing, grouping, and grading practices promote and support the long-popular model of teaching as the direct transmission to students of what is to be learned and the corresponding prevailing model of teaching as the management and control of students' learning and behavior. From here on, I will use the terms "transmission" and "management and control" either interchangeably or according to which best fits the context I am addressing.

Thus, the rationalizing, efficiency-management, and standardizing practices of modern schooling all encourage a transmission and a management-control approach to teaching. The fixed and standardized curriculum, sequenced by grade levels and further sequenced within grade levels, the standardized and graded learning materials, texts, and achievement tests—all imply that the major task of teaching is to deliver or transmit to students the knowledge and skills prescribed in the curriculum. The sequencing and grading of curricular materials and texts and the measured grade levels applied to students' performances all lead to the idea that the first task of teaching is to match the difficulty levels of materials and activities as closely as possible to the assessed achievement levels of students, and then to monitor or "move" students along to the next levels or sequences of the curriculum.

Modernist Presumptions

The modernist presumptions that the social world and its actors can be rationally ordered for progressive purposes and that, through systematic planning and the application of scientific procedures, we can achieve power and control over the objective world are played out in the practices of modern schooling. These presumptions underlie the ordering and sequencing by levels of a fixed and standardized curriculum and tests and in the measuring and labeling of students' performances according to abstract grade levels. The modernist preference for abstract and universalizing categories is seen in the way curricular levels, sequences, and objectives are universalized and in the way these universalizing categories are used to represent students' educational accomplishments, their progress, and their experiences.

The great power that these modernist presumptions and preferences have exerted over educational theory and practice is revealed in the way, a few years ago, programmed learning, with its standardized, precise, and universalized sequences of learning tasks and content, was intended to "teach" or transmit curricular skills and knowledge, or lead students through the steps of the curriculum largely independent of teachers' interactions with students. The technology of programmed learning is, of course, a rational elaboration of the earlier established practice of standardizing and sequencing the curriculum and the items of tests. The technology is also a rational elaboration of the management and control model of teaching, except that management and control of students' learning, through the universalized programmed learning materials, is by the expert programmers who are remote from the many and varied contexts and locales wherein the programmed materials are applied, and remote from the many and varied individual students who work through the materials.

If teaching consists of primarily transmitting or delivering fixed, standard, and universalized sequences of skills and knowledge to students, the standard sequences can just as well, if not more efficiently and "validly," be delivered by scientifically developed programmed materials. Similar ideas about the meaning of teaching and learning also generated interest in the technology of task analysis, a technology that has become widely used especially in special education with students who have severe handicaps. Remedial educational methods, materials, and programs also have been built generally upon an intensified model of rational ordering.

Positivist–Empiricist Epistemology Underlying Beliefs and Practices

Besides the broad values and beliefs just reviewed, Western modernity produced a positivist–empiricist epistemology that eventually came to dominate many intellectual domains, especially through the 19th century and up to the mid-20th century (Bernstein, 1976; Bohman, 1991; Bohman, Hiley, & Shusterman, 1991; Kolakowski, 1972; Radnitzky, 1973; Rosenberg, 1995; Shea, 1976; Toulmin, 1992). This epistemology contains the assumption that elements of knowledge, information, and understanding are directly impressed upon the minds of students, that students "receive" these elements as they are delivered to them by people, objects, and events in their environment. Moreover, the knowledge, information, and understandings to be transmitted to students exist objectively as bounded, definable, and separable units or elements that can be identified, codified, and listed so that they therefore can be fully prescribed and standardized in tests and curricular documents. Students, then, "receive," "absorb," or "take in" the knowledge, but this reception, if it is to be a true reception, is a re-production, a re-presentation, or a re-flection in the minds of students of the same bounded and defined elements of knowledge transmitted to them. Students then should be able to re-present or re-produce the knowledge, information, and understandings by speaking, by writing, by making pictures, or by other physical means. Again, these bounded and defined elements of knowledge, information, and understandings can be directly given or transmitted to students through telling, explaining, showing, lecturing, or directing, or these elements can be placed in texts or other media and, from these, transmitted directly to students.

Finally, if knowledge, information, and what students are to comprehend exist objectively, are bounded, definable, and separable as units or elements, they are, in turn, measurable. This means that the content represented in texts and curricular documents can be graded and measured in hierarchical levels and, as well, what students acquire and achieve of the curriculum can be graded in levels. Then, as an important part of managing and controlling students' learning and progress, teachers "match" levels of the curriculum and learning tasks to the students' current achievement levels.

Advocates of prescriptive or direct teaching methods or proponents of teaching as primarily a technical practice would, I expect, object to my presentation above on the ground that it oversimplifies and distorts their teaching beliefs and practices. I admit to having laid out the features of modern schooling and the management-control approach to teaching in a bare and unqualified way to highlight how insistently they objectify and separate what is learned from the subjectivities of learners, as well as from their social interactions and social circumstances. Perhaps few educators would hold these beliefs in quite the way I have presented them here, as there are many and varied shadings within this system of beliefs just as there are in any other major system. From my own observations, I would even maintain that teachers who profess to be strong advocates of prescriptive or behaviorist strategies often, without being aware of it, go beyond the restrictive principles of these teaching theories. Nevertheless, I insist that the features as I have identified them must predominate if we are to understand the persistent and strong attachment to tracking and ability grouping, to the dual system of general and special education, to the emphasis on prescribing the curriculum in great detail, and to the overriding importance given to objective testing and standardization in education.

That these various practices have persisted over decades and have been so resistant to change makes sense only if many believe that what is to be learned can be objectively prescribed and standardized and then transmitted directly to students, in large part, if not in entirety. In the same way, the apparent appeal and credibility of accountability systems that place major emphasis on grading and judging the work of teachers according to students' achievement scores make sense only if it is believed that those scores are a good and full representation of what those students have accomplished educationally, and only if it is believed that teachers can in important ways manage, control, or produce the educational accomplishments of their students.

Moreover, that the beliefs do predominate in the way I have laid them out also would explain why, when there is the contemplation or intent to change from a system that tracks and homogeneously groups students to a system that heterogeneously groups students and does not track, teachers and administrators alike often express the fear that the new and increased diversity among heterogeneously grouped students will be too much for teachers to handle, that teachers will be unable to accommodate sufficiently to the increased range of differences among students (Gamoran, 1996; Genest, 1996; Hunderford, 1996). This fear, expressed even by those who have apparently come to see the limitations in tracking and ability grouping, shows that they nevertheless retain some belief that teaching and learning are more efficient when students are categorized, separated, and homogeneously grouped, once again implying that students' learning and progress can be measured and controlled and the curriculum can be standardized and prescribed.

The Limitations of Modern Schooling Practices

Modern schooling practices rely heavily upon the beliefs and values of Western modernity that I mentioned earlier: objectivism and the use of abstract and universalizing categories, with a subordination of the subjective and personal, of particulars belonging to individuals, groups, and situations, and of the varieties of contexts within which social actions and interactions occur. The general consequence is that the education of students is deeply partial and incomplete.

Management and Control Model

I begin by returning to the concept of teaching as essentially the management and control of student learning. This model of teaching is extended to the notion that teaching and learning can be made more efficient and effective through the practices of age-grading, ability grouping, tracking, and grouping students by disability categories. A still further, related extension of the management and control model is the practice of assessing and matching students' ability or performance levels to the difficulty levels of the curriculum. These practices rely on the use of abstraction and universalized categories. When students are grouped homogeneously, they are grouped by categories of age, or ability, or performance in some subject, or by some combination of these categories—usually three at the most, because of practical limits. It is immediately obvious, however, that students grouped together by any one or any combination of these categories will be truly "homogeneous" only when viewed within the restriction of the abstract categories, and it also is obvious that students grouped by any of the categories will differ from each other in innumerable characteristics that fall outside the categories.

Only by restricting their views to narrow, fixed, and abstract categories are teachers able to label and grade student performance according to level or to homogeneously grouped students. Thus, to measure, grade, monitor, or match students' achievements and progress, narrowly conceived dimensions must be constructed to represent the school subjects and the subjects must be abstracted from their contexts of practical use and even from their theoretical frames of development. But the actual performances and achievements of students in the contexts of purposeful activities and projects are richly varied and textured, complex, and subtly adapted to circumstances. These richly varied, complex, and subtly adapted performances are ignored, eliminated, or suppressed when teachers confine and reduce their conceptions and actions to abstract, fixed, and narrow categories. This is one way that the education of students is made partial and incomplete: As the complex, rich, and ever-varying events and activities of practical contexts and circumstances are ignored, eliminated, or suppressed, educational opportunities and experiences, in turn, are severely reduced and narrowed.

When student performance is monitored and precisely assessed along abstract and narrow dimensions, individual differences in performances among students, ironically, are exaggerated and become a central concern for teacher management. Within the narrow dimensions and categories of learning and test tasks, students pull away from each other in their performances. The variation and spread in performances among students typically are rationalized as the natural order of things, as the natural expression of human variation. The "normal curve" often is used to represent the variation in performances among students. The normal curve is considered to be an objective expression of human variation, as given to us by the natural world, rather than as something we construct to fit our assumptions and theories about human variation. Yet, teachers often experience contradiction and tension as they struggle to manage learning and keep particular groups of students together in their progress, even as their students inevitably differentiate and pull apart from each other in their performances along narrow dimensions.

The prevailing emphasis on competitive grading, ranking, and sorting students only reinforces the focus on differences among students. Teachers often perceive the typical spread in performances among students, especially at the lower end of the distribution, as a threat to their self-image as effective managers of learning. Or they view low performances as the result of inadequacies inherent to students. Moreover, just as many other kinds of diversities among students are overlooked as teachers' perceptions and actions are confined to narrow dimensions, the many possibilities for common interest, purpose, and activity among students are overlooked and untapped.

It is easy to understand, then, why teachers caught within the management and control model of teaching would be strong supporters of ability grouping and tracking, and why they would fear the increased range of differences in student performances and behaviors they would face if special education students were to be placed in their classrooms. Later, I describe the sharply contrasting views of teaching and learning and the contrasting approach to differences among students that are offered by proponents of progressive reform and inclusion.

More generally, management and control models of teaching radically objectify knowledge, the disciplines, and the curriculum, and separate them from the subjectivities of learners or knowers. The curriculum is fixed, prescribed, and standardized external to and prior to the interactions of students and teachers. This objectification and universalization of the curriculum subordinates local activities and experiences of teachers and students created interactively and dialogically between them in particular times and places. These objectified and universalized forms of knowledge are believed to be transmitted directly to the minds of students in intact form through presentations, telling, explaining, lecturing, or directing, or through various media and displays. Here, communication is treated as if it were a one-way transmission, from source to receiver.

Communication, however, is not essentially a one-way transmission but, rather, interactional between sender and receiver, and what is communicated is subject to interpretation, creative reproduction, and understanding. The richer and more complex a communication is, the more it will tend to evoke varieties of interpretations, creative reproductions, and understandings. Therefore, students interpret, creatively reproduce, and understand their teachers' presentations, lectures, text offerings, and displays in various, indefinite, and unpredictable ways. Teachers, then, can hope to achieve full and genuine communication with students only by working toward intersubjective understanding through dialogue with and among students (Gadamer,

1988; Habermas, 1988; Iano, 1992; Ingram, 1985; Taylor, 1985; Warnke, 1987).

The ideology of management and control suppresses the demands of genuine communication and of intersubjective understanding. The suppression occurs when the major tasks of communication in teaching and learning are shifted from those of dialogue, creative reproduction, and interpretation to those of clarity in presentation by the teacher and fidelity in reproduction by the student. That is, as most standard texts on teaching purport, successful teaching is largely a matter of being able to make what is to be learned unambiguously clear to students and of being able to attract and hold their attention. Successful students, for their part, learn to "play the game" well; they learn that what is really important are not things such as the occasional, interesting, and spontaneous discussions on a topic or the interest and passion one brings to a project but, rather, those elements of lessons that can be clearly and precisely defined, that can be easily reproduced as items on objective tests, and that can be restated back to the teacher in fixed and unambiguous form. As students restate precisely what was presented to them, it appears to teachers that the narrowing of teaching and learning works, and that the learning and progress of students can be managed and controlled.

The widespread use of standardized and prescribed curricula and standardized tests, materials, and texts is based upon a one-sided, objectified view of knowledge and the disciplines. The subjective, active, and constructive aspects of knowledge and the disciplines are subordinated and obscured. The students' task is to master the settled content that authoritative others have constructed external to the students. Instead of knowledge, the content of disciplines, and curricular standards and objectives being one of the major starting points for study and inquiry, with student interests and questions being another major starting point, they become finished end-points for students to faithfully reproduce in assignments and tests. Except for those few students who attain advanced graduate or professional work within a discipline, the subjective active and constructive side of the discipline is not made prominent or easily available, and this is another way the education of students is partial and incomplete.

The beliefs that teachers can effectively manage and control the learning of their students, and that teachers can precisely match levels of student capabilities to difficulty levels of curricular tasks, seem to achieve plausibility only if educational outcomes are viewed through severely restricted categories and concepts. I mentioned earlier another reason for plausibility—that the various modernist beliefs and practices of schooling interlock and are mutually supportive. A third reason for plausibility, which I also mentioned earlier, is that these beliefs and practices tend to be self-reinforcing within their narrow categories. A fourth reason that I will suggest for plausibility is that these beliefs and practices trade on partial truths.

Partial Truths

There is partial truth in the claims that what students learn is transmitted to them and that teachers can effectively manage and control what students learn in their classrooms. Only in a general sense, however, may we claim that the cultural heritage, knowledge, language, and school curriculum are transmitted to the young and to students, and, therefore, only in a general sense may we claim that these learnings and acquisitions are managed and controlled by adults and teachers. Moreover, learnings, acquisitions, copyings, and imitations ordinarily are active, creative, and reconstructive, as they must be if they are to be useful, enduring, and personally owned and meaningful to the young and to students, and if they are to be adaptable to constantly changing and new circumstances, needs, demands, and purposes.

Therefore, what is passed on to and acquired by the young and by students for the most part is not mechanically received in intact form but, rather, is actively reconstructed and appropriated. To say that what is acquired and learned is appropriated rather than mechanically received is to emphasize that new knowledge, beliefs, understandings, and skills are not mere additive extensions of the self but, rather, are integrated with already existing structures and characteristics and represent changes or transformations in the self. Sometimes the changes are minor, sometimes major.

At times, adults and teachers do directly teach specific words, phrases, skills, facts, or subject matter, but this still does not mean they manage and control learning and progress in a step-by-step, fully prescribed, and standardized manner. Such direct, controlled, and specific transmissions are effective only within limited contexts and purposes, and when they do effectively occur, they are entirely dependent upon learners' previous acquisitions, which themselves are the outgrowth of various, broad, unspecifiable experiences and learnings that could not be specifically managed or programmed.

Similarly, adults and teachers can often, in a general way, match the difficulties of activities and tasks to the capabilities of the young or of their students (Newman, Griffin, & Cole, 1989; Rogoff, 1990; Wells & Chang-Wells, 1992; Wertsch, 1991). This is no more than we all do, usually without much conscious effort, in our everyday social interactions, as we subtly match and adapt our speech and conversation to different styles and patterns of the various groups and individuals we have come to know. More particularly, studies of early language development have shown that parents intuitively, and in a very general way, "match" their speech to their young child's level of understanding (Bryen, 1982).

Teachers of young children, too, learn to match their speaking to their students' general understanding. Yet, there is no attempt to formalize and quantify fixed levels of vocabulary or syntax, and no one could claim to know which specific words, concepts, phrases, or utterances should be taught to a given child at a particular time and in a particular context. Rather, all the children are constantly exposed to various general levels and kinds of speech from adults, their peers, and younger children, and children's levels of understanding and response vary in different contexts and circumstances.

In the same way, materials, tasks, presentations, and explanations for the various school subjects can, at times and in a very general way, be gauged or matched to students' stages of learning, although even the concept of stages or levels does not sensibly apply to many domains, subjects, or kinds of learnings. In any case, there is no way to determine precisely what specific level of words, materials, or tasks will be most efficient and effective for any given student's learning at a given time. Nor is there ordinarily any reason for teachers to attempt to achieve precise matching of learner performance levels with difficulty levels of materials and tasks. I maintain that attempts at a matching are more likely to undermine than to promote educational progress. The basis for my contention that such strategies undermine progress is that they narrow the way subjects, domains, and students' abilities are constructed for teaching and learning, thereby fragmenting students' actions and tasks and separating them from larger, practical purposes and meaningful contexts. Rather than attempt to control and monitor the precise steps of learning by severely narrowing tasks and actions, it would seem much more preferable for teachers to aim at providing a range and variety of opportunities, at the same time allowing for student initiative and self-direction.

A Summary Statement on the Management and Control Model

Let me now sum up the general effects on students and teachers of the management and control model of teaching and the heavy reliance on prescribed and standardized curricula and on standardized testing. These practices combine to place students in a passive position in their education. Students come to regard knowledge, the school curriculum, and prescribed standards as authoritatively given, as completed end points to be taken in and mastered rather than as a starting point for raising questions, or as routes to further knowledge and questions. Students learn to take direction from others in their education rather than to pursue projects and activities on their own initiative.

Students also learn that what is important for them to know are predetermined answers to close-ended questions, that knowledge and truths are not personally won and fashioned but instead reside in external authorities such as institutions, governmental bodies, teachers, and standard texts and materials. Furthermore, with the widespread emphasis on competition for grades and for placement in prestigious schools and programs, students learn that their successes and failures are strictly relative to the performances of others and determined through external rewards and signs. Textbooks and teachers that stress almost exclusively the clarity of presentation support the impression that knowledge and truths are fixed, neatly bounded, and entirely unrelated to students' current life passions, problems, questions, or interests. The broader and deeper goals of education tend to be shunted aside or suppressed—such as the goal of learning to formulate purposes that can guide ongoing activities, or learning how to deal with the ambiguities and multiple intimations of rich concepts, or the goal of learning how to overcome puzzling difficulties and obstacles often presented by challenging projects, or learning how to achieve intersubjective agreement with others in the complex interpretations engendered by challenging ideas and experiences. These kinds of broad and deep goals are discouraged or suppressed when the major concern is to manage and control the learning of students and to confine their activities and interests to that which is capable of being standardized and of being expressed clearly and explicitly in curricular materials, in teachers' presentations, and in tests.

Teachers, as managers and controllers of student learning, conceive of their main tasks as "delivering" and "covering" the prescribed curriculum, "motivating" students to work within the prescribed curriculum, and directing or channeling their students' energies and actions away from the random, chaotic, destructive, or frivolous activities that constantly threaten to disrupt the order and direction of classroom work. With this constant external management, control, and direction, students' sense of purpose and initiative wither, and it is not surprising that surveys often show that students, even those who are successful within the present system and practices, generally experience schooling as deadly dull (Clinchy, 1999; Cohn & Kottkamp, 1993; Goldberg, 1996; Kohn, 1999; Steinberg, 1996), or that researchers find that the use of external motivators tend to undermine interest in the school curriculum.

Downward Pressures From Higher Education

The higher levels of schooling exert downward pressures on the lower levels, with the result that existing practices are maintained and attempts at substantial reforms are resisted (Brown, 1995; Clinchy, 1999; Labaree, 1997). The primary and elementary levels of schooling have been less subject to those pressures than has the secondary level, so that attempts to break away from age-grading, tracking, ability grouping, and segregation of special education students, although always difficult and only sporadic, have been tried much more frequently and with greater success at the primary and elementary levels than at the secondary level of schooling.

At the secondary level of schooling, these practices have been held firmly in place since the late-19th century, in large part because of college and university admission practices (Brown, 1995; Clinchy, 1999; Labaree, 1997). These admission practices have been designed to serve primarily the interest of higher education faculty, thereby ensuring that each discipline is duly represented in admission tests and also in the required academic subjects of high school curricula. Higher education also has managed to enlist the secondary schools as early sorters and selectors in the process of producing small numbers of elite students for advanced study of the academic disciplines.

In the latter half of the 19th century, as higher education and secondary education were both rapidly expanding, the nation's high schools were independent; they developed their own distinctive and terminal educational programs, and the higher education institutions found themselves competing with high schools for students (Brown, 1995; Labaree, 1997). From the late-19th century to the early-20th century, the educational leadership of higher education urgently worked through foundations, accrediting organizations, and admission requirements to subordinate secondary schools and to eliminate them as competitors. The higher education leadership also worked to vertically integrate the nation's public schools, starting with the primary and elementary schools, upward through the secondary schools, to the advanced graduate schools (Brown, 1995; Labaree, 1997). The overall aim was to rationalize the nation's schools into a coordinated system, whereby the lower-level schools would serve as feeders and sorters for the higher-level schools.

By the early 20th century, our modern system of schooling was fully consolidated and the elementary and secondary schools alike were vertically integrated in their organization and curricula, as well as fully standardized in their curricula. Since then, tracking in the secondary schools has become a standard and locked-in practice, with the academic or pre-college track consisting of standard subject requirements shaped primarily by the admission requirements and by the academic disciplines of higher education. The admission requirements of higher education and the pressure on students and their parents to achieve or maintain class and economic status through educational certification are major factors in ensuring that the practice of tracking students, the fragmented and standardized curriculum, and the management and control approach to teaching and learning are all vigorously maintained in our schools.

We might say, then, that the organization and practices of modern schooling generally work against, and often preclude, significant progressive reform in teaching, especially at the secondary level. At the secondary level the organization of the curriculum into disciplinary subjects, separately taught by subject-specialist teachers, in separate classrooms of 45-minute periods all act as powerful restraints against reform. Furthermore, the testing and subject admission requirements of colleges and universities are major factors in maintaining the established organizational and teaching practices of modern schooling.

At the same time, there have been recurring instances of teachers—though their numbers always have been small—who have demonstrated that structures and practices at the organizational level of schooling need not absolutely determine or constrain the actions of individual teachers and particular groups of students (Bacharach, Hasslen, & Anderson, 1995; Brown, 1991; Cuban, 1984; Zilversmit, 1993). That is, some individual teachers have managed to go beyond the standard and prescribed curriculum in their teaching, actively engaging their students in the construction of their educational experiences. Again, successful instances of breaking away from standard teaching practices occur much more frequently and readily at the primary and elementary levels of schooling than at the secondary level.

When teachers have broken through the constraints of standard teaching practices at the secondary level, this has involved at least some organizational change beyond the individual classroom level and some minimal collaboration with colleagues, so that block times and integrated subjects or projects might be used (Brown, 1991; Jorgensen, 1998b). The most famous attempt at progressive reform at the secondary level is the Eight-Year Study. In the notable Eight-Year Study the kinds of organizational changes I have mentioned were made, and also arrangements with a number of leading higher education institutions to at least temporarily set aside their usual admission requirements (Kahne, 1996). In a later reform at the secondary level (Meir, 1999) the experimenters reported that projecting ahead to higher education admission requirements for the students in their study caused them to make compromises in their reforms. Even with compromises, these latter experimenters were concerned that, to an extent, they might have impaired the higher education admission chances of their students. The compromises made by the experimenters of these two studies and their concerns with respect to the admission requirements of higher education institutions attest to the power these requirements exert over secondary school practices and lend support to the claims of a group of critics (Clinchy, 1999) that until higher education is reformed, no enduring reforms can take place at the levels of schooling below.

In sum, throughout the past hundred years or so of modern schooling, there have been sporadic but continued, even persistent, reform efforts at breaking away from the dominant mode of schooling through a variety of

approaches emphasizing the active engagement of students in the construction of their educational achievements and experiences. Whether the reform efforts were by individual teachers or through more organized projects, such as the Eight-Year Study (Kahne, 1996) and the one reported by Meir (1999), these reforms all have been short-lived, and they have failed to generalize or to have a significant spread-effect to the wider school system or to other teachers, although teachers at the primary level of schooling frequently have adoped child- or student-centered approaches to teaching.

Overall, a management and control approach to teaching and reliance on a prescribed curriculum have characterized modern schooling and have proved to be remarkably enduring and resistant to change (Beyer & Liston, 1996; Cohn & Kottkamp, 1993; Cruickshank, 1995; Cuban, 1984; Goodlad & Lovitt, 1999; Kahne, 1996; Wheelock, 1995). Reform efforts in the 1980s and 1990s, however, often aimed both at progressive changes in general education and at including students with special disabilities in the regular education program, provide us with some reason to believe that these latter efforts might prove to be more enduring and also more capable of generalizing to the wider school system. Later I examine these latter reform efforts in some detail.

Before examining the reform efforts, I want to take one final look at the modern school system, this time from the perspective of the overall formulation of purpose for schooling and from the perspective of the wider societal and cultural forces that influence the character and purpose of schooling.

Overall Purpose of Schooling and Influence of Wider Social Forces

Seymour B. Sarason (1997), who has struggled mightily and for a long time, both practically and theoretically, with school reform, has much wisdom to offer. In his critique of public school governance, Sarason proposes that any system of governance, if it is to be effective, must have one overarching purpose that it is obligated to achieve—a purpose so important that only if it is achieved does the system stand a real chance of achieving any of its other purposes. According to Sarason, this overriding purpose drives the governance of education, but only at the level of rhetoric, usually expressed as, "To help each child reach his or her potential" (p. x). It is fairly well recognized, Sarason states, that the assertion amounts to only empty rhetoric and is violated every day in almost all classrooms. Also, he maintains, our current system of educational governance has not in the past, nor can it now or in the future, reflect that purpose but, instead, is against it, though not by the intention of the participants. Sarason, interestingly, further proposes that the one, overarching goal by which the school system should be organized to achieve is to create the conditions that make students want to learn. I will return later to this proposal by Sarason.

The most illuminating analysis of school purpose that I have found is by David Labaree (1997). In his *How to Succeed in School Without Really Trying,* Labaree argues that the U.S. educational system has been pulled by two opposing ideas: whether education should be considered primarily a public good and inclusive, providing shared societal benefits, or whether it should be considered primarily a private good and exclusive, providing selective individual benefits. Over the historical life of U.S. education, these competing ideas have been manifested as three competing, overall goals for education:

1. Schooling for democratic equality—a public good that entails preparing citizens.
2. Social efficiency—also a public good, which entails preparing workers for economic production.
3. Social mobility—a private good that entails preparing individuals to compete for social positions.

Labaree's analysis brings him to the claim that the historical conflict among the three competing goals has produced a contradictory structure for the educational system that has impaired its effectiveness and its legitimacy. Even more important, Labaree believes, are the consequences produced by the growing domination of the third goal—education for social mobility.

In his sociological examination of schooling and its purpose, Labaree (1997) also considers the influence of social forces from outside and beyond the schools themselves. Labaree proposes that the market forces powerfully shaping the nation's economic and social life have worked to turn education into a form of private property and the pursuit of private advantage, so that credentials have become the object rather than the byproduct of educational achievement. Our market-based society is reflected in a market-centered educational system that has allowed, or even encouraged, individual consumers to override the public interest by exploiting the system for their private benefit. As gaining competitive advantage for grades and credentials becomes the focus of individual students' efforts, the core of the curriculum and the substance of education are undermined.

This market-based society is characterized by a strong emphasis on individualism, separation and stratification of members of society, and relentless competition for goods and position. Individualism, stratification, and competition typically are reflected throughout modern schooling and teaching, resulting in the tendency to treat knowledge and education as if they were scarce commodities to be fought for and won by a select few.

Another set of broad cultural forces that also has had significant effects on modern schooling and teaching descends from the ideas of modernity that I earlier mentioned, and in their effects they seem to be both compatible with and complimentary to market forces. For example, Beyer and Liston (1996) and Wise (in Cohn & Kottkamp, 1993) cite rationalistic thinking as the source for bureaucratic and scientific management procedures of schooling and for the emphasis of schooling and teaching alike on efficiency and control. Similarly, Smith (1982) contends that the modernist outlook in our society has resulted in education being increasingly pressed into an approach to knowledge that embraces power and control, to the extent that alternative approaches to knowledge have been excluded.

Progressive Reform and Inclusion— The Prospects, the Sources

We have seen that modern schooling practices have been dominant, pervasive, and remarkably persistent in the face of constant critical assaults and attempts at progressive reform. According to critics such as Labaree (1997), Tyack and Hansot (1982), and Engel (2000), modern schooling practices are nourished and sustained largely by the combined effects of two forces in contemporary society: the market ideology and the technical–scientific rationality. Within schools themselves, modern practices apparently are sustained also by the way in which schools are organized and also by the sheer momentum of the practices being so long-established and entrenched.

Despite the overall dominance and the persistence of modern school practices, however, attempts at progressive reforms also have persisted, although the reforms have been limited in scope and lacking in endurance. And recently, both paralleling and often combining with inclusion reform, progressive reform apparently has been enjoying a resurgence, as well as bringing the promise of greater success and endurance than in the past. But why? What accounts for the reassertion and repeated attempts over the years to make progressive reforms, sometimes by individual teachers, other times by groups of educators or by schools? I propose two major sources of inspiration for repeated attempts at progressive reform:

1. The democratic tradition of our culture.
2. The strong, in-built human urge for meaning.

Let us briefly reconsider Labaree's assertion of three overall, competing goals of U.S. schooling. I find Labaree's proposal persuasive—that our market ideology is largely responsible for the predominance of the social efficiency and social mobility goals over the goals of democratic equality and preparation of citizens. Although the goal for democratic equality and the preparation of citizens is subordinated, Labaree recognizes its persistence. Thus, this latter goal, which reflects the continuing vitality and commitment to democratic ideals and values in our nation, provides, I would suggest, a source and inspiration for those who turn to the principles and aims of progressive education.

The second major source and inspiration for progressive reforms in education—the in-built and strong human urge for meaning—implies that teachers and students generally fail to find meaning and relevance in modern schooling. Here, I briefly review some prominent ways by which modern schooling practices undermine meaning and relevance for teachers and students. As we have seen, the objectification and standardization of the curriculum and of knowledge of modern schooling are dualistically one-sided and stunted, as is the use of abstract, narrow, and universalized categories. The one-sided dualism undermines meaning and relevance for teachers and students as a consequence of a failure to provide full and sufficient use of subjective understanding and purpose, a lack of opportunities for using and applying practical judgment in local, social contexts, and a failure to adequately draw on the aspects of knowledge that are reconstructive, extendable, generative, and a starting point for action, problem solving, and inquiry.

The management and control strategy of teaching turns curricular activities into externally imposed tasks to be authoritatively, passively, and arbitrarily mastered, absorbed, and faithfully reproduced as given, rather than as tasks having the intrinsic interest, meaning, and relevance that come from being personally initiated and owned by students. Finally, as Labaree has attested, the market ideology has contributed to focusing the energies and purposes of teachers and students toward competition for grades and credentials and away from the substance and meaning of the curriculum and what is to be learned.

I earlier mentioned Sarason's proposal that the one, overarching goal of the school system should be to create the conditions that make students want to learn. I further maintain that when students find tasks personally meaningful, they want to learn. Thus, the key is for educators to create the conditions of schooling that are favorable to engaging students in meaningful learning. These are the conditions of schooling that are created by the kind of progressive reforms I review in the latter part of this chapter.

To sum up, although powerful forces have contributed to maintaining modern school practices intact for more than a century, other powerful forces have driven educators and students to reform those practices. Thus, despite the influences of the market ideology and the technical–scientific ideology, despite the bureaucratic and hierarchical organization of schools, and despite the momentum of established practices themselves, if we ask what resources are available for the progressive–democratic reform of schools, the answer, I propose, is to be found in the cultural resources of our democratic tradition and also in the insistent human urge for meaning. It surely is significant that many of our leading advocates for untracking the schools and for inclusion build their rationale on democratic principles (Braddock & Slavin, 1995; Brantlinger, 1997; Cruickshank, 1995; Deever, 1995; Falvey, Gage, & Ephilian, 1989; Graves & Bradley, 1997; Hunderford, 1996; Jubala, Bishop, & Falvey, 1989; Kahne, 1996; Kelly, 1995; Oakes, 1995; Page & Page, 1995; Zilversmit, 1993).

Yet an additional resource to draw upon that has become available to us in the last two decades or so are the extensive published examples of successful progressive reform in the schools. These reforms in general education often are carried out hand-in-hand within inclusion reforms. Moreover, one of the basic principles I review next states that successful and enduring inclusion generally requires reforms in the wider educational system. In the next section, I provide a review and integration of the principles for successful progressive–democratic and inclusion reform. I have drawn these principles from various and numerous published examples of successful reform and from the consensus contained in published works of leading reform advocates.

Principles of Successful Inclusion Reform

A review of the literature on progressive reform reveals a notable phenomenon: Since the mid-1980s, the emergence of inclusion reform has paralleled a resurgence in progressive reform in general education (Ferguson, 1996; Kugelmass, 1996). Especially noteworthy is how, at the secondary level of public schooling, these reforms often have been initiated with the principal aim of "untracking"—eliminating the system of tracking students into separate programs. I earlier maintained that, as a logical extension of age-grading and tracking in the general education system, the separate system of special education emerged, with its separation of students into special programs. Therefore, it is not at all surprising that reforms aimed at untracking and at inclusion will face similar kinds of challenges and obstacles and also that those who advocate and work for each of these reforms offer us similar guidelines and principles for success.

Moreover, although untracking reform can and does occur without inclusion reform, it often happens that a reform beginning out of an initial interest in untracking gets extended to inclusion reform (Berres, 1996; Pool & Page, 1995; Schattman, 1992). And finally, advocates of inclusion at the secondary school level generally have concluded that successful inclusion can occur only in concert with general reform of secondary schooling, and this general reform has inevitably consisted of untracking as a central feature (Jorgensen, 1998b; Kugelmass, 1996). This brings us to the first guideline or principle for successful inclusion reform, which might be called "systemic reform" (Berres, Ferguson, Knoblock, & Woods, 1996).

Principle One: Systemic Reform

For reform to be deep, genuine, successful, and ultimately enduring, it cannot be limited to changing one or a few practices, and it cannot be limited to a few people, or to one or a few classrooms or teachers. The reform has to be schoolwide and, preferably, systemwide. Those who have observed, studied, or themselves been directly engaged in successful inclusion reform emphasize that inclusion must be part of wider, general school reform (Fisher, Sax, & Jorgensen, 1998; Fisher, Sax, & Pumpian, 1999, Jorgensen, 1998a; Lipsky & Gartner, 1997; Roach, 1998; Shapiro-Barnard, 1998; Villa, Thousand, Stainback & Stainback, 1992). This kind of school reform has been termed "systemic reform" (Berres, Ferguson, Knoblock, & Woods, 1996).

Similarly, those who have taken the lead in untracking at the secondary school level have insisted that untracking cannot be successful as a single, piecemeal, self-contained reform but instead must be carried out as part of a general and interrelated reform. Oakes (1995) and Wheelock (1995), well-known as pioneer reformers of secondary schools and as advocates of untracking, insist that the reforms must be more than a change in just a few practices; the reforms must involve changing the "school culture." What they mean by change in school culture I further detail below, but here I provide a brief explication by stating that a change in the culture of the school is a change in interlocking practices along with a change in beliefs about the meaning of education, teaching, and learning.

Inclusion certainly can be, and has been, accomplished in a limited sort of way by individual or small numbers of teachers in one or a few classrooms and without the benefit of systemic school reform or without the benefit of change in the wider school culture, especially below the secondary level, where organizational demands and curricular standards often are less restrictive and the pressures of the market ideology and the scientific–technical rationality are less severe. Without systemic changes and support, however, such circumscribed reforms tend to die out after the teachers or administrators involved leave the setting or after these students and their parents move on to another school setting.

For example, sometimes a few creative, passionate, and heroic parents initiate a program of full inclusion for their "special" children, but after the supportive teachers or administrators leave or after the children move to another setting, the parents find that they must begin the "battle" to persuade teachers and administrators all over again (Fisher, Sax, & Jorgensen, 1998).

The parents might fail to persuade another time, or they might become exhausted from their mighty efforts and give up trying.

Thus, our first principle, well documented and coming from a wide consensus among reformers, is that inclusion reform, to be successful and enduring, must be part of the reform of the larger school or school system of general education within which special education is located. The nature of this wider school reform is spelled out below, together with additional principles or guidelines for reform.

Principle Two: Democratic Teacher Involvement

Reform must be democratically based, especially with changes in the way teachers and students relate to each other and to school administrators. Here, I address primarily changes for teachers. Teachers must be fully involved in planning and implementing the reform and also in the day-to-day decisions and operations of the school program (Bacharach, Hasslen, & Anderson, 1995; Berres, 1996; Braddock & Slavin, 1995; Fisher, Sax, & Jorgensen, 1998; Fisher, Sax, & Pumpian, 1999; George, 1995; Goodlad, 1993; Kelly, 1995; Lockwood, 1996; Levin, 1997; Oakes, 1995; Page, 1996; Roach, 1998; Thousand & Villa, 1992; Wheelock, 1995). This fulfills the democratic principle that people experience autonomy and self-direction and that they participate and are heard in decisions that affect their lives in important ways. As Sarason (1997) concluded, from years of study and attempts to bring reform to the public schools, teachers cannot create and sustain contexts for productive learning unless these contexts exist for them. Teachers must feel ownership for the educational program, from which follows commitment and taking responsibility. A democratic approach results in what Skrtic (1991) has advocated and termed an "adhocratic" organization of schooling.

Drawing on organizational analysis and theory, Skrtic contrasts adhocratic and bureaucratic organization. Apparently, in the 1960s, organizational theorists began to recognize an emerging trend among many organizations in a move to adhocratic forms and practices, in an attempt to adapt themselves to the practical demands of their work. Bureaucracies and adhocracies are the inverse of each other in the way they address an organization's work and problems. Whereas bureaucracies rely on standardization of practices and regularization and typing of tasks and problems, adhocracies, in contrast, rely on ad-hoc and invented practices to accomplish tasks and solve problems as they emerge. Adhocracies are considered to be problem-solving organizations configured to invent new programs. Bureaucracies rely on fixed, specialized roles and a hierarchy of positions among members to get their work done, whereas adhocracies rely on democratic collaboration and reflective discussion among members and on roles that are flexible, changing according to circumstances, and often overlapping. It seems fair to say that bureaucracies represent the modernist goal of efficiently controlling and ordering the organization, its work, and its members through systematic or scientific-management procedures, whereas adhocracies represent the more recent recognition that the local and contingent elements are of prime importance for practices.

The bureaucratic organization form of modern schooling that took shape in the 19th century (Katz, 1987; Tyack & Hansot, 1982) has resulted in a hierarchical and autocratic system with an authoritarian chain of command. There is a strong tendency to externally direct and motivate teachers and to manage and control their work. In turn, teachers are impelled toward managing and controlling the learning and behavior of students, with a corresponding emphasis on external direction and motivation of students. As I have argued previously, this leads to distorted and incomplete education for students, an education lacking in opportunities for self-direction and to personally construct and own what they learn.

An adhocratic organization opens the way for practical, contingent, local, and emergent elements that are essential to a practice-based enterprise such as educating. Being practice-based, educational experiences are fully realized only as they are created in local, particular, historical places and times by particular individuals. An adhocratic organization provides the spaces and opportunities for adapting to the unexpected and unpredictable situations that constantly arise in practice. Similarly, an adhocratic organization allows room for invention, creation, spontaneity, and immediate judgment—which teachers attest are an integral part of their work. This is not to deny the role of tradition, or of general curricular standards, or of general purposes, policies, aims, and so on. Tradition, as previously maintained, however, must be continually re-created locally and historically to maintain its vitality, and general standards, policies, purposes, and aims must be applied creatively in practice, and the contingencies and particularities of practice demand frequent, immediate, on-the-spot judgments.

Bureaucracies achieve their objectives through standardization of procedures and specialization of work roles. Objectives and problems of bureaucratic organizations both are defined and categorized or typed, so that the means and strategies for achieving objectives and overcoming problems are also standardized and categorized. Thus, in the schools we find that standardized curricula and tests are given high prominence, that students are categorized or typed by grade level, by program track, and by problem or disability. Correspondingly, teachers are typed or categorized according to the category of student, program, or problem they are specialized to work with. Adhocracies, in contrast give priority to achieving objectives and solving problems through ad-hoc procedures, through flexible adaptation to emergent events, and by inventing and discovering means and solutions that fit the particulars of local situations and individuals.

Standardized methods, materials, and procedures are not eliminated, but rather than being fixed, end-points that sharply direct and channel the actions and thoughts of participants, for the most part they are starting points and general guidelines for creative adaptation and judgment as these are applied to specific circumstances and people at given times and given places. In adhocracies people are not grouped or separated according to a priori typings or categories. Instead, groupings of people follow interests, emerging purposes, or immediate opportunities, or groupings are informal, fluid, permeable, and always temporary.

Principle Three: Teacher Engagement

A third principle of reform, closely related to the second, is that the teachers who are to be a part of the reform program must be fully and deeply engaged in its planning and formulation, and they must be given generous lead time, at least a year, to study together, to discuss issues and questions with each other, to attend workshops, to visit other school sites where reform practices are successfully demonstrated, and to experiment with new ways of relating to teaching and learning (Bacharach, Hasslen, & Anderson, 1995; Genest, 1996; George, 1995; Hunderford, 1996; Norton & Jones, 1995; Wheelock, 1995). The need for generous lead time to experiment, inquire, reflect, discuss, and observe follows from the first principle, stated above, that the reform must be systemwide and must involve a change in school culture. For a school culture to change, teachers must have ample time, to work with new practices and beliefs, and also to develop a transformed vision of education and its purpose.

Principle Four: A Coming Together

The fourth principle actually embeds a number of distinctive ideas, so intertwined that it is easiest to explicate them together. As formal categorization and separation of students and teachers and as specialization of work roles are minimized, teachers are freed and encouraged to accept responsibility for all the school's students (Ferguson, 1996; Filstone, Florian, & Rose, 1998; Fisher, Sax, & Jorgensen, 1998; Lipsky & Gartner, 1997). The school, as a democratic community, becomes a place for learning, living, and socialization for all the children in the neighborhood. The school becomes a place where all can find connections with others, where all can become part of the daily activities, where all can find opportunities and openings for making a contribution to school life, and where they can explore their talents and interests. Neither students nor teachers are formally or categorically separated or segregated by track, program, ability, or disability and students are not viewed as "belonging," according to type or category, to one or another specialization of teacher.

In successful inclusion reforms based in adhocratically organized schools, special education teachers need not and do not lose their professional identity (Ferguson, 1996; Filstone, Florian, & Rose, 1998; Fisher, Sax, & Jorgensen, 1998; George, 1995; Lipsky & Gartner, 1997) as many skeptics and opponents of inclusion fear they must. Neither are special education teachers segregated in their work from the other teachers in their school, but instead, as colleagues, they work side by side with general education teachers. The adhocratic approach makes it possible for specialists to provide knowledge and skills to students based in their specialized training as opportunities arise, and also to provide any special or unusual knowledge and skills to students that are based in the teachers' personal, unique talents or unusual life experiences. At the same time, when general education teachers have unusual talents or experiences that happen to match students' special difficulties, needs, or interests, an adhocratic organization enables these teachers and students to come together.

Principle Five: Collaborative Teaching, Planning, and Problem Solving

The fifth principle consists of two closely interrelated ideas—teacher collaboration and ample time for collaborative planning and problem solving (Brown, 1991; Filstone, Florian, & Rose, 1998; Fisher, Sax, & Jorgensen, 1998; George, 1995; Murray, 1993). In bureaucratically structured schools, administrators and supervisors schedule the work of teachers so that teachers are isolated from one another for most of the day in self-contained classrooms of students and for the bulk of the school day they are assigned to teaching students. One of the key features of schools that have been successful in untracking and in inclusion reform has been the adoption of adhocratic organizational forms that promote flexible self-scheduling by teachers, with ample time for them to collaborate in planning and problem solving (Fisher, Sax, & Jorgensen, 1998; Genest, 1996; Murray, 1993). Adhocratic procedures give teachers the opportunity to achieve power, autonomy, and a sense of responsibility for their work and in how they schedule their time.

Collaborative teaching, planning, and problem solving synergistically increase the powers and capabilities of all the teachers as their diverse ideas, talents, and proposals for solving problems and for creating new strategies are brought together and combined. Once again, as teachers collaborate in adhocratic schools they are not bureaucratically restricted in their roles to their designated specialties. Rather, they are able to adapt themselves to contingencies, personalities, and circumstances, and they are able to nonprescriptively discover and develop talents and capabilities in themselves and others. Most significantly, collaboration among teachers—similar to the benefit of cooperative learning among students—produces the social interaction conditions within which most of us most easily and naturally learn and grow.

A final important benefit that collaboration and team-teaching bring is that teachers no longer have to face alone a constantly changing and boundless range of student needs, demands, and difficulties. The strategies of homogeneous grouping of students, specialization of teaching roles, and standardization of procedures are futile bureaucratic attempts to reduce and tame the student diversities that are an ineliminable feature of any grouping of school students, or of any grouping of human beings for that matter. These bureaucratic strategies only thinly cover the diversities among students, producing feelings of contradiction, tension, and frustration in many teachers, especially those who have not given up their ideals and continue to seek meaning in their work.

Thus, when teachers are faced with the prospect of including in their classrooms students who have been classified as having a disability, it is quite a natural consequence of having adjusted to the bureaucratic strategies and procedures of modern schooling that the teachers react with anxiety, lack of confidence, and fear (Gamoran, 1996; Genest, 1996; Hunderford, 1996; Lockwood, 1996; Norton & Jones, 1995), and they cannot imagine how they will be able to deal effectively with the increased diversity among their students. Yet, once they have experienced working within reform changes, including collaborative planning and teaching, teachers generally respond positively (Genest, 1996; Norton & Jones, 1995). With collaboration and team-teaching, they no longer are isolated or by themselves faced with the extraordinary task of handling all challenges and difficulties in a classroom, and, as I have already proposed, they generally find that their capabilities and powers are greatly extended. The benefits of collaboration are especially striking when teachers are faced with unusual learning or behavior problems in their students. The unity among adult teachers conveyed to students, and the collaborative development and problem solving, can significantly transform the tasks and challenges of teaching.

Principle Six: Heterogeneous Grouping

As the sixth principle of successful reform, heterogeneous grouping becomes the central procedure for grouping students (Bacharach, Hasslen, & Anderson, 1995; Fisher, Sax, & Jorgensen, 1998; Murray, 1993; Roach, 1998). The bureaucratic attempt to achieve efficiency in teaching and learning through tracking and ability grouping of students is abandoned. We may consider the principle of heterogeneous grouping to be an extension of the fourth one—that the school is to be a place for learning, living, and socialization of all the students. When secondary schools are untracked or when elementary schools are ungraded, the aim of heterogeneous grouping can be the initiating impetus for wider, systemic school reform (Jorgensen, 1998b). Moreover, the aim of including special education students in the general education program can be the initiating force for wider school reform, in which the move to heterogeneous grouping for all students becomes one of the features of the wider school reform necessary for inclusion reform to be successful (Berres, Ferguson, Knoblock, & Woods, 1996; Fisher, Sax, & Jorgensen, 1998; Jorgensen, 1998b; Lipsky & Gartner, 1997).

Yet another extension of, and complement to, the principle of heterogeneous grouping is that teachers no longer view differences among their students as a threat and a problem. Instead, the term "diversity" in the recent reform literature represents a radical change in educational philosophy and teaching–learning theory, wherein diversity among students is viewed as an inevitable feature of social life and also as a strength and resource to be valued (Bacharach, Hasslen, & Anderson, 1995; Ferguson, 1996; Roach, 1998). Then teachers no longer will have to struggle against the continual appearance of differences among their students, but, instead, student diversity becomes a core feature that enters into their teaching strategies and educational aims.

I should explain here that the principle of heterogeneous grouping means primarily the elimination of bureaucratic separations of students by fixed categories, usually by age, ability, or disability. But there are all kinds of temporary and ad-hoc groupings, sometimes according to common interest or purpose, sometimes on the basis of the educational help or support some students can offer to others, and sometimes for purposes of socialization or social growth. The Renzulli method (Erb, Gibson, & Aubin, 1995), which some secondary schools have adopted, shows how schools that have abandoned bureaucratic tracking and ability grouping and have committed to being democratic communities that value diversity in students, still incorporate special groupings or individualized study for academically talented students. When special groupings of students are temporary, varied, and constantly changing, and when no students are formally excluded from any of the groupings, students do not become identified, labeled, or segregated by groupings.

Principle Seven: Student Engagement

The seventh principle of successful reform is that students, in concert with their teachers, take an active part in developing their educational program and in setting purposes for their activities (Bacharach, Hasslen, & Anderson, 1995; Ferguson, 1996, Hill, 1995; Roach, 1998; Sarason, 1997). When students are actively engaged in this way, their educational program and learning activities in good part are an outgrowth of their purposes, understandings, curiosities, interests, and questions. Thus, management-control and transmission models are replaced by an interactive model of teaching and learning. The teacher shifts from managing and controlling the learning and behavior of students, and from the aim of transmitting a prescribed and standard curriculum to students to interactively constructing the curriculum *with* students. But, as John Dewey, our foremost advocate of democratic progressive education and an interactive approach to teaching and learning early in the 20th century, insisted (Dewey, 1964; Dewey, 1966), neither of the two poles of education—the child/student or the written curriculum—should be neglected or should be the sole focus. Rather, both the child/student and the written curriculum are included and are starting points for constructing educational activities and purposes.

Teachers and students together locally create educational programs, using the standard curriculum as a starting point for inquiry and questions, and as a guide for making judgments, for making creative adaptations, and for giving educational direction to activities. The teacher's task and responsibility are to engage students' initial interests, purposes, and understandings, and to help students direct their initial impulses toward activities and outcomes of educational quality. The teacher relies on his or her experience and knowledge, as well as on the standard curriculum, for helping students direct their interests and for helping them make judgments about the potential educational worth and quality of projects and activities. This adhocratic way of conceiving the standard curriculum and actively engaging learners is an organic part of the overall educational philosophy that views teaching and learning as interactive and knowledge as actively constructed, as the basis for further inquiry and questions, and as always up for re-creation and reconstruction.

Teachers who have exclusively known a management and control approach, both as students and as teachers, might have difficulty in "letting go" of control (Bacharach, Hasslen, & Anderson, 1995). But once teachers do experience what it is like to give up the unrealistic and tension-producing burden of managing and controlling the learning of their students, they usually find pleasure and success in interactively constructing educational programs with their students. For students, too, it can be difficult at the beginning to move toward a more self-directed approach, so the teacher often must approach the change gradually (Brown, 1991).

Principle Eight: Thematic Curricula

In the eighth principle of successful reform, teachers use broad, thematic units of study and projects as a major curricular strategy (Barta & Allen, 1995; Bacharach, Hasslen, & Anderson, 1995; Brown, 1991; Filstone, Florian, & Rose, 1998; Fisher, Sax, & Jorgensen, 1998; Murray, 1993;

Roach, 1998). Thematic units and projects integrate the disciplines or school subjects; provide a means for connecting the disciplines or subjects with student interests and purposes; and they make it possible to provide practical contexts of use for the content and skills of the disciplines or subjects. This interdisciplinary strategy coordinates well with teacher collaboration and with active learning. Curricular structures that link disciplines around common themes or questions are generally associated with collaborative and active approaches to learning, and several colleges and universities are currently experimenting with such approaches (Kelly, 1995).

The use of broad, thematic units opens the educational curriculum to a wide variety of interests and abilities, thereby ensuring that the curriculum does not exclusively serve those who have special academic interests or talents. This entails an especially radical change in approach at the secondary school level, where the standard practice has been for teachers to work as subject-matter specialists, isolated from each other in separate classrooms. At the same time, secondary schools using the Renzulli method (Erb et al., 1995) and those using the Foxfire approach (Kugelmass, 1996) have demonstrated that within these progressive reforms the integrity of the academic disciplines can be maintained and students with academic interests and talents can be provided opportunities through mini-courses and various kinds of ad-hoc study groups.

Principle Nine: Cooperative Learning

Maximum use is made of cooperative student learning in the ninth principle of successful reform (Bacharach, Hasslen, & Anderson, 1995; Barta & Allen, 1995; Fisher, Sax, & Jorgensen, 1998; Lockwood, 1996; Murray, 1993). Cooperative learning is an important component in the shift away from schooling as a striving among students for scarce positions and rewards and away from conceiving knowledge and learning as principally for private consumption and personal advantage. As schools become democratic communities, knowledge is conceived of as something to be shared and cooperatively constructed with others, and its values and benefits are considered to have unlimited potential for spreading among numbers of people.

Cooperative learning can range from the tasks and purposes being determined strictly by the teacher to students' taking more of an active role in determining tasks and purposes (Braddock & Slavin, 1995; Murray, 1993). In any case, all the various approaches to cooperative learning bring at least some active engagement by students; even when the teacher strictly determines the tasks and purposes, the students typically work together independently of the teacher for some period of time as they complete tasks and achieve outcomes or products.

Cooperative learning strategies take advantage of the way much of our learning ordinarily derives from social interactions with others. Cooperative learning provides opportunities for students to learn from each other, to work together to achieve common ends, and to share their talents and skills with others. Finally, cooperative learning provides students with all-important opportunities to engage in dialogue face-to-face and to encounter the variety of interpretations their classmates bring to concepts and topics.

Principle Ten: Authentic Assessments and Portfolios

The tenth principle of successful reform represents a shift away from an emphasis on competitive grading and testing of students to the use of authentic assessments and portfolios (Bacharach, Hasslen, & Anderson, 1995; Murray, 1993; Norton & Jones, 1995). Competitive grading and testing are suited to the modern system of schooling, which is heavily oriented toward sorting and selecting students for scarce positions and certificates and toward students' working primarily to achieve private gain and advantage. Competitive grading and testing, sorting and selecting for scarce positions, and placing personal and private gain to the fore are all contradictory to, and even destructive of, democratic-progressive reforms of schooling. Yet, even in settings of successful reform, competitive grading and testing seldom are easily or completely eliminated because of the momentum of long-established practice, the expectations of students and parents, the external and downward pressures from the wider school system and from higher levels of schooling, and also because of external political pressures (Lockwood, 1996).

Despite the difficulties and obstacles, and although most successful reform settings have not completely eliminated competitive grading and testing, reform settings have at least radically modified the usual practices to the extent that authentic assessments, evaluations adapted to individuals and to local circumstances, and portfolios have been given precedence over competitive grading and testing, especially within the classroom setting and in reporting the progress and achievements of students to parents.

Authentic assessments and portfolios, because they are based in the actual products and outcomes of classroom learning activities or in performance records, tend to be immediately useful and meaningful to students and teachers alike. Portfolios can be used to record and document the achievements and progress of students over an extended period of schooling. Portfolios are easily tailored to the unique needs, talents, and interests of individual students, or to groups of students who have worked together, or to specific and unique educational accomplishments.

Principle Eleven: Parent and Community Involvement

The last principle I propose is that the parents and the community must be involved in the study and planning for reform, and their support must be obtained for the new program and practices (Bacharach, Hasslen, & Anderson, 1995; Fisher, Sax, & Jorgensen, 1998; George, 1995; Oakes, 1995). The kinds of democratic–progressive reforms described here can come to self-contradiction and self-destruction only if the attempt is made to autocratically impose them on any of the participants who are to live with and be a part of the reforms—the students, the teachers, and the parents and immediate community members.

In the third principle I proposed that teachers must be full participants in the study of and planning for reform. In a similar way, schools that have achieved successful reform engaged parents and community members early on in the study of issues and problems and in the planning for reform (Bacharach, Hasslen, & Anderson, 1995; Fisher, Sax, & Jorgensen, 1998; George, 1995; Oakes, 1995). There is no doubt that this democratic route can lead to difficulties and resistance to the changes that educators want, especially when the minority of parents who have been most engaged with their children's schools from the start, and who also are the most politically influential, are the very same parents whose children usually benefit most from a school system oriented toward competitive and private advantage (Brantlinger, 1993; Fisher, Sax, & Jorgensen, 1998; Oakes, 1995).

In any case, if these parents are not engaged early on, they easily can turn back reform later (Page & Page, 1995). But if these parents are engaged early and become a part of the study and planning, they can come to see that the proposed reforms are aimed at improving schooling for all the students in the school and that, at the least, their children will not be harmed. Even more, they can come to realize that democratic–progressive reform and inclusion reform can bring important and desirable benefits to their children along with others (George, 1995; Page & Page, 1995).

Something More From the Inclusion Reforms

Before bringing this chapter to a close, I want to explore, in a more general way than I have in the 11 principles formulated above, just what we may learn from the many successful inclusion reforms that have been published. Notably, the inclusion reformers whose reports I have drawn upon have proceeded very differently from educators and researchers who subscribe to a positivist and scientific-technical rationale. The latter insist that before attempting to implement inclusion reforms on a wide and general basis in the schools, we must first establish, through controlled, experimental research, the methods and procedures that would universally and reliably produce positive, prescribed outcomes in the general educational setting for students with disabilities. Significantly, the scientific–technical research program is highly compatible with the modernist view that the overall purposes of schooling are the efficient production of prescribed, standardized outcomes of student learnings and behaviors and the efficient sorting of students for competitive positions. As I have made quite clear, the successful inclusion reformers I have drawn upon for this chapter have proceeded with assumptions very different from those who embrace the scientific-technical rationale.

The initial inclusion reformers, particularly those who advocated for the inclusion of students with more severe disabilities, had no previous evidence upon which to proceed; they did not have even the most informal kind of support that might be offered had there been general published reports of previous inclusion attempts. Rather than relying on prior evidence, the reformers generally proceeded with the presumption that the public schools are to be democratic communities for *all* students and that the students are the responsibility of all the teachers and administrators working in the school.

Inclusion reformers also have proceeded with a transformed vision and understanding of the overall purposes of schooling, transformed from that of the efficient production of prescribed student outcomes and the efficient sorting of students for competitive positions to that of a democratic community of learners, wherein students with divergent talents, interests, needs, goals, and abilities can build common purposes as they work and learn together.

Further, the scientific–technical rationale and the aims of modern schooling propel educators and researchers to search for ever more efficient and powerful methods for producing prescribed and standardized student learnings and behaviors. Again, these methods are to be universalizable, transferable, and intact from teacher to teacher, from student to student, and from setting to setting. If these methods are to be individualized, it only means that each different, universalized category of method is to be scientifically established as most efficient for its own universalized category of learning ability or disability, or for its own category of learning style. In short, the methods are shaped by researchers as prescriptions for teachers to use in efficiently producing prescribed learning or behavior outcomes in students.

Rather than search for efficiency, the reformers typically have sought conditions and strategies that would create opportunities for students—particularly opportunities that would capitalize on their propensities to socialize, to communicate with each other, to extend their knowledge, and to increase their powers. For example, the use of broad themes and problems for developing curricular activities provides opportunities for students with diverse interests and strengths to work together and offer their various contributions. Similarly, the use of cooperative learning offers opportunities for students to actively contribute to the formulation of activities and purposes, to coordinate their diverse understandings and interpretations, to engage in dialogue, and to learn to work together toward common objectives. Some might want to call these "methods," but they can be called methods only in the broadest sense of the term, and they are not at all like the kind of universalizable methods sought by those who subscribe to the scientific-technical rationale.

The methods offered by scientific researchers are meant to be universalizable and prescriptive, whereas the methods offered in the reform reports, such as the use of themes and cooperative learning, are offered as examples, not as prescriptions. Prescriptive methods are to be followed as faithfully as possible; they are viewed as being like carefully, or even precisely, fashioned tools, detachable and transferable from teacher to teacher, student to student, and setting to setting. As examples, the descriptions of broad themes and projects of cooperative learning activities provided in the reform reports are meant to be suggestive, inspirational, and as resources for others to draw upon.

Thus, although the examples of themes and cooperative learning are often described in considerable detail, they also are described in open-textured forms that encourage teachers and students to create their own versions adapted to their circumstances, interests, and purposes. Put another way, the scientifically created methods are intended for teachers to use with or on students as the teachers are instructed to do, whereas the examples of themes and cooperative learning are to be refashioned and re-created in each setting by the particular teacher and group of students.

Defenders of modern schooling and of special education as a system separate from general education within the public schools repeatedly assert that we still lack the research evidence necessary to move forward in replacing the current, separate system of special education with an inclusive schooling approach. Or the defenders of the current special education system sometimes claim that they are open to the idea of inclusion, or not opposed to it, but that nonetheless we first must establish, through carefully controlled research programs, to what extent, for whom, when, and how inclusion might be justified. Given the numerous and continually growing number of published reports in the professional literature of the kind that I have drawn upon here, this constant claim that we lack evidence for justifying a change from a separate special education system to an inclusive system seems odd, as does the apparent disregard for the reported successful reforms. The claim and the disregard seem strange until we remember that those defending the present system or claiming that we lack the evidence to adopt inclusion reform assume the scientific–technical rationale.

Those who assume the scientific–technical rationale count as "evidence" only that which is a product of studies that meet their criteria for being called "scientific": Scientific studies are controlled, consist of measurable variables, and are scrupulously "objective" in being distanced from any explicit commitment to an overall value or moral orientation. Further, those who assume the scientific–technical rationale also generally assume that the central purpose of schooling is to efficiently achieve standard outcomes that are objectively given. It is obvious that those who provided the reform reports I have drawn upon here did not base their reports on the scientific–technical rationale.

Although the reformers have not adhered to the scientific–technical rationale, I maintain that they have been disciplined in their approach and have created an emerging tradition for the study and development of education, particularly for the study and development of democratic–progressive and inclusive education reform (see Chapter 3, The Study and Development of Teaching, in this book). These reformers have proceeded with the understanding that, unlike natural events such as storms, floods, or river flows, and unlike essentially technical activities that have well defined and fixed objectives, education is a cultural and human practice thoroughly constituted by values and moral purposes.

The reformers have been characteristically forthright and clear from the start in their commitment to democratic and progressive educational values. As practitioner–researchers, the reformers have both studied and actively participated in developing the reforms. Further, the practitioner teachers and administrators have not been merely the "subjects" of scientific research. They have been equal partners in the disciplined study of reform and in developing and evaluating reforms. The published reports do not offer "scientific" regularities or "dependable" connections between objectively defined means and standard outcomes. Instead, the reports are detailed narratives describing the initial philosophic–theoretical commitments of the researchers and school practitioners, the kind of study, fore-planning, and development engaged in, the various obstacles met, and the strategies adopted. Many of the strategies were taken from the already existing literature, but all were adapted and modified to fit the special problems and opportunities in the local settings.

Thus, these reformers, through their published reports, have amply demonstrated that all students, as well as students labeled with disabilities, can thrive, learn, and benefit within inclusive educational settings. These reports also provide a consensus on the general conditions and strategies that educators must create to support inclusive education and ensure that it is successful. Also, the numerous reports on successful inclusion, with their careful detailing of reform procedures, strategies, and outcomes, provide a fruitful and inspiring resource for those who wish to adopt inclusive educational practices. Perhaps even more striking, a number of the reports give examples of how students with a variety of severe disabilities can receive rich and practical opportunities to develop their social and communicative competencies in the ordinary classroom setting, where a diversity of students engage daily in everyday activities and in broad educational projects.

Conclusions

Just as special education, separated as a subsystem within general education, is an integral feature of modern schooling, so the reform of special education into an inclusive system requires that the larger system of schooling be reformed according to democratic–progressive principles. In recent decades, a growing tradition of inquiry has produced a number of reform studies that are reported in the educational literature. These studies provide detailed examples of successful reforms of modern schooling and special education according to democratic–progressive and inclusive principles. What, then, are the prospects for special education in the coming years? Will special education become increasingly inclusive, so that the practices of diagnostic labeling and segregated placements of students diminish or disappear? Or will these reforms be limited and short-lived, just as previous reforms have been?

Powerful social and political forces suggest a pessimistic outlook for democratic–progressive and inclusive education. A surge of neoconservatism in recent decades is running through our politics and our culture, along with an increasing emphasis on individualism, competitiveness for scarce positions, and heavy reliance on the market ideology for setting the purposes of schooling. Nevertheless, I believe the outlook for the democratic–progressive and inclusive schooling today is better than it ever has been because of new resources available to us.

First, there is the new tradition of inquiry and development and the numerous examples of successful reform I described earlier. *Second,* and related to the new tradition of inquiry and development, since the 1960s educators increasingly have come to use alternatives to the scientific–technical model for studying and developing educational practice. *Third,* as the parents of children labeled as having disabilities, especially parents of children with severe disabilities, experience inclusion for their children or as they learn about the inclusion experiences of others, it is likely to get increasingly difficult to deny them what they see as the opportunity that inclusion offers their children for living, socializing, and learning with the other children and adults of their communities. Therefore, although oppositional forces no doubt will continue to resist the inclusion movement, and although the movement may be slowed, I believe the inclusion reform movement is less likely to die altogether as have previous school reforms.

References

Algozzine, K. M., Morsink, C. V., Algozzine, B. (1986). Classroom ecology in categorical special education classrooms: And so, they counted the teeth of the horse! *Journal of Special Education, 20*(2), 207–217.

Anderson, R. H., & Pavan, B. N. (1993). *Nongradedness: Helping it to happen.* Lancaster, PA: Technomic.

Arnstine, D. (1995). *Democracy and the arts of schooling.* New York: State University Press of New York.

Bacharach, N., Hasslen, R. C., & Anderson, J. (1995). *Learning together: A manual for multiage grouping.* Thousand Oaks, CA: Corwin Press.

Barta, J. J., & Allen, M. G. (1995). The dilemma of tracking and grouping in early childhood and middle grades. In H. H. Pool & J. A. Page (Eds.), *Beyond tracking: Finding success in inclusive schools* (pp. 95–103). Bloomington, IN: Phi Delta Kappa.

Bernstein, R. J. (1976). *The restructuring of social and political theory.* London: Methuen University Paperback.

Berres, M. S. (1996). Prologue: All children, all schools. In M. S. Berres, D. L. Ferguson, P. Knoblock, & C. Woods (Eds.), *Creating tomorrow's schools today: Stories of inclusion, change, and research.* New York: Teachers College Press.

Berres, M. S., Ferguson, D. L., Knoblock, P., & Woods, C. (Eds.) (1996). *Creating tomorrow's schools today: Stories of inclusion, change, and research.* New York: Teachers College Press.

Beyer, L. E., & Liston, D. P. (1996). *Curriculum in conflict: Social visions, educational agendas, and progressive school reform.* New York: Teachers College Press.

Bohman, J. (1991). *New philosophy of social science.* Cambridge, MA: MIT Press.

Bohman, J. F., Hiley, D. R., & Shusterman, R. (1991). Introduction: The interpretive turn. In D. R. Hiley, J. F. Bohman, & R. Shusterman (Eds.), *The interpretive turn: Philosophy, science, culture* (pp. 1–14). Ithaca, NY: Cornell University Press.

Braddock, J. H., & Slavin, R. E. (1995). Why ability grouping must end: Achieving excellence and equity in American education. In H. Pool & J. A. Page (Eds.), *Beyond tracking: Finding success in inclusive schools* (pp. 1–27). Bloomington, IN: Phi Delta Kappa.

Brantlinger, E. A. (1993). *The politics of social class in secondary school: Views of affluent and impoverished youth.* New York: Teachers College Press.

Brantlinger, E. A. (1997). Using ideology: Cases of nonrecognition of the politics of research and practice in special education. *Review of Educational Research, 67*(4), 425–459.

Brown, D. K. (1995). *Degrees of control: A sociology of educational expansion and occupational credentialism.* New York: Teachers College Press.

Brown, R. G. (1991). *Schools of thought: How the politics of literacy shape thinking in the classroom.* San Francisco: Jossey–Bass.

Bryen, D. N. (1982). *Inquiries into child language.* Boston: Allyn & Bacon.

Calhoun, C. (1995). *Critical social theory: Culture, history, and the challenge of difference.* Cambridge: Blackwell.

Clinchy, E. (Ed.) (1999). *Reforming American education: From the bottom to the top.* Portsmouth, NH: Heinemann.

Cohn, M. M., & Kottkamp, R. B. (1993). *Teachers: The missing voice in education.* Albany: State University of New York Press.

Cruickshank, K. (1995). Understanding ourselves: The ancestry of tracking. In H. A. Pool & J. A. Page (Eds.), *Beyond tracking: Finding success in inclusive schools* (pp. 21–28). Bloomington, IN: Phi Delta Kappa.

Cuban, L. (1984). *How teachers taught: Constancy and change in American classrooms 1890–1980.* New York: Longman.

Deever, B. (1995). Beyond tracking, what? Discursive problems and possibilities. In H. A. Pool & J. A. Page (Eds.), *Beyond tracking: Finding success in inclusive schools* (pp. 87–93). Bloomington, IN: Phi Delta Kappa.

Dewey, J. (1964). The child and the curriculum. In R. D. Archambault (Ed.), *John Dewey on education: Selected writings* (pp. 339–358). Chicago: University of Chicago Press. (Originally published in 1902)

Dewey, J. (1966). *Democracy and education.* New York: Free Press. (Originally published in 1916)

Engel, M. (2000). *The struggle for control of public education: Market ideology vs. democratic values.* Philadelphia: Temple University Press.

Erb, T. O., Gibson, S. O., & Aubin, P. E. (1995). Promoting gifted behavior in an untracked middle school. In H. A. Pool & J. A. Page (Eds.), *Beyond tracking: Finding success in inclusive schools* (pp. 133–140). Bloomington, IN: Phi Delta Kappa.

Falvey, M. A., Gage, S. T., & Ephilian, L. (1989). Secondary curriculum in instruction. In M. A. Falvey (Ed.), *Inclusive and heterogeneous schooling: Assessment, curriculum and instruction* (pp. 341–361). Baltimore: Paul H. Brookes.

Ferguson, D. L. (1996). Is it inclusion yet?: Bursting the bubbles. In M. S. Berres, D. L. Ferguson, P. Knoblock, & C. Woods (Eds.), *Creating tomorrow's schools today: Stories of inclusion, change, and research* (pp. 16–37). New York: Teachers College Press.

Filstone, C., Florian, L., & Rose, R. (1998). *Promoting inclusive practice.* New York: Routledge.

Fisher, D., Sax, C., & Jorgensen, C. M. (1998). Philosophical foundations of inclusive, restructuring schools. In C. M. Jorgensen (Ed.), *Restructuring high school for all students: Taking inclusion to the next level* (pp. 29–47). Baltimore: Paul H. Brookes.

Fisher, D., Sax, C., & Pumpian, I. (1999). *Inclusive high schools: Learning from contemporary classrooms.* Baltimore: Paul H. Brookes.

Fulcher, G. (1989). *Disability policies?: A comparative approach to education policy and disability.* New York and Philadelphia: Falmer Press.

Gadamer, H. G. (1988). Hermeneutics as practical philosophy. In K. Baynes, J. Bohman, & T. McCarthy (Eds.), *After philosophy: End or transformation?* (Pp. 325–338). Cambridge, MA: The MIT Press.

Gamoran, A. (1996). High quality instruction for all. In A. T. Lockwood (Ed.), *Tracking: Conflicts and resolutions* (pp. 10–20). Thousand Oaks, CA: Corwin Press.

Gartner, A., & Lipsky, D. (1987). Beyond special education: Toward a quality system for all students. *Harvard Educational Review, 57*(4), 367–395.

Genest, R. (1996). From tracking to high-quality heterogeneous instruction. In A. T. Lockwood (Ed.), *Tracking: Conflicts and resolutions* (pp. 45–54). Thousand Oaks, CA: Corwin Press.

George, P. S. (1995). Untracking your middle school: Nine tentative steps toward long-term success. In H. A. Pool & J. A. Page (Eds.), *Beyond tracking: Finding success in inclusive schools* (pp. 141–153). Bloomington, IN: Phi Delta Kappa.

Goldberg, G. (1996). *Why schools fail.* Washington, DC: Cato.

Goodlad, J. I. (1993). Access to knowledge. In J. I. Goodlad & T. C. Lovitt (Eds.), *Integrating general and special education* (pp. 1–22). New York: Macmillan.

Goodlad, J. I., & Lovitt, T. C. (Eds.) (1993). *Integrating general and special education.* New York: Macmillan.

Graves, D. K., & Bradley, D. F. (1997). Establishing the classroom as a community. In D. F. Bradley, M. E. King-Sears, & D. M. Tessier-Switlock (Eds.), *Teaching students in inclusive settings: From theory to practice* (pp. 365–383). Boston: Allyn & Bacon.

Habermas, J. (1981). *Theory of communicative action: Vol. 1. Reason and the rationalization of society* (Transl. by Thomas McCarthy). Boston: Beacon Press.

Habermas, J. (1988). Philosophy as stand-in and interpreter. In K. Baynes, J. Bohman, & T. McCarthy (Eds.), *After philosophy: End or transformation?* (pp. 296–315). Cambridge, MA: MIT Press.

Hill, H. D. (1995). Ideas and programs to assist in the untracking of American schools. In H. A. Pool & J. A. Page (Eds.), *Beyond tracking: Finding success in inclusive schools* (pp. 105–116). Bloomington, IN: Phi Delta Kappa.

Hunderford, A. (1996). Detracking with democratic values. In A. T. Lockwood (Ed.), *Tracking: Conflicts and resolutions* (pp. 56–65). Thousand Oaks, CA: Corwin Press.

Iano, R. P. (1992). Role of interpretation in the human sciences with some applications to education. In W. Stainback & S. Stainback (Eds.), *Controversial issues confronting special education: Divergent perspectives* (pp. 323–333). Boston: Allyn & Bacon.

Ingram, D. (1985). Hermeneutics and truth. In R. Hollinger (Ed.), *Hermeneutics and praxis* (pp. 32–53). Notre Dame, IN: University of Notre Dame Press.

Jorgensen, C. M. (1998a). Preface. In C. M. Jorgensen (Ed.), *Restructuring high school for all students: Taking inclusion to the next level* (pp. xxi–xxii). Baltimore: Paul H. Brookes.

Jorgensen, C. M. (Ed.). (1998b). *Restructuring high school for all students: Taking inclusion to the next level.* Baltimore: Paul H. Brookes.

Jubala, K. A., Bishop, K. D., & Falvey, M. A. (1989). Creating a supportive classroom environment. In M. A. Falvey (Ed.), *Inclusive and heterogeneous schooling: Assessment, curriculum and instruction* (pp. 111–129). Baltimore: Paul H. Brookes.

Kahne, J. (1996). *Reframing educational policy.* New York: Teachers College Press.

Katz, M. B. (1971). *Class, bureaucracy, and schools: The illusion of educational change in America.* New York: Praeger.

Katz, M. B. (1987). *Reconstructing American education.* Cambridge, MA: Harvard University Press.

Kelly, E. A. (1995). *Education, democracy and public knowledge.* San Francisco: Westview Press.

Kohn, A. (1999). *The schools our children deserve: Moving beyond traditional classrooms and "tougher standards."* New York: Houghton Mifflin.

Kolakowski, L. (1972). *Positivist philosophy.* Harmondsworth, Middlesex, UK: Penguin.

Kolb, D. (1986). *The critique of pure modernity: Hegel, Heidegger, and after.* Chicago: University of Chicago Press.

Kugelmass, J. W. (1996). Deconstructing curriculum for systemic inclusion. In M. S. Berres, D. L. Ferguson, P. Knoblock, & C. Woods (Eds.), *Creating tomorrow's schools today: Stories of inclusion, change, and research* (pp. 38–65). New York: Teachers College Press.

Labaree, D. F. (1997). *How to succeed in school without really trying: The credential race in American education.* New Haven, CT: Yale University Press.

Levin, H. M. (1997). Doing what comes naturally: Full inclusion in accelerated schools. In D. K. Lipsky & A. Gartner (Eds.), *Inclusion and school reform: Transforming America's schools.* Baltimore: Paul H. Brookes.

Lipsky, D. K., & Gartner, A. (Eds.) (1997). *Inclusion and school reform: Transforming America's schools.* Baltimore: Paul H. Brookes.

Lockwood, A. T. (1996). Introduction. In A. T. Lockwood (Ed.), *Tracking: Conflicts and resolutions* (pp. 1–9). Thousand Oaks, CA: Corwin Press.

McCarthy, M. H. (1990). *The crisis of philosophy.* New York: State University of New York Press.

Meir, D. (1999). Supposing that . . . . In E. Clinchy (Ed.), *Reforming American education from the bottom to the top* (pp. 3–14). Portsmouth, NH: Heinemann.

Murray, L. B. (1993). Putting it all together at the school level: A principal's perspective. In J. I. Goodlad & T. C. Lovitt (Eds.), *Integrating general and special education* (pp. 171–201). New York: Macmillan.

Newman, D., Griffin, P., & Cole, M. (1989). *The construction zone: Working for cognitive change in school.* Cambridge, UK: Cambridge University Press.

Norton, N. B., & Jones, C. A. (1995). Creating a nontraditional school in a traditional community. In H. A. Pool & J. A. Page (Eds.), *Beyond tracking: Finding success in inclusive schools* (pp. 225–234). Bloomington, IN: Phi Delta Kappa.

Oakes, J. (1985). *Keeping track: How schools structure inequality.* New Haven, CT: Yale University Press.

Oakes, J. (1995). More than meets the eye: Links between tracking and the culture of schools. In H. A. Pool & J. A. Page (Eds.), *Beyond tracking: Finding success in inclusive schools* (pp. 59–69). Bloomington, IN: Phi Delta Kappa.

Page, J. A., & Page, F. M. (1995). Tracking and research-based decisions: A Georgia school system's dilemma. In H. A. Pool & J. A. Page (Eds.), *Beyond tracking: Finding success in inclusive schools* (pp. 255–275). Bloomington, IN: Phi Delta Kappa.

Page, R. N. (1996). Tracking and American culture. In A. Lockwood (Ed.), *Tracking: Conflicts and resolutions* (pp. 21–32). Thousand Oaks, CA: Corwin Press.

Pool, H. A., & Page, J. A. (1995). Introduction. In H. A. Pool & J. A. Page (Eds.), *Beyond tracking: Finding success in inclusive schools* (pp. 1–4). Bloomington, IN: Phi Delta Kappa.

Popkewitz, T. S. (1991). *A political sociology of educational reform: Power/knowledge in teaching, teacher education, and research.* New York: Teachers College Press.

Radnitzky, G. (1973). *Contemporary schools of metascience* (3d ed.). Chicago: Regnery.

Roach, V. (1998). Forward. In C. M. Jorgensen (Ed.), *Restructuring high school for all students: Taking inclusion to the next level* (pp. xv–xix). Baltimore: Paul H. Brookes.

Rogoff, B. (1990). *Apprenticeship in thinking: Cognitive development in social context.* New York: Oxford University Press.

Rosenberg, A. (1995). *Philosophy of social science* (2d ed.). Boulder, CO: Westview Press.

Sarason, S. B. (1997). *How schools might be governed and why.* New York: Teachers College Press.

Schattman, R. (1992). The Franklin Northeast Supervising Union. In R. A. Villa, J. S. Thousand, W. Stainback, & S. Stainback (Eds.), *Restructuring for caring and effective education: An administrative guide to creating heterogeneous schools* (pp. 143–158). Baltimore: Paul H. Brookes.

Shapiro–Barnard, S. (1998). Preparing the ground for what is to come. In C. M. Jorgensen (Ed.), *Restructuring high school for all students: Taking inclusion to the next level* (pp. 1–14). Baltimore: Paul H. Brookes.

Shea, W. R. (1976). Introduction: Contemporary philosophy of science. In W. R. Shea (Ed.), *Basic issues in the philosophy of science* (pp. 1–14). New York: Neale Watson Academic Publications.

Skrtic, T. M. (1991). *Behind special education: A critical analysis of professional culture and school organization.* Denver: Love.

Smith, H. (1982). *Beyond the post-modern mind.* Wheaton, IL: Quest Book, Theosophical Publishing House.

Steinberg, L. (1996). *Beyond the classroom: Why school reform has failed and what parents need to do.* New York: Simon and Schuster.

Taylor, C. (1985). Interpretation and the science of man. In *Philosophy and the science of man: Philosophical papers 2* (pp. 15–57). Cambridge, UK: Cambridge University Press.

Thousand, J. S., & Villa, R. A. (1992). Collaborative teams: A powerful tool for restructuring. In R. A. Villa, J. S. Thousand, W. Stainback, & S. Stainback (Eds.). *Restructuring for caring and effective education: An administrative guide to creating heterogeneous schools* (pp. 73–90). Baltimore: Paul H. Brookes.

Toulmin, S. (1992). *Cosmopolis: The hidden agenda of modernity.* Chicago: University of Chicago Press.

Tyack, D., & Hansot, E. (1982). *Managers of virtue: Public school leadership in America, 1820–1980.* New York: Basic Books.

Villa, R. A., Thousand, J. S., Stainback, W., & Stainback, S. (Eds.) (1992). *Restructuring for caring and effective education: An administrative guide to creating heterogeneous schools.* Baltimore: Paul H. Brookes.

Warnke, G. (1987). *Gadamer: Hermeneutics, tradition and reason.* Stanford, CA: Stanford University Press.

Wells, G., & Chang–Wells, G. L. (1992). *Constructing knowledge together: Classrooms as centers of inquiry and literacy.* Portsmouth, NH: Heinemann.

Wertsch, J. K. (1991). *Voices of the mind: A sociocultural approach to mediated action.* Cambridge, MA: Harvard University Press.

Wheelock, A. (1995). Conditions that enhance the reintegration of schools. In H. A. Pool & J. A. Page (Eds.), *Beyond tracking: Finding success in inclusive schools* (pp. 29–43). Bloomington, IN: Phi Delta Kappa.

Zilversmit, A. (1993). *Changing schools: Progressive educational theory and practice.* Chicago: University of Chicago Press.

Critical Disability Studies

Thomas M. Skrtic

My task in this chapter is to characterize my current work and provide a sense of where I am headed with my intellectual pursuits and academic career. I ended Chapter 7 by noting that the path I'm on was influenced by the people and ideas I encountered during and after my 1991–92 sabbatical leave. I begin this chapter by going into greater detail about what happened to me intellectually and politically between 1991 and 1995, and how this shaped what I've been doing since then. I've already mentioned my current interest in history, democratic theory, and disability studies. Here I say more about how these interests relate to one another and to my professional and personal commitments. I also expand upon what I mean by critical social theory, which I left undefined in Chapter 7, and how it informs my current work in what I refer to as "critical disability studies" (Kent & Skrtic, in press). In the space available, I discuss what critical social theory entails as an analytical perspective and moral commitment, and why I believe such a broad intellectual and political framework is essential today in the field of disability and beyond.

Back to the Well, Again

Although the work I published between 1986 and 1991 attracted a good deal of attention (and controversy) in the field of special education, by 1991 I had gone about as far as I could with this line of inquiry based on what I had learned before, during, and after my 1985–86 professorship (see Chapter 7). And because I had been so involved in publishing and presenting my work in the late 1980s, I had done little to integrate its themes and ideas into my teaching.

With both of these things in mind, I organized my sabbatical to pursue further study in critical social theory and to integrate it into my teaching within the special education doctoral program at the University of Kansas. During the sabbatical I pursued further study in critical social theory at KU with my 1985–86 professorship mentors Bob Antonio, Gary Shapiro, and Dwight Kiel, as well as at the University of Cambridge with Anthony Giddens, the renowned British social and political theorist. I also taught a special education course in policy and administration at Syracuse University and a research methodology course at the Cambridge Institute of Education, both of which I used to develop and try new course material based on what I had learned in the 1980s and the more advanced ideas to which I was being exposed at KU and Cambridge.

As I had done during my professorship, I wrote several working papers in 1991–92, in which I integrated my past and evolving work in critical social theory and my earlier interests in qualitative research, school organization, and special education policy. After the sabbatical I used the working papers to finish *Disability and Democracy* (Skrtic, 1995) and to write and expand my chapters in the 1995 edition of the Meyen and Skrtic book (see Chapter 7).

I also used my working papers to develop an Office of Special Education Programs (OSEP) leadership grant application with Wayne Sailor in the fall of 1992. This was subsequently funded and ran from 1993–94 through 1997–98. Wayne and I used the grant to create a new special education doctoral and postdoctoral program in "interdisciplinary policy studies," focusing on service integration, which at the time was an emerging reform movement aimed at integrating education, social welfare, and health services and systems. Beyond its obvious implications for children with disabilities and their families, as well as for children and families living in poverty, I was attracted to the service-integration concept and reform movement as an opportunity to expand the substantive base of my work and to apply critical social theory to policy and practice in professional and institutional contexts beyond education and special education.

The leadership program was interdisciplinary in two senses. First, it integrated theory and practice within and across special education subfields, general and special education, and the professions of education, social work, public health, and public administration. Second, across these fields, professions, and institutions, it sought to build the integration of theory and practice upon a foundation of critical, interdisciplinary social science and humanities research. Our goal was to produce special education leaders who, drawing on a socially critical and historical understanding of the institutional development of American society, could design, implement, and evaluate integrated educational and human services policy, as well as provide integrated policy advocacy, mediation, agenda building, and technical assistance.

The interdisciplinary policy studies program had two components: a *substantive policy* component focusing on reform policies, agendas, models, and practices in the relevant fields, professions, and social institutions; and a *social foundations* component that was to identify and justify a moral, political, and epistemological framework for specific policy designs and institutional reforms. Wayne was responsible for developing the first component of the program, and I was responsible for developing the second.

The significance of the interdisciplinary policy studies leadership program for my academic career was that its service integration policy agenda and social foundations component allowed me to expand the focus of my research from public education to the American welfare state and ultimately to American democracy itself. In addition, the program gave me the opportunity to develop a sequence of social foundations courses with Bob Kent, whom I recruited as a postdoctoral fellow specifically for this purpose.

As noted in Chapter 7, I had met Bob earlier as a student in his American Studies course, "Democracy in America". My current research interests were influenced initially by what his course added to what I had been exposed to intellectually in the 1980s, and then more fully by the close collegial relationship that Bob and I developed while creating and teaching the social foundations courses. Through this association my current interests took shape—my interest in history as an indispensable disciplinary perspective for critical social theory, in democratic theory as the normative framework for my broader critical project, and in disability studies as way to integrate my professional and critical interests.

Strong Democracy and Civic Professionalism

Under the 1993–98 grant and two additional OSEP leadership grants funded in 1998 and 1999, respectively, Bob and I developed a four-course social foundations sequence integrating virtually all of my past and evolving research and teaching interests under the related concepts of "strong democracy and civic professionalism". The purpose of the sequence is to prepare doctoral candidates in special education as public intellectuals, as leaders in their profession who are instilled with a greater awareness and appreciation of the obligations of professionals to society. At the core of these courses is the idea of strong democracy—a more deliberative, inclusive, and participatory form of democracy than the weak, thin, or "elitist" form that currently exists in the United States and other liberal democracies. The question that drives the whole social foundations sequence is what sort of professional identity and practice is compatible with strong versions of democracy.

The first course in the sequence, "Democracy and Education in America," introduces the history of American public education—its mission, institutional form, and administration—and views this history critically from the perspective of democratic theory. It does so by tracing the parallel development of public education and democracy in the United States from the American Founding until the present. The second course, "Professionalization and the Origins of the American Welfare State," traces the institutional development of the American welfare state and the various welfare state professions. It is critically important in the sequence because it introduces the model of civic professionalism—a form of professional identity and practice in which professionals function as civic educators and community organizers who share knowledge and decision making with citizens, thereby empowering them in a collaborative effort to define their problems, determine their needs, and contribute to developing appropriate responses. The model of civic professionalism, which is based on the form of professionalism inspired by John Dewey and Jane Addams at the turn of the 20th century, provides a point of departure for mapping the affinities between strong democracy and a compatible form of professionalism in the welfare state professions.

The third course, "Democracy and the Prospects of Learning Organizations," differentiates bureaucratic and organic organizations—what we call learning organizations or adhocracies—and analyzes the affinities between technocrat professionalism and bureaucracy on the one hand and civic professionalism and learning organizations on the other. Finally, "Public Policy and Civic Professionalism" introduces forms of planning and policy formation based on practical rationality rather than the instrumental or technical rationality of traditional policy analysis. Here we are interested in forms of planning and policy research that are compatible with strong democracy and corresponding welfare state regimes. Unlike mainstream policy analysis, this planning and research requires substantive collaboration among professionals and citizens in the identification and resolution of social problems. By building upon affinities introduced in the previous courses, this final one in the sequence concludes with a sharp contrast between two sets of internally compatible but mutually exclusive concepts: technocratic professionalism, bureaucracy, policy analysis (planning by experts), and elitist–weak democracy *versus* civic professionalism, learning organizations, collaborative planning, and deliberative–strong democracy.

Developing and teaching these courses with a social historian and critical social theorist has been a productive learning experience for me, even more productive than the reading, studying, and writing I did during and after my 1985–1986 professorship. Teaching has been a definite advantage; it has required me to learn my subject matter more thoroughly than merely studying and writing about it. Moreover, because Bob Kent and I have been developing, teaching, or refining the courses continuously from 1993 until today, in effect, my 1991–92 sabbatical has yet to end. Although I have written and published far less than I did during and after my professorship, my relative understanding and appreciation of subject matter has been far greater.

Substantively, the experience has allowed me to develop a deeper understanding and appreciation of history as a discipline, and democracy as both a contested body of political thought and as an institutional phenomenon, globally and in the American cultural context. And, in addition to advancing my prior understanding of critical social theory, as I expected, the experience has helped me to expand my previous interests in philosophy of science, organization, and pedagogy and to integrate them into my developing understanding of history and democracy. Although most of the learning with respect to history, democracy, and critical social theory has flowed from Bob to me, at times it also has flowed the other way, particularly with respect to philosophy of science, organization, and disability. It was through this back-and-forth flow that Bob and I began to see disability studies as a way to integrate virtually all of our past and developing interests, including our long-standing shared interest in critical social theory, American pragmatism, and especially John Dewey.

Critical Social Theory and American Pragmatism

"Critical social theory" and, when used in a broad sense, "critical theory" are general terms referring to a variety of critical applications of social theory, which itself is not necessarily critical. This includes the specific form of critical social theory called "critical theory," which is associated with Max Horkheimer, Jurgen Habermas, and the Frankfurt School (Bronner & Kellner, 1989), as well as the pragmatist variant associated with John Dewey, George Herbert Mead, and the Chicago School of American Pragmatism

(Rucker, 1969; Feffer, 1993). It is this pragmatist variant of critical social theory—what, following Cleo Cherryholmes (1988), I have called "critical pragmatism" (Skrtic, 1991)—that has figured so prominently in my work since the late 1980s. Analytically, critical theorists of both Schools share the objectives of interdisciplinarity and a reciprocal integration of philosophy and empirical social science. A key difference is that the critical theory of the Frankfurt School is based on an unorthodox form of Marxism, whereas that of the American pragmatists is based on what James Campbell (1992) calls the "social pragmatism" of Dewey, Mead, and the Chicago School.

Both forms of critical social theory represent a combined political and intellectual enterprise. They are political enterprises because all critical theorists want their ideas to motivate and enlighten citizen mobilization for progressive social change. They are intellectual enterprises because they appropriate, reconstruct, and defend traditions of ethical and political theory that give meaning to the norms of justice, liberty (as autonomous self-realization), and participatory democracy (Kent & Skrtic, in press).

Politically, the audiences of both types of critical theorists are the general public and especially participants in specific social movements, such as those who seek progressive social change in the politics of class, race, gender, sexuality, and disability. That is, critical theorists want to inform the political judgment of citizens who seek a more meaningful realization of the values of justice, individual autonomy, and strong democracy in society. Intellectually, critical social theory provides both a theoretically grounded political orientation for social action and a body of empirically based substantive content to support its educational and motivational aims. Critical theorists use social theory and descriptive analysis to characterize the institutional structures and cultural patterns of a society in which social movements committed to a politics of justice, autonomy, and strong, inclusive democracy might advance their agendas for social change. As such, critical social theory provides both a grounding for social criticism and a source of hope for achieving the "good society"—a society in which these norms are more fully realized (Kent & Skrtic, in press).

In Chapter 7, I cast the evolution of my academic career in terms of seeking answers to questions that emerged from unexpected disappointments and nagging concerns about educational practices and arrangements for students with special educational needs. At first, I viewed the problem of better, more inclusive educational practices and arrangements as a simple matter of improved pedagogy. Then, when this fell short, I looked at the problem in terms of improved teacher education and targeted educational reforms. When I saw that neither of these approaches resulted in meaningful change, I recast the problem more broadly as one of transforming school organization and the professional culture of education.

Although I still see the organization and culture of schooling as a root problem, today I realize that the scope of the problem is much larger. The same structural and cultural problems that make public education far less than what it could and should be affect the entire U.S. welfare state and all of the welfare state professions. Today I believe that resolving these institutional problems ultimately requires a stronger, more inclusive form of democracy that, in turn, requires civic professionalism, learning organizations, and forms of planning and collective problem solving premised on a reflective and deliberative form of professional–citizen engagement and collaboration.

Dewey's Historicism

The intellectual dimension of critical social theory can be characterized in terms of five components: metatheory, theory, description, critique, and vision (Kent & Skrtic, in press). Metatheory is basic to the entire enterprise because it provides the philosophical grounds for choosing theory and methods of empirical description, as well as for the normative commitments and political mission that shape critique and vision. As such, grounding and interpretation of political norms requires reflection on the history of practical philosophy as well as on past and current struggles for justice, liberty, and democracy. As well, the pragmatist form of critical theory requires a particular kind of historical reflection, one that avoids both the transhistorical stance of traditional foundationalism and the relativism of pure contextualism. Given the range of options in the social sciences and humanities, justification of one's choice of substantive theory and methods of inquiry is a primary metatheoretical task, one guided by the need to match theory and method to the nature of the problem and also by normative commitments and political vision.

In carrying out this metatheoretical task, the critical pragmatist is guided by several essential features of Dewey's social philosophy, two of which I want to highlight (Kent, 2000; Kent & Skrtic, in press). The first feature is Dewey's historicism, of which two aspects are definitive. The first is his recognition that the only foundation for ethical and political ideals is the history of their meaning, a history embedded in traditions of philosophical reflection as well as in political struggles to establish particular interpretations as hegemonic. As such, Dewey is antiessentialist with respect to traditional political concepts such as justice, individual autonomy, and democracy. That is, although he constructs and defends certain interpretations of political ideals, he recognizes that there can be no appeal to timeless standards beyond the contestation of contemporary political discourses.

The second aspect of Dewey's historicism is its sensitivity to context, an appreciation of which is indispensable for him. Depending upon the object of inquiry, many contexts come into play in social analysis—cultural, institutional, political, social, psychological—each of which is replete with competing discourses about meaning and appropriate practice. For the critical pragmatist, an understanding of any human phenomenon depends upon locating it in the appropriate context, and no context can be fully understood without an appreciation of its history.

Critical Disability Studies

The problems that critical theorists address and the kinds of inquiry they pursue emerge from contemporary struggles for social justice and a stronger, more inclusive form of democracy. The politics of class, race, gender, and sexuality are well known examples of these struggles, but over the past several years, scholars of humanities-based disability studies have added the politics of disability to the list of contemporary struggles. Although there are notable exceptions (e.g., Erevelles, 2000; Oliver, 1990), most of these scholars tend to draw upon postmodernism as a guiding analytical framework. But certain forms of postmodernism are a problem for disability studies because, as Seyla Benhabib (1992) notes for feminism, they contradict the very liberationist politics they are meant to advance. That is, under what she calls "strong postmodernism," human agency virtually disappears or is collapsed into discourse, historical analysis disappears with the rejection of "grand narratives," and a critical role for philosophy is eliminated with the dismissal of metaphysics.

Under what Benhabib calls "weak postmodernism," however, the decentered self is still a creative agent, the debunking of grand narratives does not destroy the value of history, and a chastened, fallibilistic philosophy is still necessary for social criticism. According to Benhabib, only weak postmodernism is compatible with the ethical and political objectives of critical theory and the social movements it seeks to enlighten and motivate, whereas strong postmodernism most often tends to devolve into mere identity politics (Kent & Skrtic, in press).

Weak postmodernism, or what, following Antonio (1989), I have called "progressive liberal" postmodernism (Skrtic, 1991, 1995), is consistent with the ethical ideals and political commitments of critical pragmatism. This is best understood by considering the second feature of Dewey's social philosophy, fallibilism, or the idea that our knowledge of nature, self and society, and our interpretation of political norms are provisional and subject to revision (Kent & Skrtic, in press). Like postmodernists, pragmatists reject traditional foundationalism because they recognize that "there is no belief or thesis—no matter how fundamental—that is not open to further interpretation and criticism" (Bernstein, 1992, p. 326).

Furthermore, it is not just personal preferences and political commitments that are subject to correction, or even interpretations of individual autonomy and democracy. For critical pragmatists, the grounding principles and assumptions of metatheory itself may require rethinking and reframing (Antonio & Bonnano, 1996). The context for revision is a deliberative community of inquiry, either a scholarly community or an inclusive democratic one, and the medium of revision is communication. And, of course, these communities require human agency, historical reflection, and a philosophical basis for social criticism, the necessity and prospects of which differentiate critical pragmatism from strong postmodernism.

Drawing on these and other advantages of critical pragmatism, Bob Kent and I have laid out the intellectual and political dimensions of what we call "critical disability studies," an approach to disability studies premised on the pragmatist version of critical social theory (Kent & Skrtic, in press). As we see it, critical disability studies has three objectives concerned with disability, the American welfare state, and American democracy itself:

1. To increase knowledge and understanding of five social phenomena: the concept of "disability," the populations of people with disabilities, public and private care and services for people with disabilities, the disability rights movement, and the politics of disability.

2. To rethink the whole domain of care and services, framed by the project of critical social theory and guided by the norms of justice, autonomy, and strong democracy. In addition to addressing the gender issues associated with care-giving within families, there is the urgent need to redesign the American welfare state, an important point for us that we have been addressing in the interdisciplinary policy studies program (see Skrtic & Sailor, 1996).

3. To participate in reconstructing the overarching political and emancipatory project of critical theory itself. This will require working with strong democrats in the disability rights movement to move beyond identity politics and interest-group pluralism—that is, to make the disability rights movement part of a broader social movement composed of participants in the social movements concerned with the politics of class, race, gender, sexuality, age, and disability. The primary stake in all of these social movements is a resuscitation of genuinely progressive politics in the United States. This broadening of political horizons should be guided by the model of strong, inclusive democracy and a conception of justice that can accommodate demands for both cultural recognition and economic redistribution (see Fraser, 1998; Skrtic, 2000; Young, 2000).

I plan to spend the next phase of my academic career and intellectual life pursuing these three objectives.

References

Antonio, R. J. (1989). The normative foundations of emancipatory theory: Evolutionary versus pragmatic perspectives. *American Journal of Sociology, 94*(4), 721–748.

Antonio, R. J., & Bonnano, A. (1996). Post-Fordism in the United States: The poverty of market-centered democracy. *Current Perspectives in Social Theory 16,* 3–32.

Benhabib, S. (1992). Feminism and the question of postmodernism. In S. Benhabib (Ed.), *Situating the self: Gender, community, and postmodernism in contemporary ethics* (pp. 20–241). New York: Routledge.

Bernstein, R. J. (1992). *The new constellation.* Cambridge, UK: Polity Press.

Bronner, S. E., & Kellner, D. M. (1989). *Critical theory and society: A reader.* New York: Routledge, 1989).

Campbell, J. (1992). *The community resconstructs: The meaning of pragmatic social thought.* Urbana: University of Illinois Press.

Cherryholmes, C. H. (1988). *Power and criticism: Poststructuralist investigations in education.* New York: Teachers College Press.

Erevelles, N. (2000). Educating unruly bodies: Critical pedagogy, disability studies, and the politics of schooling. *Educational Theory, 50* (Winter), 25–47.

Feffer, A. (1993). *The Chicago pragmatists and American progressivism.* Ithaca, NY: Cornell University Press.

Fraser, N. (1998). Social justice in the age of identity politics: Redistribution, recognition, and participation. *Tanner Lectures on Human Values, 19,* 3–67.

Kent, J. R. (2000). John Dewey and the project of critical social theory. *Social Thought & Research, 23*(1 & 2), 1–43.

Kent, J. R., & Skrtic, T. M. (in press). Disability studies and the project of critical social theory. In S. Gabel (Ed.), *Breaking the silence: Disability studies in education.* New York: Peter Lang.

Meyen, E. L., & Skrtic, T. M. (1995). *Special education and student disability: Traditional, emerging, and alternative perspectives.* Denver: Love.

Oliver, M. (1990). *The politics of disablement.* London: Macmillan Press LTD.

Rucker, D. (1969). *The Chicago pragmatists.* Minneapolis: University of Minnesota Press.

Skrtic, T. M. (1991). *Behind special education: A critical analysis of professional culture and school organization.* Denver, CO: Love.

Skrtic, T. M. (1995). *Disability and democracy: Reconstructing (special) education for post-modernity.* New York: Teachers College Press.

Skrtic, T. M. (2000). *Civic professionalism and the struggle over needs.* (Keynote address presented at the Leadership Project Directors' Conference). U.S. Department of Education, (2000, July). Washington, DC: Office of Special Education Programs.

Skrtic, T. M., & Sailor, W. (1996). School-linked services integration: Crisis and opportunity in the transition to postmodern society. *Remedial and Special Education, 17*(5), 271–283.

Young, I. (2000). *Inclusion and democracy.* Oxford, UK: Oxford University Press.

Moving the Conversation Forward: Empiricism Versus Relativism Reconsidered

Deborah Gallagher

lternative voices in special education have been around for some time now. Among them, Heshusius, Iano, and Skrtic were, and remain to this day, three of the most eminent of those voices. In the preceding chapters they have shared the stories of their personal and professional journeys, their early work, their insights into the present, and their hopes for a better, more inclusive and participatory future for schools and society as a whole. This chapter seems to be a fitting place to reflect on what we might draw from their experiences and insights and consider what this might mean for the future.

To be sure, these authors have each advanced their concerns from somewhat different directions, but their individual pursuits for understanding all centered on epistemology—the nature of knowledge itself—and, ultimately, on ontology—how we are together in the world. In their rejection of positivism, they have unveiled the fundamental moral and practical limitations of this framework of knowledge, particularly as it has been applied to disability and special education. They have shown why positivism's claim to neutrality is illusory and how its effects diminish people and impoverish professional discourse.

"The claim to neutrality," Heshusius (in Chapter 5) asserts, "is a ventriloquist trick, a mode of speaking where the voice is smartly hidden, so smartly, that the reader/listener is made to believe that it comes from somewhere else." That the voice does not come from somewhere else, that there is no disembodied objective knowledge to which to appeal, compels us to confront the most important question of all: If we don't have neutrality or an objective foundation for our inquiry and practice, does this mean that all knowledge is relative and therefore anything goes? And if there is no disembodied voice, are all voices now equal? The answer is, of course, no.

On one side, these three people have made it clear that we no longer can hold onto the pretense of a foundation for our knowledge. There is no question that the concepts of objectivity, predictability, certainty, and control have been completely undermined by the analysis offered by these three people, and by others. On the other side stands the rejoinder to this position offered by their critics. This rejoinder claims that their nonfoundationalist stance is anti-science, is enamored of intuition, deals in art rather than science, and on and on. It is to this deep divide that I must turn in closing this book.

If one could summarize how this divide is often understood, it can be described as a search for certainty versus the supposed void of relativism. The implications of relativism are, without doubt, exceedingly daunting, but much depends upon how we understand this concept. Certainly, relativism forces us to acknowledge that there is no external or neutral arbiter to vindicate our beliefs, actions, and so forth (Smith & Deemer, 2000). Ontologically speaking, we are balancing on the moral high-wire without a net. Relativism requires letting go of the illusion of certainty—hence, control—that seemed to have brought some measure of comfort to daily life. That is why the term "relativism" is unappealing to many, if not most, people. It provokes a deep sense of misgiving that surrendering the possibility of neutrality, of value-free objectivity, plunges us headlong into the abyss of "anything-goes relativism." Given a choice between adhering to a belief in the possibility of foundational knowledge versus the abyss of "anything-goes relativism," who would choose the latter? And if this understanding of relativism is what alternative thinkers have to offer us, why should we listen to them?

My response to these questions may come as a surprise, because it is one that requires rethinking the concept of relativism. First, who would, or even could, choose "anything-goes relativism"? Nobody I know—including the alternative thinkers—could live their life as "anything goes." I raise this question because it does not come down to a choice between one or the other. To frame the issue in this way is pointless. And in that it is pointless, it is absolutely essential to draw a clearer understanding of what "all of our knowledge is relative" means.

If relativism does not, and cannot, mean anything goes, what does it mean? It means that even though we cannot ground the knowledge that informs our actions in the certainty of an objective, neutral authority, we are still responsible as moral beings. Or, put differently, it means that we are obligated to distinguish some ways of understanding and acting as being better than others *even in the absence of any final justification for making those distinctions* (see Hazelrigg, 1995; Rorty, 1999; Schwandt, 1996; Smith & Deemer, 2000). If this "predicament" initially seems disagreeable, it is because its most promising possibilities are not immediately apparent. Whether those possibilities are recognized depends upon how we respond.

One response might be to lament what Hazelrigg (1995) terms our human "deficiency" (p. 102), to take our marbles, so to speak, and go home. This kind of self-indulgent capitulation finds an easy way out of the dilemma by concluding that, because we cannot have final justification, nothing, in the end, really matters. But this is a morally vacuous, and ultimately irresponsible, version of relativism that finds absolution in the seductive embrace of nihilism.

Another response might be to deny our human inability to anchor our knowledge in an objective reality outside of ourselves by asserting and reasserting confidence in the tenets of philosophical realism or positivism. Sasso (2001) provides an example of this kind of insistence among traditionalists in special education. Such a reaction turns out to be far more common and, in many ways, far more problematic than first appearances might reveal. In fact, I would suggest that the appeal to neutrality is not, in the end, much different from a capitulation to "anything-goes relativism." Both are simply attempts to absolve ourselves of direct responsibility to others, to deflect difficult questions and evade meaningful critique.

At this juncture I wish to emphasize that understanding knowledge as relative does not require us to believe that the physical properties of the world are figments of our imagination. There is no point in claiming that physical reality is brought into existence by an act of human will. But equally so, there is no point in claiming that social reality can be anything other than a social construction. In a heavily qualified attempt to bring both physical and social inquiry under the same epistemological umbrella, Sokal ends up, apparently without full recognition on his part, accepting that there is a profound difference between the two. As he noted:

> While the *basic* epistemology of inquiry *ought to be roughly* the same for the natural and social sciences, I am of course perfectly aware that many special (and very difficult) methodological issues arise in the social sciences from the fact that the objects of inquiry are human beings (including their subjective states of mind); that these objects of inquiry have intentions (including in some cases the concealment of evidence or the placement of deliberately self-serving

> evidence); that the evidence is expressed (usually) in human lan-
> guage whose meaning may be ambiguous; that the meaning of con-
> ceptual categories (e.g., childhood, masculinity, femininity, family,
> economics, etc.) changes over time; that the goal of historical inquiry
> is not just facts but interpretation, etc. *So by no means do I claim
> that my comments about physics should apply directly to history and
> the social sciences – that would be absurd. To say that "physical real-
> ity is a social and linguistic construct" is just plain silly, but to say
> that "social reality is a social and linguistic construct" is virtually a
> tautology* [emphasis added]. (Sokal & Bricmont, 1998, p. 270)[1]

Because social reality *is* a social and linguistic construct, it is futile to appeal to the natural sciences to assert otherwise. Likewise, there is little point in trotting out the shopworn, if not downright fatuous, question, "If you don't believe in reality, does that mean that you won't die if you fall from a 20-story building?" Of course, it does not mean that. But there's a great deal of difference between kicking the physical reality of a football in the quad and kicking the constructed realities of self-concept, intelligence, or learning disability.

But to return to my main concern, there is another way to understand relativism, one that, paradoxically, presents the most hopeful and inspiring dimension of our humanity. This dimension emanates from the fundamental requirement of relativism. That we cannot have a neutral foundation for our knowledge means that we never can postpone the moral nature of our actions and thoughts. Once we realize that we construct rather than discover our social knowledge, truth, and realities, that they are of our own making, we no longer are confined to a shoulder-shrugging acquiescence that says, "Well, that's just the way things are." Instead, we can construct better ways of understanding and acting. Stated differently:

> Once we give up the idea that the point of discourse is to represent
> reality accurately, we will have no interest in distinguishing social
> constructs from other things. We shall confine ourselves to debating
> the utility of alternative constructs. (Rorty, 1999, p. 86)

Thus, our responsibility is not to get our knowledge and actions to correspond to some objective referent of "how things really are." Instead, our obligation is to recognize that our moral intentions are fulfilled in the knowledge we construct.

A Return to the Four Questions

What is a better way to look at the relativist implications of social knowledge/reality as constructed? To answer this question, perhaps it would be useful to return to the four questions I discussed in Chapter 1. The first question has to do with how we understand disability. Indisputably, no two people are exactly alike; everyone recognizes human diversity. Some of our differences are physical, and some of them are not. Socially, some of those differences seem to matter quite a bit and others matter so little that they are hardly noticed. What these differences *mean*, whether they are good or bad, desirable or undesirable, depends upon human interpretation. We decide what differences *make a difference*.

Disability, for example, is a culturally and historically conditioned interpretation of certain differences. This statement does not deny that some people cannot see, hear, walk, and so on. Many, but certainly not all, judgments of disability involve a physical or biological referent. But it is the social meaning brought to these differences that matters most in the lives of people who are seen as having a disability. This point is expressed quite cogently by Oliver (1990), who states:

> All disabled people experience disability as social restriction, whether those restrictions occur as a consequence of inaccessible built environments, questionable notions of intelligence and social competence, the inability of the general population to use sign language, the lack of reading material in Braille or hostile public attitudes to people with non-visible disabilities. (p. xiv)

When certain differences are understood as something to dread, fear, pity, or avoid, people with these differences experience exclusion, social restrictions, and the denial of autonomy and dignity.

The positivist understanding of disability attempts to ignore that its definitions and labels interpret or bring meaning to difference. From this perspective a disability is something that people have in an objective sense, apart from interpretation or social judgment. But every term has a denotation and connotation. To pretend that blind, deaf, learning disability, and so on are nothing more than objective classifications is to fail to realize that every term carries with it unspoken understandings. As the logical positivists were reminded long ago, ostensive reference is an untenable concept.

To understand disability as a relative, socially constructed concept requires us to take moral ownership of the meaning we bring to human differences. From this perspective, disability labeling is essentially an act of imposing invidious social comparisons that inevitably create injustices. We now must turn our gaze toward ourselves to ask how our interpretations rationalize the creation and perpetuation of barriers, both physical and social, imposed upon those whom we view as disabled. In what ways do our judgments about difference demean, dehumanize, exclude, and restrict? Can we alter attitudes and environmental conditions so that differences might not make much of a difference? To undertake these liberating possibilities requires us first to acknowledge our role in the conceptual, hence the environmental, creation of disability.

The second question centers on research, or the production of professional knowledge. Most special education researchers continue to assert that positivist/empiricist research methods offer the greatest possibility of "efficacious and efficient interventions" for special education students. The journal *Behavioral Disorders* has devoted an entire issue to fostering "a deeper understanding of the meaning of science and the definition of what constitutes legitimate knowledge for the social sciences" (Crockett, 2001, p. 7). The organizing focus of this effort was to reassert positivist/empiricist science as superior because, as various authors insisted, these methods can objectively ground or verify the knowledge it produces.

One article in particular claimed that analytic narrative reviews and meta-analysis techniques are methods that can sort out what teaching practices work from those that do not (Mostert & Kavale, 2001). The authors concluded by stating that these methods of synthesizing research hold "enormous potential for judging the worth of special education practices because their *relative objectivity* brings greater logic and reason to judgments about what works" [emphasis added] (p. 65). Apparently, the authors failed to recognize that they had entirely undermined their main thesis when they used the term "relative objectivity" to endorse the superiority of their methodology. The claim of relative objectivity is nothing more, and nothing less, than a contradiction in terms. No sense at all can be made of this knowledge claim unless, of course, the authors could distinguish between which aspects of their findings are relative and which are objective. Were they to attempt such an undertaking, they would encounter what Chronbach (1975) described as "a hall of mirrors that extends to infinity" (p. 119).

The insistence, however qualified, that positivist social sciences research methods are neutral, and hence objective, cannot in any case be sustained. Many philosophers of science (Hazelrigg, 1989; Hesse, 1980; Giddens, 1976) have repeatedly revealed the fundamental flaw in this notion. Chisholm (1973), for example, illustrates the circular nature of the logic underpinning the claim of methodological neutrality:

> To know whether things really are as they seem to be, we must have a "procedure" for distinguishing appearances that are true from appearances that are false. But to know whether our procedure is a good procedure, we have to know whether it really "succeeds" in distinguishing appearances that are true from appearances that are false. And we cannot know whether it does really succeed unless we

already know which appearances are "true" and which ones are "false." And so we are caught in a circle. (p. 3)

Intentionally or not, those who insist on the neutrality of their methods persuade others of the rightness and common-sense goodness of their own perspectives. To assume the position of neutrality is a rhetorical device, and an unsatisfactory one at that, in that it camouflages political positions, beliefs, and ideologies beneath the cloak of moral detachment.

In contrast, recognizing the relative nature of our research knowledge "raises questions concerning the relationship between the researcher and the researched, the notion of expertise and the issue of who controls the process of research production" (Barton, 1998, p. 62). Nonpositivist, interpretive modes of inquiry collapse all of the traditional categories of knower/known, fact/value, and subject/object. A fundamental assumption of this mode of inquiry is the impossibility of theory-free observation, or extralinguistic, mind-independent knowledge (see Smith, 1989). There is, in other words, no mantle of neutrality for the researcher to hide behind.

Accordingly, this approach recognizes the moral nature of all research endeavors. Interpretive inquirers do not pretend that they don't bring assumptions about the nature of disability to their research, or that their questions and methods are not influenced by their intentions, understandings, background, and so forth. Neither would they claim that they do not affect, and are not affected by, their research participants. Finally, interpretive researchers understand that their research has moral consequences for which they are responsible. In Chapter 8 of this book, Heshusius expresses the situation so eloquently that it bears reiteration:

> In setting aside positivist dogmas, and by engaging in research in which we interact with and listen to the other in real-life settings, we have made our "knowing selves" certainly less safe, less stable, and less secure. This helps to create more open and democratic notions of inquiry. We work directly with research participants, face to face, with no instruments between us. Our research encounters become human encounters. A rationality of method has now become a human rationality that makes it impossible to play a game of ventriloquism, and makes it more difficult to hide our own lives from the impact the contact with the other will have on the self. (p. 8)

Interpretive modes of inquiry require that we risk ourselves, and our prejudices (Gadamer, 1975), so that we do not speak entirely for, or stand over and above, those for whom we presume to speak.

Some might argue that interpretive or qualitative inquiry is inefficient and does not adequately inform educational practices because it does not lead to generalizable interventions (Mostert & Kavale, 2001).[2] That this approach to inquiry does not lead to generalizable techniques in a positivist sense is true enough. Nor does it aspire to do so. What it does aspire toward is a deeper understanding of who we are as people, as learners, and as educators. Because learning and teaching are acts of meaning construction, hence interpretation, this mode of inquiry offers complex insight, understanding, and discernment into students' learning and teachers' practices. In turn, insight, understanding, and discernment are what inform teaching practices in profound and substantial ways. I might add also that one has only to point to the legacies of people such as Burton Blatt to make the case that nonpositivist modes of inquiry have resulted in the most historically important reforms in the field of special education.

The third problem area I raise in Chapter 1 pertains to teacher preparation. More than a decade ago, Heshusius (1984), Iano (1990), and Skrtic (1991) offered penetrating insights into how positivist/empiricist assumptions that inform teacher preparation diminish teachers, students, and the profession as a whole. Drawing on their work, I discussed how the ultimate goal of this framework is to establish and train teachers to use a body of "scientifically proven" teaching interventions. The guiding assumption of this approach is that there is essentially a superior set of techniques to teach students, particularly those with learning difficulties. This skills-driven approach, however, is entirely incommensurate with a relativist understanding of knowledge, which holds that there is never one right answer and that teaching is an ongoing working out of ideas and approaches.

Teacher preparation consistent with this understanding places its focus on intellectual autonomy. One aspect of achieving this is to make a pointed distinction between what it means to be educated versus what it means to be merely trained in the practice of specific teaching skills. Though few would quarrel with teachers accruing pedagogical skills, to be skilled is not synonymous with being educated. The former means that teacher education students must have the opportunity to immerse themselves deeply in the political, historical, and theoretical scholarship that informs those skills and practices. As they experience opportunities to engage the philosophical and pedagogical critiques of their field, students become increasingly able to exert intellectual autonomy and conceptual sophistication in their analyses of the challenges they confront as professionals.

Another aspect of developing intellectual autonomy concerns an obligation to create teacher education programs that embody an ethic of free and open exchanges of ideas. This ethic draws on Habermas's (1970) description of the ideal speech community. Students should be encouraged to express their doubts or disagreements with the understanding that disagreement about ideas is healthy and desirable. Part of this ethic involves intellectual risk-taking, the willingness to offer ideas and the willingness to be persuaded by the ideas of others. In classroom discussions and in other forms of expression alike, teacher educators must demonstrate the crucial distinction between drawing precipitous conclusions versus exercising reasoned judgment. Understanding this distinction assists students in affirming the independence of mind that comes with being able to articulate in a clear and coherent fashion *what* they think and also being able to substantiate *why* they think it.

None of this can take place, of course, unless their deliberations on ideas are deeply and broadly informed. And this requires that students have the opportunity to explore disciplines of study outside of the confines of their own field. For example, one of the issues that my students and I cover in our Critical Issues in Special Education Seminar concerns the reproductive rights of individuals with disabilities. During the course of our discussions, we explore the historical origins of the eugenics movement and its influence on the Third Reich's propaganda campaign leading to the forced sterilization and extermination of individuals with disabilities during World War II. Sociological, philosophical, and literary perspectives also are brought to bear on this issue. These works assist students in informing their work as educators in practical ways, especially those who are preparing to work with adolescents and adults in postsecondary or community settings. The arts and humanities, the social and physical sciences, the law, and so on offer invaluable contributions to students' understanding of issues and practices in their own field.

If, in the preparation of teachers, we free ourselves from the mechanistic or natural sciences–technical model of teaching, we must embrace education as opposed to training. The development of intellectual autonomy leads to professional autonomy wherein teachers are not consigned to the perpetual search for the one right technique, or the next set of new and improved materials. What the concept of relativism tells us is that being prepared to be a teacher is a laborious, intellectually challenging project, a project that opens for discussion immense possibilities of a distinctly human, hence moral, character.

Special education researchers of the positivist persuasion have long contended that the fourth problem, the debate over inclusion, should be resolved through neutral evidence. In their view, segregated special education placements should remain until scientific studies conclusively confirm whether inclusive placements are as "effective" as separate ones (Hallahan & Kauffman, 2000; Kauffman, 1995; MacMillan, Gresham, & Forness, 1996; Walker et. al, 1998). The question of where the onus of proof lies notwithstanding (see, Brantlinger, 1997), no studies of this nature have been equal to the task of providing such confirmation. The main reason the question cannot be arbitrated in this manner is that inclusion is a human choice that cannot be addressed by invoking neutrality as a moral standpoint (Gallagher, 2001). We conceive the reasons for or against, and conditions that either undermine or support, inclusion depending upon the values we hold.

If we want to live in a world that most values social hierarchies and competition, we inevitably will find it necessary to create educational structures that serve these intentions. Conversely, if we want to live in a world that most values egalitarianism, and mutuality, we will find a way to promote these values in our educational arrangements. It all depends on what is most important to us.

As Brantlinger (1997) so aptly noted, the guise of neutrality is frequently invoked in the service of disguising the primary values one holds. For this reason, efforts to be fair and just are not served by claiming to be neutral. To the contrary, accusing others of being ideological while claiming to take a neutral stance is an attempt at one-upmanship that can be pulled off only before an audience that is misled into believing that neutrality is a viable concept. I suspect that this attempt is often successful because many people equate neutrality with impartiality. Hence, the invoking of neutrality appeals to well intended people who value fairness and justice, mistakenly believing that neutrality is synonymous with impartiality. The crucial distinction, though, is that neutrality is a moral stance concealed by neutral pretension. Impartiality is a moral position that is served by the deliberate effort to recognize our prejudices or self-interests so that others' interests and well-being are treated as equal to our own.

Rorty (1999) explained that it is pointless to pursue truth in some nonrelative, neutral space detached from our beliefs and values. In a quote that proposed an alternative, he stated:

> But you can aim at ever more sensitivity to pain, and ever greater satisfaction of ever more various needs. Pragmatists [nonrealist philosophers] think that the idea of something nonhuman luring us human beings on should be replaced with the idea of getting more and more human beings into our community—of taking the needs and interests and views of more and more diverse human beings into account. (p. 82)

Because Rorty is a philosopher, and not a professor of education, I was struck when I read this by how remarkably well this quote captures the essentially moral nature of the inclusion debate in education.

Confronting Our Fears

One of the reasons that so many go out of their way to try to avoid the relative nature of our human knowledge is that once we concede that there is no objectivity to hide behind, we also must recognize our complicity in creating and maintaining social injustice (Ellis & Bochner, 2000). In his well known book, *Escape from Freedom,* Erich Fromm (1964) discussed the deep sense of apprehension that humans experience when confronting responsibility for their human agency. Our fear of making the wrong choices, he told us, is so profound that we would rather submit to an external authority, no matter how dubious, than risk making choices in the absence of complete knowledge. For him, it was precisely this flight from freedom that resulted in Hitler's ability to obtain the necessary cooperation to implement his "final solution" during World War II.

Beyond the unwarranted fear of "anything goes," some resist relativism not only because it forces us to give up a false sense of moral exoneration but also because it requires giving up other privileged positions. As Heshusius discussed in Chapter 8, this threat of lost privilege relates to our need to try to "construct superior, stable, distancing, and safe selves," a need that extends itself into the professional realm. In his discussion on professionalization, Skrtic (1995) noted that, "On the basis of the claim to scientific authority, society allows the professions greater autonomy than it does other social groups" (p. 6). In addition to greater autonomy, he added, specialization in the professions has provided greater wealth and prestige. Along the same lines, Iano (1986) pointed out how the claim to scientific authority created a regrettable system of professional classes in the field of education, relegating public school teachers to the lower rungs while elevating researchers and professors to top of the professional hierarchy.

Fear of losing privileged status is conspicuous, for example, in Kauffman's (1994) article, "Places of Change: Special Education's Power and Identity in an Era of Educational Reform." In his defense of traditional special education's continuum of placements, he expressed his deep anxiety that the field's recent endangerment at the hands of its critics and dissenting voices will result in the loss of services for students with disabilities. Yet, in the title and text of the article, his fears seem to be centered primarily on the vulnerability of professionals' status, power, and identity, as the following quote illustrates: "It may be too late to save ourselves. This is a harsh and pessimistic outlook, and I hope that I am wrong in my assessment of our plight" (p. 610).

Similarly, Walker et al. (1998) proposed that the field of behavioral disorders might repair its damaged credibility through rededication to empirical (positivist) inquiry and use of their collective expertise to "achieve a degree of 'macrosocial validation' for our efforts" (p. 7). The term "macrosocial validation," they explained, refers to "recognition, approval, and valuing of a field's professional activities by the larger constituencies affected by them, such as the general public, the U.S. Congress, and policymakers" (p. 7). Although it would be entirely unfair to doubt their sincere dedication to the students whose lives they hope to improve, it also should be recognized that apprehension about the loss of professional privilege is present in the ongoing defense of positivist ideology.

A further concern expressed by those who fear that the acceptance of relativism as here defined is that it will lead to a return to the bad old days. By "bad old days," they mean a return to the times when people with disabilities were institutionalized, abandoned, mistreated, denied the right to education, and so on. The presumption here is that their science has been morally efficacious. Dissenting voices in critical special education and disability studies have argued, however, that its effect has been just the opposite. Heshusius (in Chapter 8) illustrates the ways in which positivist ideology has done more to impede social justice than to promote it. In what she terms "an epistemological civil rights movement," she describes the emancipatory potential of contesting positivism's epistemologically objectifying and silencing gaze. It also should be recognized that it was not science that launched the deinstitutionalization movement, the disability rights movement, or the inclusion movement. These movements came about as a result of advocacy on the part of people with disabilities and others who joined them. It is to their collective efforts that credit for the advances achieved so far rightly belongs.

Conclusion

If, in the end, we cannot appeal to an objective foundation for our knowledge, are we now left to an eternal lament of our human deficiency? Does it mean that nothing really matters, or that all choices are equally good? The answer to these questions is, in a word, no. Instead, we are left with far more hopeful possibilities. The work of the three scholars featured in this book points to a better way to understand the relative nature of our knowledge. They show us that, in coming to understand how the positivist and realist positions constrain our human capacities, we actually can make our future better than our present.

If this is the case, how might we begin? The answer is really quite straightforward: We begin by genuinely listening to each other. One of the primary obligations we have to each other, if we are to carry on such a conversation, is to lay to rest the question, "Is our knowledge of things adequate to the way things really are?" and substitute instead the question, "Are our ways of describing things, of relating them to other things so as to make them fulfill our needs more adequately, as good as possible?" (Rorty, 1999, p. 72). In replacing the first question with the latter one, we accept that our ways of describing things (or people) is inevitably bound to our intentions, goals and purposes. We then are confronted with the moral substance of all human knowledge.

Herein lies the hope, and the hope is this: that we can come more deliberately to some consensus, however imperfect, about what kind of choices we want to make for ourselves and each other. The need to locate our work as educators within this moral space is our task for the future.

References

Barton, L. (1998). Sociology, disability studies and education: Some observations. In T. Shakespeare (Ed.), *The disability studies reader: Social science perspectives*. London and New York: Cassell.

Brantlinger, E. (1997). Using ideology: Cases of nonrecognition of the politics of research and practice in special education. *Review of Educational Research, 67*(4), 425–459.

Chisholm, R. (1973). *The problem of criteria*. Milwaukee, WI: Marquette University Press.

Crockett, J. B. (2001). Prologue: Exploring the meaning of science and defining rigor in the social sciences. *Behavioral Disorders, 27*(1), 7–11.

Chronbach, L. J. (1975). Beyond the two disciplines of scientific psychology. *American Psychologist, 30,* 116–127.

Ellis, C., & Bochner, A. P. (2000). Autoethnography, personal narrative, reflexivity: Researcher as subject. In N. K. Denzin & Y. S. Lincoln (Eds.), *Handbook of qualitative research* (2d ed., pp. 733–768). Thousand Oaks, CA: Sage Publications.

Fromm, E. (1964). *Escape from freedom*. New York: Holt, Rinehart and Winston.

Gadamer, H.- G. (1975). Truth and method. (G. Barden & J. Cumming, Eds. & Trans.). New York: Seabury Press.

Gallagher, D. J. (1998). The scientific knowledge base of special education: Do we know what we think we know? *Exceptional Children, 64,* 493–502.

Gallagher, D. J. (2001). Neutrality as a moral standpoint, conceptual confusion and the full inclusion debate. *Disability & Society, 16*(5), 637–654.

Giddens, A. (1976). *New rules of sociological method: A positive critique of interpretive sociologies*. New York: Basic Books.

Habermas, J. (1970). Toward a theory of communicative competence. *Inquiry, 13,* 360–375.

Hallahan, D. P. , & Kauffman, J. M. (2000). *Exceptional learners: Introduction to special education (8th ed)*. Needham Heights, MA: Allyn & Bacon.

Hazelrigg, L. (1989). *A wilderness of mirrors: On practices of theory in a gray age*. Tallahassee, FL: The Florida State University Press.

Hazelrigg, L. (1995). *Cultures of nature: An essay on the production of nature*. Tallahassee: Florida State University Press.

Heshusius, L. (1984). Why would they and I want to do it?: A phenomenological–theoretical view of special education. *Learning Disability Quarterly, 7,* 363–368.

Hesse, M.(1980). *Revolutions and reconstructions in the philosophy of science*. Brighton, UK: Harvester.

Iano, R. P. (1986). The study and development of teaching: With implications for the advancement of special education. *Remedial & Special Education, 7*(5), 50–61.

Iano, R. P. (1990). Special education teachers: Technicians or educators? *Journal of Learning Disabilities, 23*(8), 462–465.

Kauffman, J. M. (1994). Places of change: Special education's power and identity in an era of educational reform. *Journal of Learning Disabilities, 27*(10), 610–618.

Kauffman, J. M. (1995). Why we must celebrate a diversity of restrictive environments. *Learning Disabilities Research and Practice, 10*(4), 225–232.

MacMillan, D. L., Gresham, F.M., & Forness, S. R. (1996). Full inclusion: An empirical perspective. *Behavioral Disorders, 21*(2), 145–159.

Mostert, M. P., & Kavale, K. (2001). Evaluation of research for usable knowledge in behavioral disorders: Ignoring the irrelevant, considering the germane. *Behavioral Disorders, 27*(1), 53–68.

Oliver, M. (1990). *The politics of disablement.* Basingstoke, UK: Macmillan.

Rorty, R. (1999). *Philosophy and social hope.* London: Penguin Books.

Sasso, G. M. (2001). The retreat from inquiry and knowledge in special education. *Journal of Special Education, 34,* 178–193.

Schwandt, T. A. (1996). Farewell to criteriology. *Qualitative Inquiry, 2,* 58–72.

Skrtic, T. M. (1990). Students with special educational needs: Artifacts of the traditional curriculum. In M. Ainscow (Ed.), *Effective schools for all,* pp. 20–42. London: David Fulton Publications.

Skrtic, T. M. (1991). *Behind special education: A critical analysis of professional culture and school organization.* Denver, CO: Love.

Skrtic, T. M. (1995). Theory/practice and objectivism: The modern view of the professions. In T. M. Skrtic (Ed.), *Disability & democracy: Reconstructing [special] education for postmodernity* (pp. 3–24). New York: Teachers College Press.

Sokal, A., & Bricmont, J. (1998). *Fashionable nonsense: Postmodern intellectuals' abuse of science.* New York: Picador USA.

Smith, J. K. (1989). *The nature of social and educational inquiry: Empiricism versus interpretation.* Norwood, New Jersey: Ablex Publishing Corporation.

Smith, J. K., & Deemer, D. K. (2000). The problem of criteria in the age of relativism. In N. K. Denzin & Y. S. Lincoln (Eds.), *Handbook of qualitative research* (2d), pp. 877–896. Thousand Oaks, CA: Sage Publications.

Walker, H. M., Forness, S. R., Kauffman, J. M., Epstein, M. H., Gresham, F. M., Nelson, C. M., & Strain, P. S. (1998). Macro-social validation: Referencing outcomes in behavioral disorders to societal issues and problems. *Behavioral Disorders, 24*(1), 7–18.

Notes

1. Of course, those who would invoke Sokal and Bricmont's (1998) work to shore up a defense of positivism are advised to read the authors' work more carefully. Sokal states quite directly that, "Readers are cautioned not to infer my views on any subject except insofar as they are set forth in this Afterword. In particular, the fact that I have parodied an extreme or ambiguously stated version of an idea does not exclude that I may agree with a more nuanced or precisely stated version of the same idea" (p. 268).

2. Positivist research methodology does not produce generalizable interventions, either. For an extended discussion of why this is the case, see Gallagher, D. J. (1998).

Name Index

Subject Index